Missional Acts

Missional Acts

Rhetorical Narrative in the Acts of the Apostles

DANIEL McGINNIS

Foreword by Steve Walton

PICKWICK *Publications* · Eugene, Oregon

MISSIONAL ACTS
Rhetorical Narrative in the Acts of the Apostle

Pickwick Publications
An Imprint of Wipf and Stock Publishers
199 W. 8th Ave., Suite 3
Eugene, OR 97401

www.wipfandstock.com

PAPERBACK ISBN: 978-1-7252-7843-1
HARDCOVER ISBN: 978-1-7252-7842-4
EBOOK ISBN: 978-1-7252-7844-8

Cataloguing-in-Publication data:

Names: McGinnis, Daniel, author.

Title: Missional acts : rhetorical narrative in the Acts of the Apostle / Daniel M. McGinnis.

Description: Eugene, OR: Pickwick Publications, 2022 | Includes bibliographical references and index.

Identifiers: ISBN 978-1-7252-7843-1 (paperback) | ISBN 978-1-7252-7842-4 (hardcover) | ISBN 978-1-7252-7844-8 (ebook)

Subjects: LCSH: Bible. Acts—Criticism, interpretation, etc. | Missions—History—Early church, ca. 30–600. | Bible. Acts—Socio-rhetorical criticism. | Rhetorical criticism.

Classification:BS2625.2 M34 2022 (paperback) | BS2625.2 (ebook)

01/12/22

Contents

List of Tables

Foreword

The theme of mission in the book of Acts is, rather surprisingly, neglected in academic biblical studies. Dr. Daniel McGinnis here provides an insightful, thoughtful, engaging and scholarly study which will be valuable to scholars, students and pastors who wish to learn from and reflect on that important theme. Four features of this book illustrate its value.

First and foremost, Dr. McGinnis provides us with a study of mission in the whole book of Acts which engages thoughtfully with the text in conversation with the best of scholarship. He mines commentaries, monographs, essays and articles which touch on this theme to illuminate how Luke portrays the mission of Acts. He argues that mission is the central theme of Acts, and that Luke is writing his book in order to persuade the church of his day of its importance. Not only that, but Luke is offering his church stimuli for mission, structures which promote mission, strategies for engaging in mission, and how to handle the inevitable suffering which mission brings. This is a book rich in insights into mission in the book of Acts.

Secondly, Dr. McGinnis organises his study clearly, and uses a helpful metaphor—the human body—to show how the four major areas fit together. Thus, mission stimuli are the heart, for they explain why mission is vital for followers of Jesus; mission structures are the hands and feet, explaining what followers of Jesus should do as they engage in mission; mission strategies are the brain, providing direction and shaping tactics, and keeping the whole body of believers functioning together; suffering highlights the backbone of the mission, the persistence required in the face of opposition and persecution. These images are accessible and clear, and will help readers as they navigate the fine detailed work in many of the book's chapters. He also regularly provides clear charts and summaries at key points which enable readers to get a clear sense of what he is saying, and from where in Acts he is drawing his ideas.

Thirdly, Dr. McGinnis recognises the vital interplay of divine initiative and power with human response and responsibility in mission. He is clear that the mission in question is God's mission, as modern missiologists frequently say. Thus he explores how the word of the Lord and the Holy Spirit are key drivers of where the mission goes and how it develops. He is equally clear that Luke portrays followers of Jesus as responsible for engaging with God in this mission by both following God's directions and being flexible enough to adapt when God does surprising things. He offers a nuanced and attentive discussion of the relationship of divine initiative and human responsibility in mission in Acts which avoids simplistic answers.

Fourthly, Dr. McGinnis writes with an eye to today's Christians and churches, particularly in his final Conclusions and Reflection, where he sketches implications from the four key areas covered in the book: mission stimuli, structures, strategies, and suffering. He recognises that to study this book of Christian Scripture is not only to study the ancient foundations of the church, but is highly relevant now. His concluding section repays careful thought in an era when it is all too easy to look for "what works" when thinking about mission, rather than asking what guidance and stimulus Scripture offers. He avoids naïvely assuming that the ways the earliest believers acted is the way believers should act today, but teases out themes and theology which will inform and shape action today.

You hold a valuable and worthwhile book in your hand; you will find it informative, stimulating, engaging, and creative.

Steve Walton
Maundy Thursday 2021

Preface

As I complete this book in early 2021, the world is in upheaval. The effects of the Black Lives Matter and #metoo movements are transforming culture and revealing many unsettling truths about our communities and ways of relating to one another. The ravages of the COVID-19 pandemic can be seen everywhere. Lockdowns are only beginning to be lifted, and the church has largely been unable to meet or to function in any semblance of normality over the past year. These challenges come in the context of a global climate emergency the world is only starting to come to terms with, along with many tragedies of poverty and conflict throughout the world.

These cultural crises precipitate a spiritual opportunity, for those with eyes to see it. As the church prepares to re-emerge post lockdown, it has the precious chance to reset and rethink what missional engagement means in the new world in which it now finds itself. Much has changed, and a guide is required. It strikes me that there are few roadmaps more relevant than the book of Acts. Its themes of multicultural church, of overcoming division, opposition, and suffering, and of loving and bold outreach have a surprising resonance with today's cultural confluences. Christ's church has the potential to be a prophetic voice of service, leadership, and influence in these turbulent times, and I am convinced that the narrative of Acts can help to show the way. It has perhaps never been needed more.

My own preoccupation with the narrative of Acts began at a young age, and it has always struck me as a marvelous story filled with exciting drama and hair-raising intrigue. When I was a university student, I was challenged to look deeper at the repeated missional themes of Acts, and I have been fascinated by that study ever since, immersing myself in the text of Acts for more than twenty-five years. During that time, I have been a church-planter, mentor, pastor, Christian leader, and theological teacher, and all these roles have shaped and informed my thinking. I have become convinced that the missional adventures which Acts describes are not merely historical particularities, but that Luke presents them as models to be followed by his readers. I continue to wrestle with questions surrounding the missional patterns Acts depicts and their relevance to church life and witness today.

These missional themes are not simply intellectually fascinating, they matter urgently for the church and the world to which it is called. I have often been struck by the way many biblical scholars seem to avoid mission. There are surely many reasons for this, but that is a question for another study. It is my sincere hope that this book will contribute to the relatively unexplored terrain of mission within biblical studies, and Acts scholarship in particular. I have attempted to present my arguments as accessibly as possible, including translating the Greek and Hebrew, in the hopes that they will also be useful to practitioners such as pastors, church planters, missionaries, and other Christian leaders. The variety of current cultural contexts and missional situations has made me hesitant to be specific or prescriptive about contemporary application, which I only briefly touch on in the conclusion, but I anticipate that the rich missional content of Acts will spark many creative ideas and innovative practices in this unique time of challenge and opportunity.

Whatever else Acts may be, it is a book filled with stories of mission in a way that is unique within the New Testament. I increasingly think of it as the missional heart of the canon, which is why the present study is called "Missional Acts," also a rather feeble play on words because Acts is brimming with so many memorable missional acts. Even though the adjective "missional" is one of the most overused and yet perhaps least understood words in the church today, I have chosen to use it frequently, partly in the hope that the narrative of Acts will inform its meaning. It seems to me that Luke writes these vivid stories to rhetorically influence his readers towards missional action, hence the subtitle "Rhetorical Narrative in the Acts of the Apostles." I am aware of the negative connotations the word "rhetoric" may carry. Readers will come to their own conclusions, but I use the term to highlight Luke's eloquent and persuasive writing, in line with ancient rhetorical conventions, and not the hyperbole, bombast, or ostentatious fabrication that many associate with rhetorical speech today. The literary genre of rhetorical narrative allows me to focus on what the text of Acts in its final form is doing, while attempting to sidestep the separate question of its historical reliability.

Acts is the second longest book in the New Testament, after Luke's Gospel, and I have undoubtedly been ambitious in attempting to deal with this substantial book in its entirety. This choice has forced me to deal in general observations rather than more detailed analysis in certain places. I have attempted to reference more thorough studies where relevant and am particularly indebted to many of the excellent recent Acts commentators. I also take full responsibility for any unintentional omission or misrepresentation of voices within Acts and mission scholarship, which may be inevitable despite my best efforts.

Many have helped me along the way. I am grateful to Jimmy Seibert, who first challenged me to think about the missional themes of Acts more systematically and inspired me to discover my own missional way of life. I am also grateful to the faculty of the Biblical Studies Department of Sheffield University for nurturing the academic environment in which I carried out much of this initial research. Professors Loveday Alexander and James Crossley proved to be excellent supervisors, whose guidance and encouragement were invaluable in shaping the direction and outline of the work. Additionally, Professor Steve Walton has provided important feedback which has helped me to develop and refine this project, as well as contributing the Foreword. Throughout my time of study and ministry my mother Betty McGinnis has been an unfailing support, encouragement, and inspiration.

The environments in which I work and lead at St Hild Theological College and the Leeds School of Theology have allowed me to teach and sharpen much of this material over the last eight years, and I have enjoyed working through it with colleagues and students alike. I am particularly grateful to my good friend and mentor Dr. Yancy Smith, who has been an invaluable companion on the journey, including reading and discussing every chapter of this project with me.

Most of all, I am indebted to my wife Jeannie and my children Madeline and Aiden, who have undoubtedly sacrificed most to allow me to complete this work. This past year we have all suffered with COVID, and as I write my wife and teenage son continue to bravely battle the mysterious effects of "long COVID." Despite the challenges of this journey, they have continued to support me faithfully. I appreciate their patient sacrifice more than I can say and am confident that better days are ahead.

This work is dedicated to my late father, Dr. Rodney McGinnis, whose life has inspired and motivated me in so many ways.

Daniel McGinnis
Easter 2021

Abbreviations

AIIFCS	The Book of Acts in Its First Century Setting
BAR	*Biblical Archaeology Review*
BDAG	*Greek-English Lexicon of the New Testament and Other Early Christian Literature*. 3rd ed.
CBQ	*Catholic Biblical Quarterly*
ET	*Expository Times*
HTR	*Harvard Theological Review*
JBL	*Journal of Biblical Literature*
JSNT	*Journal for the Study of the New Testament*
JTS	*Journal of Theological Studies*
LCL	Loeb Classical Library
LNTS	Library of New Testament Studies
LXX	Septuagint
NIGTC	The New International Greek Testament Commentary
NT	New Testament
NTS	*New Testament Studies*
OT	Old Testament
SNTSMS	Society for New Testament Studies Monograph Series
TDNT	*Theological Dictionary of the New Testament*
TynB	*Tyndale Bulletin*
WUNT	Wissenschaftliche Untersuchungen zum Neuen Testament

Introduction

But you will receive power when the Holy Spirit has come upon you;
and you will be my witnesses in Jerusalem, in all Judea and Samaria,
and to the ends of the earth.

—ACTS 1:8[1]

From Jesus's early "ends of the earth" commission in Jerusalem to Paul's preaching under house arrest in Rome at its conclusion, the book of Acts is saturated with mission. Between these narrative bookends Acts tracks the growing group of Christ-followers as they establish themselves in Jerusalem, expand outward into Judea and Samaria, and reach out to many of the great urban centers of the Roman Empire, including finally Rome itself. The book of Acts begins with 120 Jews waiting expectantly for the promised Holy Spirit and culminates in a sprawling multiethnic movement of Christian churches with a universal mission. This is the story of Acts, the story of the birth and missional expansion of the church.[2]

But what is the significance of this story, and of the missionizing that permeates it? What are readers to make of so much mission? This pervasive theme reveals the author's rhetorical purposes in writing Acts,

1. Unless otherwise noted, citations of the English Bible in chapter headings are from the NRSV, in the chapters from the author's translation, and of the Greek NT from NA27. Abbreviations of books of the Bible and standard scholarly works follow Alexander, *SBL Handbook of Style*.

2. Many commentaries discuss the introductory critical issues related to Acts scholarship, including the most encyclopedic of them all, Keener (2012–2015, 4 vols). See also Peterson (2009), Pervo (2009), Parsons (2008), Gaventa (2003), Witherington (1998), Fitzmyer (1998), Jervell (1998), Dunn (1996), Barrett (1994–1998, 2 vols), Polhill (1992), Bruce (3rd ed., 1990), Conzelmann (1987), Marshall (1980), Haenchen (1971).

and the cumulative effect is a persuasive presentation of mission as the *raison d'être of the church*.[3]

A MISSIONAL PURPOSE

This study follows the nearly unanimous tradition of the church in referring to the author of the book of Acts as "Luke."[4] Its arguments about the missional rhetoric of Acts apply equally well to audiences across the range of scholarly estimates regarding the date of Acts, from 62 to 130 CE; a more precise date and historical exigency are not central to this study's concerns.[5] There is consensus that "Luke-Acts" is one narrative unity, and therefore Acts is the literary continuation of Luke's Gospel.[6] This means that the content of Luke's Gospel is fundamental to understanding Acts.[7] The canonical configuration makes it easy to miss the profound theological and narrative connections between Luke and Acts; somewhat like Trinitarian theology, they are clearly distinct and yet they are one.[8]

---

3. Mission is here understood as the proclamation of the good news about Jesus the Savior and Redeemer, in loving word and deed; the end of this introduction further defines it.

4. Keener, *Acts*, 1:402–22. Luke is likely a co-worker and occasional traveling companion of Paul; this is the most straightforward way to understand the "we passages" in the latter parts of Acts, though this is contested. Keener, *Acts*, 3:2350–74. Little can be known with certainty about the identity of the author of Acts.

5. Witherington, *Acts*, 60–63, claims a date around 80 is sufficiently later than the last event in the book (60–63) to allow for Luke's historical perspective to develop, yet before the Pauline corpus was fully formed, about which Luke seems to know very little; it also explains the vivid detail apparent in the second half of Acts. Cf. Keener, *Acts*, 1:383–401; 4:3777–80; Peterson, *Acts*, 4–5. Pervo's recent arguments in *Dating Acts* for a second-century origin have been influential, though a majority of scholars still advocate a late first-century date.

6. "Luke-Acts" implies that the same author wrote both parts and that together they constitute a logical narrative world; Tannehill, *Narrative Unity*, 1:xiii, 1–9. Parsons and Pervo, *Rethinking the Unity* question the narrower ideas of theological, stylistic, and compositional *uniformity*. Cf. Keener, *Acts*, 1:550–74—the common authorship of Luke-Acts is rarely questioned, but issues like shared purpose and genre are ongoing debates.

7. Approaching Luke and Acts consecutively yields multiple insights, including the notion that the prologue of Luke (1:1–4) is really the prologue of all of Luke-Acts, and the brief prologue of Acts (1:1) simply recalls it.

8. Though there is general agreement on this point, Acts and Luke's Gospel have their own independent transmission histories, pointing to separate releases and distributions: "There is absolutely no manuscript evidence to support the view that Luke and Acts ever physically appeared side by side, ready for reading as one continuous whole," Parsons, "Hearing Acts," 131. "Luke-Acts" is therefore a modern designation.

What Luke is doing in Luke-Acts is unique; he is extending the Gospel genre, to underscore that the cross and resurrection are not the end of Jesus's story.[9] By adding to these the foundational stories of the ascension and the outpouring of the Spirit at the beginning of Acts, which lead directly to the genesis of the first church, he is emphasizing that the church and its mission are the continuation and culmination of the gospel story. The ministry of Jesus brings about the mission of the church, which finds its own culmination for Luke in the Pauline journeys. In writing Luke-Acts, Luke is intending that the story of Jesus becomes the story of Jesus's church.[10] Luke establishes Jesus as the "paradigm for the church's ministry" to all nations, and this is carried forward in Acts by those who act in his name.[11]

Though Acts takes the form of historical narrative, this work argues that Luke's primary purpose in writing Acts is rhetorical and didactic, as is often the case with ancient historiography. He is not merely interested in "what happened" in the past, but in how to interpret its meaning, and what the church of his day can learn from it (Luke 1:1–4). *Luke draws on his sources to construct a narrative world which functions as a provocation towards one primary thing: missional witness.* Luke articulates this overarching purpose through the mouth of Jesus himself: "you will receive power when the Holy Spirit comes upon you; and you will be my witnesses in Jerusalem, in all Judea and Samaria, and to the ends of the earth" (Acts 1:8). Luke is inviting the church of his day to take up this promise, receive the power of the Spirit, and be Christ's witnesses everywhere, even to the farthest parts of the earth. This is Luke's purpose and goal in writing Acts.

Luke goes on to take many of the missional principles of the earliest church, as he understands them, and package them in a way that they can be grasped and applied by subsequent generations. This is unique in the NT. Paul surely taught and modeled mission, but his surviving letters are pastoral and situational in nature. Luke means for Acts to function as a template and guide for missionary activity, so he shapes and presents stories which help his audience understand and imitate this central priority of the early church.

The book of Acts confronts missional apathy by painting a vivid picture of the earliest church, which highlights the disparities between that church and its readers, along with their shared challenges. Its open-ended and inconclusive "ending" stresses that the mission which drives the earliest believers is not complete, but ongoing and urgent. Understood this way,

---

9. Stevens, *Acts*, 3–4, 18.

10. Stevens, *Acts*, 11. Luke directly links the stories in Acts 1:1; Keener, *Acts*, 1:651–53.

11. Hays, *Moral Vision*, 120–22.

Acts is a compelling call to missional action, which urges its audience to reject fear, apathy, and survivalism. In addition to provoking his readers to action, Luke presents multiple missional practices and strategies throughout Acts. His rhetoric is persuasive, couched in a narrative format that draws readers in and urges them to join the expansive mission which Acts depicts. Luke's fundamental desire is to motivate his audience, and his secondary purpose is to equip them to implement his mission instructions effectively. In this regard, Acts is both motivational in its challenge and practical in its guidance.

AN OVERVIEW OF THE PROJECT: "THE BODY OF MISSION"

This work examines both the motivational and the instructive dynamics of the missional content of Acts, arranged into four overlapping categories: stimuli, structures, strategies, and suffering. These four areas of rhetorical instruction can be compared to a human body, with each part working symbiotically to keep the whole body healthy and functioning optimally.

Part 1—Missional Stimuli (The Heart)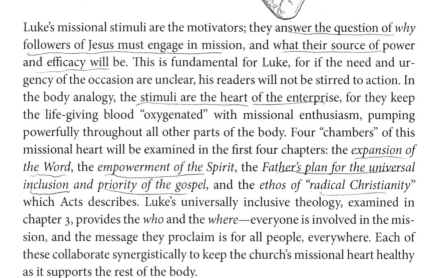

Luke's missional stimuli are the motivators; they answer the question of *why* followers of Jesus must engage in mission, and what their source of power and efficacy will be. This is fundamental for Luke, for if the need and urgency of the occasion are unclear, his readers will not be stirred to action. In the body analogy, the stimuli are the heart of the enterprise, for they keep the life-giving blood "oxygenated" with missional enthusiasm, pumping powerfully throughout all other parts of the body. Four "chambers" of this missional heart will be examined in the first four chapters: the *expansion of the Word*, the *empowerment of the Spirit*, the *Father's plan for the universal inclusion and priority of the gospel*, and the *ethos of "radical Christianity"* which Acts describes. Luke's universally inclusive theology, examined in chapter 3, provides the *who* and the *where*—everyone is involved in the mission, and the message they proclaim is for all people, everywhere. Each of these collaborate synergistically to keep the church's missional heart healthy as it supports the rest of the body.

Part 2—Missional Structures (The Hands and Feet)

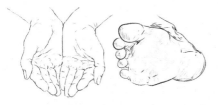

The missional structures in Acts are the building blocks; they answer the question of *what* Luke's readers ought to employ as they carry out the mission. These structures can be considered the missional hands and feet: *the church* is the hands, for it reaches out to those around it and welcomes them as they join it (chapter 5), and *the house/household* is the feet, for it is the network of relationships and the physical structure through which the mission progresses (chapter 6). These structures combine to form *the house church*, the fundamental material and social structure which facilitates mission throughout Acts (chapter 7).

Part 3—Missional Strategies (The Brain)

The missional strategies in Acts are Luke's attempt to equip the church in *how* to go about the mission to which he is calling them. These strategies are the brain, for they determine the tactics to be employed, direct the whole body at key points of decision, and keep all the members coordinated and working in harmony with one another. In the first twelve chapters of Acts mission is largely incidental, unfolding locally and then more widely as Christians are scattered by persecution. However, the church at Syrian Antioch is a significant turning point, and intentional strategies emerge during Paul's subsequent journeys in Acts 13–21, revealing through this archetypal messenger the deliberate missional activities which Luke is rhetorically advocating. Part 3 is therefore a detailed study of this crucial section of Acts: chapters 8–10 examine each of Paul's three journeys in sequence and chapter 11 summarizes the missional strategies which Paul employs in Acts.

Part 4—Missional Suffering (The Backbone)

Missional suffering in Acts is further training for *how to conduct the mission*, particularly when missionaries experience persecution or opposition. Luke's instruction about how to face persecution and even use it as a platform for further outreach functions as the backbone of the missional body—it supplies bravery, strength, longevity, and resilience, as a necessary spine in the face of opposition which keeps the body upright and correctly aligned. Part 4 examines the theme of suffering throughout Luke-Acts (chapter 12), with a particular focus on Paul's captivity and trial narratives in Acts 21–28 (chapter 13). This part closes with an examination of the rhetorical function of the open-ended conclusion of Acts.

Each of the four main parts of this work will seek to elucidate a central aspect of Luke's parenetic purposes in writing Acts: to convince his audience of the supreme value and priority of their mission, and to teach them practical ways of implementing and sustaining it. The book of Acts thus functions persuasively as a catalyst to and an equipping narrative for mission, and these two overriding aims are discernible in nearly every episode. As Maddox says, "Luke summons his fellow-Christians to worship God with whole-hearted joy, to follow Jesus with unwavering loyalty, and to carry on with zeal, through the power of the Spirit, the charge to be his witnesses to the end of the earth."[12]

SUBSIDIARY ASPECTS OF ACTS' MISSIONAL PURPOSE

Scholars have long debated Luke's purposes in writing Acts.[13] "Luke himself indicates that he authored his two-volume work not primarily for outsiders but to legitimate and confirm faith" to a Christian audience in the prologue of Luke-Acts (Luke 1:3–4).[14] In addition to this introductory statement of intent, repeated narrative themes and motifs in the text are the clearest way

---

12. Maddox, *Purpose*, 187.

13. E.g., Maddox, *Purpose*; Fitzmyer, *Acts*, 55–60; Bruce, *Acts*, 21–27; Witherington, *Acts*, 68–76; Johnson, *Acts*, 7–9; Keener, *Acts*, 1.435–58; Peterson, *Acts*, 36–39; Haenchen, *Acts*, 90–111.

14. Keener, "Paul and Sedition," 203.

to identify Luke's purpose. This work argues that Luke means for Acts to play a hortative role in influencing and equipping Christians for mission, and therefore other proposed purposes of Acts can be best understood as sub-aspects of this overriding rhetorical goal.[15] For example, many have seen that Acts is *equipping believers in how to respond when they are put on trial or face persecution*.[16] It is encouraging believers to remain faithful in their allegiance and witness to Christ, no matter what happens to them.[17] Luke sees persecution, imprisonment, trials, and other forms of suffering as fundamental aspects of the church's mission, and as opportunities to further the proclamation of the gospel. He particularly presents Paul's life as a model for how to prioritize faithfulness to the mission above all else, including one's own personal safety. Paul's trial scenes also function as models for later Christians undergoing prosecution and imprisonment. Part 4 of this work focuses on this prominent theme of missional suffering.

Acts is also *building a Christian identity, and attempting to help Christ-followers understand their identity as juxtaposed with Judaism*.[18] To this end, Luke addresses why many Jews have not received Christ, and why, conversely, what started as an internal Jewish movement has become rooted in non-Jewish society.[19] "It is a work aimed at reassuring the Christian community about the significance of the tradition and faith in which it stands . . . [Luke] writes to reassure the Christians of his day that their faith in Jesus is no aberration, but the authentic goal towards which God's ancient dealings with Israel were driving."[20] Luke emphasizes the legitimate Jewish heritage of the Christian movement and especially the Gentile mission. This validation of the church's identity, rooted in the promises of the Hebrew Bible, establishes

---

15. These further aspects of Luke's purpose in writing Acts will be expanded upon throughout this study.

16. E.g., Maddox, *Purpose*, 80–82.

17. Cassidy develops this "allegiance-witness theory," *Society and Politics*, 158–70.

18. E.g., Baker, *Identity, Memory*, sees Acts as a late first-century "identity-forming story," crafted around a reconstructed view of Peter and Paul as "prototypical" leaders in a unified and socially cohesive church. Pervo, *Acts*, 21–22 considers Acts to be a second-century "legitimating narrative," designed "to explain and defend a body that has existed for some time and whose identity has been challenged rather than, for example, to nurture a young and fragile body grappling to discover its identity." (As publication approached, it came to my attention that Coleman Baker had recently been convicted of disturbing criminal charges. I have taken steps to minimize his presence in this book. The reader should also note that Baker's work is no longer in print.)

19. Luke's Greco-Roman readers were accustomed to oriental religious movements transforming into popular cults, such as the Egyptian deities Isis and Serapis, and the Mithraic mystery religions.

20. Maddox, *Purpose*, 186.

a solid foundation from which it is able to participate in Christ's mission to the ends of the earth, through the power of the Holy Spirit.

The amount of narrative dedicated to the Apostle Paul shows an additional interest in *defending and rehabilitating the dignity of Paul*.[21] Paul's outreach to non-Jews, frequent run-ins with religious and governmental authorities, and long imprisonments would have placed him under a cloud of suspicion, and Paul remains a lightning rod for controversy in Luke's day. The book of Acts can thus be seen as a Lukan apologetic for Paul; this is essential because Paul is Luke's ideal missionary, and he uses Paul's life as a model for his readers to imitate. The rehabilitation of Paul's reputation therefore substantially strengthens Luke's rhetoric throughout Acts. Parts 3 and 4 of this work focus on Luke's depiction of Paul as a paradigmatic missionary within the Acts narrative.

A common motif in the Hellenistic-Roman world is an appeal to the authority and example of founding figures; this can be seen in both philosophical schools such as Platonists, and ethnic groups such as Romans, Athenians, and Judeans.[22] Luke writes with a similar purpose: his first volume focuses on the life of Jesus, the founder of Christianity, while his second volume focuses on the ancillary founding figures of Peter and Paul. Together these constitute an *"origin story" for the Christian church, articulating the shared values of these three paramount founders*. Luke-Acts can therefore be seen as a rhetorical call to honor and imitate the common principles and conduct of Christianity's authoritative founders, who provide examples for subsequent Christians to follow. Chief among these is a cluster of values related to the priority of the Christian mission, which finds its climactic expression in Paul's efforts in the second half of Acts. This grouping involves related themes such as the healing of division and the welcome of foreigners, each of which seeks to unleash the missional power of the united church.

The primordial enemy of cross-cultural mission is ethnocentrism and the accompanying assumptions of ethnic supremacy. *The book of Acts seeks to heal the division and conflict in the early church between Jews and Gentiles*, at least partially caused by Pauline controversy. It does this by focusing on Jewish Christians based around Jerusalem in the first half, and non-Jewish Christians as represented by Paul's largely Gentile-focused mission in the

---

21. Schneckenburger's *Über den Zweck* is the first elaborate investigation of the purpose of Acts and argues that it is directed towards Jewish Christians in Rome and is primarily interested in legitimizing Paul and his mission.

22. Balch, "Luke-Acts," 65, compares Dionysius's account of Romulus and Josephus's account of Moses. Balch, "Founders of Rome," lists 32 values shared by Dionysius's story of Rome's origins and Luke-Acts, arguing that the identical vocabulary and many shared values legitimate reading these as parallel stories of origin.

second half. The result is a picture of unity and the resolution of conflict, using the Hellenist leaders, the Ethiopian eunuch, the Cornelius episode, the church at Syrian Antioch, and the "Jerusalem Council" as focal turning points.[23] This harmonious narrative framework is meant to bring additional healing and unity in Luke's day, and paves the way for effective missionary efforts to flourish. Luke emphasizes that the healing of division is a springboard to missional activity through his presentation of Paul's burgeoning mission.[24]

Luke's goal of healing division and generating unity illuminates the related theme of *the universal inclusion of all people*. If Luke's emphasis on mission is to be implemented, it must overcome deeply ingrained ethnic and intercity prejudice, and provoke his Christian readers to welcome and include all people, especially foreigners. Luke goes to great lengths to establish this theme of universal inclusion throughout Luke-Acts, beginning in Jesus's paradigmatic founding sermon (Luke 4:18–27), continuing with Peter's declaration that, "in every nation anyone who fears him and does what is right is acceptable to God" (Acts 10:35), and culminating with Paul "accepting all" in Rome (Acts 28:30–31). Thus, one of the primary purposes of Luke-Acts is to encourage Christians to overcome prejudice and welcome foreigners in their assemblies; the missional value of such a goal is self-evident. Chapter 3 of this work focuses on Luke's universally inclusive theology.[25]

THE RHETORIC OF ACTS

The question of the historical reliability of Acts is beyond the scope of this study, which focuses on its rhetoric and narrative world.[26] The following

---

23. Acts is likely reshaping existing traditions of division in order to assure readers that non-Jewish inclusion is not a novel development, but a central part of Jesus, Peter, and Paul's message; Baker, *Identity, Memory*, 146.

24. The latter parts of Acts show that this conflict is not fully resolved. For example, Paul is alone throughout much of his trials; other Christians fail to rally to his defense or support.

25. Other purposes for Acts have been advocated, such as legitimizing Paul and/ or Christianity to a Roman legal audience, evangelizing Gentiles, defending against Gnosticism, teaching about how to endure the delay of the *parousia*, training Christian leaders, and praising friendship within early Christian communities. While some are more convincing than others, all should be viewed through the primary lens of Luke's missional agenda.

26. Keener, *Acts*, 1:166–257 summarizes the historicity debate. Many scholars argue for the "general plausibility" of Acts, particularly when judged by ancient historiographical standards, while acknowledging certain problem areas such as Theudas's rebellion and various discrepancies with Paul's letters Where it can be compared to other

pages conduct a literary and narrative analysis of the persuasive effects of Luke's words and stories, pursuing a canonical reading of the Greek text.[27] As author and redactor, Luke has thoroughly made the content of Acts his own by shaping and arranging his sources, and by employing linguistic and narrative redundancy to illuminate his meaning. The structure and composition, plot development, themes and motifs, rhetorical repetition, and prominent characterization of Acts are all narrative tools Luke uses to express his missional ideas.[28]

Luke's apologetic tendencies are revealed in his use of the available means of persuasion, that is, his rhetoric, which is a common feature of ancient historiography.[29] Aristotle has provided three well-known categories of ancient rhetoric.[30] Of the three, Acts is not primarily deliberative or judicial, though political advice is given and legal arguments are made, particularly in the latter trial sections, but is best understood as *epideictic or demonstrative rhetoric*. This third rhetorical category encourages learning from the past as a guide to the future through praise, blame, or invective, in order to reaffirm and strengthen shared community values, as an end in itself or as the basis for some policy of action.[31] Epideictic rhetoric is similar to deliberative rhetoric, in that it advises about the future, but it does this more subtly through describing the past rather than giving direct advice.[32] Luke goes to great lengths to present certain characters and groups in the best possible light, in the hopes that his hearers will not just admire them, but also emulate them. Luke's specific rhetorical strategy shows multiple

---

contemporary sources, Acts seems to be largely reliable as a historical document, but this work focuses on the separate question of its rhetorical tendencies as a literary work.

27. This study follows the Alexandrian text-type, represented by Codex Sinaiticus (א), Vaticanus (B), and Alexandrinus (A), among others, which most scholars believe is earliest and simplest, while mentioning instances when the Western text-type, chiefly witnessed by Codex Bezae (D), is relevant. The Byzantine text-type, represented by uncials H, L, P, and S, is probably from the later fourth and fifth centuries. Keener, *Acts*, 1:7–11; Witherington, *Acts*, 65–8; Peterson, *Acts*, 49–52; Metzger, *Textual Commentary*, 222–445.

28. Keener, *Acts*, 1:16–26 discusses historical and literary approaches to Acts.

29. On Luke-Acts and rhetoric, see Witherington, *Acts*, 39–51; Peterson, *Acts*, 19–23; Keener, *Acts*, 1:20–21, 25–26, 139–43.

30. Aristotle, *Rhetorica* (fourth century BCE).

31. Kennedy, *Interpretation*, 39–74. Kennedy remarks that epideictic style "tends to amplification and is fond of ornament and tolerant of description and digression" (*Interpretation*, 74). Penner, *In Praise*, provides an example by arguing that the Stephen stories of Acts 6–7 are best understood as epideictic rhetoric praising the early church as bound together by friendship and service.

32. For ancient orators such as Cicero they are closely related, though epideictic praises what deliberative oratory advises; Balch, "Acts as Epideictic History," xiii.

similarities to that outlined in the Asiatic rhetorical handbook *Rhetorica ad Herennium*, particularly in the nuanced way that he seeks to meet his audience on their own ground in order to gain their trust.[33] Such a tactic could be employed in judicial cases but could also be a corollary of rhetoric aimed at initiation or basic schooling in a religious or philosophical group.[34]

In employing this epideictic rhetorical approach, Luke praises and idealizes key missionary figures throughout Acts, in the hopes that his audience will emulate their exploits in their own time and context. This habit of presenting protagonists as models or paradigms (*exampla* or παραδείγματα), also known as characterization, is the accepted way of communicating throughout the ancient Greco-Roman world. "Exemplary discourse, then, encompasses all of Roman society, from the loftiest aristocrats to the humblest peasants, laborers, and slaves,"[35] Luke means for his readers to follow in the footsteps of people such as Paul, Peter, James, Stephen, Philip, Barnabas, Apollos, Mary, Tabitha, Lydia, Priscilla, and Aquila, at least in terms of their public words and deeds. Luke also presents churches such as Jerusalem, Syrian Antioch, Berea, and Ephesus as models for later congregations to imitate. This is essentially the argument of Jervell: "the Lucan portrayal of early Christianity is not a mere presentation of a bygone era in the history of salvation, but is taken as a binding/compulsory example, which Luke the theologian sets before the eyes of the Christians of his generation."[36]

Luke also arranges and repeats certain crucial stories in a rhetorical use of narrative redundancy to make his point. For example, the story of the Gentile expansion is book-ended by the accounts of Saul's Damascus Road encounter in Acts 9 and Acts 22, and then reinterpreted theologically in Acts 26; this is Luke's most emphasized story and demonstrates his skillful use of *prosopopoeia*.[37] Conversely, Luke holds up enemies of the Christian mis-

---

33. *Rhetorica ad Herennium* (eighties BCE) is an anonymous text traditionally attributed to Cicero or Cornificius.

34. This approach closely resembles Hellenistic stasis theory, a central chapter in the history of the rhetoric of the Second Sophistic (roughly 54–230 CE); Heath, "Substructure of stasis-theory," 114–29. For early roots of and responses to the Second Sophistic, see Winter, *Philo and Paul Among the Sophists*.

35. Roller, "Exemplarity in Roman Culture," 6. Luke's readers would therefore expect the pedagogical use of historical events and characters as models. See also Darr, *Character Building*.

36. Jervell, *Apostelgeschichte*, 50–51.

37. "The Damascus road event allows the author of Acts to unfold the theological theme that he cherishes above all else: this theme is *the power of the Risen One as a transforming force within history*," Marguerat, *Historian*, 204. *Prosopopoeia* is an exercise among the rhetorical schools of antiquity which involves recomposing a story from one character's particular point of view and adapting it to a specific audience.

sion for derision in his narrative, following typical contemporary rhetorical conventions which use blame and invective as means of strengthening the shared commitment of the audience through urging them to reject common enemies, thus making the audience well-disposed towards the speaker. This is particularly similar to the approach of *Rhetorica ad Herennium*.[38]

As rhetorical narrative, Luke's account of the dynamic mission, conversion of Jews and Gentiles, establishing of new churches, and trial and defense sequences is meant to have a parenetic function for Luke's readers. The way Luke composes, arranges, and repeats certain stories and plot themes is highly persuasive. This work will mostly avoid analyzing the *overt persuasion* in the evangelistic speeches of Acts, which scholars have studied in detail, and will focus instead on the more nuanced *covert persuasion* of Luke's narrative presentation of his characters and churches.[39] This is where Luke's masterful epideictic and exemplary rhetoric is most apparent.

DEFINING MISSION

There are multiple ways to define mission, one of which is Schnabel's definition:

> The term "mission" or "missions" refers to the activity of a *community of faith* that distinguishes itself from its environment in terms of both *religious belief* (theology) and *social behavior* (ethics), that is *convinced of the truth claims of its faith*, and that *actively works* to win other people to the content of faith and the way of life of whose truth and necessity the members of that community are convinced.[40]

Four points can be drawn from this definition. First, mission is inherently a community affair. While individuals may engage in missional activity, this is within the context of a larger community, and the goal is either to draw new believers into the existing faith community or to create a new

---

38. *Rhetorica ad Herennium*, 1.4–5: "We can by four methods make our hearers well-disposed: by discussing our own persons, the person of our adversaries, that of our hearers, and the facts themselves . . . From the discussion of the person of our adversaries we shall secure goodwill by bringing them into hatred, unpopularity, or contempt . . . We shall make our adversaries unpopular by setting forth their violent behavior, their dominance, factiousness." Cf. Acts 4:1–22; 5:17–42; 6:8–15; Paul's many opponents.

39. Keener, *Acts*, 1:258–319; Soards, *Speeches*. The evangelistic speeches are certainly models for proclamation, employing multiple rhetorical techniques. Peterson, *Acts*, 22 uses the overt and covert persuasion distinction.

40. Schnabel, *Mission*, 1:11, emphasis added. "Missional" is simply the adjectival form of mission; outreach and witness are closely related concepts.

community. Second, to engage in mission, a person must be convinced of the truth of the message he or she is proclaiming. Third, mission is intentional, and requires proactive effort and concerted focus. Fourth, mission is about integrating belief and behavior, and putting action to faith. Missional activity is the behavioral result of a missional belief system, the ethical outcome of biblical theology constructed around the idea of God's intention to save all peoples.

Further aspects of mission can be seen in the derivation of the word. The English word mission comes from the Latin words *missio* (sending) and *mittere* (to send), which are related to the ἀποστέλλω word group in the NT.[41] These words imply intentional movement, from one point to another, and the existence of an authoritative sender and an authorized "sent one" (a messenger, ambassador, missionary).[42]

Christian mission is here understood as a holistic umbrella category, under which all sorts of varied activities take place, such as relational evangelism, organized outreach, church planting, serving ministries, discipleship, social action, and many others. The Anglican five marks of mission helpfully express this expansive idea:[43]

1. To proclaim the good news of Jesus Christ and invite others to life in his name.

2. To make disciples, plant and revitalize churches, and pioneer new ministries.

3. To respond to human need with compassionate service and prayer for healing.

4. To foster the flourishing of society and challenge injustice at every level.

---

41. Schnabel, *Paul the Missionary*, 22. In the NT, ἀποστέλλω (to send or dispatch someone, usually with a specific objective) occurs 136 times in the NT, most often for Jesus having been "sent" by God and the disciples "sent" by Jesus; ἀποστολή (a sending forth, assignment, mission, apostleship) is used to describe Peter and Paul's missionary callings and ministries; ἀπόστολος (apostle) speaks of the missionary, the sent one, and occurs 80 times. Schnabel, *Paul the Missionary*, 27–28. Lampe's *Patristic Greek Lexicon*, 209–11, discusses ἀποστολή and ἀποστολικός (having a mission, pertaining to an apostle) and points to a development of the concept of mission that extends from the missionary Spirit to structures and the individual members of the church.

42. Mission does not necessarily imply geographical travel, but it does require movement and "sentness" of some kind. Cf. John 20:21: "As the Father has sent me, so I send you." In the ancient world, the "sent one" (ἀπόστολος) carries the authority of the sender, such as an ambassador, agent, or envoy; BDAG, 121–22.

43. https://anglicancommunion.org/mission/marks-of-mission.aspx. Slightly adapted for this study.

5. To safeguard creation and address the damage of climate change.

As this study will show, the book of Acts is most overtly focused on the first mark, proclamation, and the rhetoric of missional speech acts. However, there are also multiple references to the discipleship of new believers, as well as to the priorities of serving others and advocating for justice, along with hints towards care of creation as well.[44]

This broader nuance moves towards the *missio dei* conception that mission is a part of God's very nature, and that all missional endeavors originate in God's missional initiative, which is cosmic in scope. Wright's definition of mission is helpful in this regard: "Our committed participation as God's people, at God's invitation and command, in God's own mission within the history of God's world for the redemption of God's creation."[45] Acts points to a God who wants to be known, and who reveals himself through the redemption of his people and his creation. Crucially, this missional trajectory in Acts from Jerusalem to Rome, and from Israel to all the nations, "is nothing more nor less than a fulfillment of the Scriptures, and especially the prophecies of Isaiah."[46] Mission in Acts, and in the NT for that matter, cannot be understood apart from its prophetic foundations in the Hebrew Scriptures, and Luke makes it clear in the first verse of Luke-Acts that his entire missiological paradigm is based on "the things that have been fulfilled among us" (Luke 1:1). The universal mission of the church is the climax, the grand realization of the purpose for which God created Israel in the first place—to be a blessing to all peoples (Gen 12:2–3).

Direct missional practice can be divided into three sub-categories, each of which will be observed in the text of Acts:[47] *public mission proclamation*, usually through preaching and teaching; *person-to-person mission*, usually through personal conversation, relationship, and social networks; *lifestyle mission*, which involves patiently living a transformed, just, and loving life before others in the context of a larger Christian community, in a way that awakens interest in nonbelievers.[48] In this matrix, mission is expressed in

---

44. Little has been written about the theme of creation care in Acts. This missional narrative should be understood as a central chapter in God's story of redeeming and renewing all of creation, on a cosmic and an individual level (3:21). Stories such as the famine relief (11:27–30) and the repeated emphasis on God as Creator of all things (4:24; 7:48–50; 10:15; 14:15–17; 17:24–29) speak to this vital aspect of mission.

45. Wright, *Mission of God*, 23.

46. Wright, *Mission of God*, 514; Wright provides examples of this in the next 8 pages, in an unfortunately brief treatment of mission in Acts.

47. Gehring, *House*, 91.

48. On this less direct lifestyle approach missional approach see Green, *Evangelism*. Kreider, *Patient Ferment*, argues that the church grew in the Roman Empire because

both word and deed, a partnership of loving outreach and service. The traditional focus on evangelistic outreach is crucial but should never be to the exclusion of missional justice actions such as redressing economic disparity, oppression, racial inequality, climate change, and other social ills. All these diverse missional activities proclaim the gospel of Jesus as Savior and Redeemer of both the individual and the world.

CONTEXTUALIZING MISSION TODAY

In Acts, this gospel travels across multiple cultures and boundaries, from Jew to Gentile, from rural Palestine to urban Rome, from the synagogue in Pisidian Antioch to the Athenian Areopagus to court before a King and governor. This involves contextualization within the narrative itself, for every new context requires a varied approach to the proclamation of the gospel. As the paradigmatic missionary, Paul in particular alters his message and approach to be as relevant and accessible to his audience as possible. The book of Acts therefore invites thoughtful contextualization, and supplies helpful examples of this essential process, which is inevitable as the message extends to different people, places, and times.

This work focuses on the rhetoric of Acts in its ancient context. However, it is difficult to read such missional content without reflecting on the question of contemporary application. Although there are fascinating similarities, the diverse world of the book of Acts is vastly different than the myriad cultural contexts of the modern world, and so any implementation requires significant contextualization. This process revolves around understanding the trajectory of missional practice in Acts, and then imaginatively tracing this arc onwards to today. The contemporary church cannot naively mimic the exact practices it finds in Acts, but must discover its own innovative practices, doing the challenging work of reflection and contextualization, while using Acts as a helpful and inspiring guide for this crucial journey. This work's concluding chapter reflects on the relevance and value of the missional stories of Acts for present-day outreach and proposes multiple ways Acts can contribute to the church's growth in mission today.

the virtue of patience was of central importance in the life and witness of the early Christians.

CONCLUSION—A RHETORICAL
CALL TO MISSIONAL ACTION

Acts depicts the church faithfully continuing Jesus's own ministry, with mission as its *raison d'être*. This is not simply a historical peculiarity; it is an intentionally persuasive strategy, a rhetorical *tour de force*. Luke crafts the narrative world of Acts in a way that compels its hearers to move from being passive observers to active participants, primarily using ancient epideictic approaches. His mission instructions can be separated into four overlapping categories: stimuli, structures, strategies, and suffering. His main characters provide missional exemplars to emulate, and none more so than the Apostle Paul, the culmination of Luke's two-part story. This introduction paves the way for a discussion of how Luke goes about calling his audience to join in the mission which he so compellingly describes in Acts. These missional stimuli are the focus of part 1.

PART 1

Missional Stimuli in Acts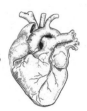

Because Luke's goal in writing Acts is to challenge and equip his readers for mission, he presents stories that function as missional catalysts for the church. After all, practical modelling of the mission will be futile if his generation of Christ-followers are not first motivated to take up the baton, live missional lives, and join in Christ's exhortation to take the message to the ends of the earth. *The why of the mission must therefore precede the* how. Luke carefully shapes his stories to help readers understand why this mission is so important, to increase their commitment to it, and to counter any sense of apathy or disengagement. In the body analogy, Luke's missional stimuli are the beating heart of his missional teaching, for they supply life-giving passion and missional energy to the whole body. Just as the human heart has four chambers which work together, so Luke presents four catalysts for mission, each of which partners with the others to motivate Luke's readers.

What does Luke claim empowers the early church to live missionally? Why does a regional band of Christ-followers based in the frontier city of Jerusalem go on to establish their churches in many of the most influential cities of the Empire within a few short decades? What is their motivation? These questions are at the heart of the book of Acts, and the focus of part 1: the missional stimuli of the church in Acts.

Chapter 1

The Expansion of the Word

So the word of the Lord grew mightily and prevailed

—ACTS 19:20

Most readers assume that Acts is primarily about the Spirit or the church. While these are prominent themes, Luke uses another concept as his fundamental impetus for mission: the triumphant Word. Marguerat claims that, "The theme of Acts is neither the history of the Church, nor the activity of the Spirit, but the expansion of the Word. The real hero of the Acts of the Apostles is the λόγος, the Word."[1] In Acts, the Word does not become flesh, as in John's Gospel, but is a *dynamic narrative personification of a three-fold Christological, ecclesiological, and missional identity.* This is the true missionary-hero of Acts.

The noun λόγος (word, message) occurs 65 times in Acts, of which at least 40 denote in some way this significant missional persona.[2] The volume

---

1. Marguerat, *Historian*, 37. "The word of God should be understood as the main character in the narrative of Acts," Pao, *Isaianic*, 49. Most commentators recognize Luke's focus on the spread of the gospel, or as he calls it, "the word of God/the Lord."

2. 2:41; 4:4, 29, 31; 6:2, 4, 7; 8:4, 14, 25; 10:36, 44; 11:1, 19; 12:24; 13:5, 7, 26, 44, 46, 48, 49; 14:3, 12, 25; 15:7, 15, 32, 35, 36; 16:6, 32; 17:11, 13; 18:11; 19:10, 20; 20:2, 7, 24, 32. It is sometimes difficult to make this distinction, e.g., 2:41. "The word of God" appears 11 times, "the word of the Lord" appears 10 times; other important phrases include: "the word of salvation" (σωτηρίας, 13:26), "the word of his grace" (χάριτος αὐτοῦ,

of references to this concept and its prominent activity indicate its importance to the Christian mission in Luke's mind.[3] He portrays the Word as
the trailblazer and "chief missionary" of the expanding church throughout
Acts, and calls believers to honor its leadership, following in the missional
footsteps of "those who from the beginning were eyewitnesses and servants
of the word" in the prologue of Luke-Acts (Luke 1:2).

THE ACTIVITY OF THE WORD

The λόγος is exceedingly active throughout Acts.[4] At Pentecost, the Spirit
initiates the preaching and dispersion of the Word.[5] From this event forward, the missionaries become *witnesses of a* Word, which they must recognize and follow. Throughout Acts, the Word leads the witnesses, acting
upon them, rather than being acted upon by them. For example, in Acts
13:44–49 the people assemble to hear (ἀκοῦσαι) the Word (not the messengers), the Word is spoken (λαληθῆναι), the Word is even praised/glorified
(ἐδόξαζον), and the Word spreads throughout the whole region (διεφέρετο
δὲ ὁ λόγος τοῦ Κυρίου δι᾽ ὅλης τῆς χώρας). It "grows/proliferates" three times
(αὐξάνω, 6:7; 12:24; 19:20). Paul is "possessed" by the Word (συνέχω, 18:5).[6]
People "receive" the Word four times (δέχομαι, ἀποδέχομαι, 2:41; 8:14; 11:1;
17:11). These occurrences describe the Word as a distinct personal being
or substance with an active will; this personification of the λόγος has been
called "the hypostatization of the Word."[7] In Acts, the λόγος takes on a life of
its own, as it vigorously leads the mission forward.

The Word also travels in Acts. Pao dissects the itinerary of the Word
of God and concludes that its journey in Acts is "one of conquest as the
word prevails in the midst of opposing forces."[8] Additionally, the journey
of the Word is linear, from Jerusalem to the Gentile nations, as opposed

---

14:3; 20:32), and "the word of the gospel" (εὐαγγελίου, 15:7).

3. Pao, *Isaianic*, 148, contrasts λόγος with ῥῆμα (a word or saying) in Acts, concluding that they are not synonymous, but that Luke uses λόγος in a special sense as a
reference to the Word of God throughout Acts.

4. This chapter follows and expands upon Marguerat's analysis of the Word in Acts,
Historian, 37–40.

5. See the following chapter for the relation between the Word and the Spirit.

6. Συνέχω can also mean seized or pressed, as when a person is gripped by, or devoted to, something; BDAG, 970–71.

7. Pao, *Isaianic*, 160–67. Many commentators simply understand "the word spread"
to be a typical Lukan phrase to summarize the success of the gospel, but Luke is making
the Word one of his primary characters here.

8. Pao, *Isaianic*, 156.

to the circular movements of the ministers of the Word. This travel theme further emphasizes that the active and personal Word is leading forward the irrepressible growth of the mission, particularly as it reaches out towards all the nations in fulfillment of Acts 1:8 and multiple Isaianic prophecies.[9]

The Word is not simply active in Acts, it is also *impossible to control or hinder*. The conflict with the religious leaders in Jerusalem (Acts 3–5) is about who controls the Word (4:1, 18), and Luke "ironically exposes the helplessness of the adversaries to censure it (24:1–4, 17; 5:17–28, 40)."[10] In Jerusalem (4:23–31) and Philippi (16:19–26) the apostles are jailed for preaching the Word and both attempts to silence them are futile against the earth-quaking power of God. Similarly, Paul's imprisonment in Rome does not prevent his bold and persuasive preaching (μετά πάσης παρρησίας ἀκωλύτως, 28:31). Luke is emphasizing that the dynamic growth of the Word is impossible to contain; ensured by God's providence, its eventual triumph is inevitable, and this is something it servants can anticipate with confidence.[11]

However, the Word's triumph in Acts does not guarantee the well-being of its bearers. Luke is not advocating a theological triumphalism on the part of the missionaries, as some have claimed.[12] The success of the Word usually comes in the context of the suffering of its messengers, and often because of their suffering. This highlights another theme of Acts: *providential failure*. For example, the apparent failure of the scattering of the Christians in Jerusalem (8:1b–4) has a positive effect on the spreading of the Word in Samaria (8:5) and results directly in the evangelization of the Gentiles in Antioch (11:19–21). Additionally, Paul's appeal to the emperor to avoid injustice results in the apostle's witness to the Word in the capital of the Empire (25:11—28:31). In each case, God sovereignly ordains failure and suffering as a vehicle for the proclamation of the Word.[13]

9. Pao, *Isaianic*, 150–56. The Isaianic roots of this are Isa 2:2–4; 40:9; 45:22–24; 55:10–11.

10. Marguerat, *Historian*, 37.

11. The providence of God, another of Acts' favorite themes, assures the Word's triumph; Squires, *Plan of God*, 37–77.

12. Käsemann, *Der Ruf der Freiheit*, 207–22, claimed that Luke had exchanged Paul's theology of the cross, of life working through death (e.g., Rom 6:6–8; Gal 2:19–20; 2 Cor 12:9–10), for a theology of glory or triumphalism, supporting this with the observation that in Luke-Acts the resurrection and not the cross is central in salvation. See also Conzelmann, *Theology of St. Luke*, 210. Gaventa, "Towards a Theology of Acts," 146–57, first opposed Käsemann's view, highlighting the suffering of the messengers of the Word, whose experience is not triumphant. Cunningham, "*Many Tribulations*," 16–17, cites multiple scholars who conclude that there is a theology of the cross in Luke-Acts, though it is different than Paul's.

13. Cunningham develops this theme, "*Many Tribulations*."

It is notable that each of the three references in Acts to the growth and expansion of the Word occurs narratively on the day after a crisis: 6:7 is after the crisis caused by the neglect of the widows; 12:24 concludes the killing of James, and the imprisonment of Peter; 19:20 completes the persecution-filled ministry of Paul in Corinth and Ephesus. "Threatened, beaten, betrayed, judged, imprisoned and stoned, the messengers do not ensure the advancement of the Word *in spite of* the bad things that happen to them, but *because of* them."[14]

This association of suffering and missional effectiveness is a narrative pattern in the Acts story.[15] At Lystra, Paul heals a paralyzed man and then is stoned and left for dead (14:19). In Philippi, Paul and Silas exorcise a demon from the "pythoness" slave girl, only to be put in prison (16:16–40).[16] God's empowering of his messengers does not spare them from failure, humiliation or martyrdom (7:54–60); as the Word advances, its bearers suffer.[17] This theme is soberly emphasized by Jesus's articulation of Paul's calling: "He is a chosen instrument of mine, to bear my name before the Gentiles and kings and the sons of Israel; for *I will show him how much he must suffer* ($\delta\epsilon\hat{i}$ . . . $\pi\alpha\theta\epsilon\hat{i}\nu$) *for my name's sake*" (9:15–16).

Marguerat summarizes this point: "Rather than a triumphal path, the route of the heralds of the Word is the road of the cross. According to Luke, this is the frame in which witness takes place."[18] In Acts, the Word irrepressibly triumphs, its witnesses suffer on the road of the cross, and the sovereignty of God in it all is absolute. "Nothing can stop the gospel but its spread still causes grief and loss."[19] The bearers of the Word must walk the way of the cross, the way of Christ, even as the mission advances.

OLD TESTAMENT ROOTS

Pao has claimed that to fully understand Acts, one must understand the OT background of the Exodus tradition as reinterpreted in Isaiah. "The scriptural story which provides the hermeneutical framework for Acts is none

---

14. Marguerat, *Historian*, 39.

15. See part 4 for more on the connection between mission and suffering in Acts.

16. Evangelization in Act often culminates in the violent rejection of the missionary, e.g., in Thessalonica, Berea, Corinth, and Ephesus (Acts 17–19). Yet the Word continues to expand.

17. Rapske, "Opposition," 235–56 itemizes the sources of persecution and opposition in Acts and demonstrates how they all reveal "the principle that if it is of God, it will be invincible," 254.

18. Marguerat, *Historian*, 40.

19. House, "Suffering," 323.

other than the foundation story of Exodus as developed and transformed through the Isaianic corpus … in the development of the identity of the early Christian movement, the appropriation of ancient Israel's foundation story provides grounds for a claim by the early Christian community to be the true people of God."[20] This is particularly true for the λόγος in Acts, and three foundational passages in Deutero-Isaiah (40–55) illustrate the connection:

- "The grass withers, the flower fades, but the *word of our God* (וּדְבַר־ אֱלֹהֵינוּ) will stand forever" (Isa 40:8);

- "From my mouth has gone forth in righteousness a *word* (דָּבָר) that shall not return: 'To me every knee shall bow, every tongue shall swear'" (Isa 45:23);

- "For as the rain and the snow come down from heaven, and do not return there until they have watered the earth … so shall *my word* (דְבָרִי) be that goes out from my mouth; it shall not return to me empty, but it shall accomplish that which I purpose" (Isa 55:10–11).[21]

Each of these emphasizes the power and supremacy of the Word of God—it stands forever, and it is unstoppable in accomplishing God's purposes.

Luke draws on this Isaianic tradition by presenting the Word in Luke-Acts similarly, particularly in its inevitable triumph and its unchanging nature. Significantly, Jesus fulfills the prophets as the bearer of the Word of God in Luke's Gospel.[22] The Word of the Lord in Acts then accomplishes the divine will "with power/might/vigor" (κατὰ κράτος, 19:20)—this phrase should probably be understood as a militaristic conquest statement.[23] The Word in Acts travels to the ends of the earth, with a two-fold goal: "to conquer the world and to create a community as the true people of God."[24] As Pao emphasizes: "Themes such as the journey of the word, the nature of the word, the growth of the word-community, and the identity of the word-community as the people of God can be properly understood only against the context of the Exodus traditions as transformed in Isaiah 40–55."[25]

---

20. Pao, *Isaianic*, 5.

21. Pao, *Isaianic*, 48–49. See also Isa 2:2–4.

22. Luke 5:1; 6:47; 7:7, 17; 11:28; 21:33, 61; 24:19.

23. Pao, *Isaianic*, 162–63.

24. Pao, *Isaianic*, 176.

25. Pao, *Isaianic*, 176; see 145–80 for the details of Pao's arguments.

In addition to Isaiah, there are other Hebrew Bible roots to the Word in Acts.[26] Luke is drawing on texts such as Ps 33:6–11: "By *the word* (בִּדְבַר) *of the Lord* the heavens were made, and all their host by the breath of his mouth . . . The counsel [plans] of the Lord stands forever, the thoughts of his heart to all generations." There are also other prophetic texts, such as when Jeremiah proclaims, "Is not *my word* (דְבָרִי) like fire, says the Lord, and like a hammer that breaks a rock in pieces?" (23:29), and when Jeremiah, Ezekiel, and Zechariah claim, "*the word of the Lord* came to me."[27] These and many other passages depict the Word as a potent force, with an emphasis on its powerful ability to accomplish God's intentions. Luke draws on this rich theological tradition and develops it into a personified vehicle and catalyst for the ongoing Christian mission.

THE THREE-FOLD NATURE OF THE WORD

The Word is first a *Christological* phenomenon in Acts; for Luke, Jesus is the incarnation of the forcefully effective OT Word of the Lord.[28] For this reason, scholars refer to it as the divine λόγος. There are parallels with Johannine theology of the pre-incarnate Word (John 1:1–14), yet Lucan theology is distinct: "For Luke, the word of God was made flesh in Jesus, but not in John's manner: it is the word of God, the word in the past addressed to the *prophets* and not pre-existent in heaven, which took on a body in Jesus (Acts 10:36f.)."[29]

Luke understands the divine Word to be the continuation of the "word of the Lord" spoken to and through the prophets, embodied and fulfilled in Jesus, and now continuing its activity among his followers. The Book of Acts is Luke's bold extension of the activity of Christ found in his Gospel to the activity of Christ's church, and the Word is one of the narrative links. Acts 10:36–43 summarizes this understanding, and connects the sons of Israel, Jesus of Nazareth, of whom all the prophets bear witness, and the ongoing call to proclaim his name as witnesses, that everyone who believes in him may be forgiven. For Luke, the λόγος is the story of the life, death and resurrection of Jesus, the present-day activity of the risen Christ in the world, and

---

26. Peterson, *Acts*, 33.

27. There are at least 64 such occurrences in these three prophetic books.

28. For a review of books and articles on Luke's Christology, see Bovon, *Luke*, 123–223, 532–36.

29. Bovon, *Luke*, 222. There is overlap between these conceptions of the word. The Johannine tradition is likely more influenced by Hellenistic philosophical concepts, as well as the OT prophetic "word of the Lord."

the fulfillment of all which the prophets of old had spoken. This is why its victory is certain—the triumph of the Word is the triumph of Christ himself.

The Word is also an *ecclesiological* concept for Luke.[30] Throughout Acts, "the growth of the Word is co-extensive with that of the Church."[31] When Luke speaks of the Word spreading three different times (6:7; 12:24; 19:20), he is actually referring to the numerical growth of the church.[32] The same verb, πληθύνω, which implies proliferation and growth, is used for both the λόγος (12:24) and the church (6:1, 7; 9:31).[33] The growth of the Word personifies the growth of the church; just as a seed possesses the power of growth, so "the word has in itself the power of life . . . This independent force of the word of God makes it the preeminent instrument of salvation."[34]

The Word's primary goal in Acts is the creation of the new community of the people of God, in the Isaianic Exodus tradition.[35] Through the Word, God is bringing his people once again out of exile and into promise, in a further new exodus. This community is also the sole possessor of the Word as their inheritance.[36] Luke views the Word and the church as interchangeable, at least as far as their irresistible growth is concerned.[37] "The community is the word as it testifies to the power and salvation of the God of Israel."[38]

This highlights the inseparable nature of Christ and his church in Lukan theology (9:1–5). The pivotal story of Saul's conversion reveals this most clearly. Acts 9:1 states that Saul is persecuting Jesus's disciples, the church, and yet in 9:4–5 Jesus says twice that Saul is persecuting him. Christ and his church are one and the same throughout Acts: "Distinctive to Luke's account is the identification of the risen Lord with the community . . . Luke could scarcely have found a more effective way of establishing the living relationship and presence of the raised prophet with those who continued to live and speak and act with his prophetic spirit."[39] For Luke, Christ and

---

30. Kodell, "Word," 505–19.

31. Marguerat, *Historian*, 38.

32. This phrase Ὁ λόγος τοῦ Θεοῦ ηὔξανε (6:7; 12:24; 19:20), used to summarize church growth, has been a "perennial source of puzzlement for translators and interpreters," Kodell, "Word," 505.

33. Marguerat, *Historian*, 38.

34. Kodell, "Word," 506.

35. Pao, *Isaianic*, 167–71.

36. Pao, *Isaianic*, 171–76.

37. For the interchangeable growth of the church and the Word, see 2:42; 5:14; 6:1, 7; 9:31; 11:21; 12:24; 13:49; 16:5; 18:10; 19:20.

38. Pao, *Isaianic*, 170.

39. Johnson, *Acts*, 168.

his church are one, brought together by his theological understanding of the divine λόγος.

Thirdly, λόγος is also a *message* to proclaim, and a *mission* to implement: "The mission itself can be described as the Word of God expanding and growing (Acts 6:7; 8:14; 10:36; 11:1; 12:24; 19:20)."[40] This nuance draws on the most natural meaning of "word," a spoken message. When the Holy Spirit fills the disciples, they are empowered to "speak the *word* of God with great boldness" (4:31). When they are scatted by persecution, they "go about preaching the *word*" (8:4). When they reach Salamis (and other destinations), they "proclaim the *word* of God in the synagogues" (13:5). In this sense, the Word and the message of the gospel are synonyms for Luke. He explicitly joins the two concepts at the Jerusalem Council when Peter refers to "the Word of the gospel" (τόν λόγον τοῦ εὐαγγελίου, 15:7; cf. 20:24). The book of Acts defines believers by their acceptance of the Word (8:14; 11:1; 17:11; cf. Luke 8:13) and calls them "hearers of the Word" (13:7, 44; 15:7).[41]

Luke announces this missional understanding of the Word as a message to proclaim and receive much earlier, in the parable of the sower (Luke 8:5–15).[42] In his explanation of this parable, Jesus identifies the seed as "the word of God" (ὁ λόγος τοῦ Θεοῦ, 8:11), and emphasizes hearing (ἀκούω) and believing (πιστεύω) the Word four times (8:12–15). This image of a life-giving seed summarizes the reproductive power of the missional proclamation: when it falls on fertile soil, it multiplies rapidly to yield a crop a hundred times more than was sown (Luke 8:8). Luke goes on to present the story of the growth of the church's mission in Acts as the beginnings of the fulfillment of this Christological promise of dramatic hundred-fold expansion. Because of their response to the Word, Luke implies that the cities of the Roman Empire are good soil for an extensive harvest.[43]

CONCLUSION—FOLLOWING THE UNSTOPPABLE MISSIONARY FORCE

Three understandings of λόγος elucidate its nature and meaning in Acts. The Word is the gospel message, the good news of the ongoing missional

---

40. Johnson, *Luke*, 23.

41. Marguerat, *Historian*, 38.

42. For other occurrences of "the word of God" in Luke's Gospel see 3:2; 5:1; 8:21; 11:28; note the emphasis on hearing and obeying the Word.

43. Kodell, "Word," 517, observes that "the flourishing of the early Christian community was proof positive for Luke that the word had fallen on good soil and was bearing fruit."

activity of Christ, through his people. It fuses together Jesus, the church, and the message which they proclaim. For Luke, these concepts are inseparable, and illuminate his understanding of the early Christian movement and its mission. The repeated language of increase and growth signifies the forward momentum of the gospel movement which the missionary Word generates.

With a theological foundation in the OT prophets and especially the Isaianic new exodus, Luke depicts the Word as an unstoppable personal force, extremely active, constantly expanding, and leading the growing mission of the church ever outward. It is the central character in the narrative, and the early church's principal missionary, which every subsequent missionary must follow. The divine λόγος, representing Christ, his church, and their collective gospel message, is the primary catalyst and most potent stimulus for Christian mission in Acts.

The Word's power and inevitable triumph is a source of strength to its messengers, especially when they suffer on its behalf. Luke's implications are clear: what was true for the earliest Christ-followers is still true as he writes. The Word is unchanging, just as Isaiah declared; therefore, it is still advancing with power in Luke's day, and it will unquestionably accomplish all that God intends for it. Luke's presentation of the Christological Word in Acts inspires his readers to become caught up in its triumphant expansion, embodied in the growth of the church, and accomplished by the missional proclamation of the gospel message.

Luke acknowledges that the Word's victory does not necessarily equate to the triumph of its bearers, but often occurs amid and even as a direct result of the suffering of those who proclaim it. Yet believers can be reassured that the Word will ultimately prevail, for God's providence guarantees this. The theological personification of the Word is therefore Luke's most compelling missional stimulus, for it invites followers of Christ to follow its continuing initiative and expansion, even at great personal cost. This can only happen by the power of the Spirit, which is the focus of the next chapter.

Chapter 2

The Empowerment of The Spirit

In the last days it will be, God declares, that I will pour out my Spirit upon all flesh, and your sons and your daughters shall prophesy

—ACTS 2:17

While the growth of the divine Word is the primary missional theme of Acts, the power and activity of the Spirit is a potent secondary motif, and more precisely the means by which the Word advances with such authority. Luke roots the witness of the Spirit, like the progress of the Word, explicitly in the Father's plan and promise (Luke 24:49; Acts 1:4–8). Luke has given the Spirit such central importance that Chrysostom famously called Acts "the Gospel of the Holy Spirit," and the record of what that "other Paraclete" said and did (cf. John 14:16).[1] Acts is plainly less about "the acts of the apostles," and much more about the acts of the Spirit.

---

1. John Chrysostom, *Hom. Act.*, 1:5, as cited in Bruce, *Acts*, 61n3. Multiple others have made similar claims, e.g., Johnson, *Acts*, 14: the "Book of the Holy Spirit." Bovon, *Luke*, 225–72, 536–40 has a bibliography and review of many of the principal monographs and articles on Luke's pneumatology. Keener, *Acts*, 1:519–37 is a recent survey of the Spirit in Acts.

AN EMPOWERING NARRATIVE CHARACTER

Scholars are nearly unanimous that the Spirit's main role in Acts is to empower the church for mission, though the precise details of this vary. Jesus's final addresses to his disciples in both Luke's Gospel and Acts present the Spirit as utterly necessary for the success of the mission, and thus urge them to wait in their witness until they have received the promised Spirit (Luke 24:49; Acts 1:4–8). The essential programmatic texts in both volumes focus on the Spirit's empowerment for mission, first of Jesus, and then of the church (Luke 4:18–19; 24:48–49; Acts 1:8; 2:17–18).[2] Luke is teaching that dependence on the Spirit's power and activity is a prerequisite for missional success.

Jesus is initially the Spirit-bearer (4:18), and the leading of the Spirit is the central focus of his ministry.[3] He is also the giver of the Spirit, and though Jesus gives the Spirit initially only to the apostles to empower their witness (1:8), Luke quickly includes all believers in all places (2:39), including eventually Samaritans (8:15–17) and non-Jewish peoples further afield (10:44–48; cf. 19:6). The Spirit's activity also supersedes all age and gender barriers (2:17–18). By democratizing the Spirit in this way, Luke is advocating that all followers of Christ, including his own audience, actively partake in this Spirit empowerment for mission, a conviction which propels the early church's remarkable growth. The book of Acts insists that all people can become "indigenous partners in mission" through the empowerment of the Spirit.[4]

Luke's conception of the Spirit is distinct from other NT pneumatologies.[5] In Pauline theology the Spirit is the source of personal faith (1 Cor 12:3, 9), and "life in the Spirit" is normative Christian experience (Rom 8; Gal 5:16–25). The Johannine Paraclete has a primary teaching function, in which he reminds the disciples of Jesus's teaching and testifies about who Jesus is by revealing him to people (John 14:25; 15:26–27; 16:13–15). By contrast, in Acts the Spirit never incites faith or glorifies the Son. Instead, Luke's Spirit provokes missional action, protects the emerging church, takes hold of communities, and engages in other active behaviors, always directed towards Christ followers.[6] The most common ground is with Paul's concept of "life in the Spirit," for Luke encourages believers to live in and by the

2. Keener, *Acts*, 1:520.

3. Dunn, *Jesus and the Spirit*, is an exploration of Jesus's experience and consciousness of the Spirit.

4. Keener, *Acts*, 1:521.

5. Shelton, *Mighty in Word and Deed*, 6–13 compares the pneumatologies of Mark, Matthew, and Luke.

6. Marguerat, *Historian*, 109.

Spirit. However, while Paul emphasizes personal transformation and particular pneumatic gifts for ministry, in Acts the Spirit's life relates almost exclusively to empowerment for missional proclamation.

Luke never explains the Spirit, but instead shows the Spirit in action. He never presents any systematic theological conception of the Spirit, but instead portrays the πνεῦμα as a prominent narrative character in the plotline of Acts, who on the Father's behalf repetitively intervenes in the lives and affairs of the other characters.[7] For Luke, as for all expert storytellers, showing is better than telling.[8] Marguerat explains the implications of such a literary strategy:

> Luke presents less a concept than a *pragmatic of the Holy Spirit*. There is no question here: this operation is not theologically innocent. To draw the Spirit into the scene of the narrative is to enroll in the programme a God who intervenes in human affairs. The pragmatic of the Spirit translates and inspires an experience of the Spirit. In his own way, Luke rejoins the situation of the first Christians, practical theologians, indwelt by the Spirit, living by him, committed to proclaiming the kerygma rather than to advancing a teaching about the Spirit.[9]

This "pragmatic" approach could indicate that Luke lacks a refined pneumatology, but this is not a foregone conclusion. Luke writes narrative theology, with a practical missional goal, and thus chooses to be more illustrative than didactic about the Spirit.

SPIRIT ACTIVITY IN ACTS

The Spirit's activity is extremely frequent in Acts. Of the 70 total occurrences of πνεῦμα, at least 58 are references to the Holy Spirit,[10] which represent

7. Shepherd, *Narrative Function*, esp. 90–98 treats the Spirit as a character in the Acts narrative and concludes that Luke's inclusion of the Spirit as a virtual substitute for God in his narrative led directly to the development of Trinitarian theology (*Narrative Function*, 254–57).

8. Shepherd, *Narrative Function*, 249: "Indirect presentation of character is the preferred method for every characterization. To let a character be presented by speech and action is a favorite authorial device."

9. Marguerat, *Historian*, 110.

10. Of the 70 total occurrences, eight refer to evil/unclean spirits: 5:16; 8:7; 16:16, 18; 19:12, 13, 15, 16; four refer to a human or other spirit: 7:59; 17:16; 23:8, 9; and the remaining 58 likely refer to the Holy Spirit: 1:2, 5, 8, 16; 2:4 [twice], 17, 18, 33, 38; 4:8, 25, 31; 5:3, 9, 32; 6:3, 5, 10; 7:51, 55; 8:15, 17, 18, 19, 29, 39; 9:17, 31; 10:19, 38, 44, 45, 47; 11:12, 15, 16, 24, 28; 13:2, 4, 9, 52; 15:8, 28; 16:6, 7; 18:25; 19:2 [twice], 6, 21; 20:22,

nearly a quarter of all occurrences in the NT; no other NT book has even half as many.[11]

Table 2.1 Concentration of Relevant Πνεῦμα Occurrences in Acts

1. The Jerusalem Community (1–7)	253 verses/21 occurrences *12.04 verses per reference* *8.3 percent* (2nd)
2. The Peter Cycle (8–12)	186 verses/18 occurrences *10.33 verses per reference* *9.7 percent* (1st)
3. The Pauline Mission (13–20)	302 verses/16 occurrences *18.86 verses per reference* *5.3 percent* (3rd)
4. Paul's Imprisonment (21–28)	266 verses/3 occurrences *88.67 verses per reference* *1.1 percent* (4th)

Some scholars have posited that there is a steady decline in total references to the Spirit from the beginning of Acts to the end.[12] However, as the above table shows, the greatest concentration per verse is actually in the Peter cycle, and the Pauline mission is not far behind. The last section of Acts has much less reference to the Spirit's activity, but there are apparent narrative explanations for this; Luke's narrowing focus on Paul's trials in the final eight chapters does not mean that the activity of the Spirit in the wider church necessarily diminishes during this time.

In addition to its *frequency*, there is also a shift in the *type* of πνεῦμα activity over the course of Acts.[13] Corporate, ecstatic interventions dominate the early activity of the Spirit, such as at Pentecost (2:1–13), the room-shaking prayer meeting (4:31), and the Cornelius episode (10:44–46). There are 18 such interventions in the Jerusalem community, 11 in the Peter cycle, four in the Pauline mission, and none in the imprisonment of Paul. As Acts unfolds, the Spirit moves from dramatic communal interventions towards personal activity, such as the Spirit forbidding Paul from speaking the Word in Asia, or entering Bithynia (16:6, 7). "Luke's narration begins at Pentecost, in fire and loud noise; it ends with the figure of the prisoner Paul preaching

---

23, 28; 21:4, 11; 28:25. This discounts the Western textual variants in 15:29 and 19:1. Richards, "Pentecost," 133–49.

11. This is even more apparent when examining the phrase "holy spirit," Keener, *Acts*, 1:520.

12. E.g., Marguerat, *Historian*, 111–13, who does not take into account the varying lengths of these sections.

13. Marguerat, *Historian*, 112. Shepherd, *Narrative Function*, 219–20, 250–53.

in Rome. The author unfolds his story of the Church between fire and the Word . . . The Church is always led by the Spirit, but the breath of God does not act in identical ways from one end to the other in Acts."[14]

Some claim that this more individual involvement, mostly on behalf of the servants of the Word, provides glimpses of the normative experience of the church with the Spirit in Luke's day, though this is not necessarily the case. This trajectory can also be explained by Luke's narrowing narrative focus, as he moves from broad community narratives to individualized stories. It is unsurprising that the Spirit's activity in Acts would follow this same pattern, from dramatic founding narratives in Jerusalem, through Paul's missionary travels and imprisonment, and it is ill-advised to make definitive conclusions about the activity of the Spirit in Luke's day based on what he selectively includes in his story.

Perhaps surprisingly, Luke avoids attributing miracles to the Spirit in Acts, but instead ascribes the miracles of Jesus (2:22), Peter (4:7), Stephen (6:8), Philip (8:10), and Paul (19:11) to "power" (δύναμις).[15] Additionally, the Spirit reaches believers in Acts, rather than non-believers. "Whether groups or individuals, in Acts it is only the followers of Jesus or the holy men of Israel who are touched [by the Spirit]."[16] This activity among believers is a trademark of Lukan pneumatology, and highlights what is central for Luke: The Spirit builds the church by empowering believers and communities for mission but is rarely if ever responsible for the conversion of an individual.

Luke generally reserves the privileged place of miracles and personal faith for the Christological Word: "Luke, with Paul, refuses to place the Spirit in the forefront. It is the Word, stimulated and accompanied by the Spirit, which is the most important."[17] Miracles in Acts are a sign of the Risen One's work; it is "in the name of Jesus Christ" that people are healed (ἐν τῷ ὀνόματι Ἰησοῦ Χριστοῦ, 3:6, 16; 4:10, 30; 16:18; 19:13). Similarly, it is the name of the Lord that saves and forgives (2:21; 4:12; 10:43; 22:16), and new believers are baptized in the name of the Lord (2:38; 8:16; 10:48; 19:5).[18] These roles are connected in Acts—miracles are often the confirma-

---

14. Marguerat, *Historian*, 113.

15. Marguerat, *Historian*, 120. Cf. Luke 11:20 ("if I drive out demons by *the finger of God*"), with its parallel passage, Matt 12:28 ("if I drive out demons by *the Spirit of God*"). Luke's hesitance to attribute miracles to the Spirit is another difference with Pauline thought (1 Cor 12:7–11).

16. Marguerat, *Historian*, 112, who points out that the πνεῦμα does not stop Saul on the Damascus road (Acts 9), or lead Julius the centurion to protect Paul (Acts 27).

17. Bovon, *Luke*, 238.

18. Marguerat, *Historian*, 121. Christ's name (ὄνομα) is exceedingly powerful in Acts; Luke refers to its role in healing and salvation at least 32 times.

tion of the Christological message, and as such lead directly to a person's faith, which is Christ's domain. Such limitations also highlight the Spirit's primary roles of advancing the mission and fortifying the church.

Though this is true, it is important to avoid overstating the point, or concluding that in Acts the Spirit's work has no relationship whatsoever to miracles or conversion.[19] For Luke δύναμις and πνεῦμα are closely linked, and power often comes from the Spirit (1:8; 8:19; 10:38; cf. Luke 1:17, 35; 4:14, 36). There are multiple instances in Luke-Acts where "power" clearly designates the Spirit, who is undoubtedly involved in performing miracles (Luke 1:35; 24:49; Acts 1:8; 4:6–8; 13:9–11).[20] Additionally, the NT appears to show early Christianity united in the conviction that miracles come from the power of the Spirit. If this is the case, analysis of the activity of the Spirit in Acts must also consider references to "power."[21]

Similarly, it is difficult to separate the Spirit-empowered proclamation of the gospel from the hearer's faith response to it. For example, in Acts 5:30–32 the preaching of repentance, the witness of believers, and the witness of the Spirit are all mentioned in close proximity. Passages like this reveal more nuance and overlap in these concepts than may have been first apparent, though Luke does subtly but consistently differentiate them. The effect of this rhetorical strategy is to highlight the Holy Spirit's focus on *the empowerment of believers for mission* in Acts rather than on conversion and miracles, which are predominantly the realm of Luke's "chief missionary," the Christological Word.

THE SPIRIT IN LUKE'S GOSPEL

Unsurprisingly, the Spirit is also a prominent theme in Luke's Gospel—there are nearly three times as many references to the Spirit in Luke as in Mark (about half its length) and 1.4 times as many as in Matthew (of similar length).[22] During the birth and infancy narratives, the Spirit fills multiple early characters, such as Mary (1:35), Elizabeth (1:41), Zechariah (1:67), and Simeon (2:25–27). However, after the Holy Spirit descends dove-like upon Jesus at his baptism (3:22), and the Father declares that Jesus is his

19. This is the extreme view of Schweizer, "πνεῦμα," 407. For arguments against this position, see Bovon, *Luke*, 242–3; Turner, "Jesus and the Spirit," 14–22.

20. Strelan, *Strange Acts*, 59–63 explores the association of the spirit with power.

21. There are nine occurrences of "power" (δύναμις) in Acts: 1:8; 2:22; 3:12; 4:7, 33; 6:8; 8:13; 10:38; 19:11.

22. Keener, *Acts*, 1.520.

"beloved," only Jesus possesses the Spirit in Luke's Gospel.[23] The angel of the Lord declares that Jesus will be "filled with the Spirit even from the womb of his mother" (πνεύματος ἁγίου πλησθήσεται ἔτι ἐκ κοιλίας μητρὸς αὐτοῦ, 1:15), and Luke repeatedly emphasizes that Jesus is "full of the Holy Spirit" (πλήρης πνεύματος ἁγίου, 4:1), "in the power of the Spirit" (ἐν τῇ δυνάμει τοῦ πνεύματος, 4:14), and "rejoices in the Holy Spirit" (ἠγαλλιάσατο [ἐν] τῷ πνεύματι τῷ ἁγίῳ, 10:21).

Luke underscores this exclusive connection with the Spirit in the inaugural scene of Jesus's ministry in the Nazarene synagogue when Jesus declares, "The Spirit of the Lord is upon me—" (πνεῦμα κυρίου ἐπ᾽ ἐμέ, 4:18). Most scholars see this as the programmatic text for the entire Gospel, if not all of Luke-Acts. In this pivotal moment, Jesus claims the Spirit's empowerment for his mission, which functions as a prototype anticipating the church's Spirit-empowerment to reach the ends of the earth later in Acts (Luke 24:48–49; Acts 1:8; 2:17–18). Luke also stresses the exclusive bond between Jesus and the Spirit in the fact that Jesus does not give the Spirit to his disciples until after his ascension at Pentecost (cf. John 20:21–22). After his baptism Jesus alone is continually inhabited by the Spirit in Luke's Gospel.[24]

A fundamental pneumatological shift happens with the resurrection and ascension of Jesus. Now that Jesus is absent (Acts 1:9–11) the Spirit comes upon believers (Acts 2; cf. John 16:7). Luke wants every reader to understand that the church is born not of human effort or activity, but from God: "Being *exalted* (ὑψωθείς) at the right hand of God, and *having received* (λαβών) from the Father the *promise of the Holy Spirit*, he [Jesus] has *poured out* (ἐξέχεεν) this that you both see and hear" (2:33). This important verse merges two Jewish traditions: bestowing the Spirit on the Isaianic Messiah (Isa 11:2; 42:1; 61:1), and distributing the Spirit to God's people (Num 11:29; Ezek 39:29; Joel 3:1).[25] It is also a hermeneutical key to Luke's pneumatology, for it links the exaltation of Jesus, the Father's promise of the Spirit, and its fulfillment in the Spirit being poured out on believers. As possessor of the Spirit, Jesus gives the Spirit to his followers to empower their ministry, and the church is born.

---

23. Marguerat, *Historian*, 114 argues Jesus is the sole bearer of the Spirit but ignores others at the beginning of Luke.

24. Schweizer, "πνεῦμα," 404–5, claims Jesus's mastery over the Spirit, yet a more balanced view is that this is a mutual relationship; Dunn, *Jesus and the Spirit*; Turner, "Jesus and the Spirit," 3–42.

25. Marguerat, *Historian*, 115.

THE SPIRIT AND WITNESS

Jesus assigns this Spirit, poured out at Pentecost, a specific function: "*You will receive power* (δύναμις) when the Holy Spirit comes upon you; and *you will be my witnesses* (μάρτυρες) in Jerusalem, in all Judea and Samaria, and to the ends of the earth" (Acts 1:8). The Spirit is here a source of power, with the particular role of enabling the disciples to be Jesus's witnesses from their current location to the neighboring regions, and on to the ends of the earth. With this verse, Luke locates the beginning of the Christian mission in the founding gift of the Spirit, and stresses that this power not only inaugurates the mission but will also sustain it for its duration to all the earth. In Acts, the Spirit leads and empowers God's people in witnessing as a "co-witness" to Jesus: "We are *witnesses* (μάρτυρες) of these things; and *so is the Holy Spirit*, whom God has given to those who obey him" (5:32).[26]

Acts 4 sheds light on how the Spirit expresses witness alongside God's people. After imprisoning Peter and John, the Jerusalem authorities release them, threatening dire consequences if they continue to teach in the name of Jesus (4:18, 21, 29). They promptly ignore this warning and focus on continuing the mission: "Lord, take note of their threats, and grant that your servants may *speak your word with all boldness* (μετὰ παρρησίας πάσης λαλεῖν τὸν λόγον σου), while you extend your hand to heal, and signs and wonders take place through the name of your holy servant Jesus" (4:29–30). The response is dramatic: "the place where they had gathered together was shaken, and they were all *filled with the Holy Spirit* (ἐπλήσθησαν ἅπαντες Πνεύματος Ἁγίου) and began to speak the word of God *with boldness*" (μετὰ παρρησίας, 4:31).[27] God's immediate response concerns boldness (παρρησία) to witness, but not the requested healings and signs and wonders (until 5:12–16): this boldness results from the filling of the Spirit.

In Acts, there is a compelling connection between the Spirit and bold proclamation of the Word, which recalls Jesus's earlier promise to give his followers the Spirit's assistance in case of persecution (Luke 12:11–12). It is "filled with the Spirit" that Peter speaks to the people of Jerusalem (4:8). Wisdom and the Spirit give Stephen's words their authority (6:10), and the same is true for Barnabas in his evangelistic ministry at Antioch (11:24).[28]

This theme of proclamation is underlined by Peter's message at Pentecost: "*I will pour out My Spirit* (ἐκχεῶ ἀπὸ τοῦ πνεύματός μου) on all mankind; and your sons and your daughters shall *prophesy* (προφητεύσουσιν) . . .

26. Marguerat, *Historian*, 115.

27. The shaking is a sign of divine assent and fulfillment in the ancient world, cf. Acts 16:6; Keener, *Acts*, 2:1174–5.

28. Schweizer, "πνεῦμα," 406–13.

in those days *I will pour out My Spirit*," and Luke adds for emphasis, "and they will prophesy" (προφητεύσουσιν, 2:17–18; quoting Joel 2:28–32; cf. Num 11:29). This emphatic repetition accentuates Luke's point: The Spirit is a Spirit of prophecy, who enables the authoritative communication of a prophetic message.[29] Each of the instances of *glossolalia* (γλῶσσα, Acts 2:4; 10:45–46; 19:6) is explicitly linked to the filling of the Spirit in Acts, and reinforces this theme of Spirit-inspired proclamation.

As the quotation from Joel shows, Luke derives the idea that the Holy Spirit is a spirit of prophecy from the OT. The parallel between the *ruach* (רוּחַ), which inspires ministry and revelation, and the NT prophetic Spirit, is evident.[30] Early Jewish prophetic inspiration included prophetic activity and verbal inspiration, so the Spirit inspires both prophetic speaking and action in Luke-Acts.[31] For Luke, Jesus is the idealized prophet as confirmed by the disciples on the Road to Emmaus, who explain that Jesus is "a prophet, powerful in word and deed before God and all the people" (Luke 24:19).

This highlights Luke's theological schema—the OT prophets find their fulfillment in Jesus and the church is the continuation of his mission, mighty in prophetic word and deed. The implication is that the same Spirit that animated the prophets and Jesus empowers Christians in their prophetic witness; God leads them just as he led the prophets of old. This may be an apologetic towards Judaism: "the end-time Spirit (Acts 2:17) earmarks the true community of God's Messiah."[32] However, it also stems from Luke's conviction that the Christian mission to all nations depicted in Acts is the continuation of the Spirit's prophetic empowerment, revealed in Elijah, Elisha, Joel, the other OT prophets, and ultimately in Jesus.

In Luke-Acts, the Spirit's work is nearly always a missional witness of the Word, a work of bold prophetic proclamation. The Spirit can lead to secondary outcomes like joy or wisdom, but these remain linked to the prophetic witness.[33] Shelton concludes, "The role that seizes Luke's attention the most . . . is that of Spirit-inspired witness . . . Spirit-inspired witness dominates the one quarter of the NT that we call Luke-Acts."[34]

---

29. Turner, "Spirit of Prophecy," 68–72 presents a list of ways the "Spirit of prophecy" empowers preaching and witness in Luke-Acts.

30. Luke stresses the prophetic dimension of the OT (e.g., in the infancy narratives, Luke 1:46, 67; 2:25–27), and of John the Baptist in his Gospel (1:15, 17).

31. Keener, *Acts*, 1:524. See 1.529–37 for influences on Luke's view of the Spirit, including possible Jewish and non-Jewish backgrounds.

32. Keener, *Acts*, 1.523.

33. Acts 13:52: "the disciples were continually filled with *joy* (χαρά) and with the Holy Spirit"; also 11:23, 24; 13:52; Luke 10:21.

34. Shelton, *Mighty in Word and Deed*, 13. He identifies what is uniquely Lukan

In addition to empowering direct missional proclamation, the Spirit is also *strategist and tactical director of the broader outreach of the church* (1:8; 4:29–31).[35] "Luke hardly held that the apostles, or even the Church, were custodians of the Spirit, that He was theirs to impart. The Church did not control the Spirit; the Spirit controlled the Church. Where He led, the Church must follow."[36] This can be seen in the way the Spirit firmly guides and oversees Philip's ministry in Samaria (8:26, 29, 39–40). Similarly, Cornelius and Peter both receive a supernatural visitation (10:3–6, 10–15), and then the Spirit decisively instructs Peter to go to Cornelius's household (10:19–20; 11:12). As Peter is still preaching, the Spirit dramatically falls on Cornelius's household in a way that mirrors Pentecost (10:47; 11:15). This episode shows the Spirit directing the mission and opening it to non-Jews.

The Spirit also guides Paul's mission. The Spirit initiates Barnabas and Paul's commissioning at Antioch (13:2, 4), forbids Paul from speaking the word in Asia on his second journey (16:6), restricts the evangelization of Bithynia (16:7), and re-directs him towards Europe (16:8–10). Paul's journey to and arrest in Jerusalem are explicitly directed by the Spirit (20:22; 19:21) and are confirmed by the Spirit-inspired prophetic activity of other Christians (20:23; 21:4, 11). The Spirit also provides power for confronting opponents of the message (4:8; 5:32; 7:55; 13:9; Paul's defense speeches, 22–26). As a central part of the Spirit's work of enabling witness, Luke shows the Spirit directing the church's missional activity throughout Acts.

THE SPIRIT BUILDS THE CHURCH

Pentecost establishes the church as a missionary community in which Christians receive the Spirit in order to witness to the risen Christ. It is also the occasion of a new declaration or *kerygma* to the wider world, to the whole list of nations present (2:9–11). The rapid expansion of this community marks the early chapters of Acts (1:15; 2:41; 4:4), and Luke's dramatic vocabulary in the first seven chapters highlights this miraculous growth,[37] which is unquestionably the work of the Spirit. From that starting point,

---

material in the Gospels ("L material") and demonstrates the dominance of Spirit-inspired witness throughout Luke-Acts.

35. Cf. Shelton, *Mighty in Word and Deed*, 125–56: "the Holy Spirit as Director of Missions."

36. Hull, *Holy Spirit in Acts*, 178.

37. "The multitude" (πλῆθος): 2:6; 4:32; 5:14, 16; 6:2, 5; "many" (πολύς): 1:3; 2:40, 43; 4:4, 17, 22; 5:12; 6:7; "to increase" (πληθύνω): 6:1, 7; 7:17; "to add" (προστίθημι): 2:41, 47; 5:14; "big" (μέγας): 2:20; 4:33a, 33b; 5:5, 11; 6:8; 7:11, 57, 60; 32 occurrences of πᾶς and five of ἅπας express totality.

the boundary-breaking Spirit enlarges the church, continually prodding the believers to venture beyond the cultural boundary of Israel (8–11), the religious boundary of the Law (10:10–16; 15:7–11), and the geographical borders of Asia (16:6–10).[38]

Pentecost or the Festival of Weeks is the only annual Jewish pilgrim festival unmentioned in the other Gospels. It marks the spring harvest in ancient Israel, and in Acts becomes a fitting setting and motif for the founding and spread of the church, with its distinctive Pentecostal emphases of divine forgiveness, harvest bounty, harvest joy, and harvest inclusiveness.[39] Pentecost is the founding event of the church, the beginning of the church's missional harvest, and at each subsequent stage in its growth, some echo of the first Pentecost is present.[40] "The Spirit and the Pentecost theme provide the link between the Christian mission and the divine plan."[41]

First, Philip evangelizes Samaria, and the Samaritans "receive the Holy Spirit" (8:17) at the hands of Peter and John. Then the opening of the gospel to the Gentiles comes with the encounter of Peter and Cornelius, where Peter emphasizes continuity with Pentecost by claiming, "The Holy Spirit fell on them *just as on us at the beginning* (ὥσπερ καὶ ἐφ᾽ ἡμᾶς ἐν ἀρχῇ) . . . *God gave the same gift* (τὴν ἴσην δωρεάν) to them as he gave to us after believing" (11:15–17).[42] After this, the Spirit selects Barnabas and Saul for the first intentionally cross-cultural mission amongst the Gentiles (13:2, 4). Then the Spirit forces Paul and Silas to leave Asia and enter Europe (16:6–10). Another "mini-Pentecost" takes place in Ephesus around Paul, with the outpouring of *glossolalia* (19:6), an intentional echo of Pentecost, and the beginning of Paul's urban mission in Asia. Finally, Paul, "compelled/bound by the Spirit" (20:22), departs for Jerusalem under the Spirit's leadership.

Luke presents each of these episodes as a new phase of the mission, and in each of them, the Spirit draws the believers towards God's ultimate plan. Luke is showing through this Pentecost motif that the Spirit births the church, and then builds it stage by stage. As Richards explains:

> Luke uses the Pentecost theme to . . . present the unfolding of the
> divine plan, and to trace the missionary activity of the "absent"

38. Marguerat, *Historian*, 116.

39. Stevens, *Acts*, 20, 37–71. The church's missional harvest emerges directly from these four central themes.

40. Richards, "Pentecost," 133–49. In addition to the following "echoes" of Pentecost, Richards, 135 includes Acts 4:31 (the community at prayer).

41. Richards, "Pentecost," 145.

42. This should be regarded as Peter's conversion more than Cornelius's, for nothing in the text indicates a change in Cornelius, though this may be implied, but there is much that changes in Peter (10:9–48).

Lord and his witnesses . . . The Spirit for Luke is a pervading reality throughout this divine schema, whose presence accounts for
the origin, life, and mission of the community, and which grants
the believer boldness, comfort, and peace . . . Thus, Pentecost
for Luke, is a paradigmatic episode that, in parallel with Jesus'
reception of the Spirit, signals conferral of power for and the
beginning of the mission and witness to the ends of the earth.[43]

While this repeated theme is evident in the text, the uniqueness of
the first Pentecost in Acts 2 should also be acknowledged.[44] The subsequent
"Pentecostal echoes" are further explosions of the Spirit's activity and rever-
berations of the initial paradigmatic episode, which singularly marks the
inception of the new Christian community and mission.

Acts 9:31 attributes the growth and building up of the church to the
work of the Holy Spirit: "So the church throughout all Judea and Galilee
and Samaria had peace, *being built up* (οἰκοδομουμένη) and moving along
(πορευομένη) in the fear of the Lord and in the encouragement of the
Holy Spirit (παρακλήσει ἁγίου πνεύματος), *it continued to increase greatly*
(ἐπληθύνετο)." The Spirit is not the origin of faith in Acts, but initiates testimony once a person has responded to the Word in faith, which causes the
continued missional growth of the church. The book of Acts repeats this pattern of Christological faith preceding the receiving of the Spirit and the call
to be a witness with the Samaritans (8:5–17) and the Ephesians (19:1–6).[45]
As previously, Luke "situates faith exclusively in relation to Christ, while
missionary activity is the Spirit's realm."[46]

The Spirit also builds up the church in Acts by protecting its unity.
Luke emphasizes that the original community of the Twelve is one (1:12;
2:1), and the three early summary passages accentuate the unity of the
church (2:42–47; 4:32–35; 5:12–16).[47] These summaries contain multiple
unity phrases: "together" (ὁμοθυμαδόν, 2:46; 5:12; ἐπί τὸ αὐτό, 2:44, 46);[48] "of
one heart and soul" (καρδία καί ψυχή μία, 4:32); they shared according to
everyone's needs (2:45), to the point where no one was needy among them

43. Richards, "Pentecost," 148.

44. Witherington, *Acts*, 134–5 accentuates the differences between the original Pentecost and subsequent activity of the Spirit in Acts.

45. Cornelius's household follows a somewhat different pattern (10:44–48).

46. Marguerat, *Historian*, 118.

47. The many imperfect verbs in all three summaries indicate the enduring quality
of the community.

48. Ἐπί τὸ αὐτό is a somewhat awkward Septuagintalism which should probably
be translated as "of one accord," occurs 55 times in the LXX, and is also used for the
Qumranic community (1QS 1:1; 3:7); Barrett, *Acts*, 1:167.

(4:34). Luke is using common friendship language here to praise the unified early community in its close relationships.

There is a strong connection with the Spirit in each of these passages.[49] The first summary (2:42–47) is the conclusion of the single Pentecost narrative sequence, which focuses on the outpouring of the Spirit, and culminates in the first believing community's formation.[50] The implication is that the intervention of the Spirit leads ultimately to a loving and unified community, the church: "The irruption of the breath of God creating the Church finds its ethical concretization in the unity of the believers."[51]

The second summary explains the sharing of possessions, illustrated by the positive example of Barnabas (4:32–37). The negative example of Ananias and Sapphira follows (5:1–11), whose death sentence is carefully justified with a double reference to the Spirit: "Why has Satan filled your heart *to lie to the Holy Spirit* (ψεύσασθαί σε τὸ πνεῦμα τὸ ἅγιον) . . . Why did you agree together *to test/try to trap the Spirit of the Lord?*" (πειράσαι τὸ πνεῦμα κυρίου, 5:3, 9). They have not simply lied to the Spirit: "the Greek expression is even stronger than that—he 'belied,' he 'falsified' the Spirit. His action was in effect a denial, a falsification of the Spirit's presence in the community."[52] This is also an ironic unity here, in light of Luke's previous emphasis: "Ananias and Sapphira were together in this deed (συνεφωνήθη; cf. σύν in v. 1), but it was the wrong sort of togetherness. It was a togetherness that violated the togetherness of the Christian community."[53] Marguerat explains this scandal:

> The crime is not in financial withholding, but in offending against the principle of sharing everything in common (4:32). Ananias and Sapphira have not sinned against morality, but against the Spirit in his function of constructing unity . . . The reader learns how the Church, in its origin, was directed by the Spirit while also being exposed to Satan and how God has (terribly) protected it from the attacks of Evil.[54]

In these summary passages Luke memorably establishes the Spirit as the creator and guardian of the unified fellowship of the community. For Luke, such unity gives concrete expression to the action of the Spirit, and guarding

---

49. Marguerat, *Historian*, 122–3.

50. There is no narrative transition at 2:42, while the new location at 3:1 signals a conspicuous episodic break.

51. Marguerat, *Historian*, 123.

52. Polhill, *Acts*, 157.

53. Witherington, *Acts*, 218.

54. Marguerat, *Historian*, 123.

it is one of the primary ways that the Spirit actively builds up the church. To violate the early community's togetherness is patently shameful, and the conclusion of this episode shows the resulting fearful reverence: "great fear (φόβος μέγας, cf. 2:43) seized the whole church and all who heard about these events" (5:11). "Luke depicted it as a unique period, the new people of God in Christ, filled with the Spirit, growing by leaps and bounds. There was no room for distrust, for duplicity, for any breach in fellowship. The same Spirit that gave the community its growth also maintained its purity."[55]

There is no doubt that the Spirit's primary occupation throughout Acts is the empowerment of Christ's people for missional proclamation, and that unified relationships are an important prerequisite to and catalyst for this witness. Some scholars argue that this is the exclusive focus of the Lukan Spirit's activity.[56] Though the Pauline transformation and growth of the individual is not Luke's primary interest, this can be explained by his focus, which is the meta-narrative of the church's growth, and by his historiographical genre, which contrasts with Paul's more personal corre-spondences.[57] Despite this, it does appear that Luke is aware of the Pauline emphasis on the personal transformation aspect of the Spirit's work, for Acts contains hints of the Spirit moving in this way in the four "full of the Spirit" statements: the Hellenist seven are "full of the Spirit and *wisdom*" (σοφίας, 6:3); Stephen is "full of *faith* and the Holy Spirit" (πίστεως, 6:5); Barnabas is a "*good man* (ἀνὴρ ἀγαθός), and full of the Spirit and *faith*" (πίστεως, 11:24); finally, the disciples are "filled with *joy* and the Holy Spirit" (χαρᾶς, 13:52). This demonstrates some connection between the Spirit and these four char-acter attributes; how explicit the connection is, and whether causality is implied or not, is not definite, though it is likely. All these characteristics are familiar signs of the Spirit for Jews and can be found in the LXX, so readers should assume a direct correlation.[58]

55. Polhill, *Acts*, 161; also Marshall, *Acts*, 110–14.

56. Menzies, *Empowered for Witness*, 44 is extreme: "Luke never attributes sote-riological functions to the Spirit and his narrative presupposes a pneumatology which excludes this dimension . . . Luke consistently portrays the Spirit as the source of prophetic inspiration, which . . . empowers God's people for effective service." Turner, *Power from on High*, 111 debates him, presenting a more balanced view. For Menzies's view of the four "full of the Spirit" passages, see 258–59.

57. Marguerat, *Historian*, 124, claims that Luke's emphasis on κοινωνία is as close as he comes to the personal sanctifying transformation and regeneration of the Spirit in the lives of believers (Pauline pneumatology).

58. Turner, *Power from on High*, 418, claims that this should be assumed, given the Jewish and Christian presuppositions along these lines, and itemizes the individual's strengthening: 1) the revelatory gift that makes a person aware of God's presence and leading; 2) the source of spiritual wisdom which fuels personal discipleship, prayer and

These references hint at a sanctifying work in the personal life of the believer, parallel to Paul's "fruit of the Spirit" (Gal 5:22–23). They demonstrate the Spirit's personal effect on a person, not simply in a moment of empowering charisma, but also in the long-term transformation of character; the same Spirit of prophecy which fuels and directs the mission of the church also strengthens the individual as well.[59] For Luke a life filled with the Spirit should result in growth in traits such as wisdom, faith, joy, and "goodness" of character, alongside direct empowerment for mission. These are results of the Spirit's influence in Acts, but they also contribute to effective witness, which is Luke's consistent priority; a person filled with increasing wisdom, joy, goodness, and faith will make a more effective missionary, enhance the health and unity of the church, and offer a more attractive example of following Christ.

CONCLUSION—SPIRIT EMPOWERMENT FOR MISSION

Luke expresses the Spirit's role in founding, building, nurturing, and protecting the church more strongly than any other NT author. He involves the Spirit thoroughly in the details of the church; even setbacks are the work of the Spirit (8:1, 4; 16:6–7; 20:22).[60] He shows the Spirit empowering believers for bold testimony about Jesus and leading them as the "Director of Missions."[61] *The essence of Lukan pneumatology is prophetic proclamation.*

The Spirit is a primary missional stimulus in Acts, for it is the Spirit that motivates and empowers believers to engage in evangelism, and that carries the Word forward in its unstoppable momentum. "For Luke, baptism in the Spirit offers more than the optimum results of human obedience by adding an obviously divine dimension."[62] The Spirit's activity in Acts shows that the church is not left to depend on its own strengths or abilities, but on God's power.

Additionally, the Spirit is not given to the church primarily for its own sake, or its selfish enjoyment, but for the blessing of others; bearing witness is the church's purpose, through the power of the Spirit.[63] At Pentecost and its many echoes in Acts, Jesus gives the Spirit to all believers to build the

---

doxology; 3) the enabling to take part in the communal life and witness of the church.

59. Turner, *Power from on High*, 408–12.

60. Marguerat, *Historian*, 128.

61. Shelton, *Mighty in Word and Deed*, 125–27.

62. Keener, *Acts*, 1:521.

63. Hull, *Holy Spirit in Acts*, 178.

church, to inspire mission, and to protect the unity of the developing community. The Spirit also aids in the personal transformation of individuals within that community, though this is not Luke's primary focus.

Because Acts is a story, Luke never explains the work of the Spirit, but instead describes it, weaving the Spirit into the narrative in memorable and vivid fashion. "By establishing a narrative role for the Holy Spirit, Luke has taken a significant step towards the eventual theological recognition of the Holy Spirit as a 'person.'"[64] This personalized "pragmatic of the Spirit" does leave undeniable gaps, for Luke's goal is not systematic theological instruction, but compelling rhetorical narrative.[65] Acts directs readers not to comprehend the Spirit, but to live in and from the person of the Spirit, and to follow the Spirit's cross-cultural missional journey throughout human history and across the earth. The same prophetic Spirit that inspired the prophets of old and filled Jesus's life is available, powerful, and compelling. Luke does not leave his readers to their own ability but offers the Spirit's power to join the mission and receive personal transformation in the process. In all these ways, Luke presents Spirit-empowerment as a vital stimulus to Christian mission.

64. Johnson, Acts, 15.

65. Luke never teaches about the discerning of spirits, as do the letters of Paul (1 Cor 14), and John (1 John 4:1–6). Nor does he address the relationship between conversion, baptism, and the coming of the Spirit on the believer. Dunn, Baptism in the Holy Spirit, 90–102, attempts to decipher Luke's convictions on these issues.

Chapter 3

The Father's Universal Offer of Salvation

There is salvation in no one else, for there is no other name under heaven given among mortals by which we must be saved.

—ACTS 4:12

The Word and the Spirit combine to create a potent missional force in Acts, which catches missionaries up in its irresistible momentum. However, Luke is clear this is all according to the Father's plan and purpose (Luke 24:49). The Spirit is the Father's "promised gift" (Acts 1:4). It is the Father who decides "dates and times" by his own authority (Acts 1:7), who reveals the Son to whom he will according to his good pleasure, and who has handed over all things to the Son (Luke 10:21–22). The Father decides where and when the peoples of the world live so that they may seek and find him, as he is close to every person (Acts 17:26–28). The Father appoints the Day when he will judge the world through the Son, and the Father treats all nations with mercy, overlooking their faults for their ultimate salvation (17:30–31). "As Father, God sends the Son and Messiah, promises the Holy Spirit, and includes the followers of Jesus, both Jews and Gentiles, in his family. The father metaphor brings to the foreground the authority, faithfulness, mercy, and tenacious love of God."[1] *For Luke, the church's mission to all nations in Acts is a "Fatherly" enterprise*: the saving actions of the Father of Israel, Jesus, and Jesus's followers on behalf of his children, within the ethos of his loving and inclusive family.[2]

The Father's invitation into his family, or offer of salvation, has a universal scope and priority in Acts, missionally focused on the Son. "Jesus is the *one* Savior for *all* peoples and this is why he must be proclaimed to *all* peoples."[3] Luke expresses this emphatically in Acts 4:12, which claims salvation (σωτηρία) comes through Christ alone (cf. 4:10); ἄλλῳ οὐδενί underlines that salvation is found in "no one else, not even one." "The primary meaning of salvation is detachment from the world of the unbelieving and disobedient and attachment to the true people of God of the last days, the ἐκκλησία, the community which is constituted on the one hand by its loyalty to Jesus, and on the other by his gift of the Spirit, which makes possible a new life conformed to the new loyalty."[4]

According to Luke, the Father's offer of salvation through Jesus has implications for everyone, everywhere.[5] It is universally relevant and germane—ethnically, geographically, and socially inclusive—and it affects every part of a person's life.[6] In Luke-Acts this all-encompassing redemption is the Father's loving initiative, and functions as an additional persuasive stimulus to his people. God the Father and Creator's plan to make Jesus the Savior of all people in all places amplifies the urgency of the mission.

GEOGRAPHICALLY UNIVERSAL

Luke arranges his narrative in an intentional geographical fashion, which is not unusual for Greek historians.[7] He also employs a form of geographical

---

1. Chen, *God as Father*, 240. Chen describes the Fatherhood of God as "the neglected image in Lukan theology," 1, and "the hub of Lukan Theology," 239.

2. This is Chen's conclusion, *God as Father*, 239–41; see her work for more detail.

3. Witherington, *Acts*, 71.

4. Barrett, *Acts*, 1:231. This community of God is the father's family.

5. Rosner, "Progress," 220 highlights elements of universalism in Luke's Gospel: 1) Simeon's prophecy quoting Isa 42:6 (2:32); 2) John's ministry to Roman soldiers (2:1; 3:1, 14); 3) Jesus's reading of Isa 61 and commendation of the gentiles (4:16–30); 4) Jesus's friendship with tax collectors and sinners (7:34), and those on the margins of Jewish society (5:27–39; 19:5–7); 5) the prominence of women—Elizabeth and Mary, Mary and Martha, women witnesses of the resurrection; 6) the response of Samaritans to Jesus (9:51–56; 10:25–37; 17:11–19; cf. Acts 8:4–24).

6. Witherington, *Acts*, 68–72 lays out these strands of universal theology in Acts.

7. Drews, "Ephorus' *kata genos* History," 497–98.

theology in which locations and movement possess theological significance. Luke's Gospel and Acts are geographical mirror images of each other.[8] In the Gospel everything moves towards Jerusalem (Luke 9:51, 53), and Jesus must go from Galilee, through Samaria, to Jerusalem. By contrast, Acts begins with the disciples waiting in Jerusalem for the outpouring of the Holy Spirit (Acts 1:4), who then propels them outwards through Samaria, to other locations further afield. This mirrored literary structure indicates that the outwardly expanding mission in Acts is not haphazard but unfolds according to the Father's "purposeful plan" (βουλή, Acts 2:23; 4:28; 13:36; 20:27).

Jewish expectations of salvation help to explain the geographical orientation of Luke's Gospel: Jesus must go up to Jerusalem, for it is the spiritual center from which the Jews have always looked for salvation, and Jesus makes reference to this often (Luke 9:51; 13:22, 33, 35; 17:11; 18:31; 19:11, 28).[9] Luke locates Jesus in the line of OT prophets (13:33) and presents Jesus's life, teaching, and the completion of his earthly work in Jerusalem as a fulfillment of multiple prophetic texts within the Hebrew Scriptures (4:18–21; 16:31; 18:31; 24:27, 45). Many of Luke's unique episodes reinforce the theological importance of Jerusalem, such as Jesus going up to the temple as a boy (2:41–52) and the prophecies of Simeon and Anna in the temple about Jesus being the world's savior (2:25–38).

At the end of Luke's Gospel, Jesus appears to the disciples, and "opens up their minds" by saying, "*It is written*, that the Christ would suffer and rise again from the dead on the third day, and that repentance for forgiveness of sins would be proclaimed in his name *to all the nations* (πάντα τὰ ἔθνη), *beginning from Jerusalem*" (Luke 24:45–47).[10] This saying sets the stage geographically and theologically for the universal emphasis of the gospel proclamation to all nations that is to come in Acts, while maintaining its Jewish prophetic roots and the importance of Jerusalem as the origin of the universal mission.

Jerusalem is the place from which salvation comes, and the place from which the Father's commission to proclaim salvation comes (Luke 24:47, 53; Acts 1:4). For this reason, the disciples wait in Jerusalem for power from on high (Acts 1:4–5). Acts 1:8 sets a geographical framework for the Acts story, and functions as its basic outline: "You will be my witnesses in Jerusalem [Acts 1–7], and in all Judea and Samaria [Acts 8–9], and to the ends of the earth [Acts 10–28]." This momentous verse has its roots in the Isaianic

---

8. Witherington, *Acts*, 69; Johnson, *Acts*, 10–11.

9. Witherington, *Acts*, 70.

10. Cf. Matt 28:19: "Go and make disciples of *all the nations* (πάντα τὰ ἔθνη)." The geographical goal is identical, though the specific instructions vary slightly. "It is written" clearly references Scripture (Luke 24:44).

Servant Songs, which speak of the message of salvation going out to the earth's limits (e.g., Isa 49:6; 62:11).[11] Acts can be represented by a series of five overlapping circles, originating in Jerusalem, and stretching ever further to the north and west.[12]

Table 3.1 Geographical Expansion in Acts

1. The martyrdom of Stephen forces believers outside of Jerusalem (8:1b–4) into *Judea and Samaria* (Acts 8–9).

2. They make their way to *Phoenicia, Cyprus, and Syrian Antioch* (11:20).

3. Paul's first journey takes him as far west as *Pisidian Antioch and Attalia* (13:4—14:28).

4. Paul's second and third journeys take him as far as *Thessalonica and Berea in Macedonia, and Athens and Corinth in Achaia* (15:39—21:17).

5. Paul's imprisonment carries him to *Rome, the power center of the Empire* (28:16–31).

Haenchen rightly says of Acts 1:8, "the whole action of Acts becomes the fulfilment of Jesus' word, and this is much more than a mere table of contents: it is a promise!"[13] This promise is reemphasized as a divine command (ἐντέλλομαι) with identical language in Paul's mission: "I have set you to be a light for the Gentiles, to bring *salvation to the ends of the earth*" (σωτηρίαν ἕως ἐσχάτου τῆς γῆς, 13:47; Isa 49:6). Is Rome the fulfillment of this ends of the earth promise? Geographically, the Acts narrative ends like an open book, for Acts 1:8 is not yet accomplished; Rome is the center of the Empire, and not the end of the earth. "There is no evidence that any Jew, Greek, or Roman around the first century A.D. ever conceived of Rome as being at the end of the earth."[14] Therefore the promise of Jesus remains unrealized in Acts, implying that the geographical mandate must continue until salvation has actually reached the ends of the earth (cf. Matt 24:14).

---

11. Isaiah is Luke's favorite prophetic book, and this Isaianic theme of universality is highlighted both early and often in Luke-Acts (cf. e.g., Luke 3:6, "all flesh shall see the salvation of God," to Isa 52:10). Moore, "End of the Earth," 389–99 shows how the Isaianic background of Acts 1:8 signifies Luke's universalistic perspective regarding the expansion of the gospel, and how this has *both* geographic and ethnic significance.

12. Witherington, *Acts*, 77–86. See maps in chapters 8–10, 13 of this work for visual depictions.

13. Haenchen, *Acts*, 145–6.

14. Thornton, "To the End of the Earth," 374. The limits of the west were further, to Spain (cf. Rom 15:24, 28).

The Acts narrative is only the beginning of the fulfillment of Christ's commission, which implicitly gives readers a responsibility to continue the worldwide geographical mission until all nations are reached, and the ends of the earth hear. This sort of reader response is one of Luke's primary rhetorical objectives—he intends to draw his audience into the church's ongoing universal mission, foretold in the ancient scriptures. The text compels others to go to the ends of the earth, to "every nation," for what has begun in Acts must be completed; Christ's promise requires fulfillment.[15]

ETHNICALLY UNIVERSAL

A related theme is the church's theology of universal ethnic inclusion in Acts, announced through Simeon's early prophetic prayer in the Temple: "My eyes have seen your *salvation* (σωτήριον), which you have prepared in the presence of *all peoples* (πάντων τῶν λαῶν, all the tribes, people groups), *a light for revelation to the Gentiles* (ἐθνῶν, nations, ethnicities), *and for glory to your people Israel*" (λαοῦ σου Ἰσραήλ, Luke 2:30–32). This grouping of "all peoples" and ethnicities underscores Luke's conviction that God offers salvation to every ἔθνος and λαός on the face of the earth. As with the geographical "ends of the earth," this does not fully happen in Luke-Acts— Luke's story is only the beginning of the church's inclusive engagement with every ethnic group.

Ethnic prejudice is a prevalent problem in Luke's world, and multiple contemporary writers deal with this theme, including Dio Chrysostom, Juvenal, and Lucian.[16] In response to this challenge, Luke goes to great lengths to establish the theme of welcoming all throughout Luke-Acts, beginning in Jesus's paradigmatic founding sermon (Luke 4:18–27), which sees in Isa 61:1–2 inspiration for a global mission, and a church overcoming these prejudices by embracing all ethnicities: "The Spirit of the Lord is upon me, because he has anointed me; he has sent me to bring good news to the poor (εὐαγγελίσασθαι πτωχοῖς) . . . to summon the inclusive year of the Lord (καλέσαι ἐνιαυτὸν κυρίου δεκτόν, Luke 4:18–19)." The final phrase has also been translated, "to declare God's age open and welcoming to all."[17]

---

15. See the end of chapter 13 for more on the rhetorically incomplete "ending" of Acts.

16. Dio Chrysostom, *Discourses*, 36, 38, advocates *homonoia* (ὁμόνοια, concord, oneness of heart and mind) as a way of honoring the emperor; in a literary parallel Luke emphasizes the importance of *homonoia* amongst Christians, in the Judean church, in incorporating Hellenistic Jews, and in shaping unity between Jewish and non-Jewish Christians. Juvenal (*Sat.* 3.60–77) and Lucian (*Parliament* [ἐκκλησία] *of the Gods*) satirize the people's failures to live up to the ideal of welcoming foreigners. Balch, "Luke-Acts," 98.

17. Translations of Luke 4:19 from Lane McGaughy and Gary Pence respectively;

This prophetic passage contains not only the proclamation of the gospel to the poor, but also reflects God's "acceptance, welcome, inclusion" (δεκτός) of other ethnicities.[18] Jesus then proceeds to re-emphasize this inclusiveness by celebrating two examples of God welcoming and blessing foreigners (the Sidonian widow and Naaman the Syrian, 4:25–27), in direct contrast to "many" Jewish widows and lepers, and purposefully omits Isaiah's next statement, "and the day of vengeance of our God" (Isa 61:2). Leaving out the idea of vengeance (on foreigners) and adding stories about God's welcoming kindness to them explains why the Nazareth Jews are "all filled with rage" (ἐπλήσθησαν πάντες θυμοῦ), and attempt to kill him—they cannot accept this inclusive welcoming of foreign peoples (4:28–29). The way Luke constructs this crucial founding sermon shows his interest in the universal welcome of all people and sets the stage for what will come in Acts.

This same theme is highlighted at the pivotal point during Peter's speech before Cornelius's household, when he declares that, "in every nation anyone who fears him and does what is right is acceptable/welcome (δεκτὸς) to God" (Acts 10:35) and models such behavior by baptizing the foreigner Cornelius. The final scene of Acts importantly depicts Paul in Rome "accepting all" (ἀπεδέχετο πάντας, Acts 28:30–31). This three-fold repetition of the theme of universal acceptance links Luke-Acts together missionally; Acts is the story of the church learning to implement Jesus's paradigmatic instructions in his founding sermon.

Thus, one of the primary purposes of Luke-Acts is to encourage Christians to "accept, welcome, include" (δεκτός, δέχομαι) "foreigners, outsiders" (ἀλλόφυλοι, Acts 10:28) in their assemblies.[19] Titus had likely burned Jerusalem and the Temple long before Luke writes, so Luke is not focused on ethnic tensions in Judea.[20] Luke writes to "Christians" (Acts 11:26; 26:28) throughout the Roman world to persuade them to open domestic, ecclesial doors to those with different customs, laws, and ethnicities, as a fundamental aspect of his call to missional action.

The Pentecost story also demonstrates Luke's universal outlook. Because it is the Festival of Pentecost, Jerusalem is inundated with Jewish pilgrims of many different ethnicities during the initial outpouring of the Spirit.[21] Acts 2:5 speaks of, "devout people *from every nation under heaven*"

Balch, "Luke-Acts," 82.

18. Balch, "Luke-Acts," 98.

19. The δεκτός word group underscores this crucial theme; ἀποδέχομαι only occurs in the NT in Luke-Acts.

20. Balch, "Luke-Acts," 68.

21. Also called the Feast of Weeks, *Shavuot* (שָׁבֻעוֹת, "weeks," Deut 16:10), the Feast of Harvest (Exod 23:26), and the day of first fruits (Nu. 28:26), Pentecost is the fiftieth

(ἀπὸ παντὸς ἔθνους τῶν ὑπὸ τὸν οὐρανόν), and then lists 16 of them: "Parthians, Medes, Elamites, residents of Mesopotamia, Judea and Cappadocia, Pontus and Asia, Phrygia and Pamphylia, Egypt and the parts of Libya belonging to Cyrene, visitors from Rome . . . Cretans and Arabs" (Acts 2:9–11).[22] The phrase "every nation under heaven" has significant LXX roots.[23] In Luke's eschatological theology, the missionary movement originating in Jerusalem will reach all peoples, but these same peoples will also be gathered back to Jerusalem.[24] "For Luke, Jerusalem was more than merely the center from which the centrifugal movement of the gospel went out to the ends of the earth; rather, Jerusalem was the center to which, in corresponding centripetal movement, the eschatological people of God must constantly return."[25]

Pentecost is a direct fulfillment of Isa 49:6, which encompasses both the restoration of Israel and the call to be a guiding light to the nations: "It is too light a thing that you should be my servant to raise up the tribes of Jacob and to restore the survivors of Israel; *I will give you as a light to the nations, that my salvation may reach to the end of the earth.*" Paul and Barnabas quote this verse in the Pisidian Antioch synagogue as a justification for going to the Gentiles (13:47). It also reflects Isa 66:18–20, the most overt expression of universalism in the OT, and a central influence on Luke's outlook. This passage refers to the ingathering of all nations and tongues, but also to the missional sending of "those who have been saved to the nations" to declare God's glory. It is likely the first biblical reference to "the sending of individuals to distant peoples in order to proclaim God's glory among them."[26]

Luke understands Pentecost to be the fulfillment of the eschatological pilgrimage of the nations to worship in Zion.[27] Similar to Jesus' inaugural

---

day after the Sabbath of Passover week (Lev 23:15–16).

22. All these nations have known Jewish Diasporan populations and are places to which Israel and Judah had been exiled centuries earlier; Polhill, *Acts*, 102–4. The "table of nations" in 2:9–11 alludes to the table of nations tradition of Gen 10 (just before the Tower of Babel), reformulated in 1 Chr 1:1—2:2. The Pentecost table of nations also reflects multiple OT passages with an eschatological outlook, e.g., Ezek 38–39 and Dan 11. Scott, "Acts 2:9–11," 110–23 summarizes the debate about its origins and meaning.

23. Deut 2:25; 4:19; 30:4–5; Jer 38[31]:8; Scott, "Acts 2:9–11," 107–8.

24. Since the exile, Israel expected the remnant of God's people to return to Jerusalem (Mic 2:12–13; 4:6–8; Zeph 3:14–20). This ingathering sometimes takes the form of a meeting in Jerusalem including the entire world, in which every nation worships Yahweh (Isa 60:1–14; Mic 4:1–5; Isa 2:1–5). Scott, "Acts 2:9–11," 109.

25. Scott, "Acts 2:9–11," 108–9.

26. Westermann, *Isaiah*, 425.

27. Scott, "Acts 2:9–11," 103–4, proposes that Luke is influenced by the Book of Jubilees, which makes Pentecost the most important of the annual festivals in the Jewish liturgical calendar (Jub 22:1), and links it with the Noahic covenant, incumbent upon

speech in Luke (4:18–21), this episode sets the universal agenda in Acts: many different ethnicities hear the good news in their own language, implying that the message is for all tongues and peoples. "This Pentecost event is an anticipation of the whole mission to the nations which unfolds in the rest of the Book of Acts . . . the Diaspora Jews who gathered in Jerusalem represent 'every nation under heaven' (Acts 2:5) and point to the universalistic thrust of the Book of Acts."[28] Pentecost is a hermeneutical key to Luke's inclusive theology, which is emphasized when Peter declares, "*everyone* (πᾶς) who calls on the name of the Lord will be saved" (Acts 2:21; Joel 2:23).

Philip's later encounter with the Ethiopian eunuch (Acts 8:26–40) also demonstrates Luke's universalized ethnic convictions, because the eunuch will actually reach "the ends of the earth" as he travels back to Ethiopia. In an intentional mirroring, Luke emphasizes that the two meet and then separate through the intervention of the Spirit (8:26, 39). Ethiopia is often referred to as the ends of the earth in antiquity, and there is already a lengthy interest in Ethiopians by the time Luke-Acts is written.[29] People would see those at or beyond the fringes of the Roman Empire as living "at the ends of the earth."[30]

Luke is referring to the Nubian kingdom whose capital was Meroë, south of Egypt, between the fifth and sixth cataracts of the Nile, in modern-day Sudan; "Ethiopia" was considered the southern edge of the earth, bordering the great sea Oceanus.[31] For Luke, the Ethiopian eunuch is an example of the promise of the prophets of old being fulfilled (e.g., Isa 52:10), as distant ethnic groups are reached, and the actual ends of the earth hear of God's salvation.[32] This narrative is about "the reaching of those from the parts of Africa that were at or beyond the borders of the Empire, those that

---

all humanity after the flood (Jub 6:15–19).

28. Scott, "Acts 2:9–11," 122.

29. Herodotus, *Hist.*, 3.25.114: "march against the Ethiopians . . . in *the uttermost parts of the earth*"; Strabo, *Geogr.*, 1.1.6: "the Ethiopians live at the ends of the earth . . . the farthermost of men"; Homer, *Odyssey*, 1.23: "the Ethiopians . . . at the world's end" (αἰθίοπας . . . ἔσχατοι ἀνδρῶν). This interest goes as far back as Herodotus and is because of their racially distinctive features. Snowden, *Blacks in Antiquity*, 101–68.

30. Including some of those whom the Greeks call βάρβαροι, meaning non-Greek people, living on the Empire's fringes (cf. Acts 28:2; Col 3:11).

31. Meroë was the capital of a world power from at least 540 BCE until 339 CE. Witherington, *Acts*, 295.

32. "Blackness and the Ethiopian were . . . synonymous. The Ethiopian's blackness became proverbial," Snowden, *Blacks in Antiquity*, 5. Snowden emphasizes that there is *no* evidence in antiquity of prejudice against people simply because of their color or distinctive features. Instead, there is an appreciation and respect for black people; cf. Herodotus, *Hist.*, 3.114–15.

were at the ends of the earth."[33] Luke presents the Ethiopian eunuch as a foreshadowing of what is to come: the advancement of the gospel into every ethnic region of the Roman Empire, and beyond its borders to the people groups living at the ends of the earth.

There is another significant dimension to this story—Deut 23:1 specifically prohibits eunuchs from the assembly of the Lord.[34] When Philip offers salvation to this foreign official, he overlooks this prohibition, in fulfillment of Isaiah's inclusive promise (Isa 56:3–5). What was excluded is now being included, which explains why the eunuch "goes on his way rejoicing" (χαίρων, Acts 8:39). In a dramatic reversal, Luke is illustrating how Christ's salvation welcomes people who were previously barred from faith and fellowship.[35]

The story of the Ethiopian eunuch is an example of Luke's hermeneutical approach to the Hebrew Scriptures. The book of Acts draws on Jewish traditions which are universal and inclusive in scope, such as these four direct OT quotes:

- Joel 2:28–32 ("I will pour out my Spirit on all flesh . . . everyone who calls on the name of the Lord will be saved," Acts 2:16–21);
- Gen 22:18 ("all the families of the earth will be blessed," Acts 3:26);
- Isa 49:6 ("a light to the nations," Acts 13:47);
- Amos 9:11–12 ("all the Gentiles called by my name," Acts 15:16–18).[36]

In siding with these voices and others such as Jonah, Luke rejects contrasting voices such as Ezra and Nehemiah, which accentuate ethnic purity and the rejection of foreign peoples (Ezra 9–10; Neh 13:1–3). In doing this, Acts is turning on its head significant portions of canonical literature, and holding out others, all based on the Christ event and its inclusive implications. This is emphasized by the eschatological dimensions of the universal mission in

---

33. Witherington, *Acts*, 293.

34. Εὐνοῦχος normally refers to a man who has been castrated and often dismembered; this was common for those in charge of a king's harem or who had duties involving close contact with the queen. Eunuchs could not become full Jewish proselytes, for they could not be properly circumcised. Keener, *Bible Background*, 346, points out that Jews were opposed to the practice, though "God could certainly accept even foreign eunuchs" (Isa 56:3–5; Jer 38:7–13); Marshall, *Acts*, 160–62. It is possible this word is simply a synonym for a court official, and therefore Luke may intend the eunuch to be seen as a full Jewish proselyte.

35. Such reversal is also evident in the story of Ruth; Deut 23:2–8 excludes Moabites from Israel "until the 10th generation," yet "Ruth the Moabite" is not only accepted but becomes David's ancestor.

36. Meek, *Gentile Mission* is a thorough study of each of these four quotations.

the NT: "the mission [to all nations] is the precondition to the end and is thus an eschatological necessity."[37]

Luke stresses the Jewish foundations of Christianity throughout Acts, particularly in its rootedness in the Scriptures and temple and synagogue communities. However, most strands of first-century Judaism are internal, ethnically narrow, and unable or unwilling to accommodate the ethnic universalism of the Jesus movement. This point of discord leads to the eventual break of the Christians with Judaism: "It is hard to doubt that what determines the discontinuity is this universalistic agenda—those facets of Judaism that make difficult or impossible the welcoming of other ethnic groups into the people of God purely on the basis of faith must either be critiqued or be seen as obsolescent [by Christians]."[38]

> The fact was that *religious* conversion wasn't sufficient [for Judaism] . . . the Jewish leadership demanded that all "nations" become fully Jewish; there was no room for Egyptian-Jews or Roman-Jews, let alone Germanic- or British-Jews, but only for Jewish-Jews. Given the remarkable success they achieved, this ethnic barrier to conversion probably was the sole reason that the Roman Empire did not embrace the God of Abraham. It was not a mistake that Paul let Christianity repeat . . . What Christianity offered the world was monotheism stripped of ethnic encumbrances. People of all nations could embrace the One True God while remaining people of all nations.[39]

This clarifies why God-fearers are particularly receptive to the Christian message in Acts—they find a version of monotheism with similar ethical emphases and the same Scriptures that does not require their circumcision or loss of ethnic identity. This distinction eventually gives Christianity a substantial strategic advantage; by accommodating the welcoming inclusion of all peoples, the church becomes a missional "light to all nations."

SOCIALLY UNIVERSAL

Luke's universal theological outlook goes beyond places and ethnicities. He is eager to show the movement's *horizontal* expansion across nations, and

37. Thompson, "Gentile Mission," 27.

38. Witherington, *Acts*, 70. Much of the theological content of Acts is the hashing out of this conviction.

39. Stark, *Cities of God*, 6–7; he may be over-simplifying ancient Judaism, and scholars debate him on this point, but it is true that many Jews were not interested in missional engagement in the same way Christians were. Keener, *Acts*, 1:511–16.

the gospel's *vertical* spread up and down the social status spectrum of the Empire, from the least to the greatest.[40]

The Underprivileged Lower Classes

Luke goes to great lengths in his Gospel to show Jesus's concern for the least, last, and lost.[41] When Jesus articulates his mission in Luke 4:18, he identifies four "focal groups": "The Spirit of the Lord is upon me, because [1] he has anointed me to preach the gospel to the poor (εὐαγγελίσασθαι πτωχοῖς). [2] He has sent me to proclaim release to the captives (κηρύξαι αἰχμαλώτοις ἄφεσιν), and [3] recovery of sight to the blind (τυφλοῖς ἀνάβλεψιν), [4] to set free those who are oppressed (ἀποστεῖλαι τεθραυσμένους ἐν ἀφέσει)." The Holy Spirit anoints and sends Jesus to minister to these groups, which are generally located at the bottom of society.[42] This focus continues in Acts through Jesus's people.

Luke states in an early summary passage that the early community in Acts cares for the poor among them to such an extent that, "there was no one needy (ἐνδεής) among them, for all who were owners of land or houses would sell them and bring the proceeds of the sales" (4:34; cf. 2:45). The practice of selling property to care for the poor is indicative of the extent to which the community follows in Jesus's footsteps, providing for those in need.

This can also be seen in the choosing of the seven to serve the Hellenistic widows (6:1–7). The "daily distribution/service" (τῇ διακονίᾳ τῇ καθημερινῇ, 6:1) of food to the needy in the early community demonstrates the apostles' interest in caring for people's material needs, as well as their spiritual needs. The apostles emphasize that the seven candidates must be of good reputation, full of the Spirit, and full of wisdom (6:3). This high standard, along with the formal commissioning the seven receive (6:5), reveal the value the apostles place on this generous public ministry to the needy. This story underscores the Judeo-Christian idea of charity, of giving without

40. For the social stratification of ancient Roman society, see Gehring, *House*, 166–67; Verner, *Household of God*, 47–54; Meeks, *Moral World*, 32–39; Friesen, "Poverty in Pauline Studies," 323–61, "Injustice or God's Will," 240–60; Longenecker's critique of Friesen's model, "Middle," 243–78.

41. E.g., *the last* (ἔσχατοι): Luke 13:30; 14:9–10; *the least* (μικρότεροι): Luke 7:28; 9:48; *the sick* (κακῶς): Luke 4:40; 5:31; 7:2; 10:9; 14:13; *the lost* (ἀπολωλός): Luke 15; 19:10; *the poor* (πτωχοί): Luke 4:18; 6:20; 7:22; 14:13, 21; 16:19–31; 19:8; 21:1–3.

42. The poor are lower class by definition, as are most prisoners/captives. People spiritually oppressed or infirmed could be drawn from any class, but someone with a long-term illness would often suffer social ostracism and disgrace, making them more likely to be on the lower ends of the social spectrum.

thought of return and being "gracious"—grace/gift (charis, χάρις) is the root of "charity."[43]

Tabitha's story (Acts 9:36–42), and particularly the background material about Tabitha's life, also shows the early church's care for the poor in Acts.[44] Luke says that Tabitha is "continuously abounding with good works and giving alms/charity" (πλήρης ἔργων ἀγαθῶν καὶ ἐλεημοσυνῶν, 9:36). Tabitha makes tunics and garments for widows (9:38), and her ongoing ministry to these poor women gains her special respect and honor within the church, as the details of her funeral and presentation back to the community alive show (9:37, 39, 41).[45] Luke is highlighting the value the church places on caring for the poor and the needy in this story, and particularly unattached widows, one of the groups living in most poverty in ancient society. Tabitha is a prototypical "female disciple" (μαθήτρια, the only NT instance) who Luke holds up as an exemplum for women.[46]

Although care for the poor is a priority for the Jerusalem church, it is notably less prominent in later parts of Acts. Luke has established this theme in his Gospel, where it is conspicuously highlighted at least ten times in the ministry of Jesus.[47] Luke also depicts the practice as normative behavior in the Jerusalem community, as the above examples show, and the reader can assume this is an important aspect of the church's continuing missional practice, based on its emphasis in the life of Jesus and the Jerusalem church.

In addition to the poor, Luke shows the Christian community caring for the long-term ill and disabled through four prominent examples in Acts.[48] Peter and John heal the beggar crippled from birth (χωλὸς ἐκ κοιλίας μητρός) at the temple gate Beautiful (3:1–10).[49] Peter heals Aeneas,

43. In the Greco-Roman world a gift sets off a chain of reciprocity and usually one only gives to achieve honor or gain and only to those who are able to reciprocate (in money, votes, vocal support, etc.). Witherington, *Acts*, 249.

44. Tabitha is a person of some means, to be able to live as she does. The mention of her upper room suggests a larger house, which may be where the church meets (cf. Acts 1:3, 13; 20:8; Barrett, *Acts*, 1:483). She may be a patroness or benefactor for the Joppa Christian community, which explains why her loss is a blow to the Joppa church; Keener, *Bible Background*, 349.

45. Neither of these honorary actions happen in the previous story, the healing of Aeneas.

46. Witherington, *Women*, 150.

47. Luke 4:18; 6:20; 7:22; 11:41; 12:33; 14:13, 21; 18:22; 19:8; 21:2–3

48. Although illness does not necessarily indicate low social status, this would largely be the case for people with long-term chronic illness or disabilities in ancient society; many would interpret this as judgment from the gods for sin (John 9:2–3).

49. This first physical miracle of Acts comes just after the Pentecost narrative, when the church begins to grow with the first converts to the Christian movement. It parallels

a paralytic (παραλελυμένος) who has been bedridden for 8 years, in Lydda (9:32–35). Paul heals another man who has been lame from birth (χωλὸς ἐκ κοιλίας μητρός) in Lystra (14:8–10);[50] and Paul heals Publius's father in Malta, who is suffering from fever and dysentery (28:8–9).

There are also three summary passages in Acts about people with illnesses or disabilities. In Jerusalem, Peter's shadow heals the sick and excited crowds gather, bringing many "sick and troubled by unclean spirits" (ἀσθενεῖς καὶ ὀχλουμένους ὑπὸ πνευμάτων ἀκαθάρτων) to be healed (5:15–16).[51] This story is meant to impress upon Luke's audience the astounding power working through Peter for healing.[52] Similarly, in Samaria Philip heals many paralytics and people "possessed" (ἐχόντων) by unclean spirits, resulting in "great joy in that city" (8:6–8). This significantly happens at the hands of Philip, who is not an apostle, and with Samaritans beyond Judea's borders. In Ephesus, handkerchiefs and aprons from Paul's work cure multiple illnesses and cause evil spirits to leave (19:11–12).[53]

All of these memorable episodes demonstrate that a primary task of the early church is caring for and healing the sick, and offer a parenetic example to be emulated by readers as they engage with Christ's mission.[54] Both Christian and pagan sources confirm that Christians are known for doing this over the next centuries, even in times of widespread epidemics, and this is undoubtedly a vital contributor to Christianity's missional success.[55]

The church in Acts also cares for the *spiritually sick*. Luke shows this ministry to oppressed people in Philip's Samaritan ministry: "With loud shrieks, unclean spirits came out of many" (πνεύματα ἀκάθαρτα βοῶντα

Jesus's similar healing of the paralytic man (Luke 5:17–26), which comparably follows the calling of his first disciples (5:1–11).

50. Note the identical description of the crippled beggar at the temple gate Beautiful (3:2; 14:8)—Luke is claiming that Paul's healing ministry is parallel to and as powerful as Peter and John's.

51. The idea of a shadow being an extension of the soul or spiritual life force of a person is not uncommon in antiquity (cf. Luke 1:35); Witherington, *Acts*, 227.

52. Polhill, *Acts*, 164: "So widespread was the fame of his healing powers . . . One is reminded of the woman who shared a similar hope that the fringe of Jesus' garment might heal her (Luke 8:44)."

53. "Handkerchiefs" (σουδάρια) refer to kerchiefs worn on the head (cf. Luke 19:20; John 11:44; 20:7), while "aprons" (σιμικίνθια) refer to aprons, or possibly belts. As Paul's reputation as a miracle worker spreads, people come to see him while he works, and he gives them items of clothing used in his trade (as a leather worker or tentmaker, Acts 18:3). Bruce, *Acts*, 410; Trebilco, "Asia," 313–14.

54. Not to mention the myriad instances of healing in Luke's Gospel.

55. Stark argues that this is central to Christianity's triumph in the Roman world, *Rise of Christianity*, 73–94.

φωνῇ μεγάλῃ, 8:7).[56] The exorcism of the girl with the "python spirit" (πνεῦμα πύθωνος) is another example of this kind of ministry (Acts 16:16–18).[57] She is a slave-girl (παιδίσκην), and therefore a representative of the lower class. Paul casts the demon out of her, even at the price of his own welfare (16:19–24).

Acts 19:11–12 says that after Paul's handkerchiefs and aprons touched people "the evil spirits left them" (πνεύματα τὰ πονηρὰ ἐκπορεύεσθαι). This is in Ephesus, widely known as the magic capital of Asia Minor. The implications of Christianity's triumph in Ephesus would not be lost on Luke's readers. This confrontation between Paul's God and the pagan gods climaxes in the burning of the infamous Ephesian scrolls related to sorcery (19:18–20).[58] Luke goes to great rhetorical lengths to show that even in this haven of hostile spiritual powers, the word of God has authority and will be victorious, as underscored by the result: "In this way the word of the Lord spread widely and grew in power" (19:20).

In ministering to spiritually oppressed people, Christians follow in the footsteps of Christ, who demonstrates his compassion by performing multiple exorcisms in Luke's Gospel (4:33; 6:18; 7:21; 8:2, 29; 9:42; 11:24). Luke highlights this connection in Peter's summary of Jesus's ministry at Cornelius's house: "God anointed Jesus of Nazareth with the *Holy Spirit and power*, and he went around doing good and *healing all who were under the power of the devil* (ἰώμενος πάντας τοὺς καταδυναστευομένους ὑπὸ τοῦ διαβόλου), because God was with him" (Acts 10:38). This powerful healing activity is a central part of the church's mission in Acts, and concrete evidence that God is with them.

---

56. This sort of deliverance ministry is commonplace in the ancient world, as evidenced by the story of the Seven Sons of Sceva, of whom Luke casually says, "some Jews who went around driving out evil spirits" (19:13). Josephus, *Ant.* 8.42–49 is a revealing passage about Jewish exorcists. Witherington provides an overview of miracles and magic in antiquity and in Acts, *Acts,* 577–79.

57. The girl's python spirit means that she is inspired by Apollo. It was believed that Apollo was embodied at the oracle at Delphi by a Python, which came to be associated with ventriloquism; see Plutarch, *De Defectu Oraculorum,* 9.414E. She is in essence a fortune-teller, offering answers to questions people ask about their futures, clearly a lucrative business for her owners. Fontenrose, *Delphic Oracle,* 10; Barrett, *Acts,* 2:785.

58. The phrase "Ephesian writings" (ἐθέστια γράμματα) was used for spells and magical formulas, recited by those possessed by demons; Plutarch, *Table Talk,* 7.5.706E: "sorcerers advise those possessed by demons to recite and name over to themselves the Ephesian letters." These books have a value of fifty thousand drachmas, or silver pieces (19:19), the equivalent of about fifty thousand days of a day laborer's pay. The practice of burning books seen as dangerous or subversive is well known in this era; Trebilco, "Asia," 314–15.

Luke emphasizes ministry to the disadvantaged throughout Acts. This practice flows directly out of Christian ethics, and is a catalyst to missional growth, as Stark explains:

> The truly revolutionary aspect of Christianity lay in moral imperatives such as "Love one's neighbor as oneself," "Do unto others as you would have them do unto you," "It is more blessed to give than to receive," and "When you did it to the least of my brethren, you did it unto me." These were not just slogans. Members did nurse the sick, even during epidemics; they did support orphans, widows, the elderly, and the poor; they did concern themselves with the lot of slaves. In short, Christians created "a miniature welfare state in an empire which for the most part lacked social services."[59]

The consistent example that Luke paints of the care of the early Christians for the disadvantaged lower classes provides an inspiring example for readers of Acts to emulate, and it seems that they do go on to follow it. In 362, as Emperor Julian attempts to revitalize paganism, he writes a letter to a pagan priest: "Why do we not observe that it is their *benevolence to strangers* . . . and the *pretended holiness* of their lives that have done most to increase atheism [Christianity] . . . For it is disgraceful that . . . *the impious Galileans support not only their own poor but ours as well.*"[60] In Acts, those at the bottom of Roman society such as widows, orphans, beggars, the disabled, and those with long-term illness, are welcomed in the Jesus movement. The gospel is good news for the underprivileged, and this is one of the primary reasons for Christianity's eventual triumph.

Social concern in Acts involves both compassion and empowerment. Christ-followers do more than give charity; they restore broken lives, bring freedom to people suffering from oppression, and heal the sick. The marginalized are invited not simply to receive aid, but to actually join the fellowship of the Christian community; in this way they are not simply objects of charity, but become active participants, empowered to help others, just as they have been helped.[61] The Spirit is not merely interested in acts of justice, but in the creation of a new spiritual community in which participants are dependent on God and one another, and equipped to join and contribute to the unfolding mission themselves (2:41–47; 4:31–35). This repeated narrative theme demonstrates the church's commitment to the inclusive

---

59. Stark, *Cities of God*, 30–31.

60. Novak, *Christianity and the Roman Empire*, 181–83.

61. Keener, *Acts*, 1:526.

empowerment of all people, and functions as a compelling and persuasive model for Luke's readers to imitate.

The Privileged Higher Classes

If social inclusion is to be universal, it must be for those on the lower end of the social ladder *and* for those on the upper end. Luke is eager to show how the good news is for the oppressor as well as the oppressed, for those with money, power, and influence as well as those with none. In Luke's Gospel, Jesus certainly focuses more on the lowly and the poor, but there are also multiple interactions with people higher up the social ladder. Jesus eats with Levi and a crowd of tax collectors (Luke 5:29), and with Simon the Pharisee, a householder (7:36; cf. 11:37; 14:1). Jesus befriends Zacchaeus, a tax collector and "wealthy man" (πλούσιος, 19:1–10). He points out that there is more faith in a Roman centurion, a representative of the emperor Caesar, than in all of God's chosen people (7:1–10). Finally, he calls an "exceedingly rich" (πλούσιος σφόδρα) young ruler to follow him (18:18–23).

Luke continues to show the gospel reaching the upper classes in Acts, such as in Philip's encounter with the Ethiopian eunuch (Acts 8:26–40). This man is described as a man of power, an official (δυνάστης) of Candace, queen of Ethiopia, who is "in charge of all her treasure" (ἐπὶ πάσης τῆς γάζης αὐτῆς, 8:27), as her chief financial officer.[62] That this eunuch is reading is another indication of his status,[63] along with his ownership of a scroll of Isaiah and a chariot which can seat at least three people.[64] Finally, the eunuch's elegant Greek is a clue to his social status.[65] Though there are many hints of his prestige in this story, his identity as a eunuch and a foreigner also makes his status ambiguous and questionable in Jewish eyes.

Another person of higher status in Acts is Cornelius, a centurion in the Italian Regiment (Acts 10:1—11:18).[66] Centurions are persons of impor-

---

62. Δυνάστης implies a ruler/officer of great authority. That he is in charge of all of the queen of Ethiopia's finances/treasures (γάζης) is an indicator of his status in Ethiopia.

63. He is reading aloud, as is almost always the case in an oral culture; scrolls have no word separation and have to be read syllable by syllable to understand where the divisions come. Witherington, *Acts*, 297.

64. The eunuch, a driver, and Philip; Bruce, *Acts*, 227; Marshall, *Acts*, 162.

65. "How could I be able unless someone will guide me" (8:31) uses the optative mood (expressing a wish) with ἄν, a sign of education or conscious style; Barrett, *Acts*, 1.428. Luke uses the optative in other "educated" speeches, such as the Epicurean and Stoic philosophers (17:18), and Paul before Agrippa and Festus (26:29).

66. He may be named after P. Cornelius Sulla, the Roman general who in 82 BCE freed 10,000 slaves who then took his name. This Cornelius may be the descendant of

tance in antiquity.[67] Luke presents Cornelius as a pious and devout person (εὐσεβής), a "God-fearer" (φοβούμενος τὸν Θεόν) who prays regularly and gives many donations to the people (ἐλεημοσύνας πολλὰς τῷ λαῷ, 10:2, 4), an indicator of status and financial means.[68] His career provides upward social mobility, and this story emphasizes that the Spirit directs the early church to reach out not just to the lowly majority, but also to those on the upper ends of society's social strata.

There are multiple other references to people of influence in Acts. In Antioch, there is Manaen, "who had been brought up with Herod the tetrarch" (Ἡρῴδου τοῦ τετράρχου σύντροφος, 13:1). Σύντροφος literally means that Manaen had the same wet nurse as Herod Antipas, but also commonly refers to an intimate friend, in this case in Herod's court.[69] In Cyprus, the proconsul (ἀνθύπατος) Sergius Paulus, a member of the local elite ruling class and the governor of the senatorial province of Cyprus, is converted (13:7–12).[70] In Thessalonica, a number of the "leading women" (γυναικῶν τε τῶν πρώτων) are converted (17:4).[71] In Berea "a number of prominent Greek women and men" believe (τῶν Ἑλληνίδων γυναικῶν τῶν εὐσχημόνων καί ἀνδρῶν, 17:12).[72] "Christianity seems to have been especially successful among women. It was often through the wives that it penetrated the upper classes of society in the first instance."[73]

---

one of those freedmen; Witherington, *Acts*, 346.

67. The Roman legion (6,000 men) was divided into ten regiments of 600 men, each of which had a designation, such as the Italian, Imperial, or Augustan (Acts 27:1). A centurion (ἑκατοντάρχης) commanded sixty to eighty men and provided stability to the entire military system; Keener, *Acts*, 2:1742–44.

68. Every centurion mentioned in the NT has noble qualities (e.g., Matt 27:54; Luke 7:1–10; Acts 22:25–26; 27:1, 6, 11, 31, 43). Gospel writers are eager to show that neither Jesus nor his followers are antagonistic towards the Roman presence in the East, and that certain influential Roman soldiers even find Christianity appealing.

69. See 1 Macc 1:6; 2 Macc 9:29 on σύντροφος. Manaen could have been a source of information for Luke about the Herods; Witherington, *Acts*, 392; 165–73 on Luke's sources in Acts more generally.

70. Cyprus was ruled by a civil administration; Schnabel, *Mission*, 2:1083.

71. It is possible that γυναικῶν τε τῶν πρώτων refers to wives of leading men, and the Western text reads this way, omitting the τε and adding καί; Metzger, *Textual Commentary*, 453. There is an anti-feminist tendency in the D text (1:14; 17:12; 18:26); Witherington, "Anti-Feminist Tendencies," 82–84. Schaps, "Women Least Mentioned," 72, gives evidence that "first of women" may be an honorary title.

72. Εὐσχημόνων means proper, noble or honorable, indicating prominent status. Though it follows the word women, it likely also refers to the men. That the high-status women are mentioned first suggests that more of them converted. The anti-feminist tendency in D can be seen here as well.

73. Chadwick, *Early Church*, 56. Brown notices that "women were prominent"

In Athens, Dionysius the Areopagite is converted (ὁ Ἀρεοπαγίτης, 17:34); membership in the Athenian Areopagus indicates extremely high social standing.[74] In Corinth, Crispus the synagogue ruler (ὁ ἀρχισυνάγωγος) is converted, along with his family (18:8).[75] Apollos is in Ephesus, "a learned/eloquent man, with a mighty knowledge of the Scriptures" (ἀνὴρ λόγιος . . . δυνατὸς ὢν ἐν ταῖς γραφαῖς, 18:24).[76] In Ephesus, Paul has friends (φίλοι) amongst the elite Asiarchs (Ἀσιάρχαι, 19:31), high officials who introduce motions in the assemblies of the city council, dedicate buildings, build statues, and organize festivals and games.[77] There are multiple others of some social status mentioned throughout Acts, such as Barnabas, a land-owner (4:36–37), Lydia, a home-owner (16:13–15, 40), and Tabitha (9:36–43).

In all of these, Luke's recipient Theophilus might recognize himself, for as Luke's patron he also probably originates in the upper classes.[78] Acts even shows the gospel going to influential governors and kings (24:10; 25:6; 26:2), and hints at the highest of all, Caesar himself, hearing it (25:11–12, 21; 26:32; 27:24). These stories emphasize the appropriateness of the very highest in society hearing the gospel. In highlighting these frequent cameos of high-status people, Luke is making a case for prioritizing people of influence and means, who offer multiple strategic opportunities to the Christian mission.[79]

Women in the Christian Mission

In addition to this distinctive emphasis on reaching people of higher status, another of the defining themes of Acts is the prominent role of women in its

among upper class Christians and that "such women could influence their husbands to protect the church," *Body and Society*, 151. Osiek and MacDonald, *Woman's Place*, discuss multiple examples of prominent female leaders of households and Christian assemblies (144–63), female patrons in the Christian house churches (194–219), and women as agents of missional expansion in the early church (220–43).

74. Church tradition says this Dionysius becomes the first bishop of Athens; Eusebius, *Hist. Eccl.*, 3.4.11; 4.23.3.

75. Converting an ἀρχισυνάγωγος would lead others to follow suit. See 1 Cor 1:14–16, Crispus's baptism.

76. Ἀνὴρ λόγιος could mean that Apollos is a learned man (the classical usage), or an eloquent man, trained in rhetoric. Keener, *Bible Background*, 377, suggests it means "formally skilled in rhetoric, the more practical form of advanced learning to which well-to-do pupils could attain (the other was philosophy)."

77. Schnabel, *Mission*, 2:1225. It is uncertain whether they are Christians, but they are "friendly" towards Paul and the Ephesian church; Paul's acquaintance with them is likely the result of his missionary work in Ephesus.

78. Witherington, *Acts*, 64–65.

79. This strategic theme will be further explored in part 3.

narrative. Involving women in the church's mission and growth is a strategic tactic which underscores Luke's universal inclusion and is unconventional in a patriarchal society. Pragmatically, it doubles the available workforce, and multiplies the potential effectiveness of the church's outreach. In a domestic house-church context this may be reasonable, but it should still be seen as a noteworthy rhetorical ploy which challenges and critiques wider cultural expectations.

The programmatic declaration in Acts 2:17–18 (quoting Joel 2:28–32) sets the stage for this: "I will pour out my Spirit upon *all flesh* (πᾶσαν σάρκα), and *your sons and your daughters* (θυγατέρες . . . νεανίσκοι) *will prophesy* . . . Even upon my *male and female slaves* (δούλους . . . δούλας), in those days I will pour out my Spirit; and *they will prophesy*." At Pentecost, the barrier-bursting Spirit is breaking down gender barriers, alongside ethnic and cultural barriers—God calls all people to prophetically speak his message in Acts. Luke regards such activity as normative missional practice.

Acts contains five cameos of principal Christian women.[80] *Mary*, the mother of John Mark, is a patroness and benefactor to the early Christian community in Jerusalem (12:12–17). The reference to "many" gathering in her household (12:12) suggests a house of considerable size, as do the references to a courtyard gate and a female gatekeeper; Luke implies that this is a regular meeting place for the church in Jerusalem.[81] *Lydia, a purple* cloth dealer from Thyatira, becomes the patroness and early host of the Christian community in Philippi (16:12–40).[82] The Philippi narrative climaxes with Paul's final Christian meeting in Lydia's house, which is a strategic venue for outreach into that Roman colony.[83] *Tabitha* (9:36–43) is a notable female disciple (μαθήτρια) who has an influential ministry to Christian widows. Luke mentions *Philip the evangelist's four daughters* (θυγατέρες), who prophesy (προφητεύουσαι, 21:8–9) and fulfil the prophecy of Joel Peter reinterprets in Acts 2:17: "Your sons *and daughters* will prophesy." Luke calls

80. Witherington, *Acts*, 338.

81. This may be the location of the upper room where the Last Supper is held (Mark 14:13–15; Acts 1:13), and/or the place of prayer of Acts 4:31. See discussion in part 2.

82. Luke portrays Lydia as a person of social importance and means; such women are not uncommon in Macedonia, which unusually had allowed women important roles since at least the Hellenistic era; Marshall, "Roman Women," 108–27. The extent of Lydia's actual leadership in the Philippian church is uncertain.

83. Lydia's home serves as a base for fellowship and outreach and is thus crucial to the existence and growth of Christianity in Philippi. If Jews are forced to meet outside the city gate in Philippi (Acts 16:13), Christians would not fare much better apart from a wealthy sponsor. Lydia's home lends credibility to this new movement and causes it to be seen more like a club or society, which commonly meet in large homes, rather than a foreign cult; Witherington, *Acts*, 487.

his most eminent characters prophets or prophetesses;[84] he uses this terminology to refer to a select group of church leaders, and expects that they will be involved in the church's missional proclamation.[85] Finally, there is Luke's reference to *Priscilla*, the female teacher of the notable evangelist Apollos and Pauline co-worker (18:2, 18, 24–26).[86] Luke's portrayal of Priscilla is entirely positive, implying that he approves of women engaging in this type of teaching ministry.[87]

Luke's portrayal of women performing these functions in the early church shows his support of the role of women in the advancing Christian mission. He also highlights women being converted or serving the Christian movement in eight churches: Jerusalem (1:13–14; 12:12–17), Joppa (9:36–42), Philippi (16:11–15), Thessalonica (17:4), Berea (17:12), Athens (17:34), Corinth (18:1–3), and Ephesus (18:19–26). Luke mentions multiple women by name in Acts,[88] and emphasizes their speaking ministries as prophets and teachers.[89]

Though there is much to be appreciated, Luke's depiction of women in Acts can also be critiqued. Many of his female characters are named and do significant things, which is a marked improvement on other NT sources such as Mark or Matthew. However, Luke fails to fully acknowledge the historical role which women played within the Pauline churches and the early missionary movement, as co-workers, leaders, patrons, and even apostles.[90]

---

84. E.g., John the Baptist, Jesus, Peter, Paul, Agabus, Elizabeth, Mary, Anna, Philip's daughters. Luke sees these prophets and prophetesses as both discerning the fulfillment of OT prophecies by the Spirit's insight (e.g., Acts 2), *and* giving new predictive prophecies (e.g., Acts 11:28; 21:11; 27:10, 23–24, 31, 34).

85. See Acts 15:22, 32: these prophets point to another prophetic function, to "encourage and strengthen" the church.

86. In nearly every reference to Priscilla and Aquila, Priscilla's name is first (Acts 18:18, 26; Rom 16:3; 2 Tim 4:19), suggesting higher status, or greater prominence in the church. The Western text omits Priscilla in 18:2, 18, 21, and places Aquila's name first in 18:26, implying that he leads in teaching Apollos.

87. John Chrysostom, the first great commentator of the book of Acts, underscores the significance: "He sailed to Syria . . . *and with him Priscilla—Lo, a woman also—*and Aquila. But these he left at Ephesus with good reason, namely that they should teach"; *Homilies*, 145.

88. Schaps, "Women Least Mentioned," 323–30, shows that women normally mentioned in public by name are women of questionable reputation, women connected with the speaker's opponent, or dead women, while reputable women are excluded.

89. MacMullen, "Women in Public," 208–18, points out that women are rarely found in roles which involve public speaking; therefore, they can be seen but are not to be heard. There are also significant roles for women in Luke's Gospel, e.g., 1:24, 45–55; 2:36–38; 24:6–9, 22.

90. E.g., Romans 16:1–12 (Phoebe, Priscilla, Mary, Junia, Tryphena, Tryphosa); 1

Most of the women in Acts are involved in the story, but not in leadership or official positions, and though they have speaking roles, none of them actually speak.[91] This suppression of what Paul actually practiced, according to his letters, demonstrates Luke's tendentiousness, possibly in order to make his story more acceptable to his perceived audience.

Some scholars conclude that Luke treats women negatively, while others are more neutral or positive.[92] "Luke's version of the life of Jesus and of the first believers cannot be reduced either to a feminist treasure chamber or to a chamber of horrors for women's theology. It contains elements that bring joy to 'dignity studies' and other elements that give support to 'misery studies' . . . The Lukan construction contains a double, mixed message."[93] Witherington suggests that Luke, "shows how the Gospel liberates and creates new possibilities for women . . . we find women being converted or serving the Christian community in roles that would not have been available to them apart from that community."[94] Keener concludes that, "Luke favors the approach of more progressive cosmopolitan contemporaries rather than that of extreme traditionalists, even though this approach could have appeared scandalous to more traditional minds."[95]

The way that Luke repeatedly highlights the contributions of women in his story shows that he is willing to challenge the prevailing cultural norms in such matters. Even if they are not included in formal leadership in Acts, as they are for Paul, Luke is advocating a strategic involvement and role for women in the growth and advancement of the church's mission, and this is

---

Cor 1:11 (Chloe), 16:19 (Priscilla); Col 4:15 (Nympha); Phil 4:1–3 (Euodia, Syntyche); Balch, "Luke-Acts," 72–76; also, Westfall, *Paul and Gender*; Peppiatt, *Unveiling Paul's Women*; Keener, *Paul, Women, and Wives*.

91. Luke reinforces this by beginning many of the speeches in Acts with the typical rhetorical address "men, brothers, Israelites" (ἄνδρες, ἀδελφοί, Ἰσραηλῖται; 1:16; 2:22, 29; 3:12, 17; 6:3; 7:2; 13:16; 15:7, 13, 23; 22:1).

92. Jervell, "Daughters of Abraham," 146–57, argues that Luke portrays women as living up to all the traditional patriarchal expectations of withdrawn submission, with no more freedoms than any other religious setting. Fiorenza, *In Memory of Her*, 49f., 161–67, says that Luke's presentation of women has contributed to the "conspiracy of silence" and invisibility surrounding prominent women in the early Christian movement. Reimer, *Women*, 252, concludes that Luke suppresses stories about early female Christian leaders, such as Thecla or Mary Magdalene.

93. Seim, *Double Message*, 249. Levine, *Feminist Companion* contains multiple articles on women in Luke's Gospel which analyze this complex question from both positive and negative perspectives.

94. Witherington, *Women*, 156–57. This may be somewhat overstated; recent evidence has shown that women do have certain important positions outside of the church in the ancient world.

95. Keener, *Acts*, 1:597–638 is a summary of women and their roles in antiquity.

a decisive rhetorical move which he hopes his readers will note and emulate. Acts thus moves significantly in the direction of inclusive partnership for men and women in the church's universal mission.

SOTERIOLOGICALLY UNIVERSAL— SALVATION FOR THE ENTIRE PERSON

Luke not only emphasizes that God's salvation is for every person, everywhere, but he argues that it is for the entire person and will affect every aspect of his or her being. This is a different kind of universality; it is relevant to all parts of a person, comprehensive in its impact on a person's life. Luke's soteriology has social, moral, mental, emotional, physical, and spiritual dimensions, enhancing the well-being of the entire person who experiences it.[96]

Ancient paganism has little interest in "eternal life" or being "saved" in the Christian sense: "The 'salvation' most ancients looked for was salvation from disease, disaster, or death in this life, and the 'redemption' many pagans cried out for was redemption from the social bondage of slavery . . . Pagan religion, even when the subject of salvation did come up, was decidedly this-worldly in its focus, aims, and perceived benefits."[97] This is also true of the mystery religions,[98] and generally of ancient Judaism.[99] The Hebrew words for salvation (יְשׁוּעָה) and deliverance (תְּשׁוּעָה, פֶּלֶט, הַצָּלָה), "seldom, if ever, express a spiritual state *exclusively*: their common theological sense in Hebrew is that of *a material deliverance attended by spiritual blessings* (e.g., Isa 12:2; 45:17)."[100]

---

96. Cf. Witherington's analysis of the concept of salvation in Luke-Acts, *Acts*, 143–44, 821–43.

97. Witherington, *Acts*, 821. MacMullen, *Paganism*, 57: "'Savior' . . . or 'salvation' had to do with health or other matters of this earth, not of the soul for life eternal." Judaism has some discussion of the afterlife by the first century. Foerster and Fohrer, "σῴζω," 965–1024 is a study of the σῴζω/σωτηρία word group.

98. E.g., the cults of Isis and Serapis, or Mithraism; Gill, "Behind the Classical Façade," 86–100.

99. There is no reference to purely religious, spiritual, or eternal benefits of σωτηρία in Josephus. Forgiveness of sins is a familiar concept in the OT, but is never called salvation.

100. Driver, *Notes on the Hebrew Text*, 119, emphasis added. Driver explains that the meanings of Hebrew words such as יְשׁעה (*yeshuah*) and תְּשׁוּעה (*teshuah*) were enlarged to include spiritual blessings over time in these passages, but this was never their exclusive meaning. For Luke's Jewish contemporaries, such as Josephus, σῴζω/σωτηρία and their cognates "are not theologically freighted terms," Foerster and Fohrer, "σῴζω," 987.

Luke employs such natural conceptions of salvation, using σῴζω in the sense of rescue, heal, deliver, and keep safe frequently throughout Luke-Acts.[101] For Luke, God's salvation has undeniable worldly implications, such as survival from shipwreck (Acts 27:34).[102] Luke uses the word to refer to the physical healing of the crippled beggar (4:9).[103] He also speaks of physical rescue or deliverance as "salvation" from Egyptian captivity (7:25) and from shipwreck (27:20), a usage that would be familiar to both Jews and Greeks.[104]

However, Luke's soteriology is broader than the conventional secular understanding of the first-century world. Of the 17 uses of the noun forms σωτήρ, σωτηρία, σωτήριον in Luke-Acts, only Acts 7:25 and 27:34 have no clear "spiritual" overtones.[105] Luke uses the verbal form, σῴζω, but never the noun forms when relating stories about the healing of the sick, or the raising of the dead.

> For Luke, Christ's death and resurrection are at the very heart of God's saving plan for humankind . . . Salvation at its very core has to do with God's gracious act of forgiving sins through Jesus which causes the moral, mental, emotional, spiritual, and sometimes even physical transformation of an individual . . . Salvation is something which can happen in the present, and involves the character transformation of a human being . . . Certainly "salvation" for Luke has social consequences, but equally clearly it is a spiritual transformation of human personality that leads a person to see the logical social consequences of receiving Jesus.[106]

This can be seen in the story of Zacchaeus (Luke 19:1–10). There is no mention of Jesus healing Zacchaeus physically, or exorcising a demon, or delivering him from foes or from danger. Instead, Jesus says that "today salvation (σωτηρία) has come to this house" (19:9), and "what is meant is the recovery of a spiritually lost person by means of Jesus' gracious behavior towards the man."[107] The evidence of Zacchaeus's conversion and transformed

101. Σῴζω occurs 17 times in Luke and 13 times in Acts; Luke 6:9; 8:36, 48, 50; 9:24; 17:19; 18:42; 23:35, 37, 39; Acts 4:9; 14:9; 27:20, 31 are "natural," unspiritual references.

102. Paul urges his storm-battered fellow travelers to eat, for it is necessary for their σωτηρία, their survival or preservation; Bruce, *Acts*, 524–5; cf. Thucydides, *Hist.*, 3.59.1; Heb 11:7.

103. Peter uses σέσωται to refer to a physical healing. Jesus often uses it in this sense in Luke (8:48; 17:19; 18:42), but after Pentecost σῴζω never involves healing alone, but also spiritual benefit; Bruce, *Acts*, 151–52.

104. This is a common usage of σωτηρία in the LXX (Acts 7:25).

105. Witherington, *Acts*, 831. Possibly also Luke 1:47, 71.

106. Witherington, *Acts*, 837–38.

107. Witherington, *Acts*, 838.

character is his desire to give generously to the poor and return fourfold to all from whom he has stolen (19:8). This theme of the internal, spiritual transformation of the human being, which has implications in every area of their lives, continues throughout Acts (e.g., 4:12; 13:26, 47; 16:17; 28:28).

Luke states the means of salvation through the mouth of Peter at the theologically pivotal Jerusalem Council: "We are saved (σωθῆναι) through the grace (χάριτος) of the Lord Jesus" (Acts 15:11); salvation is available through Christ's graciousness. Jesus is the only source of salvation in Acts: "There is salvation in no one else; for there is no other name under heaven that has been given among men by which we must be saved" (δεῖ σωθῆναι ἡμᾶς, Acts 4:12). There is no other name to appeal to than the name of Jesus.[108]

For Luke, salvation is something that comes from and belongs to God. This conviction is a theological "book-end" to Luke-Acts: Simeon's eyes have seen "your salvation" (τὸ σωτήριόν σου, Luke 2:30); Paul says that "the salvation of God" (τὸ σωτήριον τοῦ Θεοῦ) has been sent to the Gentiles (Acts 28:28). Therefore, salvation is something humans receive from God. The only required human response is faith, as shown by the repeated phrase "your faith has saved/healed you" (ἡ πίστις σου σέσωκέν σε).[109] In Acts 16:30–31 when the jailer asks, "what must I do to be saved?" Paul and Silas reply, "Believe (πίστευσον) in the Lord Jesus, and you will be saved (σωθήσῃ), you and your whole household." While God initiates the offer of salvation, a person must respond in faith to receive it.

Forgiveness of sins is the primary meaning of salvation throughout Acts.[110] It is this gracious act of forgiving sins through the death and resurrection of Jesus which causes the holistic transformation of the individual who believes. Acts 13:38–39 summarizes these concepts: "I want you to know that *through Jesus the forgiveness of sins* (ἄφεσις ἁμαρτιῶν) *is proclaimed to you. Through him everyone who believes is justified* (πᾶς ὁ πιστεύων δικαιοῦται)."

At the heart of Luke's soteriology is the idea that *the Father has done something new through Christ's life, death, and resurrection, which has made possible a sort of salvation not previously available.* This decisive historical event is the beginning of the eschatological age, in which the dominion of God breaks into human history, fueled by the outpouring of the Spirit at Pentecost. All of this is the fulfillment of the prophetic promises of God (e.g.,

---

108. As in other places, salvation has spiritual, physical, and social dimensions, as the presence of the healed man in this Sanhedrin session demonstrates; Johnson, *Acts*, 78.

109. E.g., Luke 7:50; 8:48; 17:19; 18:42; also 5:20.

110. Foerster and Fohrer, "σῴζω," 997: "again and again in Acts the content of σωτηρία is the forgiveness of sins, 3:19, 26; 5:31; 10:43; 13:38; 22:16; 26:18."

Isa 25:9; 26:18; 45:17; 61:1).[111] As this salvation touches lives, the transformation works itself out in every external and internal aspect of the person's life. "Luke's salvation at its very core has to do with God's gracious act of forgiving sins through Jesus which causes the moral, mental, emotional, spiritual, and sometimes even physical transformation of an individual."[112] Social transformation can also be added to this list. The social dimension can be seen in Luke's concern for the poor and the release of the captives, which includes liberation from spiritual oppression. In addition, salvation expresses itself in family reconciliation in the parable of the prodigal son (Luke 15).

Salvation is a holistic and all-encompassing transformation in Luke-Acts, with implications for every aspect and need of an individual's life.[113] The Christian mission in Acts offers this universal salvation to everyone. This would encourage Christian missionaries and provide them with confidence and motivation. By portraying a Christian salvation that can meet every need and address every concern in a person's life, Luke seeks to strengthen the missional convictions and commitments of his readers.

CONCLUSION—AN ALL-ENCOMPASSING THEOLOGY OF UNIVERSAL RELEVANCE

Salvation in Acts is spiritual intervention with physical ramifications. It is particular, in that it is attained by believing in one name, the name of Jesus. It is also universal, in that it is for all places, all ethnicities and genders, all parts of the social spectrum, and every aspect of a person's life. This *universality* and *particularity* are both the fulfillment of the promises of the prophets, in the person of Jesus of Nazareth. This results in a comprehensive universal vision. There is no person for whom the gospel is not applicable and relevant, and there is no part of the person to whom it does not apply its transforming power, through Christ. For Luke, the gospel is for all of everyone (cf. 1 Tim 2:4).

111. "Luke focuses on the inbreaking of divine salvific activity into human history with the appearance of Jesus of Nazareth among [hu]mankind. Jesus did not come as the end of history . . . He is rather seen as the end of one historical period and the beginning of another, and all of this is a manifestation of a plan of God to bring about the salvation of human beings who recognize and accept the plan," Fitzmyer, *Luke*, 179.

112. Witherington, *Acts*, 837.

113. Luke focuses on salvation's individual and social/communal aspects because his goal is to strengthen mission in the church. It is uncertain whether he is aware of salvation's wider cosmic dimensions (mostly found in Paul), though power encounter episodes such as Paul and the "python spirit" may hint at this (16:16–18).

> The theme of universality is found in the way the Christian mission is made available to all kinds of people, whether powerful or weak, wealthy or poor, male or female: the message is constantly enunciated through proclamation or through merciful action, to poor widows (9:39) and provincials (14:15–18) and merchants (16:14), and jailers (16:30–32), and sailors (27:25) as well as powerful military officers (10:34–38), proconsuls (13:7), governors (24:10), kings (26:2), and philosophers (17:18).[114]

Luke presents this inclusive theological worldview as a potent stimulus for mission in the church. As Witherington says, "The whole gospel must be proclaimed to the whole person in the whole world, for there is one, all-sufficient Savior for all, and therefore all must be for this one."[115] Christians are empowered and motivated by the idea that the message they carry, advanced by the powerful Spirit, is relevant to all people, and that it possesses the power to transform the entire person, through the offer of holistic salvation. This realization creates an urgency to carry and communicate it to everyone. If the message really is for every person, a messenger is required, to take this good news to every person. Universal relevance leads to universal proclamation.[116]

Paul articulates a similar idea in Rom 10:12–15. He begins by claiming the universal relevance of the gospel to all people, "Jew and Greek, for the same Lord is Lord of all and is abundantly generous to all ($\pi\lambda o u \tau \tilde{\omega} \nu$ εἰς πάντας) who call on him" (10:12). He then says that people cannot call on the name of the Lord unless someone is sent to proclaim the message of salvation to them (10:13–15). The cumulative effect of Luke's universal theology is virtually identical to Paul's conclusion: missionaries must be sent to declare the gospel to all people, that they might hear, have the opportunity to believe, and be saved.[117]

Luke is seeking to inspire and motivate his readers to involve themselves in the Jesus movement. He is attempting to generate the next wave of missionaries, "sent" as "preachers," "proclaiming good news of good things" (εὐαγγελιζομένων τὰ ἀγαθά, Rom 10:14–15). By claiming that the message is

---

114. Johnson, *Acts*, 17.

115. Witherington, *Acts*, 72.

116. The universal relevance of the gospel does not result in universal acceptance; many people receive the word in Acts, while others reject it (e.g., 13:45–47; 14:2; 17:5, 32; 18:6; 19:9; 22:22; 26:24–28; 28:24–28).

117. Luke probably also believes Christ can reveal himself to people directly through dreams, visions, and trances, as these are prominent themes in Acts, though generally for guidance to Christians (e.g., 2:17; 9:10–12; 10:3; 12:9; 16:9; 18:9; 22:17). Even in this case, a missionary would ideally reiterate the message.

relevant to every person, and applies to every part of life, Luke is pursuing a response: active missional engagement. The only reply to Luke's universal theology is universal mission, on a personal level in individual relationships, and throughout the earth. The recipients of God's salvation in Christ are not merely objects of mission; they are invited into the community of the church and empowered by the Spirit to help extend the mission in their own social networks and contexts. In this way they become participants and leaders in the church's expanding outreach. Luke's universalized theology permeates the Acts narrative and serves as a persuasive stimulus for the missionary efforts of the early church. The Father's loving offer of salvation is for everyone. It also requires a radical response of faithful discipleship in return, as will be seen in the next chapter.

Chapter 4

Radical Christianity

They rejoiced that they were considered worthy to suffer dishonor for the sake of the name. And every day in the temple and at home they did not cease to teach and proclaim Jesus as the Messiah.

—ACTS 5:41–42

In Acts, the all-encompassing message of the gospel requires everything of both its hearer and its bearer. The holistic salvation the Father offers, which transforms every aspect of life, produces faithful devotion in its recipients and involves a total discipleship response. This wholehearted response is the core of Luke's understanding of radical Christianity, and he uses rhetorical characterization throughout Acts to model this sort of radical lifestyle and to challenge his readers to emulate it in their personal lives. "Radical" is understood here as extreme, uncompromising, activistic, passionate, nonconformist, and even revolutionary.[1]

1. Rowland, *Radical Christianity* focuses on early Christianity in its prophetic power and protest as a model for contemporary discipleship, social justice, liberation theology, revolutionary change, and cultural transformation.

THE INTENSIFICATION OF DEMANDS IN LUKE-ACTS

One of Luke's characteristic themes is the intensification of discipleship demands.[2] Jesus's requirements of those who receive God's gift of salvation in Luke's Gospel are strenuous and often intensified from parallel passages, as the following five examples demonstrate.

Table 4.1 Intensification of Discipleship Demands in Luke

1. Luke 9:23—"If any want to become my followers, let them deny themselves and take up their cross *daily* (καθ' ἡμέραν) and follow me"; the parallel passages (Matt 16:24; Mark 8:34) do not contain "daily," making the Lukan form more extreme.

2. Luke 9:62—"*No one* (οὐδείς) who puts his hand to the plow and looks back is fit for the Kingdom of God"; this is a unique Lukan saying (cf. John 6:66).

3. Luke 14:26—"Whoever comes to me and does not *hate* (μισεῖ) father and mother, wife and children, brothers and sisters, *yes, and even life itself* (τὴν ψυχὴν ἑαυτοῦ), cannot be my disciple"; Matt 10:34–37 does not contain "hate," or mention hating one's life in comparison to allegiance to Christ.

4. Luke 14:33—"None of you can become my disciple if you do not *give up all your possessions*" (πᾶσι τοῖς ἑαυτοῦ ὑπάρχουσιν); there is no parallel to this saying, indeed all of Luke 14:25–35, about the high cost of discipleship, is unique to Luke.

5. Luke 18:22—"Sell *everything you have* (πάντα ὅσα ἔχεις) and distribute the money to the poor, and you will have treasure in heaven; then come, follow me"; the parallel passages (Matt 19:21; Mark 10:21) do not contain "everything."[3]

None of these intensified demands have an *exact* parallel in the other Gospels, and they all express Luke's unique understanding of strenuous Christian discipleship. The twin Lukan parables of building a tower and going to war against another king (Luke 14:28–32) show that one should never take following Jesus lightly, or underestimate the cost it will require. For

2. Witherington, *Acts*, 71.

3. Peter's response, "we have left *all we own* to follow you" (Luke 18:28) shows that the disciples understand this to be relevant to them, not just the wealthy ruler.

Luke, complete surrender is the only way to follow Jesus: *daily* self-denial and sacrifice, *never* looking back, renouncing *all others* and even one's own life, and giving up *everything* are simply what it means to follow Jesus and respond to such a great salvation.

These radical discipleship demands are all found in Luke's Gospel, where the disciples mostly fail to fulfill them; Jesus's teaching sets the standard, and only he realizes them in his personal life, epitomized at the cross. Jesus's personal example is presented as a source of strength and inspiration to his disciples. Yet his discipleship standards seem impossible to fulfill, and the disciples fail repeatedly in Luke's Gospel, particularly as the end of Jesus's ministry draws near. They do not understand what is happening, are characterized by fear rather than boldness and by desertion and denial rather than loyal devotion, and they are more interested in self-preservation than self-denial.[4] In all of this, they are relatable to Luke's readers.

It is not until Acts that Christ's followers realize these lofty standards. The death and resurrection of Jesus, coupled with the outpouring of the Spirit at Pentecost, empower the disciples to successfully live the strenuous discipleship norms which Jesus has set forth. Luke is teaching that apart from God's Spirit-empowerment, people can never live as God intends. The death and resurrection of Jesus provide this power, and a new era of salvation history begins.

After Pentecost, the disciples are demonstrably transformed. Peter, who has recently denied that he knows Jesus three times (Luke 22:56–62), now risks his life by boldly and publicly proclaiming the arrival of the kingdom of God (Acts 2:14–40), and in dramatic fashion three thousand people are added to their numbers (2:41). This leads to the first summary passage, in which the early believers selflessly sell their possessions and give to anyone who has need (2:42–47). In the next summary, Luke claims that there are no needy persons among them, so great is their sacrificial sharing with one another (4:32, 34–35).[5] These are direct fulfillments of Jesus's radical demands (Luke 14:26, 33; 18:22), and divine proof that the church is composed of the legitimate followers of Jesus, for they are now realizing his discipleship requirements by the Spirit's power.

In addition to selfless generosity, the early church continues to be characterized by fearless boldness; nothing will deter them.[6] After being flogged and ordered not to speak about Jesus, they leave the Council, "rejoicing that

4. E.g., Luke 9:33, 40–41, 46, 54–55; 10:20; 18:31; 22:34, 41, 45–46, 50–51, 57–62; 23:26–56. Each is a direct failing of the discipleship standards which Jesus articulates.

5. Luke then holds up Barnabas as a good example of this sort of radical living (4:36–37), and Ananias and Sapphira as a poor example (5:1–11).

6. E.g., Acts 4:13, 19–20, 29–31; 5:29–32, 41–42; multiple other examples.

they had been considered worthy to suffer shame for the Name. And *every day* (πᾶσάν τε ἡμέραν) . . . *they never stopped* (οὐκ ἐπαύοντο) teaching and proclaiming Jesus the Christ" (5:41–42).[7] The daily and continual emphases call attention to the fulfillment of Jesus's discipleship demands.

This early theme of boldness to the point of sacrificial suffering culminates with the preaching and martyrdom of Stephen (7:54–60). In the violent narrative climax Stephen is serene as he gives up his life for Christ's sake.[8] This event sparks widespread persecution (8:1–3), yet "those who had been scattered preached the word *everywhere they went*" (8:4). Physical threats and death itself do not deter these believers. Self-preservation is replaced by obedience as the highest value. After Stephen's death, Saul the persecutor (8:1; 9:1–2) encounters the risen Christ and receives a call to go to the Gentiles (9:15–16). The remainder of Acts contains stories of Paul bravely risking his life that all would hear the gospel.

This sort of bold witness in Acts is the ultimate example of selflessness, and the best way to "deny yourself, take up your cross daily, and follow me" (Luke 9:23). When a person understands that the direct result of this is likely to be persecution, suffering, and even martyrdom, this is the essence of "hating your own life" (Luke 14:26). Additionally, many of the missionaries in Acts leave their homes and families behind without looking back (Luke 9:62); thus, they "hate" their families in comparison to their devotion to Christ (14:26).

For Luke, this kind of extreme discipleship, characterized by radical devotion to God, is the fulfillment of the discipleship demands Jesus articulated and modeled in his Gospel. The contrast between the pre- and post-Easter disciples is an intentional literary device. Filled with the Spirit, the disciples do not fear suffering or death.[9] They do not count their possessions as their own but give to those in need. They leave behind the comforts of home and family to spread the gospel. They are swept up in the irresistible advance of the Word and surrendered to the leadership of the Holy Spirit, even when this brings personal sacrifice.

Luke is using characterization here; this high standard of sacrificial and uncompromising devotion to God is meant to inspire his readers to

7. The ancient values of shame and honor are reversed, and flogging becomes an honor, because it is a result of their bold witness for Jesus.

8. It is a common conviction in the ancient world that martyrdom legitimates one's witness. For the early church, martyrdom is not something to be sought, nor is it something to avoid, as it is an honor to suffer on behalf of Christ. Like Jesus, Stephen offers nonviolent resistance and a bold prophetic witness against the corrupt temple hierarchy; Talbert, "Martyrdom and the Lukan Social Ethic," 99–110.

9. They do need a bit of reassurance and help from time to time: Acts 4:23–31; 7:55–56; 18:9–10; 22:17, 18; 23:11; 27:23–24. Notice that it is often Jesus himself who brings this.

follow the example of these earliest Christians. His message is that this way of living is impossible, apart from God's empowerment. Through the death and resurrection of Jesus and the sending of the Spirit, the Father has provided a way for normal people to fulfill Jesus's radical discipleship standards. It is now possible—God's people can live in the faithful and sacrificial way that he desires, as they receive the Spirit's empowerment to enter his missional purposes.

As the bearer of the Spirit before Pentecost, Jesus is Luke's original model for a person living out these radical discipleship demands. Alongside the Spirit's empowerment, Luke provides another significant insight into what enables Jesus to live so faithfully and sacrificially in his Gospel. The pivotal event which launches Jesus' ministry is his baptism, at which the Holy Spirit descends on him like a dove, and the voice of the Father speaks: "You are my Son the beloved (σὺ εἶ ὁ υἱός μου ὁ ἀγαπητός); in you I take pleasure/delight" (ἐν σοὶ εὐδόκησα, Luke 3:22).[10] This baptismal experience merges the empowering of the Spirit and the Father's loving affirmation. This "belovedness," this sense of being loved by and pleasing to the Father, is the foundation for Jesus's identity, and the springboard for his spiritual influence, as emphasized by the next verse which speaks about the beginning of his public ministry (3:23).

This close relationship between Father and Son is reaffirmed on the Mount of Transfiguration, at which the same paternal voice speaks from the cloud about Jesus's sonship, chosenness, and spiritual authority: "This is my son the chosen one (ὁ υἱός μου ὁ ἐκλελεγμένος); listen to him" (Luke 9:35). It is reemphasized at the return of the seventy disciples when Jesus rejoices in the Holy Spirit and praises the Father (ἐξομολογοῦμαι σοι, πάτερ) for taking such pleasure in revealing himself to little children (Luke 10:21). The next verse reveals Jesus's three-fold conviction that all things have been given to him by his Father, that no one knows him except the Father, and that no one knows the Father except those to whom the Son decides to reveal him (10:22). This important statement shows that Jesus's relationship with the Father is the source of his spiritual authority, of his identity as the Son, and of his particular redemptive role in revealing the Father to others.[11] Finally,

10. These words of commissioning draw together Isa 42:1 and Ps 2:7 and should be understood as the anointing of Jesus by the Spirit for the ministry of Isa 61:1–2 (Luke 4:18–19). "Here the emphasis is on the unique filial relationship to God which is to be the basis for the messianic role"; Nolland, *Luke 1–9:20*, 165.

11. Each of these aspects of Jesus's relationship with the Father is significant as a model for later Christ followers to imitate. The Father provides his children not only love and acceptance, but also identity, spiritual influence, and missional power to help others to also come to know him. There are of course certain elements of Jesus's relationship with the Father that may be unique, but the general trajectory is meant to be imitated.

this intimate relationship is affirmed at the crucifixion in Jesus' dying words to the Father: "Father, forgive them, for they do not know what they are doing . . . Father, into your hands I commit my spirit" (Luke 23:24, 46). These prayers of trusting surrender show that in Luke's Gospel Jesus's own sacrificial obedience to God flows out of this baptismal relationship, this personal awareness of God as his loving Father.

Luke goes to great lengths to stress Jesus's devoted relationship with God as Father; his purpose is to demonstrate that being a disciple of Jesus does not simply mean following his example of obedience and sacrifice, but also following in his intimate relationship with the Father. This is the opportunity made available at Pentecost: "Being therefore exalted at the right hand of God, and having received from the Father the promise of the Holy Spirit, he has poured out this that you both see and hear" (Acts 2:33; cf. 1:4, 7). This moment is the theological sequel of Jesus's baptism, for here Jesus pours out the same Spirit he received from the Father at his baptism onto the church. This Spirit is "the promise" of the Father, and with it comes the same fatherly affection, the same affirmation, and the same empowerment for mission. It is this connection which enables God's radical discipleship demands to be met, for the Father is the One who calls and equips his children.

For Luke, an essential aspect of following Jesus is to imitate him in his relationship with the Father. This is the foundation for and wellspring of radical discipleship, ministry, and mission in Acts, and in the church to which Luke is writing. It also means that Pentecost is a revelation of both the Spirit and the Father, for it is from this empowering Father who Christ knows so intimately that the promised Spirit of empowerment is sent to Christ's followers (Acts 1:4, 7; 2:33). Pentecost can only be fully understood in the light of Jesus's close baptismal relationship with the Father, as revealed throughout Luke's Gospel. Luke implies that the Spirit continues to lead disciples into deeper relationship with the Father in Acts and beyond (Acts 7:55–56), and the resulting identity as children of God and commissioning for spiritual influence are significant components of their empowerment for mission. In this way, Luke offers his readers the solution to fulfilling Jesus's radical discipleship demands.

THE APOSTOLIC ETHOS

According to Luke, an ethos emerges in the early church, particularly among its leaders and missionaries, which is epitomized by Jesus's intensive discipleship demands.[12] Certain shared traits make up this ethos, which capture

12. Because Acts is narrative, Luke never articulates this ethos in a systematic way (similar to the person and activity of the Spirit), but he tells story after story which

the distinctive character of the early Christians and are expressed through their attitudes, habits, actions, beliefs, and aspirations. This becomes an ideal environment in which missionaries can be trained and mission can flourish. This defining culture can be called the apostolic ethos.[13]

A _willingness to suffer_ and even die on behalf of Jesus and the advancement of the gospel is the heart of the apostolic ethos which pervades the book of Acts. The rationale for this is simple: if Jesus suffered, his followers will also suffer.[14] Christ's suffering is a prominent theme in Acts, particularly in the evangelistic speeches (3:18; 17:13; 26:23); this has its theological roots in the prophetic servant songs (Isa 42:1–7; 49:1–6; 50:4–9; 52:13—53:12). Christians in Acts consider it an honor to follow Jesus's example and suffer for his name (5:41).[15]

This theme can be seen in Jesus's calling of Saul: "This man is my chosen instrument . . . I _will show him how much he must suffer for my name_" (ὅσα δεῖ αὐτὸν ὑπὲρ τοῦ ὀνόματός μου παθεῖν, Acts 9:15–16). For Christ-followers, following Jesus inevitably involves suffering; the two are intertwined. The bearers of the Word suffer humiliation, threat, shipwreck, beating, stoning, imprisonment, and even martyrdom with alarming frequency in Acts.[16] There is at least one reference to the theme of opposition and suffering in every chapter of Acts except for the first, third, and tenth chapter.[17]

Paul and Barnabas's sobering teaching to the newly established churches in Galatia underscores the all-pervasive reality of suffering: "We must go through many hardships/pressures (πολλῶν θλίψεων) to enter the kingdom of God" (14:22). These words clarify that suffering for loyalty to one's faith is not simply for the apostles and leaders, but for the average Christ-follower in the Galatian churches as well. Following Jesus is indeed costly, as he had warned (Luke 9:22–26). Yet the messengers continue, undeterred by threat or suffering. The ability to endure resistance, persevere through pain, and

---

illustrate it.

13. This "apostolic ethos" does not refer to the apostolic office (Eph 4:11), but to the meaning of the word ἀπόστολος: a sent one, messenger, delegate, or missionary. BDAG, 122.

14. See chapter 1, the suffering of the messengers of the Word in Acts, and Luke's theology of providential suffering, and part 4, about missional suffering in Acts. Also, Keener, _Acts_, 1:505; Cunningham, "_Many Tribulations_," 337–40.

15. Cf. Rom 8:17; 2 Cor 1:5–6; Phil 1:29; 2 Tim 1:8; 2:8–12; Jas 5:10; 1 Pet 5:9.

16. See 1 Cor 4:11–13; 15:30–32; 2 Cor 4:8–11; 6:4–10; 11:23–29 for Paul's recounting of his sufferings, which validate his claims to apostleship.

17. E.g., 2:13; 4:1–7, 21; 5:17–18, 33, 40; 6:8–14; 7:54–60; 8:1–4; 9:1–2, 16, 23–25; 11:1–3; 12:1–5; 13:8–50; 14:4–5, 19, 22; 15:2, 5, 39; 16:22–24; 17:5–7, 13, 32; 18:12–13; 19:23–40; 20:3, 22–24; 21:11, 27–36; 22:22–24; 23:12–14, 30; 24:5–9; 25:6–7; 26:9–11; 27:13–42; 28:4, 16.

proclaim the gospel no matter the cost becomes a sub-culture within early Christianity, which enables the church to flourish and grow amid opposition and persecution.

Before Paul arrives at Jerusalem for the last time, the Caesarean believers use prophetic ministry to urge him not to go (Acts 21:10–12). Paul's response is full of pathos: "Why are you weeping and breaking my heart? I am ready not only *to be bound* (δεθῆναι), but also *to die* (ἀποθανεῖν) in Jerusalem *for the name of the Lord Jesus*" (21:13).[18] This scene reveals a vulnerable Paul; he uses emotionally expressive language, speaking of their words "crushing" (συνθρύπτοντες) his heart to pieces, as if to deprive him of courage. Yet he remains resolute, prepared not simply to suffer through imprisonment and torture for Christ, but also to give his life for Jesus's name. Paul's readiness to suffer epitomizes the apostolic ethos Luke is advocating.

In addition to this willingness to suffer, a *pioneering spirit*, determined to take the gospel to new frontiers and expand its boundaries to include people who have never heard, also characterizes the apostolic ethos in Acts. This is set in place by Jesus's foundational mandate to be his witnesses to the ends of the earth (Acts 1:8). The earliest church struggles to grasp this concept, waiting comfortably in Jerusalem. But the persecution triggered by Stephen's martyrdom initiates an unintentional process of missional expansion (8:1–4), and the Cornelius episode concretizes God's desire that the good news would go to all places and people in the minds of the church leaders (Acts 10–11, 15).

The Antioch church grasps this concept most clearly: "While they were worshiping the Lord and fasting, the Holy Spirit said, 'Set apart for me Barnabas and Saul for the work to which I have called them.' So . . . they placed their hands on them and sent them off" (Acts 13:2–3). This Spirit-initiated episode (13:4) is a watershed moment in the life and mission of the early church, for they begin to understand that God really does want them to take the good news beyond their locality, to all peoples everywhere.[19] After this commissioning, Paul and his associates go on to expand the boundaries of Christianity, often engaged in frontier outreach where the gospel has never been preached (Acts 13–21).

In the last version of Paul's conversion story, Jesus refers to this pioneering calling on Paul's life: "I will rescue you from your own people and from the Gentiles. I am *sending* (ἀποστέλλω) *you to them to open their eyes*

18. Cf. Paul's sobering descriptions of apostolic ministry in 1 Cor 4:9–13 and 2 Cor 6:4–10.

19. Luke's universal theology discussed in the previous chapter links with this—the conviction that the good news is for all people, in every location, motivates the early missionaries in their efforts to spread the Word in new places.

and turn them from darkness to light, and from the power of Satan to God" (26:17–18). Paul is the primary carrier of this apostolic mandate in Acts, broadening the influence of early Christianity in the Empire as he embodies the pioneering spirit.[20]

A third characteristic of the apostolic ethos is *miraculous power*—mission is intertwined with miracles throughout Acts.[21] There are at least eight distinguishable types of miracles in Acts, each with multiple occurrences.[22] These miraculous events form repeated narrative patterns; Luke means for his readers to understand that this is how God works, and therefore miracles are a central part of the unfolding mission.

Table 4.2 Miracles in Acts

1. *Physical healing* (12 at least)—3:1–10; 4:14; 5:15–16; 8:7; 9:8, 18, 33–35; 13:11–12; 14:8–10, 20; 19:12; 28:8, 9

2. *Miraculous knowledge* (5)—2:6–11; 5:3–4, 9; 27:10, 31, 34

3. *Raising from the dead* (2)—9:36–42; 20:8–12

4. *Casting out unclean spirits* (4)—5:16; 8:7; 16:16–18; 19:12

5. *Miraculous release from prison* (3)—5:19–21; 12:7–10; 16:25–26

6. *Miraculous protection* (2)—14:19–20 (?); 28:3–6

7. *Angelic intervention* (7)—5:19; 8:26; 10:3—11:13; 12:7–11, 15, 23; 27:23

8. *Miraculous speech* (3)—2:4; 10:46; 19:6

There are 38 distinct miraculous events in Acts, an average of more than one per chapter. These do not include other divine "miracles" such as the establishment of the church in new locations, the spiritual guidance of missionaries, or the salvation of individuals, all spiritually powerful events in their own right. In fact, the entire narrative of Acts can be seen as one large miraculous event:

20. Paul articulates this desire to go where nobody else has gone and open new frontiers for the faith in Rom 15:19–21; cf. 2 Cor 10:15–16.

21. Keener, *Acts*, 1:320–82 discusses miracles in Acts and antiquity more generally and concludes: "Whether or not in the end one shares the early Christian worldview concerning signs, it is ethnocentric to simply despise it. And whether or not in the end one despises it, one cannot objectively expunge from the record the clear evidence that early Christians (and many people since then) believed that they experienced or witnessed these phenomena." Keener, *Acts*, 1:537–49 contains more on the function of miracles in Acts, and Luke's expectation that they will continue to feature prominently in the church's mission.

22. Witherington, *Acts*, 220; Hemer, *Acts*, 435–36.

Miracles are . . . in Luke's understanding of the matter, part and parcel of the entire mission of witness. The whole is miraculous, in so far as it is a continuous mighty work of God. By the divine power the gospel is preached, converts are made, the Church is established in unity and brotherhood, the opposing powers, whether human or demonic are conquered . . . The whole mission . . . [is] effected by supernatural power, whether in the guidance given to the missionaries, in their dramatic release from prison or deliverance from enemies or shipwreck, or in the signs of healing and raising from the dead . . . It is consequently difficult to pick out the miraculous from the non-miraculous in Luke's story.[23]

For Luke, one of the hallmarks of the apostolic ethos is this spiritual power in operation; signs and wonders happen when the church is functioning apostolically as God intends it to function (cf. 2 Cor 12:12).

Miracles are normative Christianity for Luke, typical attributes of the apostolic ethos of the Christian community, and they take place in the context of one sweeping miracle, the wider Christian movement. These miracles function as divine confirmations of the gospel message which missionaries proclaim. Additionally, the miraculous stories Luke recounts are a crucial plank in his evidence for living in the eschatological age of the outpouring of the Spirit when the prophecies of the Hebrew Scriptures are coming to pass. The age of fulfillment has dawned, and signs and wonders are a primary confirmation of this reality.[24]

In Acts, a fourth characteristic of the apostolic ethos is an *evangelistic commitment.* The church's chief goal is that people would hear the universally good news of the gospel and have the chance to respond to it for themselves. There is an almost constant stream of evangelistic activity in Acts, which points to this being the normal way of life of the early believers. This

23. Lampe, "Miracles," 171.

24. On remaining "open" to the possibility of miracles when reading Luke-Acts, see Marshall, *Luke*, 28–32; Hemer, *Acts*, 17; Bruce, *Acts*, 31, Keener, *Acts*, 1:380–82; Witherington, *Acts*, 224: "These stories will no doubt continue to create problems for some moderns who rule out in advance the supernatural . . . and dismiss all history writing that includes such tales as pre-critical and naïve in character. I would suggest that such an apriori approach to miracles is equally uncritical and naïve, not least because science has hardly begun to plumb the depths of what is and is not possible in our universe, and especially because we are regularly being warned by scientists (particularly physicists) that assumptions about natural laws and a closed mechanistic universe and the like do not cover all the known data. One must also take into account that in every age of human history there have been numerous claims about the miraculous, many of which were made by highly intelligent and rational persons not readily given to superstition. Luke seems to have been one such person."

missional *modus operandi* is not simply for the spiritual elite. Whether this takes the form of public proclamation, person to person relational evangelism, or lifestyle and community-based mission, there is a form of mission in Acts for every follower of Christ.

Paul summarizes his commitment to evangelism before the Ephesian elders at Miletus: "I do not consider my life of any account as dear to myself, so *that I may finish my course and the ministry which I received from the Lord Jesus, to testify solemnly of the gospel of the grace of God*" (διαμαρτύρασθαι τὸ εὐαγγέλιον τῆς χάριτος τοῦ Θεοῦ, Acts 20:24; cf. 20:27). This speech reveals Paul's motivation and captures his willingness to suffer (20:19, 23) and his pioneering spirit (20:20–21). Paul explicitly desires that his personal life will challenge and inspire these leaders to aspire to the same kind of lifestyle (20:18, 34–35). Luke also means for this passage to motivate his readers towards a similar response.[25]

Luke emphasizes that Paul is fully under the leadership and guidance of the Holy Spirit—he is "compelled by the Spirit" (δεδεμένος τῷ πνεύματι, 20:22). Even when the Spirit warns him that suffering awaits him, he will still obey (20:23). Paul is not interested in preserving his own life (cf. Phil 3:7–11). Instead, his preoccupation is with accomplishing the ministry (διακονία) given him by the Lord Jesus (cf. 2 Cor 5:18),[26] "to testify to the good news of God's grace" (Acts 20:24),[27] and he will stop at nothing in fulfilling this task. Paul knows that no obstacle can deter the advancement of God's Word, for it is a part of the Father's eternal plan, and therefore guaranteed by the power of God himself.[28]

In Luke's picture of the early church a willingness to suffer, pioneering spirit, miraculous spiritual power, and evangelistic commitment combine to generate radically committed missionaries. This is most true of the leaders that Acts profiles. However, a defining culture or apostolic ethos forms around these character traits. Luke implies that everyone in the church is influenced by this. For example, they may not all experience miracles regularly, but they are familiar with miracles, and have likely seen them

25. Chapter 10 of this study analyzes the rhetorical function of this important Pauline speech in more detail.

26. "Finish my course" is an athletic metaphor of which Paul is fond (1 Cor 9:24; Phil 3:14). The closest parallel is 2 Tim 4:7: "I have finished the race." This, along with other linguistic parallels, has led some scholars to conclude that Luke wrote the pastorals on Paul's behalf; Witherington, *Acts*, 622.

27. Though this precise formulation is not found in Paul's letters, it is a concise summary of Paul's gospel.

28. This theological framework is at the heart of what drives and empowers the early Christians in Acts. Luke wants to give his readers confidence: the advance of God's Kingdom is truly inevitable.

first-hand at some point or know people who have. The merger of these characteristics creates an environment of faith, boldness, and power, which infuses the early Christian mission with dynamism and purpose. Every Christian is sent by Christ himself—they all are influenced by this culture, and in turn contribute to it. Luke is using demonstrative rhetoric to inspire the church to intentionally cultivate a similar apostolic ethos in their day.

DISCIPLINED SPIRITUAL DEVOTION

A final aspect of the radical Christianity of the church in Acts is their enthusiasm for God, expressed through personal and communal spiritual devotion. Although Luke is not primarily interested in the internal life of the Christian community, he does include episodes which give his readers insight this aspect of their life together. These reveal a robust personal connection with God, which manifests itself in several ways, and functions as another stimulus for mission in Acts.

The first of these is *prayer,* and as if often the case in Luke-Acts, Jesus initially models this practice. Luke's Gospel depicts Jesus as a man of prayer and makes a point of mentioning Jesus's regular habit of prayer at least seven times (Luke 3:21; 5:16; 6:12; 9:18, 28; 11:1; 22:39–45), while also showing Jesus frequently teaching on prayer (6:28; 11:2; 18:1; 22:36). The church goes on to follow Jesus's recurrent example: the noun προσευχή occurs nine times in Acts,[29] while the verb προσεύχομαι occurs an additional 16 times.[30] This regular practice of prayer is a crucial part of the church's praxis. The earliest group is "*continually devoting themselves with one mind to prayer*" (προσκαρτεροῦντες ὁμοθυμαδὸν τῇ προσευχῇ) in Jerusalem (1:14). Note Luke's emphasis on the continual nature of their choice to devote themselves to prayer, expressed through the present participle. During this time, they also pray (προσευξάμενοι) about who will replace Judas, before choosing Matthias (1:23–26). With these two references, Luke establishes the central role of prayer in the lives of the earliest Christians, even before the paradigm shifting events of Pentecost.[31]

Directly after the coming of the Holy Spirit, Luke re-emphasizes the crucial role of prayer as the new converts immediately *devote* themselves to

29. 1:14; 2:42; 3:1; 6:4; 10:4, 31; 12:5; 16:13, 16.

30. 1:24; 6:6; 8:15; 9:11, 40; 10:9, 30; 11:5; 12:12; 13:3; 14:23; 16:25; 20:36; 21:5; 22:17; 28:8.

31. They are naturally following the example and instruction of Jesus, and following typical Jewish prayer practices (Acts 3:1; 16:13, 16). In addition to his private practice, Luke shows Jesus intentionally modeling this to his disciples (Luke 9:28; 11:1; 22:41).

prayers (προσκαρτεροῦντες . . . ταῖς προσευχαῖς, 2:42). Later, the apostles appoint new leaders so that they can _devote themselves_ to prayer and the ministry of the word (τῇ προσευχῇ καὶ τῇ διακονίᾳ τοῦ λόγου προσκαρτερήσομεν, 6:4). In three of the previous four examples, the concept of deliberate and steadfast personal devotion (προσκαρτερέω) is linked directly to the object of prayer (προσευχή, 1:14; 2:42; 6:4). This pairing is another way Luke emphasizes prayer's importance to the community and the significance of the choice to devote oneself to it. Prayer for the early church is not casual, but a matter of wholehearted and loyal devotion.

Prayer is employed in commissioning a person to a task three times, for the seven new leaders in Jerusalem (6:6), Paul and Barnabas at Antioch (13:3), and the elders of the churches they establish (14:23). Prayer is also instrumental in people receiving the Holy Spirit (8:15) and receiving healing: Tabitha is raised from the dead (9:40) and Publius is healed from fever and dysentery (28:8). Prayer is employed in times of crisis and persecution, such as the threats from the Jerusalem authorities (4:24), Peter's imprisonment (12:5, 12), and Paul and Silas's imprisonment (16:25), and at times of sentimental goodbyes, such as with the Ephesian elders (20:36) and the Tyrian disciples (21:5). Prayer is a shared point of missional contact with Jews and God-fearers in Philippi, leading to the establishment of the Philippian church (16:13, 16). Christian leaders, such as Peter and John (3:1), Peter (10:9;[32] 11:5–10), and Paul (9:11–12; 22:17–18) make private prayer a habitual practice. In the last four examples, prayer is also linked with the reception of a spiritual vision which directly leads the mission forward, another important narrative pattern. In Acts, devotion to prayer is a way of following in Jesus's footsteps, and a primary catalyst for the ongoing expansion of the mission, integral in commissioning leaders, healing ministry, receiving the Spirit and boldness in times of crisis, and in the reception of spiritual visions. This recurrent narrative pattern throughout Luke-Acts forms a clear model for Luke's readers to follow.

In addition to regular prayer, and often in conjunction with it, the early believers have a habit of _fasting_ in Acts, in direct fulfillment of Jesus's emphatic prediction about the time following his departure: "the time will come when the bridegroom will be taken from them; in those days _they will fast_" (νηστεύσουσιν, Luke 5:35). The community at Antioch fasts together as they seek the will of God. They are ministering to the Lord (λειτουργούντων δὲ αὐτῶν τῷ Κυρίῳ) and fasting (νηστευόντων) when the Holy Spirit instructs

---

32. Peter likely goes to the roof for quietness and privacy so he can focus on prayer; Bruce, _Acts_, 254.

them to set apart Barnabas and Saul for the work to which he has called them (13:2). In response, they fast and pray (νηστεύσαντες καὶ προσευξάμενοι), and then send them away on God's mission (13:3). Luke repeats their fasting to emphasize its importance, and to show that this habit is one of the keys to their subsequent effectiveness. Early Christians fast at pivotal times, such as when appointing elders to help lead new churches: "having prayed with (plural) fastings (προσευξάμενοι μετὰ νηστειῶν), they commended them to the Lord" (14:23).[33] Saul also fasts, not eating or drinking anything for three days after his conversion experience (9:9).[34] Fasting may also be indicated in 10:10; Peter has not eaten and is hungry (πρόσπεινος) when he experiences the enigmatic but pivotal vision of a sheet descending and ascending filled with animals. For Luke, the self-denial and hunger of fasting is an important aspect of the spiritual devotion of the early Christians, particularly when paired with prayer and personal devotion; it prepares the individual to hear or receive from God, and often leads to decisive spiritual breakthrough in the life of the church.

In addition to prayer and fasting, the Christian church in Acts is a *worshipping community*. Jesus provides the model for this in the way that he praises the Father with joy (Luke 10:21). In Acts this is most evident when Paul and Silas are in prison, having been severely beaten and put in stocks, and are praying (προσευχόμενοι) and singing hymns of praise to God (ὕμνουν τὸν Θεόν, 16:25).[35] This extraordinary episode reveals the substance of the early disciples; when they are under threat and should be most hopeless and disheartened, they lift their voices in worshipful song. Such experiences of suffering and pressure show what a person is made of.[36] Acts also mentions Paul going to Jerusalem to worship (προσκυνήσωμεν, 24:11), and the God-fearing Ethiopian eunuch going to Jerusalem to worship (προσκυνήσων, 8:27).[37] These last two examples highlight an unmistakable connection—the

33. Multiple manuscripts, such as p50 and Bezae, also use νηστεύω at 10:30, to describe Cornelius's piety.

34. This may not be voluntary, but it fits with a general definition of fasting: abstaining from food for spiritual reasons. This encounter shakes Saul's spiritual foundations, and he is in a state of shock. Bruce, *Acts*, 236.

35. Cf. Col 3:16; Eph 5:19. For the singing of hymns in the OT, see 1 Chr 16:9; 2 Chr 23:13; 29:30; Ps 21:22; 70:8; 136:3; Dan 3:24. For similar experiences in prison, Epictetus says, "Then we shall be emulating Socrates, when we are able to write paeans in prison" (*Discourses* 2, 6, 26–27), and in the Testament of Joseph, 8.5, the patriarch "sang praise in the house of darkness," Johnson, *Acts*, 300.

36. "The prison experience is one that tests one's mettle," Johnson, *Acts*, 300. They have resolved that they will worship God, no matter what happens; worship is primary in their lives, independent of their circumstances.

37. Λατρεύω (to serve, worship) is another important concept: Acts 7:7, 42; 24:14;

theological roots of the devotion of the early Christians to prayer, fasting, worship, and other spiritual disciplines are found in the Hebrew Bible, and particularly in the rhythms of prayer based around the Psalms which Jews observe during the Second Temple period. Luke's portrayal of the lengthy devotion of Anna the prophetess ("for eight four years") epitomizes this: "she never left the temple, worshiping (λατρεύουσα) with fasting and prayer (νηστείαις καὶ δεήσεσιν) night and day" (Luke 2:37).

Luke presents this triad of prayer, fasting, and worship as central to the health of the church. When Christians are in prison, they worship; when they are persecuted, they pray; and when they have crucial decisions to make, they fast and seek God. Their mission is forged in the crucible of spiritual habits and flows out of this disciplined devotion to the God they serve. The fervency of their inner devotion produces a dynamic outward expression of mission, and the strength of their outward testimony is proportional to the vitality of their inward connection to God, cultivated through the primary spiritual disciplines of prayer, fasting, and worship.

The church at Antioch is the best example of this paradigmatic connection between enthusiastic spiritual devotion to God and the expansion of the mission (13:1–3). The link is explicit in the text, for the disciples are ministering (λειτουργούντων) to the Lord at Antioch, including prayer and fasting (twice emphasized), when the Holy Spirit directs them to set apart Paul and Barnabas, and their paradigm-shaping missional journeys begin. In Acts, mission flows directly out of devotion, and is sustained and strengthened by it as well (e.g., Paul and Silas in jail). This fervent personal allegiance to God, expressed through various spiritual disciplines, is thus a potent missional catalyst, and Luke wants his readers to grasp this important lesson for the health of their own outreach efforts.

CONCLUSION—REDEFINING NORMAL

The characters Acts highlights seem larger than life. They are fearless, disciplined, selfless, devoted, generous, bold, unflinchingly committed to the cause, and infused with miraculous power, truly "radical." This is intentional—Luke portrays the early disciples as normal and relatable people in his Gospel, who are filled with the Spirit of the Risen Christ in Acts.[38] This Spirit is redefining normalcy for the church. What was impossible before is now attainable; radical devotion is the new norm, by the empowerment of

---

26:7; 27:23.

38. Even Paul, the most heroic of them all, is a confused persecutor of the church before Jesus intervenes.

the Spirit and through loving relationship with the Father. This is particularly true for the intense discipleship standards and the disciplined devotion—these are goals for all believers in Luke's mind. The apostolic ethos is a culture they live in, which should most characterize the leaders of the church. But the essence of the radical standards that Luke presents in Acts is meant to be a challenge and inspiration to all his readers.

Luke uses characterization, semantic repetition, and narrative patterns in Acts to present all of this as an implicit challenge to his readers. Are they attaining to Jesus's radical discipleship standards? Are they embodying the apostolic ethos, willing to suffer, walking in miraculous power, reaching out consistently, and taking the gospel to new frontiers? Are their personal lives characterized by spiritual devotion to God, with primary habits of prayer, fasting, and worship? In short, are they living in the fullness of the power and possibility that God's Spirit provides? It may seem impossible, but God has made this kind of radical way of life accessible.

By tapping into the dynamic power source of the Spirit, promised by the Father, the readers of Acts will be able to live in the intensely missional way the earliest church lives, and experience the fruitfulness that they experience. Embracing a lifestyle of radical devotion, attaining to the discipleship demands of Jesus, and living out the apostolic ethos of the early church is the inner reality of the call to action that Acts issues to the church. For Luke, anything less than this is missing the mark. *Radical Christianity becomes normal Christianity in Acts.*

PART 1

Conclusion

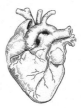

Acts, A Call to Missional Action

Part 1 has identified four missional stimuli which fuel the growth of the early church in Acts. The triumphal spread of the Word is primary, advanced forcefully by the power of the Spirit. The Father's plan of salvation is the source of all this saving activity, and his inclusive invitation to all people results in the universal mission of the church. In response to these Trinitarian themes, the early believers attain to the radical intensification of discipleship demands and live out an apostolic ethos and an enthusiastic personal devotion to God. These concepts combine to form a catalytic matrix in Acts, the stimuli that empower and motivate the church for mission. Importantly, these are first and foremost God's initiative, and the Father, Word, and Spirit enable peoples' faithful actions in response to God's empowering leadership.

These are not merely "historical" points of interest for Luke. The book of Acts is a rhetorical call to action, based upon his readers' identification with its vivid portrayal of the paradigmatic heroes of the early church. In this sense it is a provocation to Luke's readers to rekindle their missional fervency. The Word is still advancing with authority; Luke implicitly urges his readers to join with it. The Spirit is still empowering with dynamic influence; through his stirring story Luke invites his readers to receive and follow it. The Father's salvific invitation is still universally relevant and inclusive; Luke encourages his church to proclaim it with boldness. And the radical patterns of devotion in which the early Christians live are still attainable through God's power; Luke urges his readers to embrace them. In short,

Luke is rousing believers from apathy, and inviting them to join in the eschatological mission, inaugurated by the death and resurrection of Jesus and the coming of the promised Spirit. Understood in this way, Acts is a clarion call to missional action.

These stimuli are of primary importance for Luke because they are what spark mission and set it in motion. They are the essential crux of the missional enterprise Luke depicts, just as the heart is to the body. Before structures and strategies can be discussed, what is fueling and empowering the mission must be unmistakable. Without "the why" firmly in place, all the best planning and strategizing is doomed to failure, which explains why these themes are introduced prominently in the early parts of the Acts narrative. With these catalysts established, Luke can commend strategies and approaches to mission which maximize the potential for success. These are the topics of the remainder of this study.

PART 2

Missional Structures in Acts

History shows that Christians manage, in three short centuries, to transform themselves from a regional Jewish sect into the dominant religion of the Roman Empire. The book of Acts is Luke's story of how this begins in the first few decades after Christ's departure. As Luke unfolds the narrative, he presents the earliest believers as examples to be followed by later generations. The previous chapters examined the stimuli which play a prominent role in motivating and activating the church's outreach and expansion in Acts. *This part identifies the structures which contribute to the success of the mission in Acts.*

Luke highlights both material and social structures in his account. The *oikos* culture is fundamental to all first-century human life and interaction so it is no surprise that in Acts mission focuses on reaching households and then emerges from them. However, in Acts this is always to establish or strengthen the church, which is Luke's fundamental missional structure. Church happens primarily in the home so the concluding chapter of part 2 will examine house churches as the structural key that facilitates the expanding Christian mission.

In the body analogy, the church is the hands of the mission, for it reaches out to people and welcomes them as they join in. The house/household is the feet, for it is the network of relationships that carries the mission forward and facilitates its progress. These structures are fundamental to enabling the success and spread of the mission throughout Acts.

Chapter 5

The Church Assembly

Meanwhile the church throughout Judea, Galilee, and Samaria had peace and was built up. Living in the fear of the Lord and in the comfort of the Holy Spirit, it increased in numbers.

—ACTS 9:31

The church assembly (ἐκκλησία) is at the heart of mission in Acts, and it gives structure and context to every expression of early Christianity. Wherever Christ-followers go, they *never* merely establish converts or "make disciples," but they gather these believers into small communities, which they call churches. Establishing and growing the ἐκκλησία is the goal and the vision.[1] The church assemblies which Luke describes, scattered throughout the eastern Empire, are the irreplaceable structure that facilitates the advancing mission.

THE MEANING OF ΕΚΚΛΗΣΙΑ

᾽Εκκλησία is grammatically related to ἔκκλητος (summoned, selected, often to arbitrate on a point), which has the verbal form ἐκκαλέω (to summon, to

---

1. ᾽Εκκλησία occurs 115 times in the NT, showing the importance of this concept to early Christian writers.

call out).[2] It should be understood as "the called-out ones," or "those who are summoned," and in common ancient usage simply equates to an "assembly" or "gathering."

This generalized meaning can be broken down into three sub-categories in the first-century Greco-Roman world.[3] The most common meaning of ἐκκλησία is a regularly summoned legislative body, or regular statutory assembly.[4] This is the meaning in Acts 19:39, 41, which refers to the "lawful assembly" (ἐννόμῳ ἐκκλησίᾳ) in Ephesus, summoned by the city clerk when the craftsmen of Ephesus riot, protesting against the way Paul's ministry is harming their business.[5] Ἐκκλησία can also refer to a casual gathering, which is often a tumultuous and disorderly assembly which erupts spontaneously as people gather together.[6] Luke calls the Ephesian riot an ἐκκλησία (19:32).[7] He contrasts this spontaneous assembly with the formal legal assembly to which the protesters are invited in 19:39, yet in the same passage uses ἐκκλησία to describe both.[8]

A third meaning of ἐκκλησία is a group of people with a shared belief system, otherwise known as a community or congregation.[9] The LXX often uses it of the Israelite assembly or congregation, as the Greek rendering of the Hebrew קָהָל, qāhāl.[10] Luke uses τῇ ἐκκλησίᾳ ἐν τῇ ἐρήμῳ in this sense

---

2. It is a compound of ἐκ (out of), and a derivative of καλέω (to call).

3. BDAG, 303–4. See also Schmidt, "ἐκκλησία," 501–36, who analyzes its usage in Acts and the NT, the Greek world, the OT and Judaism, and church history, and examines its textual and literary criticism, Hebrew and Aramaic equivalents, and etymology.

4. Josephus, Ant., 12.164: "Joseph went up into the temple, and called the multitude together to a congregation"; 19.332: "This man got together an assembly."

5. The Ephesians would ordinarily hold this regular civic meeting three times a month. For inscriptional evidence of the ἐκκλησία in Ephesus see Hicks, Ancient Greek Inscriptions, III/I.481.340: "ἐκκλησιαν επανω της σελιδος"; III/I.481.395: "πασαν ἐκκλησιαν εἰσ το θεατρον."

6. E.g., 1 Kgdms 19:20 LXX: "when they saw a group of prophets (τὴν ἐκκλησίαν τῶν προφητῶν) prophesying"; 1 Macc 3:13; Sir 26:5: "There are three things that my heart fears . . . the slander of a city, the gathering together of an unruly multitude, and a false accusation."

7. Luke also refers to this riot using στάσις (19:40), meaning a popular uprising, insurrection, or uproar.

8. Cf. Josephus, J.W., 1.550: "Herod accused the captains and Tero in an assembly of the people"; 1.666: "the rest of the multitude together to an assembly, in the amphitheater at Jericho"; 4.159: "when they were assembled together in crowds."

9. Cf. the community of Pythagoras, according to Hermippus, quoted in Diogenes Laërtius, Lives, 8.41; in Himerius, Orationes, 39.5, Orpheus even forms for himself "an assembly of wild animals," whom he enchants with his music in the Thracian mountains.

10. E.g., Josh 8:35; Deut 31:30; Judg 20:2; 1 Kgdms 17:47; 3 Kgdms 8:14: "While the whole assembly of Israel was standing there, the king turned around and blessed them";

(7:38), to refer to the Jews assembled in the desert to hear and receive the words of the law.[11]

This third sense of ἐκκλησία is the most familiar Christian usage of the term, traditionally translated in the NT from at least the mid-1600s as "the church."[12] The Greek word is not a new or technical term for church, but a term borrowed from the surrounding culture. The English word "church" etymologically derives from the Greek adjective κυριακός, meaning "of or belonging to the Lord/κυρίου" (1 Cor 11:20: "the Lord's supper"; Rev 1:10: "the Lord's day"). Κυριακός belongs to a different semantic domain than ἐκκλησία and the two concepts should not be confused. The *place* where believers meet together came to be called "the Lord's house" (κυριακόν δῶμα or οἰκόν) later in church history, and this led to the English word "church," which somewhat confusingly is now the common translation of ἐκκλησία in English bibles.[13] With this in mind, it is vital to remember that while ἐκκλησία it may be translated "church" in English today, the underlying Greek word ἐκκλησία simply means a gathering or assembled community, usually of God's people. First-century individuals would only think of *people* when they think of the ἐκκλησία. No mental images of buildings or steeples cloud the meaning, not to mention denominations or professional clergy, because these things do not yet exist. These groupings of people can meet anywhere—in a home, outdoors, in a coliseum, even the temple—but the point is the assembled people themselves.

Early Christians use ἐκκλησία to designate their assemblies for at least two reasons.[14] First, it affirms continuity with their Israelite roots, for the Septuagint uses it often as the traditional label for God's community, translating קָהָל (*qāhāl*—assembly, convocation, congregation).[15] Second,

---

PssSol 10:6; TJob 32:8: "Are you the one who had the censers of the fragrant *assembly*"; Josephus, *Ant.*, 4.309: "Moses called the people together, with the women and children, to a *congregation.*"

11. Cf. Deut 4:10; 9:10; 18:16; Ps 21:23 LXX; Heb 2:12.

12. Witherington, *Acts*, 219.

13. Κυριακόν (neuter, literally "the Lord's thing"), became "*Kirche*" in German, and "*chirche*" in Middle English (Scottish *Kirk*). Luther uses "*Gemeinde*" (roughly "local community") to translate ἐκκλησία, not "*Kirche.*" Similarly, Tyndale uses "congregation" rather than "church" in 1536 to preserve the separate concepts. But within the next 100 years and ever since, all English translations use the word "church" to translate ἐκκλησία. Luke uses the term to reference gatherings or communities of Christians, in line with other ancient usages, and not more modern associations such as buildings (basilicas), organizations, or denominations.

14. BDAG, 303.

15. Qumran texts indicate that this usage remained familiar among Jesus's contemporaries: 4QpPs 37 (4Q171) III, 16; Keener, *Acts*, 2:1696. Other related Hebrew words:

claiming to be a legal assembly may help to alleviate suspicions that Christians are an unlawful group, particularly in political circles.

While ἐκκλησία in the NT is most often associated with "the church" as the gathered people of God, what this means requires categorization. First, it can refer to a specific individual Christian group or assembly, ordinarily involving worship and the discussion of matters of concern to the community. It is in this sense that Jesus says, "speak to the gathered assembly" (εἰπὲ τῇ ἐκκλησίᾳ, Matt 18:17; cf. 16:18; 18:15). Matthew uses ἐκκλησία in opposition to the Jewish synagogue (συναγωγῇ, Matt 12:9; 13:54; 23:6, 34), to emphasize the emerging Christian self-awareness as distinct from Judaism's gatherings. Luke's usage of ἐκκλησία in Acts likely has a similar goal. This meaning of ἐκκλησία occurs frequently in the NT, and often refers to the assembly of Christians in the home of a patron, the house church.[16] This is the most common usage in Paul and the other epistles.

A second use of ἐκκλησία in the NT references a congregation as the totality of Christians living and meeting in a particular locality or geographical area, and not necessarily limited to one specific meeting place. This broader definition of "the church" denotes a connected network of local congregations, or house churches, spread across a city or region. Sometimes in Acts and other parts of the NT, this does not have a geographical qualifier.[17] However, it is more frequent in a geographically specified way, usually in particular cities, such as "the church in Jerusalem" (Acts 2:47; 8:1; 11:22; 15:4, 22), Antioch (13:1), Cenchrea (Rom 16:1, 23), Corinth (1 Cor 1:2; 2 Cor 1:1),[18] Laodicea (Col 4:16; Rev 3:14), Thessalonica (1 Thess 1:1; 2 Thess 1:1), and Colossae (Phlm 1). The NT also refers to the plural ἐκκλησίαι in certain areas.[19] Ἐκκλησία is used in this sense to refer to the Christian communities in a geographical region, such as the church in Judea (Gal 1:22; 1 Thess 2:14), Galatia (Gal 1:2; 1 Cor 16:1), Asia (1 Cor 16:19; Rev 1:4, 11, 20), or Macedonia (2 Cor 8:1).

עֵדָה (edah—congregation, assembly; e.g., Exod 12:3; Num 20:8; Judg 14:8; usually translated in LXX with συναγωγῇ); מוֹעֵד (moed—appointed time, place, or meeting; e.g., Num 8:9; Lev 8:4); כָּנַס (kanas—to gather together, collect; e.g., 1 Chr 22:2; Neh 12:44).

16. E.g., Rom 16:4, 5; 1 Cor 14:33; 16:19; Col 4:15; Phlm 1:2; 1 Tim 5:16.

17. Acts 5:11; 8:3; 9:31; 11:26; 12:1, 5; 15:3; 18:22; 20:17. Also in 1 Cor 4:17; Phil 4:15; 1 Tim 5:16; Jas 5:14; 3 John 9; 1 Clem 44:3: "with the consent of *the whole church*"; Hermas, *Visions*, 2.4.3: "the elders that preside over *the church*."

18. Cf. 1 Clem 47:6: "the very steadfast and ancient church of the Corinthians."

19. E.g., Acts 15:41; 16:5; Rom 16:16; 1 Cor 7:17; 2 Cor 8:18–19, 23–24; 11:8, 28; 12:13; Rev 2:7, 11, 17, 23, 29; 3:6, 13, 22; 22:16.

Ἐκκλησία is thirdly used to designate the global community of Christians, the universal church, which encompasses all Christ-followers in every location.[20] This worldwide universal meaning is found in the NT almost exclusively in Paul's writings.[21]

The lack of ἐκκλησία is notable in the Gospels. It only occurs in Matthew, where Jesus uses the term ἐκκλησία three times (Matt 16:18; 18:17). Scholars debate whether Jesus actually used the term ἐκκλησία, or whether this is Matthean redaction. Whether Jesus used ἐκκλησία is not important to this study—he almost certainly taught in Aramaic anyway[22]—because he developed small missional communities, modeled them, and trained his disciples to do the same.[23] His followers grasp this and go on to emulate it throughout Acts and beyond. Jesus put into motion the forces which led to the establishment of what is later called the Christian ἐκκλησία, regardless of whether he ever used the word.

THE NATURE OF ΕΚΚΛΗΣΙΑ IN ACTS

All the meanings of ἐκκλησία in the ancient world occur among its 23 occurrences in Acts.[24] Ἐκκλησία is a legal assembly (ἐννόμῳ ἐκκλησίᾳ, 19:39, 40), an informal and riotous assembly (19:32), and refers to the Israelites assembled in the desert to receive the law (τῇ ἐκκλησίᾳ ἐν τῇ ἐρήμῳ, 7:38).[25] However, Luke's most common usage of ἐκκλησία refers to the Christian assembly, a local or regional congregation with a shared belief system.

20. This triple connotation—local, regional, and universal—can be seen particularly in Paul's writings.

21. E.g., 1 Cor 6:4; 12:28; Eph 1:22; 3:10, 21; 5:23–25, 27, 29, 32; Col 1:18, 24; Phil 3:6; possibly Matt 16:18; Acts 9:31. In this universalized sense it is also referred to as: 1) "the church of God"—ἐκκλησίᾳ τοῦ θεοῦ, 1 Cor 1:2; 10:32; 11:16, 22; 15:9; 2 Cor 1:1; Gal 1:13; 1 Thess 2:14; 2 Thess 1:4; 1 Tim 3:5, 15; Acts 20:28; Origen, Contra Celsum, 1.63.22; 2) "the churches of Christ"—ἐκκλησίαι τοῦ Χριστοῦ, Rom 16:16; Origen, Contra Celsum, 5.22.14; 3) of both God and Christ combined—τῇ ἐκκλησίᾳ Θεσσαλονικέων ἐν Θεῷ πατρὶ καὶ Κυρίῳ Ἰησοῦ Χριστῷ, 1 Thess 1:1.

22. In the Aramaic NT, the Peshitta, the Aramaic word עדה (edah) is used for ἐκκλησία, the equivalent to the Hebrew עֵדָה.

23. See chapter 7 for more detail. If Acts is the story of the birth of the church, the new people of God, it makes sense that Luke would save the word for this section of his narrative.

24. 5:11; 7:38; 8:1, 3; 9:31; 11:22, 26; 12:1, 5; 13:1; 14:23, 27; 15:3, 4, 22, 41; 16:5; 18:22; 19:32, 39, 40; 20:17, 28.

25. Luke is familiar with the LXX and its usage of ἐκκλησία. In the OT the Lord acquired a people by performing powerful acts in Egypt; now he has acquired a people by the shedding of Christ's blood (Acts 20:28).

Those who gather in Christ's name form a community: ἡ ἐκκλησία of a given town or area.

Seventeen of the nineteen total references to ἐκκλησία with this meaning in Acts refer to specific groupings of Christians in a particular geographical city or area: the assembly in Jerusalem (5:11; 8:1, 3; 11:22; 12:1, 5; 15:4, 22); Antioch (11:26; 13:1; 14:27; 15:3); Caesarea (18:22);[26] and Ephesus (20:17).[27] Acts also uses the plural ἐκκλησίαι to refer to the groups of Pauline converts in three particular geographical regions: Syria and Cilicia (15:41), Phrygia and Galatia (16:5), and Pisidia and Pamphylia (14:23).[28]

This leads to the conclusion that Luke's ecclesiology is simple, even rudimentary; he understands the ἐκκλησία to be one of the first two types, either the local congregation (singular), or a network of congregations in a larger area (plural). However, there are two other references in Acts to the Christian ἐκκλησία which have attracted the attention of scholars because they may point to a more developed and "catholic" (Pauline) ecclesiology. The first is 9:31: "The church throughout all Judea and Galilee and Samaria (ἐκκλησία καθ᾽ ὅλης τῆς Ἰουδαίας καὶ Γαλιλαίας καὶ Σαμαρείας) had peace, being built up (εἶχεν εἰρήνην οἰκοδομουμένη); and going on in the fear of the Lord and in the comfort of the Holy Spirit, it continued to increase (ἐπληθύνετο)."[29] Note the singular ἐκκλησία and verbs and participles.

Giles argues that Acts 9:31 is a problematic occurrence of ἐκκλησία because it is unique in the NT; nowhere else is it used in the singular of Christians spread out in different locations, and when Paul uses it in the universal sense of the worldwide church he never limits it geographically.[30] Giles proposes two possible solutions, one that the text originally contained the plural ἐκκλησίαι with plural verbs and participles (referring to multiple "churches"), or that it was actually the singular ἐκκλησία, but with plural verbs and participles. If the second option is the case, Luke would be giving a report on the Jerusalem congregation, which was recently scattered throughout "Judea, Galilee and Samaria" by persecution

26. This may refer to the church in Jerusalem; Barrett, *Acts*, 2.880–81.

27. That these are local congregations can be demonstrated from context in each of these texts, though Luke makes it explicit in three places: 8:1 and 11:22, "the church in Jerusalem"; 13:1, "the church at Antioch."

28. The distributive phrase in the singular κατ᾽ ἐκκλησίαν implies the plural.

29. This may be the beginning of a wider geographical meaning for ἐκκλησία in Acts, but it may also indicate a "local" church which resided in more than one town; Barrett, *Acts*, 1:472–75; 2:lxxxviii.

30. Giles, "ΕΚΚΛΗΣΙΑ," 135–42. This does not follow Luke's normal usage of ἐκκλησία, where he always uses the singular of a specific congregation, and the plural to refer to multiple congregations in an area.

(8:1).[31] In either case, Giles argues that Luke is not referring to the wider "catholic" church in 9:31.

Giles's first proposed solution is unconvincing, because the textual evidence favors the singular.[32] His second proposal is possible; it may be that Luke is completing the story he began in 8:1 and reporting on the progress of the Jerusalem Christians who have been scattered by persecution throughout wider regions. However, 8:1 does not mention Galilee, which is further north than Judea and Samaria, centered on Jesus's hometown Nazareth. Additionally, Luke has rhetorical reasons for focusing on individual Christian communities throughout Acts, but this does not mean he is not familiar with the wider catholic concept of the church. Keener says, "Luke here uses 'church' in a much broader way than merely the local assembly in Jerusalem, suggesting that the expanding Christian movement carried with it its concept of the disciples as God's 'assembly.'"[33] Similarly, Peterson claims, "The entity in view now is *the church throughout Judea, Galilee and Samaria*. Luke, who normally uses the word *church* in the singular to refer to a congregation in a given place, here refers to the sum of Jewish believers over a large area, corresponding to the boundaries of ancient Israel."[34] This broader usage with geographical qualifiers is not as problematic as Giles implies.

The second atypical reference is Acts 20:28: "the church of God which he purchased with his own blood" (τὴν ἐκκλησίαν τοῦ Θεοῦ, ἣν περιεποιήσατο διὰ τοῦ αἵματος τοῦ ἰδίου). This is problematic, because both the developed doctrine of "the church of God" and the redemptive interpretation of "his own blood" are unique in Acts, and are characteristically Pauline.[35] However

31. This would be a summary of the same story started in 8:1, and a report on how this one congregation was doing, meaning Luke is not actually speaking of a church in Galilee (he has not mentioned any evangelistic outreach there after Pentecost), but is speaking of the Jerusalem church, which has been scattered by persecution throughout these regions. It also helps to explain his use of the distributive expression καθ' ὅλης— they were scattered throughout that area. Giles proposes a possible textual history which would explain these variations.

32. Giles claims the textual evidence only slightly favors the singular, but this is not the case, as p74, ℵ, A, B, C, and many others have the singular, ἐκκλησία; only a few Western and Byzantine MSS contain the plural, which the KJV and NKJV follow. Peterson, *Acts*, 317–18n78, further discusses the textual evidence.

33. Keener, *Acts*, 2:1696.

34. Peterson, *Acts*, 317.

35. "Church of God," which implies a divinely ordained and initiated institution, appears 9 times in the NT, with each of the other 8 in Pauline epistles. The idea of substitutionary atonement is also characteristically Pauline, with Lukan soteriology focusing more on the individual's response to the gospel in repentance or faith (see chapter 3); cf. Eph 5:25–27, where Christ's death is for the ἐκκλησία.

one interprets the obscure reference to the blood of God,[36] many scholars view 20:28 as speaking of a single worldwide body of all Christians, the *ecclesia catholica*, though it clearly references the Ephesian church in this context.[37] Giles argues that these are not Luke's own theological ideas,[38] but that they are either Paul's direct ideas,[39] or traditional ideas, which sound like Paul's ideas.[40]

The argument that because Luke may not use a word elsewhere in a certain way he must not know that connotation is misleading. The most straightforward way to read the occurrences of ἐκκλησία in both Acts 9:31 and 20:28 may be that they refer to a more expansive view of the wider church. However, in 20:28 Luke is calling the Ephesian elders to shepherd the congregations in Ephesus and Asia, and his emphasis is on the worth of the church: "obtaining the church by such precious blood suggests an infinite cost (cf. 1 Pet 1:19). Thus, it communicates that God's church is of priceless value to him; woe to those who do not care for it lovingly."[41] Peterson similarly emphasizes this idea:

> Such language can be applied to the church as the whole body of Christ (cf. Eph 1:14; Titus 2:14; 1 Pet 2:9), but there is great significance and rhetorical force in recognising its immediate reference to the Ephesian situation. Each congregation which is brought into existence because of the saving work of Jesus is

36. This may refer to Christ as God: "with the blood of his Own," that is, Christ (cf. Rom 8:32); Metzger, *Textual Commentary*, 426; Walton, *Leadership*, 94–98. Keener claims it could refer to Christ or God, and that the emphasis is on the close relationship between the Father and Jesus, and on the costliness of the church to God, *Acts*, 3:3040. On Christ's blood, cf. Rom 3:25; 5:9.

37. That ἐκκλησία is used in a nonlocal sense here is the predominant view, but it is debated; Witherington, *Acts*, 624. The Ephesian elders are clearly being asked to shepherd their particular flock, and not the church universal. If Luke uses ἐκκλησία for both local gatherings and the universal church, this implies that for Luke each local grouping of Christians is actually the total church in the place in which it exists; Barrett, *Acts*, 2.lxxxviii. Paul emphasizes this idea (Gal 1:13; 1 Cor 11:22; 1:2; 2 Cor 1:1).

38. Luke never rejects these ideas, nor does he develop them. They do not "sound like" his theology.

39. The context of this saying is without doubt the most "Pauline" section of Acts, with various parallels with the Pauline epistles (see discussion in chapter 10). It is in one of the "we sections" of Acts, meaning that Luke is likely present for this speech, and may have used shorthand to take notes.

40. If ancient historians did not have exact sources, they would compose speeches appropriate to the occasion and the speaker.

41. Keener, *Acts*, 3:3037.

precious to God and should be so treated by those appointed to be its leaders![42]

Luke is likely aware of both the simpler local congregational view, and the broader (Pauline) universal view of the church. Paul and his theology has surely influenced him, through their travels and relationship, and Luke's writings show glimpses of this influence, including various Paulinisms. He appreciates the importance of nuanced Pauline theological perspectives such as the universal church, whether he fully grasps their implications or not, and he attempts to faithfully convey them "as Paul would have" in 20:28.[43]

However, Luke's goal is different than Paul's; Luke is writing practical missional instruction for his readers in Acts, without concern for such theological subtleties. He focuses on the ἐκκλησία as the local group of gathered believers, linked to others in a loose network of relational connections, because this is the pragmatic missional structure that he is rhetorically advocating throughout Acts. His primary purpose is not that his readers would grasp that they are part of a worldwide body of believers; instead, Luke is calling them to reproduce the local, tangible expression of the ἐκκλησία everywhere they go. Thus, this work's thesis sheds light on the question of Luke's ecclesiology, and helps the reader to understand the reasons why Luke presents the local ἐκκλησία as he does, without precluding the idea that Luke is aware of the universalized view of the church.

ΕΚΚΛΗΣΙΑ IN ACTS—NARRATIVE ANALYSIS

It is perhaps surprising that ἐκκλησία does not occur in the earliest Jerusalem stories. This may be because the Christian church is not yet sufficiently distinct from Judaism in Luke's mind.[44] Luke first uses ἐκκλησία in Acts 5:11, in the context of the sobering story of Ananias and Sapphira: "great fear came over the whole church" (ὅλην τὴν ἐκκλησίαν).[45] Luke wants to stress at this point that the followers of Jesus have a distinctive sense of self-understanding, of being a corporate entity. This also explains God's fierce response to

---

42. Peterson, *Acts*, 569.

43. Luke may not fully grasp the implications of Paul's universal ecclesiology, or his redemptive atonement Christology; if this is the case, he is certainly not alone (2 Pet 3:15–16).

44. Although D has it in 2:47, this is likely a later scribal addition. The language reflects the move from more to less Semitic language, as the narrative progresses from more to less Semitic settings; Witherington, *Acts*, 220.

45. This fearful (φόβος μέγας) response to the holy is common in Luke-Acts: Luke 1:12, 65; 2:9; 7:16; 8:37; Acts 2:43; 5:5; 7:32; 9:31; 10:4, 35; 19:17. Witherington, *Acts*, 219.

Ananias and Sapphira's violation of this holy community; no breach of fellowship or disloyalty can be tolerated amongst the vulnerable new people of God, the ἐκκλησία.[46] The ensuing consequence vividly reminds the people of who they are—the community in which the Spirit dwells, and which that same Spirit jealously protects. This instance introduces Luke's primary theological connotation: the ἐκκλησία is the new people of God, the called-out ones, the unique community of believers, worth protecting and preserving at any cost.[47]

The second occurrence is 8:3: "Saul began ravaging the church (ἐλυμαίνετο τὴν ἐκκλησίαν), entering house after house (κατὰ τοὺς οἴκους), and dragging off men and women, he put them in prison." This underscores a secondary theme of the ἐκκλησία in Acts: it will be the recipient of much persecution, even to the point of imprisonment and death.[48] It also establishes the fundamental structural expression of the Christian ἐκκλησία, house to house, which will be discussed in the following chapter.

The third (9:31) summarizes the health of the church in the Jewish regions and sets the stage for further outward geographical expansion. It also lists Luke's ideal ecclesial characteristics: peace (εἰρήνην), being built up (οἰκοδομουμένη), the fear of the Lord (τῷ φόβῳ τοῦ Κυρίου), and the comfort and exhortation of the Holy Spirit (τῇ παρακλήσει τοῦ Ἁγίου Πνεύματος). These qualities allow the church to continue to grow and missionally increase (ἐπληθύνετο), which is an indication of a church's well-being in Acts.

From 9:31, Luke continues to develop and reinforce this theme of the called-out people of God, established not just in Jerusalem and its surrounding areas, but also in Antioch (11:19–21), Ephesus (19:1–10), and many other areas of the Empire (13:4—18:11). This culminates in the final occurrence of the word in Paul's emotional goodbye speech to the Ephesian elders (20:28), where the ἐκκλησία may point to the universal body of Christians, and is set apart and redeemed by the bloody sacrifice of God (or Christ).[49] This final reference underscores the incalculable worth of this new people of God, an important message as Luke calls his readers to devote themselves faithfully to these local congregations through Paul's words to the Ephesian leaders.

---

46. Polhill, *Acts*, 161; Marshall, *Acts*, 113–14.

47. Like the community at Qumran, they claimed to be "the new people of God," Barrett, *Acts*, 1:271.

48. This theme of the suffering of the people of God is repeated throughout Acts. Persecution and suffering are to be expected, particularly if the church takes its missional calling seriously. See part 4 of this work.

49. See previous discussion on this verse, and Barrett, *Acts*, 2:974–7; Witherington, *Acts*, 623–24. Definite parallels with Pauline theology are unusual in Acts. Giles, "ΕΚΚΛΗΣΙΑ," 137.

CONCLUSION—LUKE'S MISSIONAL AND ECCLESIOLOGICAL PURPOSES

This chapter has analyzed the 23 uses of ἐκκλησία in Acts, concluding that Acts employs all the conventional meanings in the ancient Greco-Roman world. For Luke, the most important of these is the group of gathered Christians in a particular locale with a shared belief system. Throughout Acts, Luke is establishing a distinctively Christian identity. Although ἐκκλησία is not a new word, its connotations point toward the new people of God, Jew and non-Jew united, the called-out ones whom God has appointed to follow him and to further expand his mission.[50]

In Acts, the followers of Jesus hold the community as the highest priority. Whether it is establishing it, broadening its influence, guarding its unity, or training and supporting it, they *always* focus their efforts on the church assembly. Luke is arguing in Acts that the ἐκκλησία is *the* irreplaceable structure of the early Christian missionary movement. It is both the springboard for its missional proclamation, and the vehicle for its ongoing advancement and growth. Mission must emerge from local networks of churches, and result in the establishment and growth of local churches; otherwise, it is a departure from the precedent set down by the earliest missionaries. Gaining converts and influence is not enough; missionaries must establish and nurture church communities, which in turn carry the outreach ever further.

Luke seeks to strengthen the church's unique sense of Christian identity and self-understanding amidst the complex religious milieu of the Empire by presenting the church this way in Acts.[51] For Luke, the new people of God is worth protecting and defending at all costs (5:11; 20:28). As such, believers should expect suffering and persecution (8:3).[52] Luke's challenge to his readers is to preserve the church's distinctive community and persevere in trial and persecution, trusting that God's purposes will prevail. Paul's trial narratives (Acts 23–26) are a model for later Christians in positions of trial and imprisonment. Similarly, the way that the church responds to persecution, such as by praying for more boldness (4:29–31), obeying God rather

---

50. This "new" church is of course in continuity with Israel, as the fulfillment of its promised election to Abraham, but for Luke (and Paul) it has nothing to do with a national Israel (Acts 1:6–7).

51. Luke is attempting to justify the growing separation between the Christian church and Judaism; he may also be drawing deliberate contrasts with other Greco-Roman religions as well, particularly the Imperial Cult.

52. Both Peter (1 Pet 4:12–13) and John (1 John 3:13) have a similar goal in their writings.

than people when threatened (5:29), continuing to move forward with the mission (8:1–4), and even praying and worshipping (16:25), are examples for Luke's readers to imitate. He continually exhorts them not to lose sight of their missional purpose, even amid suffering.[53]

In Acts, the healthy ἐκκλησία is filled with peace, continually being built up, and characterized by the fear of the Lord and the comfort of the Holy Spirit; when it is thriving in this way it is missional at the core, constantly expanding (9:31). Acts 1:8 and the overarching geographical progression of the Acts narrative show that Luke's ultimate vision is that the church would grow into every place on earth, that the worldwide church would unify in mission and become truly universal in its influence. For this reason, Luke's presentation of the ἐκκλησία is mostly pragmatic and local. He is calling his readers to reproduce this flexible missional structure everywhere. For Luke, this happens best house to house (κατὰ τοὺς οἴκους, 8:3).

---

53. This is the lesson of Acts 8:1–4: the church is scattered by persecution, yet everywhere they go they proclaim the gospel and the church continues to advance.

Chapter 6

The House and Household

And every day, in the temple and from house to house,
they did not cease to teach and proclaim Jesus as the Christ.

—ACTS 5:42

Nearly every scholar agrees that until the fourth century, when Constantine begins building basilicas throughout the Empire, Christ-followers regularly gather in private homes built for family use (οἶκος), not in buildings constructed for public worship services.[1] While most people live in tall tenement flats or *insulae*, the space early Christians use is most likely the *triclinium* (and courtyard) of larger *domus*-style homes.[2] This does not mean they *only* meet in homes; there are examples of citywide church gatherings in Acts,[3] as well as possibilities of other group meetings in public places such as the street or marketplace.[4] However, there is no record of the ἐκκλησία

---

1. Gehring, *House*, 1; this work is a summary of research on house churches in the early church and the contemporary church.

2. Gehring, *House*, 140–41, 313–20; Schnabel, *Mission*, 2:1591, 1600, 1624–25 have floor plans and reconstructions of various housing styles revealed by archaeology.

3. The earliest Jerusalem church has access to the temple (Acts 2:46; 3:1–10; 5:21–24, 42). This does not mean other early churches hold regular large, citywide meetings, for they would not have the venue to do so. It seems that the entire Antioch church gathers in 15:30; where is not known.

4. Adams, *Meeting Places*, claims that NT scholars have overdrawn evidence to

gathering consistently in any location other than a home; the "church" and the house church are essentially synonymous in Acts. Because Christians do not have the status of a recognized religion in their first centuries, there is no possibility of a legal public meeting place, so early Christians primarily make use of the most convenient facilities available, the private dwellings of supportive families.[5] For primitive Christianity, church is nearly always in a house, for there are few other options.

THE ΟΙΚΟΣ SOCIETY

The reliance of early Christians on the household mirrors trends within their society. Scholars agree that the οἶκος is the fundamental building block of ancient society and economy.[6] The social dimension of the ancient οἶκος is the household, which consists of the father, mother, children, slaves, clients, and often the extended family. These relationships significantly determine daily life, and have financial, familial, social, and legal implications. A person gains a sense of identity and belonging through their οἶκος.

The physical dimension of the ancient οἶκος is the house itself. It is a home in which people live, and a "launching pad" for an individual's outer life. People enter into relationships from the οἶκος, and build the πόλις, the ancient city-state, and with it the entire social and political system.[7] The ancient οἶκος "is not just one social and economic form among others but rather the basic social and economic form not only for the ancient world and the New Testament but presumably for every pre-industrial sedentary culture as well."[8] This is the reason scholars refer to the NT world as an "οἶκος society." The dominance of the οἶκος in Greco-Roman culture helps to explain why early Christians (perhaps unconsciously) choose house churches as their primary way of ordering their communities. This is the default position in an οἶκος society.

---

suggest that houses are the only place early Christians meet for worship. He argues from literary and archaeological evidence that more weight should be given to other meeting options, including shops, bathhouses, storehouses, and outside locales.

5. Murphy-O'Connor, "House-Churches," 129–38 reconstructs how a thoroughly excavated Roman villa in Corinth may have contributed to the problems Paul discusses concerning the Eucharist (1 Cor 11:17–34).

6. E.g., Judge, *Social Pattern*, 49–61; Verner, *Household of God*, 27–81; Meeks, *Urban Christians*, 75–78; Filson, "Significance," 105–12, who is one of the first to link house churches and the rapid expansion of early Christianity.

7. Gehring, *House*, 17.

8. Lührmann, "Neutestamentliche Haustafeln," 87; Gehring, *House*, 17.

If one of the defining characteristics of the οἶκος is the private domestic house in which the extended family lives, the other is the structure of the patronage system. This is a hierarchical social phenomenon based around the head of household, or house father/mother, who exercises authority in nearly all things within his or her οἶκος. Patrons tend to be wealthy individuals, who either own or rent their accommodation. They are usually educated, have experience as teachers within their οἶκος, and manage their households financially and administratively. In addition to their family, they take on "clients," for whom they have responsibility and protective duties. In return for their patronage, their clientele affords them honor, service, and loyalty. These mutually beneficial relationships are based on values such as obligation and reciprocity.[9] According to Judge, such patronal relationships are the hermeneutical key to the daily functioning of ancient Roman society:

> The republic recognized not only the sweeping powers the Roman *pater familias* enjoyed over his personal family, bond and free alike, but also the rights and duties imposed by the relationship of *clientela*. Freedmen, who had formerly been members of a household through slavery, retained their link with it, and in some respects their obligations, as its clients. Others also freely associated themselves with it for their mutual benefit. Loyalty to the household interest was expected, though the authority of the patron was grounded in his trustworthiness, which guaranteed that the material and social needs of the client's family were met.[10]

This patronage system is significant for the early Christian mission and its rapid expansion.[11] It helps to explain the "οἶκος formula": "he/she was baptized [or came to faith] with his/her [entire] household." This is found four times in Acts, referring to Cornelius (11:12b–14), Lydia (16:14–16), the Philippian jailer (16:30–34), and Crispus (18:8).[12] Another example of householder conversion is Jason in Thessalonica (17:1–9). If a householder is converted and baptized in an οἶκος culture, their entire household is expected

---

9. Chow, *Patronage and Power*, chapters 2 and 3; Sampley, *Pauline Partnership* examines how Paul uses the Roman legal concept of consensual *societas*, a partnership contract linked to the patronage system.

10. Judge, *Social Pattern*, 31.

11. Holmberg, *Paul and Power*, 104–7; Elliot, *Home*, 188–99; White, *Building God's House*, 77–85, 140–48.

12. 1 Cor 1:16 has an identical phrase (about Stephanas), corroborating this Pauline practice. Matson, *Household Conversion*, 86–200 is a literary study of the household conversion narratives in Acts and their implications for the unity of Luke and Acts.

to follow their example.[13] The patronage system also demonstrates why Paul targets homeowners in any new mission venture.[14] By recruiting a house-holder, he is able to convert an entire household to Christ and quickly set up a base of operation in their house for further local and regional mission.[15] This accelerates the expansion of the church by creating micro-communities of faith, which then become the seeds of the churches that develop in that area.

ΟΙΚΟΣ IN ACTS AND THE ANCIENT WORLD

Ancient literary references to οἶκος are predictably abundant. As the various meanings of οἶκος are explored, all 25 of the occurrences of the word in Acts will be noted, and the various ways that Luke uses οἶκος and its diminutive οἰκία (12 occurrences) will be analyzed.[16]

The most common meaning of οἶκος is a physical house,[17] or a place of dwelling,[18] and sometimes certain rooms within the house.[19] Acts frequent-

13. Crossley, *Why Christianity Happened*, contains examples of the conversion of households to Christianity and Judaism, and the related practice of circumcising the Gentile male slaves of a converted household, 100, 157–71. Crossley discusses the example of Onesimus, in Paul's letter to Philemon, which is likely a household conversion (led by Philemon) in which Onesimus has not fully converted, or at least is not fully obser-vant, because of his involuntary incorporation into the Christian community, 161–63.

14. Cf. 1 Cor 1:14–16: Crispus, Gaius, and Stephanas were all householders; Geh-ring, *House*, 185–87. Paul presumably establishes his own reciprocal patron/client re-lationships with these householders, in which they owe him their allegiance in return for his spiritual assistance.

15. Gehring, *House*, 187. Taylor, "Social Nature," 128–36 deals with the social im-plications of household conversion and identifies three levels of Christian conversion: 1) the *conviction* that Christian belief is true, 2) the *social reorientation* into Christian community, and 3) the *conformity* to the discipline of the community. Early Christian-ity attracts converts who display varying degrees of commitment and are incorporated into the community to varying degrees. Their abandonment of previous beliefs, prac-tices and relationships also varies accordingly. Household conversion plays a role in this, as people who are involuntarily incorporated into the Christian community gener-ally display lower levels of devotion and adherence, at least initially.

16. Οἶκος: 2:2, 36, 46; 5:42; 7:10, 20, 42, 46, 47, 49; 8:3; 10:2, 22, 30; 11:12, 13, 14; 16:15 [twice], 31, 34a; 18:8; 19:16; 20:20; 21:8; οἰκία: 4:34; 9:11, 17; 10:6, 17, 32; 11:11; 12:12; 16:32; 17:5; 18:7 [twice]; πανοικί: 16:34b.

17. Plato, *Phaedrus*, 1: "at the *house* of Morychus; that *house* which is near the temple"; Josephus, *Ant.*, 4.74: "the various *private homes*"; Diodorus Siculus, *Library*, 17.28.4: "to go each to his own *house* and there, enjoying the best of food and drink with their families."

18. Homer, *Iliad*, 24.471, 572: Achilles's dwelling place; Homer, *Odyssey*, 9.478: the Cyclop's cave; Gen 31.33: a tent.

19. Xenophon, *Symposium*, 2.18: "a moderate-sized *room* [οἶκος] large enough for

ly uses οἶκος to refer to a person's dwelling place, such as the house with the upper room in Jerusalem (2:2), Pharaoh's home (7:20), the houses that Saul enters to persecute Christians (8:3), Cornelius's house in Caesarea (10:22, 30; 11:12, 13), Lydia's house in Philippi (16:15b), the Philippian jail keeper's house (16:34a), the house in which the seven sons of Sceva are humiliated in Ephesus (19:16), and Philip's house in Caesarea (21:8). Luke also refers to the church meeting κατ᾽ οἶκον in two summary passages (2:46; 5:42), and in Paul's reference to house-to-house teaching (20:20).[20]

Luke also uses οἰκία 12 times in Acts to refer to a person's physical dwelling: the houses sold for the poor in Jerusalem (4:34), the house of Judas in Damascus (9:11, 17), the house of Simon the tanner in Joppa (10:6, 17, 32; 11:11), the house of Mary in Jerusalem (12:12), the house of the Philippian jailer (16:32), the house of Jason in Thessalonica (17:5), and the house of Titius Justus in Corinth (18:7; twice).

The meanings of οἶκος and οἰκία are generally identical in the ancient world.[21] Though οἰκία can refer to a social household or family,[22] Luke never uses it in this way in Luke-Acts, but always as the physical structure in which people live. Cornelius's house is always an οἶκος (10:22, 30; 11:12, 13), while Simon the tanner's house is an οἰκία (10:6, 17, 32; 11:11). This implies that for Luke there is a distinction between the words, probably that οἰκία refers to a smaller house and οἶκος a larger house.[23] However, Luke is more ambiguous about the Philippian jailer's house, which is both an οἰκία and an οἶκος (16:32, 34). This indicates that Luke may use the words interchangeably, or perhaps that this particular house is neither obviously large nor small.

Οἶκος is also used in the ancient world to designate a significant structure, which may or may not be a private dwelling, such as the king's palace,[24]

---

me (just as but now this room [οἴκημα, the proper word for a room] was large enough for the lad)"; Homer, *Odyssey*, 1.356; 19.514, 598.

20. This distributive sense of κατ᾽ οἶκον is best translated "house to house" or simply "at home." 2:46 and 5:42 are both contrasting the church's private house meetings with their public temple meetings.

21. Liddell and Scott, *Lexicon*, 1203. Cf. Homer, *Iliad*, 6.15; 20.64; *Odyssey*, 12.4.

22. Matt 12:25; 13:57; Mark 3:25; 6:4; John 4:35; 1 Cor 16:15

23. This difference is not apparent in ancient literature in general: οἰκία can refer to palaces (Herodotus, *Hist.*, 1.35, 41, 44, the house of Croesus; 1.98, the royal palace), and other larger structures.

24. Josephus, *Ant.*, 9.102: "the king's *house* [οἶκος τοῦ βασιλέως]"; 2 Kgdms 11:8 LXX: "'Go down to your *house*, and wash your feet.' And Uriah went out of the king's *house*"; 15:35: "the king's *house*."

the "house of prayer,"[25] the house of God,[26] or specifically the temple in Jerusalem.[27] Luke refers to the Jerusalem Temple twice as the οἶκος built for God (Acts 7:47, 49, quoting Isa 66:1, 2). It can also refer to what is inside of a house, such as a person's estate or possessions.[28] The only place in the NT that fits this description is in Acts, when Stephen speaks of Pharaoh making Joseph governor over Egypt and his whole house (ὅλον τὸν οἶκον αὐτοῦ, 7:10; cf. Gen 41:40).[29] Finally, οἶκος is also used figuratively in the NT, referring to the body as the dwelling place of God (1 Pet 2:5); Luke similarly refers to the body as the metaphorical habitation of unclean spirits (Luke 11:24).

In addition to the physical house, οἶκος is also the social structure of the household, the people who live within the house.[30] The best way to tell the difference in Acts is to ask whether the οἶκος repents or receives salvation—if so, this indicates the household rather than the physical house, though these are overlapping concepts, for the family's identity is closely tied to their home. Luke's Gospel refers to this social dimension in Jesus's missional instructions to his disciples (10:5–7), and when mentioning Zacchaeus's household (19:9). In Acts, Luke speaks in this way of the households of Cornelius (10:2; 11:14), Lydia (16:15a), the Philippian jailer (16:31), and Crispus (18:8).[31] He also uses the derivative πανοικί (πᾶς + οἶκος), "the whole household," referring to the Philippian jailer's household (16:34b).

Οἶκος is also used in the ancient world to refer to a clan or tribe of people descended from a common ancestor, such as "the house of David," or "the house of Israel."[32] This is a common LXX usage,[33] and Luke refers to

25. Matt 21:13; Mark 11:17; Luke 19:46 (quoting Isa 56:7): "my house shall be a house of prayer" (ἔσται ὁ οἶκός μου οἶκος προσευχῆς).

26. Herodotus, *Hist.*, 8.143: "set fire to their [the gods'] *houses*"; Plato, *Phaedrus*, 24e: "Hestia alone abides at *home* in the *house* of heaven"; Matt 12:4; Mark 2:26; Luke 6:4: "the *house* of God (τὸν οἶκον τοῦ Θεοῦ)."

27. 3 Kgdms 7:31 LXX: "in the *house* of God"; John 2:16: "stop making my Father's *house* a place of business."

28. See e.g., Herodotus, *Hist.*, 3.53: "the Magus that Cambyses left in charge of his *household*"; Josephus, *J.W.*, 6.282: "packing up the baggage there in your *house*."

29. Pharaoh does not make Joseph the ruler of his family, but puts all of his possessions in his governorship.

30. Artemidorus, *Oneirocritica*, 2.68: "with all of your *household*" (μετά ὅλου τοῦ οἴκου). Metaphorically, the church is God's household (1 Pet 4:17; 1 Tim 3:15); God is the head of household or housefather, and his people his loyal οἶκος.

31. For other similar formulas in the NT, see Tit 1:11; 1 Cor 1:16; 2 Tim 1:16; 4:19; Heb 3:2–6; 1 Tim 3:4–5.

32. E.g., Josephus, *Ant.*, 2.202: "the *house* of the Israelites"; 8.111: "our *house*, and of the Hebrew people."

33. E.g., 3 Kgdms [1 Kings] 12:19; 13:2; Amos 5:25; Jer 9:25; 38:31, 33; Exod 19:3;

ὁ οἶκος Δαυίδ in his Gospel three times (Luke 1:27, 69; 2:4). In Acts, Peter refers to ὁ οἶκος Ἰσραήλ in his evangelistic speech at Pentecost (2:36).[34] Stephen uses the same expression in his speech (7:42, quoting Amos 5:25), and uses σκήνωμα τῷ οἴκῳ Ἰακώβ (7:46).[35]

This brief analysis has revealed that Luke's usage of οἶκος is diverse, encompassing every meaning of the word known in the ancient world. Yet his preferred usage refers to the physical dwelling, with the social household a close second. The two primary meanings can both be seen in 16:15: "when she [Lydia] and her *household* (ὁ οἶκος αὐτῆς) had been baptized, she urged us, saying, '. . . come into my *house* (τὸν οἶκόν μου) and stay.'" Another comparable verse is 16:34, where the jailer "brought them into his *house* (τὸν οἶκον αὐτοῦ) and set food before them, and rejoiced greatly, having believed in God with his *whole household* (πανοικεί)."[36] These verses show that while the two primary meanings of οἶκος are overlapping, their distinction is important for Luke. The physical house and the social structure it contains are both objectives for and facilitators of mission in Acts.

In addition to these explicit occurrences in Acts, Luke implies οἶκος multiple other times. The first post-ascension episode takes place in the upper room (1:13–14). Though Luke does not use οἶκος here, the disciples are definitely waiting in a private residence.[37] This episode sets the stage for all of Acts; houses are the primary physical structure throughout the narrative. The final episode in Acts also takes place in a private home, where Paul stays for two years in his own rented quarters (ἐν ἰδίῳ μισθώματι) and preaches the Kingdom of God boldly and unhindered (28:30–31).[38] Once again, missional activity emerges directly out of a private home. By framing the Acts narrative with episodes that take place in houses, Luke underlines the significance of the οἶκος structure to Christian mission.

Isa 2:5.

34. For similar NT usages, see Matt 10:6; 15:24; Heb 8:10.

35. This is textually uncertain, but is in multiple textual variations (p74, ℵ, B, D, and others), and is the more difficult reading. Keener, *Acts*, 2.1414–15 argues that whatever the textual history is, in context it likely means "dwelling place of the house of [the God] of Jacob."

36. They could not have eaten "in" a social network, and a house cannot believe in God. Though πανοικεί is a derivative of οἶκος, it refers to the entire household and is a synonym for πᾶς ὁ οἶκος (11:14).

37. Whether this is the same house as at Pentecost, when the noise like a wind fills "the whole *house*" (ὅλον τὸν οἶκον, 2:2), is unclear; see discussion in the next chapter.

38. Μισθώμα has the root μισθόω (to hire or rent, cf. Matt 20:1).

CONCLUSION—THE MISSIONAL SIGNIFICANCE OF THE OIKOΣ

Οἶκος functions missionally in Acts in two distinct but interrelated ways. Both the dwelling place and the household it contains are strategic aims for Christian missionaries. Because ancient society is composed of these interlinking social networks, the primary missional goal is to reach out within an existing οἶκος. When a missionary approaches a new city or area, their first thought is how to engage with and enter the relational networks of an established οἶκος.[39] This explains the householder evangelism patterns in Acts, for by gaining one convert, a missionary can quickly reach an entire οἶκος, which can then become an embryonic church with an already established social network. Similarly, if a household or other member of an οἶκος converts, he or she has a place of influence which yields promising missional opportunities with the other members of the household, which an outsider would not have. All these factors make the οἶκος the ideal objective for Christian outreach.

For Luke, the οἶκος is also the ideal launching-point for further outreach.[40] The built-in community, cohesion, leadership structure, outward credibility, relational influence, and social networks (business, associations, and community involvement) of an οἶκος and its head of household make it perfectly suited as a social base for mission. Similarly, the physical aspects of a house, with its resources, gathering spaces, food, and shelter, make it an ideal material base for mission. These two functions of the οἶκος create a missional cycle. The household functions as an ideal initial goal for missionaries. When it receives the gospel, it then becomes a base for mission into other households around it. These in turn begin the process again, in a cycle of outreach, establishing, and further outreach.

Luke is not simply "reporting" on all of this in Acts; he is advocating it. He wants his readers to understand that the οἶκος is *still* the most effective target and base for mission. Luke is challenging the church of his day to emulate the earliest churches, and engage in οἶκος-focused, householder evangelism. He is urging them to establish οἶκος-based churches, and to think in terms of strategic social networks and the people of influence who lead them. These

---

39. This can be seen in Paul's missional strategies, examined in part 3. He always searches out the οἶκος with which he has the most natural connection and rapport when approaching a new city in Acts.

40. The οἶκος is not the only missional launching point in Acts. In Athens, Paul evangelizes in the public synagogue, marketplace (ἀγορᾷ), and Areopagus (17:17–19); in Ephesus, in the synagogue and school of Tyrannus (19:8–10). Given the repeated pattern in Acts, one can assume these communities still gather in private homes, which function as the starting points for further outreach in their cities and regions.

new churches can then become active hubs for mission, reaching out to their communities and regions. In Acts, Luke presents the οἶκος as the crucial missional structure for both the initial contact and the ongoing outreach of the church assembly. When the οἶκος becomes a base for mission, with its own patterns of worship and community, it has become a house church.

Chapter 7

The House Church

They broke bread from house to house and ate their food with glad and sincere hearts

—ACTS 2:46

The ἐκκλησία and the οἶκος combine to create the ἐκκλησία κατ' οἶκον, or church at home, within early Christianity.[1] A "house church" is a group of Christians that meets in a private home, and possesses its own religious life, including regular gatherings for worship, which contain evangelistic and instructional proclamation, the celebration of baptism, communion, prayer, and fellowship.[2] Organizational structures are further indications of a fully developed house church.

BACKGROUND

The basic structural influence on early Christian churches is the οἶκος, which emphasizes the hospitality of the head of household as the key to the

---

1. See Gehring, *House*, 1–27 for a history of scholarship on the house church up to 2000. More recently, see Keener, *Acts*, 1:1030–31; 2:1895–1900; 3:2746–49; Adams, *Meeting Places*.

2. Gehring, *House*, 27.

gathering place, and is profoundly embedded in everyday life in ancient society.[3] It is also possible to apply other models from early Christianity's religious, intellectual, and social environments to the house church.[4] For many scholars, the synagogue is the primary *direct* influence on the formation and structure of the early house churches, and Luke's frequent references to the συναγωγή in Acts support this idea.[5] The claim is strengthened if one accepts that many of the earliest Christian converts come from the synagogue setting, and if it can be shown that house synagogues are already common during the time of the NT, not only in the Diaspora but in Palestine as well.[6]

Scholars propose many other possible influences, including the private gatherings of the Imperial cult and the various mystery religions.[7] Others argue that the first Christians imitate associations, whether *collegia*,[8] or voluntary associations.[9] Others maintain that Pauline house churches are

---

3. See Keener, *Acts*, 1:1030–31; 2:1895–1900; 3:2744–50, for other uses of private homes in antiquity, and how this would be the default practice for the earliest Christians: "apart from community centers (such as synagogues), temple courts, or gathering outdoors, where else would disciples meet?" (*Acts*, 1.1030). Adams, *Meeting Places*, 137–79 suggests shops, workshops, barns, warehouses, taverns, hotels, and bathhouses as other possible locations.

4. These models cannot be pursued in depth here but will simply be mentioned as important background.

5. Luke references synagogues in 10 locations in Acts: 6:9 (the Freedmen, Jerusalem); 9:2, 20 (Damascus); 13:5 (Salamis); 13:14, 42, 43 (Pisidian Antioch); 14:1 (Iconium); 15:21; 17:1 (Thessalonica); 17:10 (Berea); 17:17 (Athens); 18:4, 7 (Corinth); 18:19, 26; 19:8 (Ephesus); 22:19; 24:12 (Jerusalem); 26:11.

6. For the debate about the NT's portrayal of extensive Jewish house synagogues, see Gehring, *House*, 30. Neusner, *Formative Judaism*, maintains along with others that it is anachronistic. For the evidence (mainly in Josephus, Philo, and the rabbinical sources), and a reconstruction of the emergence of the synagogue prior to 70 CE, see Riesner, "Synagogues," 209: "There is nothing anachronistic in Luke's and the other evangelists' picture that there were many synagogues in Galilee and in Jerusalem"; Levine, "Second Temple Synagogue," 7: "By the end of the Second Temple period, the synagogue had become a central institution in Jewish life. It could be found everywhere, in Israel and the Diaspora, east and west, in cities as well as in villages."

7. E.g., Isis, Serapis, Cybele, Mithras cults, Orphism. For a treatment of the different models, see Meeks, *Urban Christians*, 75–84; Verner, *Household of God*, 6–9; Keener, *Acts*, 2:1895–900; Harland, *Associations*.

8. *Collegia* are legal associations which function as professional guilds and social clubs.

9. Hatch, *Organization*, 36; Judge, *Social Pattern*, 40–48; Harland, *Associations*, 28–53, proposes five categories of associations: 1) household, 2) ethnic or geographic, 3) neighborhood or location, 4) occupational, 5) temple or cult. All types of associations are influenced by the household in their organizational structures (esp. in architecture and the conventions of benefaction), and in their language of familial affection ("mother," "father," "brothers," "sisters") to express identity and feelings of belonging.

patterned after Hellenistic schools of philosophy,[10] or a combination of *collegia* and philosophical schools.[11] Others see influences from the Qumran community.[12]

These social arrangements are not exclusive in the ancient world, but exist in overlapping involvements with one another, and Christian converts would be involved in and influenced by all of them to varying degrees. Each has a configuration of social networks, which use and adapt private, usually domestic settings, and which depend on patronage for ongoing expansion. It is therefore likely that all the aforementioned models have some influence on early Christian structures at least *indirectly*, through their influence on the Jewish synagogue. Early Christians must establish their churches outwardly within the confines of Roman law, e.g., as a household-based voluntary association, or possibly a corporation of foreigners, yet their theological self-understanding as the ἐκκλησία, or the family/house (οἶκος) of God, is most directly influenced by the Jewish synagogue.[13]

Jesus's Usage of Houses

The foundations for Christian οἶκος usage in Acts are found in the ministry of Jesus. As has been seen, Jewish synagogues are probably commonplace at this time, and it can be assumed that particularly in poorer areas, such as Galilee, these are house synagogues rather than separate purpose-built structures.[14] The Gospels report multiple synagogue locations in Galilee.[15] This means that Jesus and his disciples would be accustomed to meeting and

10. E.g., Platonism, Peripateticism, Cynicism, Epicureanism, and Stoicism, which offer ideas, language patterns, and a social model comparable with the house churches. See Acts 19:9, "the school of Tyrannus," for a possible example of this; 17:18: "Epicurean and Stoic philosophers" in Athens; 17:21.

11. Judge, "Early Christians," 4–15, 125–37.

12. Particularly for the Jerusalem community of goods; Mealand, "Community of Goods," 96–99. This view is contested, as scholars know relatively little about the Essene model.

13. Gehring, *House*, 21.

14. See Levine, *Ancient Synagogues*, 19–62 for synagogues excavated at Masada, Herodium, Gamla, and Capernaum; Riesner, "Synagogues," 184–87.

15. Matt 4:23/Mark 1:39; Matt 9:35; Luke 4:14–15. Luke uses συναγωγή 15 times in his Gospel: Luke 4:15 (Galilee); 4:16, 20, 28 (Nazareth); 4:33, 38 (Capernaum); 4:44 (Judea); 6:6; 7:5; 8:41 (Capernaum); 11:43; 12:11; 13:10; 20:46; 21:12.

worshipping in private homes.[16] The many home meetings in Luke's Gospel are an important precursor to later Christian house churches in Acts.[17]

Luke reports that Jesus trains his disciples in house-to-house outreach (Luke 10:1–20).[18] In this mission discourse, which is foundational to all of Luke-Acts, Jesus announces that the harvest is plentiful but the workers are few, and sends out his disciples to the harvest in pairs (10:1–2).[19] There are two stages in the mission: the house/household (οἰκία, 10:5–7) and the town (πόλις, 10:8–12). Jesus instructs his disciples to begin with a household and focus on building relationship with the head of household, as the doorway into a pre-existing social network (10:5–7). Once they are welcomed, they spread from that household through relational attachments, healing the sick and proclaiming the kingdom, until the entire town or city has heard the message of the coming kingdom (10:8–9).

The disciples are to select a house and give their "peace greeting" to the one they enter (εἰρήνη τῷ οἴκῳ τούτῳ, 10:5). "Peace be upon this household" is a common greeting, which should be seen as a transfer of power, which can return to the greeter if the recipient is not receptive (10:6). It is a missional announcement of the arrival of the kingdom of God for Luke (10:9, 11). According to cultural customs, only the head of household can accept or reject this greeting of peace. If receptive, the householder extends the invitation of hospitality, indicating acceptance of the message *and* the messenger. This signifies the host's identity as a "person/son of peace" (υἱὸς εἰρήνης, 10:6), and the rest of the household generally follows suit.[20] This practice of seeking a person of peace points towards an intentional habit of "householder evangelism."[21]

The household (οἶκος) which receives the messenger and the message then becomes a base for missionary outreach into the surrounding areas,

16. Gehring, *House*, 29.

17. Luke 5:29; 7:36–37; 8:51; 9:4; 10:5–7; 14:1; 19:5; 22:11; Keener, *Acts*, 1:1030. Gehring, *House*, 28–48 argues that Jesus's use of houses directly contributes to later house churches; Adams, *Meeting Places*, 50 critiques Gehring's reconstruction as speculative eisegesis.

18. Cf. Matt 10:1–40; Mark 6:7–13; also 1 Cor 9, esp. 1 Cor 9:14 and Luke 10:7. Paul appears to be referring to a Jesus saying here, indicating that a mission discourse tradition exists by the time he writes 1 Corinthians (ca. early 55); Fjärstedt, *Synoptic Tradition*, 77.

19. According to OT witness regulations, in which two or more witnesses authenticate the message: Deut 17:6; 19:5; Num 35:30; cf. Matt 18:16; 26:59–60; John 8:17; 2 Cor 13:1; 1 Tim 5:19; Heb 10:28.

20. A host would reciprocate the messenger's offer—material assistance for spiritual assistance.

21. Gehring, *House*, 59. This approach is also seen in the Pauline mission.

and an embryonic community of faith and expectation of the coming kingdom.[22] It offers Jesus's disciples shelter, room and board, the material requirements for their survival as they can carry nothing with them (10:4), a social network to minister within, credibility in the larger community, and perhaps most importantly, a family community and a home, as they have left their own residence.[23]

Though these pre-Easter Kingdom-expectant household communities cannot be considered full house churches, for as practicing Jews they still undoubtedly worship in local synagogues, they are for Luke the sociological and theological forerunners of the Christian house churches that develop a few years later in Acts. Luke intentionally draws parallels between the way Jesus models and teaches mission and the way the early church practices mission, particularly regarding their οἶκος-oriented structures. Luke wants his readers to understand that the first Christian leaders are not operating in a vacuum as they establish the earliest churches after Pentecost.[24] Instead, they are applying the missional structures and practices which Jesus has already taught them. *The post-Easter house-churches evolve naturally from the homes of the Jesus movement.* In Luke's Gospel, Jesus trains his disciples in the missional use of the οἶκος through his teaching in the mission discourse (Luke 10:2–16), and then gives them vital experience in how to build household communities by sending them out to do it (9:6; 10:1, 17–24). For Luke, this Christological seal of approval is the ultimate validation for the house church movement that develops in Acts. The house church is Jesus's missional structure, endorsed by Christ himself, and readers of Luke-Acts would do well to imitate this, just as the earliest Christians in Acts do.

THE EARLY JERUSALEM COMMUNITY—ACTS 1-7

There has been a recent challenge to the scholarly consensus that early Christian meeting places are "almost exclusively houses," led largely by Adams's book *The Earliest Christian Meeting Places*. Adams's work proposes multiple other potential meeting venues, and helpfully questions the assumptions underpinning this consensus. However, Adams admits that, "The book of Acts offers the clearest and fullest New Testament documentation of the

22. Gehring, *House*, 61.

23. See Luke 18:29–30 for Jesus's promise about houses and family that his followers leave for his sake, which is fulfilled "in this age" through the house communities.

24. This can be seen in the way that they instinctively gather in homes after the ascension and before Pentecost (1:12–15). Jesus has trained them to function this way, so it is a natural choice for them.

use of houses as Christian meeting places."[25] It is important to distinguish between definite references to house churches in Acts and more ambiguous or speculative inferences. However, Adams's arguments strengthen the core claim of part 2 of this work, which is that Luke intentionally presents the house church as the primary missional structure in Acts, more so than any other NT author does.

As the next sections examine the evidence for house churches in Acts, they will rank each textual occurrence on the following scale of certainty:[26]

[4] *Definite*—the text is explicitly clear

[3] *Likely*—the text is not explicit, but there are multiple significant hints

[2] *Uncertain*—the text is unclear, but there is at least one hint

[1] *Unlikely*—the text is ambiguous, with no additional information

House Churches in the Early Jerusalem Community

In his last days with his disciples, Jesus instructs them to wait in Jerusalem until the outpouring of the Holy Spirit (Acts 1:4–5). After observing his ascension on the Mount of Olives, they obediently return to Jerusalem and assemble in the "upper room" (ὑπερῷον) of the house where they are staying (1:12–14).[27] This first reference to a house in Acts is an embryonic prototype of early Christian worship: Christ-followers experience community with one another (1:12–13), "join together constantly in prayer" (1:14), may meet there at Pentecost (2:1–2),[28] and later probably use it for worship services (2:46; 5:42; 8:3; 12:17).[29] This is the location of the earliest Christian house church, and the base for the community's fellowship, mission, and emerging collective identity.[30]

25. Adams, *Meeting Places*, 51.

26. The rationale for each ranking will be presented. Adams also examines the text of Acts, *Meeting Places*, 51–67, and classifies most of the following texts as unambiguous, debatable, or speculative.

27. The upper room is common in Palestinian houses (Mark 14:15; Luke 22:12; Acts 9:37, 39; 20:8). It is a place for relaxation, with a possible capacity of 120 people; Blue, "House Church," 140–44, 198–204; Murphy-O'Connor, "Cenacle," 318–21.

28. Most recent commentators suggest that the temple is the more likely Pentecost venue.

29. Gehring, *House*, 66. The owner of this house with the large upper room is wealthy; some have speculated that it is Joseph of Arimathea, a council member (Luke 23:51), or Joanna, the wife of Chuza, one of Herod's administrators (Luke 8:3).

30. Early Christians do not yet consciously understand themselves as separate from

Adams maintains that "the text does not demand that the room be understood as the setting of the meeting Luke goes on to describe in 1:15–26."[31] Whether 1:15 signals a new location is debatable. Even if Adams is correct that the text implies a separate meeting place to replace Judas, such as the temple premises, Luke still draws attention to consistent prayer meetings in this private house with the upper room, perhaps implying that this is the same upper room that hosted the Last Supper (Luke 22:11–12), and even that this is the site of a post-resurrection appearance (24:33–36).[32] It is evidently a "base" for the earliest Christian community, even before Pentecost. As a place of prayer and fellowship, it points to an early practice of home-based community, and is therefore ranked as a [3].[33]

Acts references another early Jerusalem house church, the house of Mary, the mother of John Mark (12:12).[34] After being released from prison, Peter goes to this house to find Christians assembled there in prayer and asks them to "report these things to James and the brothers there" (12:7–17). Peter expects to find believers gathered in this house, indicating that it is likely an established house church. The place to which Peter directs them may be the house with the upper room from Acts 1.[35] This data from 12:17, along with "many" (ἱκανοί, 12:12),[36] suggests that "James and the brethren associated with him met in a different place from Peter's company—that they belonged, to use Pauline language, to a different house church."[37] Nearly all scholars agree that Mary's house is a reference to a full house church,

---

Judaism, but the process of distinctive self-understanding begins in this house. Peter presides over this first house church, and when he leaves, James, the brother of Jesus, becomes its leader (Acts 12:17; 15:13–21).

31. Adams, *Meeting Places*, 56. He also claims that 120 persons meeting in this home is problematic, and therefore "another unspecified location makes better sense."

32. Keener, *Acts*, 1:739.

33. Whether it is a full house-church, with preaching and sharing of the Lord's Supper, is not explicit in the text.

34. According to Col 4:10, John Mark is cousin to Barnabas, a Levite from Cyprus (Acts 4:36–37), so this family belongs to the Cypriot Diaspora Jews, who are wealthy and can afford to resettle in Jerusalem. Blue, "House Church," 136 suggests that a house church meets in this house from an early date.

35. Adams, *Meeting Places*, 53 acknowledges that there is a place of regular meeting in Mary's house, and agrees that Peter references a second group with "James and the brothers," but denies that this may be the same group as that mentioned in the upper room (1:13).

36. "Many," *not all* of the believers were gathered there, implying there were others gathered elsewhere.

37. Bruce, *Men*, 88. Some also reference the "house" where Pentecost happens (2:2), but this is an ambiguous reference, more likely the temple precinct or a room within it; Witherington, *Acts*, 132; Barrett, *Acts*, 1:114.

and that "James and the brothers" references a second distinct house, giving both a ranking of [4] for certainty. The book of Acts thus explicitly presents two early Jerusalem house churches.

The early summary passages additionally refer twice to multiple homes and their role in the early church: "Breaking bread *from house to house*" (κλῶντές τε κατ' οἶκον ἄρτον, 2:46), and "every day, in the temple and *from house to house*" (ἐν τῷ ἱερῷ καὶ κατ' οἶκον, 5:42). This strengthens the thesis that the earliest Christians organize themselves primarily in homes, first in the house with the upper room, and later in multiple private residences throughout Jerusalem, including Mary's house. Adams concludes, "the use of believers' dwellings as meeting places by the fledgling Jerusalem church is thus clearly and indisputably indicated. In both verses, Luke underlines the regularity of meeting and receiving instruction at home."[38] Both of these references can be given a ranking of [4] for definitely indicating the existence of multiple early house churches.

According to Acts, the church expands quickly after Pentecost: "about three thousand souls were added" (2:41); "the Lord was adding to their number day by day" (2:47); "the number . . . came to be about five thousand" (4:4); "multitudes . . . were constantly added" (5:14); "the number of the disciples continued to increase greatly" (6:7). These new converts begin meeting in homes (κατ' οἶκον, 2:46),[39] which would require a plurality of house churches. Luke admits that his counting is not strictly precise, using "about" multiple times (ὡσεί, 1:15; 2:41; 4:4 [ὡς]). Even if these numbers are not taken literally, and many converts return to their hometowns, the two houses would not have the capacity to hold any real surge in numbers. If even half of the new converts Luke reports join a house church, and they have an average size of 10–20 members (the typical house would have no more capacity than this), this would create at least 100–150 house churches; such numbers would have quite an effect on the social culture of Jerusalem.

One final Jerusalem reference is relevant: in Acts 8:3 Saul forcefully enters multiple Jerusalem houses (κατὰ τοὺς οἴκους) to arrest Christ-followers.[40] These could be private homes but given the pattern of homes as church meeting places Luke has already established, it is very likely some of them also host house churches. Adams includes this in his "debatable" category, claiming this verse underscores the extent and intensity of Paul's quest,

38. Adams, *Meeting Places*, 52–53.

39. Gehring, *House*, 87 claims this is a distributive rather than a locational sense; also, White, *Building God's House*, 155–62. Codex D gives the plural κατ' οἴκους. Whether translated "in individual homes" or "from house to house," multiple houses are implied.

40. Gehring, *House*, 88; cf. Paul's accounts: 1 Cor 15:9; Gal 1:13, 23; Phil 3:6.

rather than drawing attention to the role of houses as Christian meeting places.[41] Because the text is not explicit, this reference receives a ranking of [3] for likely alluding to multiple Jerusalem house churches.

Luke also mentions early Christian gatherings in the temple courts, using Solomon's Porch as a public meeting place (2:46; 3:1–11; 4:1; 5:12, 20–25, 42).[42] However, the temple is clearly unique to Jerusalem, and not available in other locations. Additionally, the normative pattern in the Acts narrative is churches meeting in private homes, and this is confirmed in multiple later episodes. It is therefore reasonable to assume that other places of mission and community are also based around the house church structure, even if Luke does not make this explicit in the text. By analogy, Luke does not mention the appointing of elders in every new Pauline church, but because this is highlighted at the beginning (14:23) and end (20:17) of his journeys, the reader can reasonably conclude that this is Paul's common practice. Similarly, Luke provides a detailed example of a Pauline synagogue speech (13:16–31) and a speech to Gentiles (17:22–31), and the reader can assume other evangelistic messages before similar audiences will broadly follow these patterns. When a house church is not explicit in the text this must be acknowledged, hence this chapter's rating system. However, it is unreasonable to expect Luke to mention house churches in every location, for he is necessarily selective in what he records, providing a pattern of a few normative examples and leaving the reader to fill in the blanks in other similar contexts.

Life in the Jerusalem House Churches

As well as encouraging the use of house churches in the early parts of Acts, Luke also provides an idealized rhetorical picture of these early gatherings in Acts 2:42–47.[43] Προσκαρτερέω is the central word in Acts 2:42: "to persist

41. Adams, *Meeting Places*, 58.

42. This reminds readers that in their own self-understanding Christians are still a sect within Judaism in the early days. Luke uses αἵρεσις to describe the Christians (Acts 24:5, 14; 28:22), which is a Jewish separatist group; Filson, "Significance," 109, 112.

43. Barrett, *Acts*, 1:166: "Luke gives an idealized picture of the earliest church—idealized but not for that reason misleading. That it is not misleading appears at once if negatives are inserted [in 2:42]: they ignored the teaching of the apostles, neglected the fellowship, never met to take a meal together, and did not say their prayers. This would be nonsense. The idealizing is in the participle προσκαρτεροῦντες ('continuing faithfully,' 'remaining constant'), and that Luke did not intend it to be understood as unmarked by exceptions is shown by his story of Ananias and Sapphira (5:1–11). There is no ground for doubting the outline of Luke's account; if he had not given it, we should doubtless have conjectured something of the kind." For another exception to the community of

obstinately in . . . adhere firmly to . . . be faithful to . . . devote oneself to."[44] In the context of local house churches, the Jerusalem community devote themselves in this faithful way to four things.

1) *The apostles' teaching* (τῇ διδαχῇ τῶν ἀποστόλων): They listen to the apostles when they teach, and practice what they hear from them.[45] This instruction likely carries on the teachings of Jesus, and gives direction to the fledgling Christian community.[46] It also probably contains early forms of a Christian confessional tradition, and interpretation of the Hebrew Scriptures (LXX), with an emphasis on their eschatological fulfillment in Christ.[47]

2) *The fellowship* (τῇ κοινωνίᾳ): "The sharing in common of something with someone else in community," whether that is relationship, food, prayer, possessions, or anything else, in the context of close connection and relational cohesiveness.[48] In this sense, all the details that follow in this passage are aspects of Christian κοινωνία.[49] The οἶκος provides the ideal familial environment for this kind of intimate and generous community to develop, and offers an evangelistic example to others through its unified lifestyle together (2:47).

3) *The breaking of the bread* (τῇ κλάσει τοῦ ἄρτου): Probably a combination of a fellowship meal and an observance of the Lord's Supper.[50] This can only be understood in light of Luke 24:30–35, where the recognition

---

goods, see the Hellenistic widows, 6:1–3.

44. Liddell and Scott, *Lexicon*, 1515. Προσκαρτερέω occurs five other times in Acts: joining together constantly in prayer (1:14), continuing to meet together (2:46), giving attention to prayer and the ministry of the word (6:4), following Philip (8:13), and being a personal attendant (10:7). Paul uses it to speak about devoting oneself to prayer (Rom 12:12; Col 4:2), and about rulers devoted to being servants of God (Rom 13:6).

45. Barrett, *Acts*, 1:163. Cf. 5:28; 13:12; 17:19, all instances of public preaching, while here it appears to be internal teaching.

46. Marshall, *Acts*, 83.

47. Gehring, *House*, 81–82; Goppelt, *Apostolic*, 43–45. The way the apostles preach and interpret the LXX can be seen in the evangelistic speeches in Acts, e.g., 2:16–36; 3:22–26.

48. Κοινωνία does not appear elsewhere in Acts, though its root, κοινός, "common," occurs at 2:44 and 4:32, referring to the practice of holding all things in common. Paul uses κοινωνία 3 times (Rom 15:26; 2 Cor 8:4; 9:13), referring to the contribution he is collecting for the Jerusalem church. Thucydides, *Hist.*, 3.10.1 and Plato, *Gorgias*, 507e use κοινωνία in connection with φιλία (friendship) to refer to an association or fellowship. It may also be the best way to translate the Qumran Community Rule's Hebrew references to their community (1 QS 6:7; 5:1). Barrett, *Acts*, 1:163.

49. Witherington, *Acts*, 160. Cf. Calvin's definition: "the mutual association, alms, and other duties of brotherly fellowship," *Acts*, 1:85.

50. Pesch, *Apostelgeschichte*, 1:130 advocates both meanings for the breaking of bread; Barrett, *Acts*, 1:165.

and presence of Jesus is directly associated with the breaking of the bread.[51] According to Luke this fellowship meal is central to early Christian worship, as the unique mark of their community (Luke 22:14–20; Acts 2:42, 46; 20:7, 11).[52] The house churches allow the early Christians to practice distinctively Christian worship and fellowship in safety and privacy from the earliest of days, and enable the emergence of a discrete Christian identity.[53]

4) *The prayers* (ταῖς προσευχαῖς): The plural, as opposed to 1:14, indicates a specific set of Christian "prayers." These early prayers are likely a combination of reflection on the Lord's Prayer and other Christological teaching (Matt 6:9–13; Luke 11:2–4), excerpts from the Psalter, early Christian psalms and hymns, and prayers of thanksgiving.[54]

These four elements form a summary picture of the inner life of the early house communities in Acts. The material and social context of these activities is the household (2:46), and they may be elements of a house worship service, possibly an order of worship.[55] These practices contribute to the devotion (προσκαρτερέω) of the early church, to the vitality of Christian household fellowship (κοινωνία), and therefore to the success of the early Christian mission as Luke presents it.

One tangible outworking of early Christian κοινωνία is their community of goods, the way that they "had everything in common" (εἶχον ἅπαντα κοινά, 2:44).[56] This is a voluntary and mutual arrangement, based on friendship rather than obligation.[57] There is a parallel to this practice

51. Witherington, *Acts*, 160. Cf. Mark 14:22–25; 1 Cor 11:18–30; Acts 20:7. Marshall, *Last Supper*, 76–140.

52. Dix, *Shape of the Liturgy*, 16–18. This breaking of bread celebration is "totally unique in their world . . . the notion of a sacramental 'communion' is foreign to both Judaism and the Essenes," Goppelt, *Apostolic*, 47. Jews fellowship around meals, but the Lord's Supper is different, for it celebrates Christ's redemptive sacrifice for their sins, which would be heretical for Jews. For Luke this practice of the Lord's Supper distinguishes Christians from Jews from the beginning and requires private places of worship where it can be performed.

53. Gehring, *House*, 85–86. The theological separation largely caused by the Christians' Christology, becomes more pronounced over time. It seems that in Luke's day Christian identity is still being explored, and Christian-Jewish relations are still being worked out.

54. For the distinctive practice of Christian prayer, found in Jesus's manner of addressing the Father personally, "Abba, Father!" (Mark 14:36; cf. Rom 8:15; Gal 4:6 for early Christian application of this practice), and the older Aramaic prayer form, "Marana tha," מרנא תא, μαράνα θά ("Come, our Lord!"; cf. 1 Cor 16:22 with 11:26; Rev 22:20), see Goppelt, *Apostolic*, 47. The Jewish community would forbid praying like this.

55. Gehring, *House*, 79–86.

56. Κοινά is a cognate with κοινωνία.

57. As opposed to a political/economic system, such as communism. Nowhere is

among the Essene community.[58] Sharing in a friendship context is a well-known Greco-Roman ideal, and outsiders would look favorably upon it.[59] The community of goods is further explained in Acts 4:32–35, where Luke claims that it is so effective that "there was not a needy person among them" (οὐδὲ γὰρ ἐνδεής τις ἦν ἐν αὐτοῖς, 4:34).[60]

Multiple factors may prompt Christians to practice the community of goods:[61] 1) their eschatological beliefs about the impending end of the world;[62] 2) the radical teachings of Jesus about selling all and sharing;[63] 3) an attempt at survival for poor members, who have been cut off from Jewish charities; 4) a missional strategy which makes Christianity more attractive to nonbelievers. Each of these likely contributes to the development of the community of goods, but the missional significance of this practice should not be overlooked. Through carefully crafted rhetoric, Luke is showing his readers that the fellowship of the early church, expressed in this habit of sharing their possessions generously, is attractive to outsiders, and leads to evangelistic conversations and other forms of person-to-person mission. This is underscored by the conclusion to this section, where "day by day the Lord added to their number those who were being saved" (2:47). This community practice is appealing particularly because this generous way of living is a widely known, though rarely obtained, ideal of Greco-Roman lifestyle.[64]

---

there any indication that this is a mandatory or involuntary practice, and Acts shows Christians still owning private property later in the narrative; Marshall, *Acts*, 84–85.

58. "That they might form a community in Torah and possessions . . . to form a communal spirit with regard to the Law and to wealth," 1 QS 1:11f; 5:2. Josephus comments on this Essene practice: "These men are despisers of riches . . . Nor is there any one to be found among them who hath more than another; for it is a law among them, that those who come to them must let what they have be common to the whole order, insomuch that among them all there is no appearance of poverty, or excess of riches, but every one's possessions are intermingled with every other's possessions; and so there is, as it were, one patrimony among all the brethren," *J.W.*, 2.122. For the differences between the Christian and Essene form, see Witherington, *Acts*, 162.

59. "That friends share all things is one of the most widely quoted maxims in ancient literature," Barrett, *Acts*, 1:168. Cf. Plato, *Laws*, 5.739; Aristotle, *Eth. Nic.*, 9.8; Cicero, *De Officiis*, 1.16.51. See also Mealand, "Community of Goods," 96–99; Keener, *Acts*, 1:1012–23.

60. Luke then gives a positive (Barnabas, 4:36–37) and a negative example (Ananias and Sapphira, 5:1–11).

61. Barrett, *Acts*, 1:168 contains a more thorough treatment of this question.

62. Thompson, "Gentile Mission," 18–27.

63. E.g., Matt 6:19–21. Cf. Luke 12:13–21, and Jesus's intensification of discipleship demands discussed in chapter 4.

64. It is also a fulfillment of Jesus's promise in John 13:35, which explicitly links community-based love for one another and mission. This is a common theme in the

The community of goods is Luke's best example of the extent to which the early church lives in unified κοινωνία fellowship, and the house church is the ideal structure in which to practice and display these attractive qualities.

Mission in the Early Jerusalem House Churches

The introduction identified three primary dimensions of outreach: public proclamation, person-to-person relational outreach, and lifestyle mission through living the Christian life in community in a way that attracts the curiosity of observers. Each of these forms of mission can be observed in Luke's account of the early Jerusalem church.

Luke depicts early leaders preaching publicly in Jerusalem: Peter at Pentecost (2:14–40) and at Solomon's porch in the temple (3:12–26), Peter and John after being miraculously released from prison (5:21–32), and Stephen to the Sanhedrin (7:2–53). This focus on gospel proclamation is captured in the prayer that God would help them to continue to speak his word with boldness (παρρησίας πάσης λαλεῖν τὸν λόγον σου, 4:29), after Peter and John are threatened with punishment if they continue to preach. This is a turning point—in the face of danger, they refuse to back down from courageous proclamation. 5:42 reports that they preach every day (πᾶσάν τε ἡμέραν), both in the temple and house to house. Luke wants the reader to understand that regular public proclamation is a primary factor in the rapid expansion of the Jerusalem church.

Public preaching alone cannot explain the rapid growth of the early church, which points to a grassroots evangelistic movement fueled by the empowerment of regular believers. Most Christians possess a missional attitude, but the manifestation of this varies.[65]

> One of the most striking features in evangelism in the early days was the people who engaged in it. Communicating the faith was not regarded as the preserve of the very zealous or of the officially designated evangelist. Evangelism was the prerogative and the duty of every Church member. We have seen apostles and wandering prophets, nobles and paupers, intellectuals and fishermen all taking part enthusiastically in this the primary task committed by Christ to his Church. The ordinary people of the Church saw it as their job: Christianity was supremely a lay movement, spread by informal missionaries ... The spontaneous

---

NT: John 15:12, 17; Rom 12:10–15; 13:8; Gal 5:13, 14; Eph 4:1–6; 1 Thess 3:12; 4:9–10; 5:13; 2 Thess 1:3; 1 Pet 1:22; 4:8; 1 John 3:10, 11, 23; 4:7–12; 2 John 1:5.

65. Gehring, *House*, 91.

outreach of the total Christian community gave immense impetus to the movement from the very outset.[66]

In Acts, when persecution breaks out in Jerusalem after Stephen's martyrdom, "they were all scattered . . . *except the apostles* (πλὴν τῶν ἀποστόλων) . . . those who had been scattered preached the word wherever they went" (διασπαρέντες διῆλθον εὐαγγελιζόμενοι τὸν λόγον, 8:1, 4). These are explicitly not the "elite evangelists," they are fleeing persecution, yet they share the gospel everywhere they go. Philip is one of these, and his interaction with the Ethiopian eunuch is one of the clearest examples in Acts of person-to-person mission (8:26–39).[67] Philip shares with the Ethiopian eunuch in Samaria, and travels about, "preaching the gospel in all the towns until he reached Caesarea" (8:40). Luke is emphasizing here that early believers evangelize naturally, even under intense pressure.

To underscore this point, Luke later reveals that, "those who were scattered because of the persecution . . . made their way to Phoenicia and Cyprus and Antioch, *speaking the word* (λαλοῦντες τὸν λόγον) . . . there were some of them . . . who came to Antioch and began *speaking* (ἐλάλουν) *to the Greeks also*" (11:19–20). These are nameless, regular believers, carrying out the mission by informally "speaking" the word of Christ to others. Green says of these unnamed believers that:

> They were evangelists, just as much as any apostle was . . . They were scattered from their base in Jerusalem and they went everywhere spreading the good news which had brought joy, release and a new life to themselves. This must often have been not formal preaching, but the informal chattering to friends and chance acquaintances, in homes and wine shops, on walks, and around market stalls. They went everywhere gossiping the gospel . . . naturally, enthusiastically, and with the conviction of those who are not paid to say that sort of thing.[68]

The οἶκος structure also reveals something of this grassroots missional dynamic. The ancient household provides a social network conducive to relational person-to-person mission, along with the ideal structure in which to organize and mentor converts. Householders share with householders, and slaves with slaves; a dinner invitation provides an avenue for relational

66. Green, *Evangelism*, 274.

67. "If public proclamation of various types and the private use of the home were crucial factors in the spread of the gospel, no less important was personal evangelism, as one individual shared his faith with another . . . One of the most striking examples in the New Testament is that of Philip and the Ethiopian Eunuch," Green, *Evangelism*, 223–24.

68. Green, *Evangelism*, 173.

outreach, as a form of house-to-house evangelism.[69] The conversion of Cornelius's household is an example of this kind of private, οἶκος-based relational outreach (Acts 10:23–48).[70] Aquila and Priscilla, who use their house-based tentmaking shop as a base for sharing the gospel in their networks in Corinth, are another snapshot of this kind of ministry (18:1–4). The book of Acts indicates that the growth of the church owes as much to the grassroots person-to-person efforts of ordinary Christians in their businesses, homes, and social networks as it does to the public preaching of the apostolic missionaries.

The οἶκος groups offer their members multiple benefits, such as a personal, family-like setting, the opportunity to develop mutually beneficial relationships, and practical support and encouragement, even in material concerns.[71] Early Christians become "one in heart and soul" (καρδία καὶ ψυχὴ μία, 4:32), and the οἶκος fellowships have a significant inward impact in areas such as unity, discipleship, personal growth and pastoral care.

But their fellowship also has an outward impact on those around them: "The way Christians lived in community with one another in spite of their social differences, the fact that they made the needs of one the concern of all . . . all of this generated a power that flowed out from their community, requiring and producing a response . . . these (house) groups were compellingly attractive, drawing others into their midst."[72] Acts makes this explicit in 2:46–47, which describes the vibrant house communities of the early church, and speaks of them having the favor of all the people (ἔχοντες χάριν πρὸς ὅλον τὸν λαόν), which results directly in people being added to their numbers day by day.[73]

Put simply, people are drawn to loving and healthy community. This vibrant Jerusalem fellowship is grounded in Jesus's teachings about love,[74] and contrasts with many other religious experiences around it.[75] The rela-

69. Gehring, House, 92.

70. Though this occurs in Caesarea, it surely happens in Jerusalem as well. Luke rarely records the details of mission behind closed doors, leaving his audience to read between the lines.

71. Gehring, House, 93.

72. Vogler, "Die Bedeutung," 788–89; translated by Gehring, House, 93.

73. Acts 5:12–14 implies a similar pattern.

74. Jesus's commandments to love God and neighbor (Mark 12:28–34), and to love one's enemies (Luke 6:27–36/Matt 5:38–48) would be foundational; Gehring, House, 94.

75. With the possible exception of the Essenes, Lohfink, Jesus and Community, 149–63, 181–85. Most scholars agree that there is an Essene presence in Jerusalem by this time; Capper, "Community of Goods," 1730. This may be a motivating factor for the church, which cannot afford to live a lifestyle less ethically attractive than its neighbors. Essenes probably do not practice the other forms of mission mentioned above,

tionally based οἶκος structure of the house churches empowers early Christians to live out this attractive and missionally effective form of κοινωνία and Luke presents this as one of the primary reasons why they grow so rapidly. The way they live attracts outsiders and sparks multiple missional contacts and relationships.

Gehring makes the following conclusion: "House churches . . . were a training ground for Christian koinonia fellowship inwardly and a showplace of Christian fellowship outwardly. This missional expansion of the gospel was due not so much to the mission-strategic initiatives of individuals as to the powerful attraction of a Christian community actively practicing koinonia fellowship."[76] While his point is compelling, he overstates his case. For Luke, early Christian success is due to the combination of all three forms of mission: public proclamation, relational evangelism, and lifestyle mission. To elevate any one above the others in importance is a mistake; Luke stresses that it is in their blending that they are most effective. However, in Acts the house church structure promotes person-to-person mission by catering to the οἶκος networks which provide the necessary relationships and facilitates lifestyle mission by displaying the attractiveness of household-based κοινωνία fellowship to the watching world.

Luke's rhetorical point is that there is a missional niche for every Christian, and the diversity of styles in Acts is what makes the church's mission so effective. He implicitly invites his readers to discover what works best for them. For the majority, the house church driven relational and lifestyle mission styles will be their preference, lived in the context of their home fellowships. However this works out, Luke urges every Christian to involve themselves in the mission.

House Church Leadership Structures in Jerusalem

Luke's presentation of the Jerusalem house churches also has leadership implications, which are another important aspect of his missional structures. One of the purposes of ancient rhetoric and historiography is to provide leadership development. In Luke's world history is didactic: "historians trained leaders for the *polis*, inculcating Greek or Roman ethics for their readers."[77] Luke is similarly instilling Christian leadership and political values through his recounting of the mission of the early church, in an attempt to equip a new generation of leaders in the church.

---

which explains why they do not grow in the same way.

76. Gehring, *House*, 94.

77. Balch, "Acts as Epideictic History," xiv.

Acts 1–2 records the status transformation of the disciples, as they grow from being followers (μαθητής) to missional leaders (ἀπόστολος) within the Christian community.[78] In presenting this leadership transition, Luke solves the leadership crisis created by Judas's betrayal, and launches a "massive propaganda campaign" to restore the leadership integrity and reputation of the early leaders.[79] The transformed leadership team of "the twelve" (οἱ δώδεκα, 6:2) emerges from scandal to lead the earliest community, with Matthias replacing Judas (1:15–26). Peter is the natural leader of this group,[80] while John, son of Zebedee, is a secondary leader,[81] and together with his brother James they form an informal oversight team for the primitive church.[82] Their community initially gathers around the house with the upper room as a place for fellowship, prayer, worship, and teaching (1:13–14).[83]

Under Peter's leadership, the events involving the Hellenists led by Stephen unfold, resulting in another influential early leadership team (6:1–6). This event reveals a key to leadership development in the church, for the twelve instruct the congregation to, "choose seven men from among you (ἄνδρας ἐξ ὑμῶν) who are respected and known (μαρτυρουμένους) to be full of the Holy Spirit and wisdom" (πλήρεις Πνεύματος Ἁγίου καὶ σοφίας, 6:3). These leadership qualifications are significant. The first is that they must be "from among you," established and well-known members of the community. The second is similar; μαρτυρέω in Acts often refers to people of good reputation, who are respected because a good report is spoken about them (10:22; 16:2; 22:12). Finally, the apostles seek people who are *known* to be full of the Spirit and wisdom.[84] Each requirement highlights a central issue: relational respect, reputation, and longevity within the community. The Apostles affirm these characteristics when they formally commission

78. Estrada, *Followers to Leaders*, uses rituals of status transformation to trace each step of this transformation in Acts 1–2: Separation, Transition (Liminality-Communitas, and Ritual Confrontation), and finally Aggregation.

79. Estrada, *Followers to Leaders*, 230–37.

80. E.g., Acts 1:15–22; 2:14–41; 4:8–12; 5:3–15, 29.

81. The text emphasizes Peter and John as a leadership pair: Acts 3:1–11; 4:1–3, 6–19; 8:14–25.

82. Jesus focuses on training these three for ministry: Luke 8:51 (the healing of the synagogue official's daughter); 9:28 (the Transfiguration); cf. Mark 13:3 (private questioning); 14:33 (in Gethsemane).

83. The anonymous owner of this house plays a crucial role as patron of the early community; the twelve would not be able to buy houses after three years of itinerant ministry.

84. Being full of the Spirit is a theme in Acts (2:4; 4:8, 31; 6:5; 7:55; 9:17; 11:24; 13:9, 52), and being full of wisdom echoes one of the attributes assigned to the development of Jesus (Luke 2:40, 52). Parsons, *Acts*, 84.

the seven by prayer and the laying on of hands (6:5–6). This episode illustrates the early church's practice of relationally selecting and developing "home-grown" leaders and teams, and Luke emphasizes God's blessing in the community's resulting growth, including the surprising conversion of many Jewish priests (6:7).

Because this is an οἶκος culture, many of the early Christian house church leaders gain the experience needed to carry out their positions through being Jewish housefathers or Greco-Roman *pater familias*.[85] As such, they have responsibility and protective duties for their household, are wealthy enough to own or rent their own home, are equipped for administrative tasks as the financial managers of their homes, are educated, have experience in teaching their households, and are natural leaders in local community affairs, as patrons possessing a degree of social honor and privilege.[86] For this reason, in general, "the church in the house came with its leadership so to speak 'built in,'" as householders naturally become house church leaders.[87] The house churches in turn serve as the training grounds for the emerging overseers of the citywide and regional church. By developing their leadership skills, growing in character and maturity, learning basic theology through regular study and teaching, developing pastoral care skills, and proving themselves to be capable leaders in the house church environment, they become ideal candidates for positions of oversight within the wider church.[88]

Herod Agrippa I eventually kills James, the brother of John, and then goes on to arrest Peter (12:2–3). Despite his miraculous escape from prison, Peter decides to leave Jerusalem (12:17). In Peter's absence two distinct groups of leaders emerge to provide oversight: the apostles and the elders (ἀπόστολοι καὶ πρεσβύτεροι, 15:2, 4, 6, 22). Luke implies that the apostles become informal overseers of the wider church as it emerges extra-locally, while the elders have specific responsibilities within the local network of Jerusalem house churches. Jesus's brother James becomes the head of the elders (12:17; 15:13; 21:18), and the church begins to organize itself in a more structured way. From this time on, James and a team of elders lead the congregation,[89] and this proves to be a stable presbyterial organization until

---

85. Gehring, *House*, 97; Goppelt, *Apostolic*, 51, 53.

86. Gehring, *House*, 194–95.

87. Campbell, *Elders*, 126. This proves to be important in the emerging leadership of the Pauline churches.

88. Gehring, *House*, 97–98. The emerging church leaders could also prove their trustworthiness in other ways, such as business, the marketplace, the synagogue or temple, or as a teacher in someone else's home.

89. Five uses of πρεσβύτερος in Acts relate to the Jerusalem church after Peter has left and James is leading: 15:2, 6, 22; 16:4; 21:18. 11:30 also points towards this time. Two

James is martyred.[90] This stretch of relative calm under James's leadership provides invaluable stability, especially after the tumultuous adjustments of the first few years of the church, allowing the community to establish and strengthen itself in Jerusalem and elsewhere.

Where do these "elders" (πρεσβύτεροι, and later ἐπίσκοποι) come from?[91] The words likely begin as informal terms of honor, possibly linked to the status of householders or house church leaders.[92] Keener claims that the early Christians probably adapt the term "elder" from contemporary Judaism.[93] As the church grows in complexity they evolve into increasingly formal leadership positions to match the church's needs.[94]

Luke's presentation of the church in Acts emphasizes certain leadership characteristics. Most importantly, church leadership is based on relationship and emerges out of community; spiritual influence is earned through trust and proven reliability over time (6:1–6). Leadership is also fluid and flexible, with only the minimal necessary structure applied.[95] There should be space for leaders to develop naturally in their own way, facilitated by the house church networks. There is a degree of relational training and mentoring for those being prepared for leadership,[96] and many non-apostles have leader-

---

further references are to Pauline churches: 14:23; 20:17. Eldership appears to become a model for church leadership under James's leadership in Luke's story. Πρεσβύτερος is also used of the Jewish Council of the elders eight times: 4:5, 8, 23; 6:12; 22:5; 23:14; 24:1; 25:15. The Jewish eldership likely influences early Christian leadership structures.

90. See Josephus, *Ant.*, 20.200. The death of James and other early leaders is a crisis for the church, and Luke may be writing partly to address this.

91. Ἐπίσκοποι are not mentioned until 20:28 of the Ephesian elders. Luke appears to use πρεσβύτερος and ἐπίσκοπος interchangeably, using both words to refer to the Ephesian elders at Miletus (20:17, 28).

92. Gehring, *House*, 104–5.

93. Keener, *Acts*, 2:2187; for a broader discussion of elders, 2:2184–9.

94. There is no formal "office" of elder presiding over the services of the Jewish synagogues. Rather, elders in the ancient world in general, and in the synagogues in particular, are people with honor and seniority, but not necessarily office, rank, or function. This is thus a stronger Christian contribution than many earlier scholars have recognized. Campbell, *Elders*, 44–45, 95, 111–12, 160; Harvey, "Elders," 332: "we know virtually nothing about the functions and privileges of Christian elders for at least the first century of their existence . . . we should not any longer cloak our ignorance with a spurious picture of them drawn from a totally supposititious Jewish 'eldership.'"

95. See the progression from ἀπόστολος to πρεσβύτερος to ἐπίσκοπος in Acts.

96. Acts implies that Barnabas mentors Paul (11:25–26; 13:1–7; note their name order); Paul mentors younger leaders, e.g., Timothy, Silas, Gaius (15:40—16:3; throughout his journeys); Priscilla and Aquila mentor Apollos (18:24–26). This is likely modeled on Jesus's close rabbi/disciple mentoring relationships with his disciples in Luke's Gospel.

ship and influence in the early church.[97] Finally, Acts stresses the synergy of team leadership and ministry. From the upper room (1:13–14), through Pentecost (2:1, 14, 41), Peter and John (3:1–31), the choosing of the Seven (6:1–6), the Antioch leadership (13:1–3), and the elder teams (15:2, 6, 22; 16:4; 21:18), the normative pattern is team,[98] so much so that it is difficult to find any leader alone in Acts, and never for any extended period.[99]

Luke wants the reader to understand that all these characteristics contribute to a fluid and dynamic leadership culture in the church and are instrumental in its missional development. The church's ability to produce quality leaders at all levels and to empower every person in its midst to engage with missional ministry are two of the keys to its ultimate success. The οἶκος structure directly benefits and supports all these aspects of the leadership culture of the early church. For Luke, this is further justification of the house church structure, which he commends to his readers throughout Acts. He urges the church of his day to cultivate relational leadership networks and teams, organic local leadership development, intentional leadership mentoring, and a focus on the empowerment of the congregations. These all happen best in a house church network, an effective missional leadership structure with a simple and fluid organization.

THE HOUSE CHURCH BETWEEN JERUSALEM AND THE PAULINE MISSION—ACTS 8–13

After Stephen's martyrdom (Acts 7), persecution breaks out in Jerusalem and scatters the church throughout the surrounding regions (8:1–4).[100]

---

97. E.g., the unnamed preachers and missionaries (8:1–4; 11:19–20); the Hellenistic seven (6:1–3), particularly Stephen (6:5, 8, 10, 15; 7:55–60), and Philip (8:5–8); Silas (15:22–40; 16:19, 25, 29; 17:4, 10); Priscilla and Aquila (18:2, 18, 26); Apollos (18:24–28). Additionally, one must wonder who establishes and leads the churches at Damascus (9:2–22), Antioch (11:19–21; 13:1–3), and Rome (18:2), who the elders in the Pauline churches are (14:23: 20:17–38), who the "brothers" in Puteoli (28:13–14) and Rome (28:15–16) are, and how all these leaders are trained. Many people in the Acts narrative outside of the apostles are placed into positions of effective leadership within the early church.

98. Additionally, Paul travels with Barnabas, John Mark, Silas, Timothy, Luke, Aquila, Priscilla, Sopater, Aristarchus and Secundus, Gaius, Timothy, Tychicus, and Trophimus. All these ministry teams create natural leadership training environments.

99. Philip seems alone in Samaria (8:4–40), Peter may be alone in Lydda and Caesarea (9:32—10:48), and Paul is only rarely on his own (14:11; 17:14–34; 18:21, 23; 17:15 shows Paul's discomfort while traveling alone).

100. Damascus, Caesarea, and Antioch are Hellenist centers, along with Alexandria, and possibly Rome; Bruce, *Men*, 60. For background on the Hellenists see

Ironically, the expulsion from Jerusalem accelerates the spread of Christianity and brings the fulfillment of Acts 1:8 closer.

Philip, Saul, and Peter

Philip carries the gospel beyond its previous Jewish boundaries to the God-fearers and Samaritans (8:4–13, 26–40).[101] He develops an itinerant village to village ministry, similar to Jesus's approach (8:5–7, 26–28, 40: "he traveled about preaching the gospel in all the towns," πόλεις πάσας).[102] Luke implies that he eventually sets up residence in Caesarea (21:8–9),[103] and then targets the villages and cities in the surrounding area in a regional missional strategy, healing the sick, casting out demons, demonstrating God's power, and preaching the gospel. Luke records that many believe the message, are baptized, and subsequently receive the Holy Spirit (8:12–17). The normative pattern of Acts is that when people believe they join house communities, and so these stories probably suggest that new house fellowships begin in Samaria. Because the text is not clear about this, Philip's Samarian outreach receives a rating of [1].[104]

Saul travels to persecute the church in Damascus, which must be another early Christian center (9:1–19).[105] After his encounter with Jesus, Paul stays in the house of Judas on Straight Street (οἰκία Ἰούδα), is baptized, and receives instruction from Ananias for "several days" (ἡμέρας τινάς, 9:10–19). This may point towards a house-based training program for new converts,

---

Witherington, *Acts*, 240–51; Stevens, *Acts*, 73–111, 211–85. Penner, *In Praise* analyzes the Stephen material in this Hellenist section of Acts, and argues that Acts is best understood as epideictic historiography.

101. Gentile Palestinian cities such as Gaza (8:26), Ashdod, and Caesarea (8:40) are pivotal in his mission.

102. Gehring, *House*, 106. See Luke 8:1; 9:56; 10:38; 13:22; 17:12, for Jesus's village to village ministry.

103. Acts 21:8–9 reveals that Philip is a homeowner in Caesarea; a house church likely meets in his home, as it is large enough to offer Paul and his companions hospitality. Along with Cornelius's house, this may be a second Caesarean house church; Gehring, *House*, 106. Caesarea is a larger urbanized area than any other "city" the Christians have ministered in, and a stepping-stone towards urban ministry in Antioch, the third largest city in the Empire. Johnson, *Paul*, 145–50.

104. Philip encounters the eunuch during this time, who returns to Ethiopia rejoicing (8:39), and possibly starts churches there as well.

105. It is unknown how the Damascus church starts, possibly through the Hellenists, or Diaspora Jews who convert at Pentecost. It must be sizeable by this point to attract Paul's attention. For a concise review of proposed sources for Acts 9:1–19, see Jervell, *Apostelgeschichte*, 291n60.

as Gehring argues, though this is uncertain.[106] There are hints of a large congregation in Damascus, which could have met in Judas's house, among others (9:2, 19; 22:5). However, "Luke gives no indication that Judas is a believer let alone a 'house-church' host. While Ananias is introduced as 'a disciple,' no such descriptor is applied to Judas."[107] This passage illustrates the caution scholars must exercise in interpreting references to houses in Acts, particularly when they are not explicitly linked to church meeting places. However, the passage does show Paul's early training happening in a private home, and so receives a ranking of [2].

Like Philip, Peter also employs an itinerant ministry approach (9:32—10:48) similar to Jesus's mission discourse (Luke 10:1-12).[108] He "travels around from place to place" (διερχόμενον, 9:32), visits Lydda, where he heals Aeneas (9:33-35), and then continues to Joppa. Peter's raising of Tabitha from the dead takes place in a personal home in Joppa (9:36-43), in another upper room (ὑπερῷον, 9:37, 39).[109] Luke says that this miracle "became known all over Joppa, and many people believed in the Lord. And Peter stayed in Joppa *many days* (ἡμέρας ἱκανάς) with a tanner named Simon" (9:42-43), implying that this house becomes a missional hub for that area. However, Luke gives no definitive indication that Simon's house serves in this way, so once again, scholars must not read too much into this reference to Simon's house. The text is explicit that Simon's home hosts the initial raising of Tabitha, and hints at subsequent missional activity in Peter's extended stay there, so this episode receives a ranking of [3].

While Peter is staying at Simon's home in Joppa, a God-fearing householder named Cornelius invites Peter into his home, receives the peace greeting, and gives him shelter (10:22-24). Cornelius's entire household receives the word of God, following their head of household (10:44-48; 11:1). After this, the family invites Peter to stay a few days, presumably to establish this new house church through further teaching and discipleship instruction (10:48). In Luke's narrative world this serves as the foundation story of the Caesarean church, and the reader is left to surmise that Cornelius's

---

106. Gehring, *House*, 107 argues that new converts would have to live in such a household community at this time. Luke does imply that those in Damascus help to influence and mentor Paul in these earliest days of his Christian faith. See Acts 22:12–16 for Paul's recounting of Ananias's influence on him.

107. Adams, *Meeting Places*, 62.

108. The difference is that rather than going "randomly" from house to house, the Spirit instructs Peter, particularly in the case of Cornelius's house. Gehring, *House*, 107.

109. Luke also uses ὑπερῷον of the pre-Pentecost upper room (1:13), and of the upper room in Troas where Eutychus falls from the window (20:8). Upper rooms may have theological significance in Luke's story, or they may simply be the natural gathering space in larger private homes. The word does not appear outside of Acts in the NT.

house becomes a base of operations for outreach to the city and surrounding area, thus fulfilling the second stage of the missional progression Jesus had laid out to Peter and the other disciples (Luke 10:1–20). The Cornelius episode thus parallels Jesus's outreach instructions, and indicates an οἶκος mission approach in Caesarea.[110] The Caesarean community develops into a significant regional church over the following years (18:22; 21:8, 16).

This episode shows a house and regional mission strategy in which a seed is planted and grows into a church with a regional impact, all based around Cornelius's οἶκος. Luke focuses on the original evangelistic sermon and household conversion, and "the text does not inform us of further developments regarding the house of Cornelius."[111] Cornelius's house is a meeting place for missional proclamation and the gathering of the new church/household, regardless of the uncertainty about the future, so this episode receives a ranking of [4].

Luke is highlighting the centrality and versatility of the οἶκος structure in these stories, for private homes function as indispensable venues for missional activity. Whether they become fully fledged "house churches" or not, Luke is advocating the missional use of the οἶκος structure. While caution must be exercised when Luke does not make this explicit in the text, Luke has established a narrative pattern of house church growth in the earlier parts of Acts and means for readers to assume that this continues to be the case when he mentions households in similar contexts in later portions of the narrative, particularly in light of Jesus's foundational example in Luke 10:1–20.

The Church at Syrian Antioch

Some of the persecuted Christians flee Jerusalem and relocate to Antioch,[112] where they establish a church (11:19–21).[113] "The summary of the establishment of the church in Antioch presents an important new development, both geographically and ethnically. The gospel reaches a major city of the

110. Gehring, *House*, 108.

111. Gehring, *House*, 108.

112. Syrian Antioch (on the Orontes) is the third city of the Empire after Rome and Alexandria (Josephus, *J.W.*, 3.29); as the capital of the province of Syria and a commercial center with a population of at least half a million, it is the first cosmopolitan city where Christianity establishes itself. Witherington, *Acts*, 366.

113. These are men originally from Cyprus and Cyrene; there is a large and well-established Jewish community in Antioch by this time. Estimates for the Jewish population of Antioch at the time of Augustus vary from 45,000 (Kraeling, "Jewish Community," 136, 147) to "around 22,000" (Meeks and Wilken, *Jews and Christians*, 8).

empire and finds a ready response from people of Greek culture, including Gentiles."[114] This church evangelizes its own city, and the surrounding area, and ultimately becomes the launching point for an international mission.

Luke reveals that those at Antioch begin speaking to the "Hellenists/ Greeks" (Ἑλληνιστάς, or possibly Ἕλληνας, 11:20).[115] Intentional multicultural church is first attempted here, as Gentiles and Jews seek fellowship and unity, and out of this the first Gentile-focused mission is born.[116] Luke emphasizes three times how responsive the city is, and how quickly the church grows numerically (11:21, 24, 26). Their contribution (διακονίαν) to the "mother church" in Jerusalem also highlights the strength and wealth of this church (11:28–30). Finally, Luke mentions that the disciples are first called "Christians" in Antioch (Χριστιανούς, 11:26).[117] This new name suggests a distinguishable and visible group, presumably because of the many Gentiles involved, and because of the size of the community.[118] A group that stands out like this in cosmopolitan Antioch would have a significant social impact on the city.

"That the church in Antioch met κατ' οἶκον in the private domestic houses of affluent members as in Jerusalem is probable simply because this was the case for the overwhelming majority of all believers in the early Christian movement for the first three centuries."[119] There are likely multiple wealthy homeowners in the early stages of the development of the

---

114. Tannehill, *Narrative Unity*, 2:146.

115. The textual variant is debated, but the context implies Greek speaking Gentiles as well as Hellenized Jews; Witherington, *Acts*, 369.

116. Slee, *Church in Antioch* analyzes the conflict and resolution between Jews and Gentiles at Antioch. She examines Acts 15, Gal 2:1–14, the Didache, and Matthew's Gospel for models of how the problems of Gentile entry and Jewish-Gentile table fellowship are handled, concluding that though the Antioch church is almost destroyed by these issues, it produces an effective solution, which restores unity and ensures its survival.

117. Literally, "the disciples in Antioch transacted business (χρηματίζω) for the first time [under the name of] Christians," Bruce, *Acts*, 274. Χριστιανούς means those belonging to, identified with, or following Christ. The term occurs here, Acts 26:28, and 1 Pet 4:16, all from others speaking about Christians, probably initially as a term of contempt and ridicule. Christians do not adopt this name until the second century (Ignatius), instead preferring to call themselves disciples, believers, saints, brothers and sisters, or followers of "the Way." Mattingly, "Origin," 26–37, compares it to the Augustiani, Caesarani, etc.

118. This does not necessarily imply a separate group outside of Judaism, as the Herodians, loyal to Herod the Great and his dynasty (Mark 3:6; 12:13; Matt 22:16) are an example of a distinguishable group within Judaism. However, the Gentiles involved at Antioch suggest a growing separation.

119. Gehring, *House*, 109.

Antioch church, who act as patrons for the emerging house communities.[120] The established leadership team of the church (13:1)[121] indicates that the church has already grown beyond the initial phase of development, where it consisted of merely one or a few house churches, into a citywide organization, with a plurality of local house fellowships.[122] Though the text is not explicit about Antioch house churches, many of these gatherings throughout the city certainly meet in private homes, given the implied size and wealth of the church and the pattern already established in Acts, so this episode receives a ranking of [3].

Acts 13:1–3 is a rare glimpse into the inner workings of a missional community, and a turning point in the narrative of Acts. Barnabas and Paul have taught and lived with this church for a year (11:25–26),[123] as two of the five "prophets and teachers" (προφῆται καὶ διδάσκαλοι) who oversee the church (13:1).[124] This is another important leadership team in Acts which oversees the network of house groups and the emerging extra-local outreach.[125]

Luke presents this church as a dynamic spiritual environment, in which regular fasting (νηστευόντων, twice), prayer (προσευξάμενοι), and "ministering to the Lord and the community" (λειτουργούντων τῷ κυρίῳ) permeate the community (13:2–3).[126] As a result of this seeking of God's presence and will, the Holy Spirit directs them towards mission (ἀφορίσατε δή μοι, "set apart for me!"),[127] and they commission the designated people ("release them," ἀπέλυσαν) with more prayer and fasting and the laying on

120. All those listed in 13:1 are probably homeowners of significant social status; Nicholas the proselyte from Antioch can also be counted (6:5). God-fearers and proselytes tend to be wealthier, and there are many living in Antioch; Kraeling, "Jewish Community," 147.

121. Gehring, *House*, 112 proposes that these may be outstanding house church leaders, who form a leadership council for the citywide network of house churches in Antioch.

122. This is also supported by the fact that others give them the name "Christians," indicating a size considerable enough to stand out in a cosmopolitan center.

123. Presumably this is outreach ministry done in the city and region, laying foundations for later mission work.

124. It is best to understand these five as both prophets and teachers—Paul is certainly both (11:26; 13:9–11).

125. Luke implies that the Antioch church is flourishing, and this allows it to extend outreach to other areas. This leadership team includes "Simeon called Niger," suggestive of an African origin; Johnson, *Acts*, 220.

126. Λειτουργούντων τῷ κυρίῳ implies serving the Lord by taking care of the community needs on his behalf, and includes the Lord, the church, and the wider community which it serves.

127. Probably spoken through a prophet.

of hands (ἐπιθέντες τὰς χεῖρας, 13:3).[128] For believers in Antioch, mission emerges directly out of the vibrancy of their spiritual connection with God and with one another.

The missionaries then embark on their itinerant journey of outreach and return to the church to give a report upon completion of their task (14:26–27; cf. Luke 10:17–20).[129] This incident "represents the first deliberate and professional missionary activity . . . the spread of the Gospel can no longer take place haphazardly but is to be a planned activity of the Church, carried out by certain people on behalf of the whole Church."[130] They model their outreach on Jesus's mission instruction tradition for radical itinerants (Luke 10:1–20), traveling in pairs, renouncing the right to marry, to own personal property, and to have a permanent residence, and operating as exorcists and healers.[131] It follows, therefore, that they pursue an intentional household strategy, reaching heads of households and their οἶκος relationships to establish hubs for mission, which then develop into city-wide, regional, and eventually extra-regional οἶκος-based movements. In time they send out their own missionaries to repeat the process again.[132] In this way, the missional cycle reproduces itself many times over, in multiple different regions, loosely following the pattern Jesus sets in Luke 10:1–20.

These events at Antioch represent a watershed in the missionary endeavors of the early church. Although Gentiles have already been converted (Acts 8, 10), this is the first attempt at planned evangelism of Gentiles as well as Jews. "Here in Acts 13:1–3 they are commissioned to the full-time and intentional pursuit of the Gentile mission. As such it marks a major division in the story of Acts."[133] It is also the first intentional effort at extra-regional or international outreach, and thus a further fulfillment of Jesus's promise in Acts 1:8.

---

128. "The church that selflessly gave to relieve fasting imposed by famine (11:27–30) now engages in fasting for religious purposes," Parsons, *Acts*, 185. In addition to Paul and Barnabas, other missionaries are sent out from Antioch, including Mark and Silas (Acts 15:38–39; 13:1).

129. Gehring, *House*, 109. This accountability is crucial to the long-term sustainability of the Antioch model.

130. Best, "Acts 13:1–3," 345, 348.

131. 1 Cor 7:7; Phil 4:11–13; 2 Cor 6:10; 11:27; Acts 4:36–37. Jesus's instructions are sometimes modified slightly, for instance, at times they attempt to provide for themselves. Cf. 1 Cor 9:6, 12–18 with Matt 10:9–10. For healing and exorcism, see Acts 13 and 14. Gehring, *House*, 110.

132. This is certainly true of Paul's missionary journeys, see next section and part 3.

133. Parsons, *Acts*, 185.

Luke presents the Antioch church to his readers as the model missional church, impacting not just its immediate surroundings but many other areas as well.

Table 7.1 Missional Characteristics of the Church at Antioch

- A *vibrant spiritual environment* in which people devote themselves to God's presence, live a lifestyle characterized by prayer, worship, and fasting, and the Holy Spirit speaks (13:2–3; 11:26).
- *Team leadership* with primary prophetic and teaching functions (13:1).
- A *diverse demographic* of people from varying ethnic and social backgrounds (11:20; 13:1).
- A *group of wealthy patrons and donors* to resource the mission (11:30; 13:1; 6:5).
- A *broad geographical vision* which takes seriously Jesus's mandate to the ends of the earth, resulting in the sending of missionaries to faraway places (13:3–4; 14:26; 15:40; 18:23).
- A *mission team concept*, training and commissioning missionaries in groups (13:3; 14:26; 15:39–40).
- A *simple, home-based church model* which is easily reproduced (11:26; Paul's journeys).
- A *bold missional ethos* which inspires people to grow the church locally and travel great distances to spread the gospel (11:20–21, 24, 26; Paul's journeys).
- A *large and growing local congregation*, possessing the "strength in numbers" to generate the momentum required to birth a church planting movement (11:21, 24, 26).
- A *prevalent "culture"* in which the lives of local members exude Christlikeness (11:26).
- A *practice of pastoral care and accountability* that ensures those sent out have follow-up and long-term relationships (14:26; 18:22–23).[134]

These characteristics combine to create a sustainable and reproducible church planting movement. Luke describes this exceptional Antioch church

---

134. On "accountability" in Acts, see discussions in part 3 about Antioch as Paul's missionary base.

in such rare detail because it illustrates the dynamic potential of a missional church and he wants his readers to emulate its example.

HOUSE CHURCHES IN THE PAULINE MISSION—ACTS 13-21

The most famous missionary who emerges from the Antioch church is the Apostle Paul.[135] Everywhere he goes, he either starts a new house church, or supports an existing house church.[136] In Acts 20:20 Luke shows that Paul makes the home the hub of his ministry: "I did not shrink from . . . teaching you publicly and from house to house (κατ᾽ οἴκους)."[137] This summary statement reveals a regular practice of teaching and proclamation in homes during Paul's lengthy Ephesian ministry, and so receives a ranking of [4].

There are ten additional possible references to house churches in the Pauline mission in Acts.[138] Lydia and her household in Philippi (16:14–15, 40) are the first. There is consensus that this is a fully developed house church, largely indicated by the description in 16:40, so this receives a ranking of [4].[139] The second is the jailer and his household in Philippi (16:29–34); some see this as another Philippian "church origin" report,[140] though others disagree.[141] The account is ambiguous, though Luke may hint at a second house church forming here, so it receives a ranking of [2]. The third is the house of

135. Because Luke chooses to focus on him; there are others sent out from Antioch in similar fashion, such as Barnabas, Mark, and Silas. The book of Acts is a selective recounting of a much larger story.

136. Paul starts a church in nearly every city in which he spends any significant time: Pisidian Antioch (13:48–49), Iconium (13:1–3), Lystra (14:6–21), Derbe (14:21), Philippi (16:13–15, 40), Thessalonica (17:4), Berea (17:12), Athens (17:34), Corinth (18:8), Ephesus (19:8–12, 17, 20). Luke mentions 18 cities in Paul's travel and in nearly all of these his visits are for the founding, building up, or encouragement of the mission churches.

137. The structure of the churches is identical to the ones with which Paul is already familiar, house churches.

138. It can be assumed that Sergius Paulus's household is also involved in Paphos (13:6–12), though Luke never explicitly mentions his house. Similarly, Paul must have a householder's offer of hospitality in every location in which he stays, including Pisidian Antioch, Iconium, Lystra, Derbe, and Perga. This section is only summarized as part 3 will deal with these instances in more detail.

139. Hemer, *Acts*, 114.

140. Matson, *Household Conversion*, 154–68; Gehring, *House*, 124; this is largely based on supposed allusions to the Lord's Supper, which are not entirely convincing.

141. Adams, *Meeting Places*, 58–59: "Taking v. 40 into account, we might infer that the jailer and his dependents join with the 'brothers' meeting in Lydia's house."

Jason in Thessalonica (17:1–9). Blue claims Jason's house is a meeting place for Thessalonian believers;[142] Adams responds, "this is not an unreasonable deduction, but we are not explicitly informed by Luke that Jason's house is an assembly venue."[143] In Luke's narrative world this is very likely a reference to an early house church, so this episode receives a ranking of [3].

The next three possibilities are all in Corinth, beginning with the house of Aquila (18:1–4). It may be reasonable to assume Priscilla and Aquila do in Corinth what they go on to do at Ephesus and Rome (1 Cor 16:19; Rom 16:5), as Murphy-O'Connor and Giles both argue.[144] However, as Adams reminds readers, "Luke does not actually mention here a church in their home."[145] Due to the conjecture required here, this instance receives a ranking of [1]. The fifth occurrence is the house of Titius Justus (18:7). The text indicates that Paul moves from the synagogue as his "preaching center" to the house of Titius Justus, though it could also be translated as Paul left Aquila's house to live in Titius Justus's home. There is no definite mention of this house serving as a venue for Paul's Corinthian preaching and ministry, though it is implied, and so receives a ranking of [3].[146] The sixth possible instance is the house of Crispus (18:8). Crispus's whole household believes in the Lord, which hints at the birth of another house church, but there is no unequivocal mention of his house functioning as a church meeting place, so this receives a ranking of [2].[147]

The seventh reference is the large house in Troas with the upper room (20:7–12). This episode appears to be a weekly worship service, including a communion celebration and preaching, and most are convinced this is a house church, so this instance receives a ranking of [4].[148] The eighth concerns Paul's visit to Philip the evangelist at Caesarea (21:8–14). The text refers to gathered Caesarean Christians and may refer to Philip's house as the gathering place,[149] but this is not explicit, so this episode receives a ranking of [3].[150]

142. Blue, "House Church," 187.

143. Adams, *Meeting Places*, 60.

144. Murphy-O'Connor, "Prisca and Aquila;" Giles, "House Churches," 6.

145. Adams, *Meeting Places*, 62.

146. Barrett, *Acts*, 2:867; Adams, *Meeting Places*, 60–61.

147. Adams, *Meeting Places*, 64.

148. Adams, *Meeting Places*, 54.

149. Neyrey, "Teaching You," 90.

150. Adams, *Meeting Places*, 61.

The ninth reference is Mnason's house in Jerusalem (21:16). Blue believes this is a Jerusalem house church,[151] and Adams concedes that this could be the case, but Luke does not confirm this;[152] for this reason, this episode receives a ranking of [2]. The final reference is Paul's rented home in Rome (28:16–31). Paul's house functions as a venue for missional proclamation over a two-year period, as well as being a teaching center for Christians, but it is not explicitly a full house church as some claim,[153] so it receives a ranking of [3].[154]

Luke implies that all these private houses play a significant missional role in their city.[155] Though not always explicit in the text, each may be a church origin account in Acts, founded upon an existing house and household.[156] Luke depicts houses and households as strategic missional structures, regardless of whether he means for each of them to be understood as fully developed house churches. This Pauline practice of planting house churches is no surprise, given how influenced he and Barnabas are by the Jerusalem and Antioch churches.[157] Paul's missional strategies will be examined in more detailed in part 3.

This confirms a normative pattern: Paul continues the practice of community and mission formation around a core family in private domestic homes, just as has been seen in Jesus's teaching and ministry, in the early Jerusalem church, and in the outreach of Philip and Peter. "Houses served as community centers for the life of the church and as operational bases for missional outreach; as such they were a powerful force for the mission enterprise in all these places."[158] The house church's flexibility is ideally suited to the morphing Christian movement as it spreads across the Empire.

---

151. Blue, "House Church," 176.

152. Adams, *Meeting Places*, 63.

153. Gehring, *House*, 146.

154. Adams, *Meeting Places*, 55.

155. Gehring, *House*, 128–30. There are locations in Acts in which houses are not explicitly mentioned, such as Athens and Ephesus.

156. For more discussion on most of these, see Gehring, *House*, 121–55; Adams, *Meeting Places*, 51–67.

157. There are multiple references to other Pauline house churches in his own writing, including the church in Nympha's house in Laodicea (Col 4:15, a disputed Pauline letter, but almost certainly a Pauline church), in Aquila and Priscilla's house in Corinth (1 Cor 16:19) and in their house in Rome (Rom 16:3, 5; cf. 14–15, 23), and in the home of Archippus, likely in Colossae (Phlm 1–2, 21–22). There are other indirect references, particularly to Corinth (1 Cor), and to Phoebe in Cenchreae (Rom 16:1–2).

158. Gehring, *House*, 116.

CONCLUSION—THE IMPORTANCE
OF THE HOUSE CHURCH

This chapter has surveyed possible examples of house churches in Acts and commented on how mission and community structures function in these various locations. It has examined 22 total possible references to house churches, categorized into the following ratings.

Table 7.2 Possible References to House Churches in Acts, Ranked by Likelihood

[4] Definite—the text is explicit (8 occurrences, half in Jerusalem)

- Jerusalem—12:12, 17 (two house churches)
- Jerusalem—2:46
- Jerusalem—5:42
- Cornelius in Caesarea—10:1—11:18
- Lydia in Philippi—16:14-15, 40
- Large house in Troas—20:7-12
- Ephesus—20:20

[3] Likely—the text is not explicit, but there are multiple significant hints (8 occurrences)

- Jerusalem—1:12-14
- Damascus—8:3
- Joppa—9:33-43
- Antioch—11:19-30; 13:1-3
- Jason in Thessalonica—17:1-9
- Titius Justus in Corinth—18:7
- Philip in Caesarea—21:8-14
- Paul's rented house in Rome—28:16-31

[2] Uncertain—the text is unclear, but there is at least one hint (4 occurrences)

- Judas in Damascus—9:11-19
- The jailer in Philippi—16:29-34

- Crispus in Corinth—18:8

- Mnason in Jerusalem—21:16

[1] Unlikely—the text is ambiguous, with no additional information (2 occurrences)

- Philip in Samaria—8:4–13, 26–40

- Aquila in Corinth—18:1–4

While this methodology is admittedly somewhat subjective, the results are nevertheless revealing. It is noteworthy that there are 8 instances rated [4], 8 rated [3], 4 rated [2], and 2 rated [1], meaning that 16 of the 22 possible occurrences in Acts either definitely or likely depict actual house churches, and only 2 are ambiguous and unlikely. Even if only the 8 certain references are considered, this is ample evidence to demonstrate Luke's consistent advocacy of the house church, and in reality at least 20 of the above 22 examples should be considered in this exploration. Of course, not every reference to a house in Acts refers to a fully developed house church, underscored by the fact that there are 38 total occurrences of οἶκος, οἰκία, or πανοικί in Acts, but this study provides overwhelming evidence that Luke is advocating the house church as the principal missional structure of the early church.

Adams emphasizes that there are multiple other settings for mission and community in Acts, including the Jerusalem temple (3:1—4:3), synagogues (9:20; 13:5, 14–43; 14:1; 17:1–3, 10, 17; 18:4, 19; 19:8), Lystran city gates (14:13–18), Philippian place of prayer (16:13), Athenian marketplace and Areopagus (17:17, 22–31), "school" of Tyrannus in Ephesus (19:9), Miletus harbor (20:18–38), and Tyrian beach (21:5).[159] While these are all non-house locations, they are also mostly special one-time gatherings, usually for an evangelistic speech or individual Christian meeting. None of them is a venue for regular church gatherings, with the possible exception of the Jerusalem temple and the school of Tyrannus in Ephesus. Notably, both of these locations possess explicit evidence for multiple house churches in Acts (2:46; 5:42; 12:12, 17; 20:20), which defeats any argument that perhaps Luke is implying that the Jerusalem or Ephesian church communities do not regularly meet in homes.

Adams is helpful in challenging the assumptions scholars make about passages that are ambiguous or speculative when it comes to the existence of a house church, and his comments have helped to guide the analysis in this chapter. However, his proposals for other locations of Christian community

159. Adams, *Meeting Places*, 63–66.

in Acts are less convincing. He helpfully concludes, "the book of Acts bears strong textual witness to houses as church-meeting locales."[160] However, his final comment is misleading: "The evidence in Acts, therefore, does not comport with the consensus view that the earliest Christian meetings were 'almost exclusively' in houses."[161] If anything, this survey of Acts has come to exactly the opposite conclusion, that the earliest Christian meetings in Acts *are* "almost exclusively" in houses, and Acts proposes very few if any viable alternatives for regular church meetings than the private home.[162] For this reason, it is unwise to eradicate the category of "house church" from NT and Early Christian studies, as Adams recommends.[163]

According to Luke, the basic structure for Christian mission is the house church. This is largely because the Greco-Roman world is fundamentally an οἶκος society; the household is the architectural, social, and economic foundation for life, and therefore the ideal structure for the missional advancement of the church. The early church leaders capitalize on the potential of this all-pervasive structure in an intentional and effective way. By building the church within the οἶκος, and focusing on householders in the existing patronage system, they tap into an already intact social and economic organization, which enables the church to grow naturally and rapidly within existing social and material structures.

In Acts, Christians adopt the house church as their primary base for mission, and a way to "gather the harvest" as it comes in (Luke 10:2; cf. John 4:35). This can be observed in at least four stages of the early Christian mission: Jesus introduces this approach in nascent form in his village and regional ministry and teaching (Luke 10:1–20); the primitive church in Jerusalem develops it in their city-wide outreach (Acts 1–7); those who flee from Jerusalem adapt it in their urban and regional outreach (Acts 8:1—13:3); and Paul employs it in his multinational center-oriented mission journeys (Acts 13–20). The structure of the house church has implications for missional strategy and practice, church community and daily life, leadership development and structure, and virtually every other aspect of the life of the early church in Acts. Luke presents it as one of the primary reasons for the dazzling success of the Christian mission in his narrative, to help avoid modern "house church" connotations.

160. Adams, *Meeting Places*, 67.

161. Adams, *Meeting Places*, 67.

162. Adams's argument is stronger for other parts of the NT, especially the Gospels and Paul's letters.

163. Adams, *Meeting Places*, 202; this agrees with Osiek's review of Adams's book, 185–86. Perhaps new vocabulary, such as "house communities" or "home gatherings" would be helpful.

PART 2

Conclusion

Structures That Facilitate Mission in Acts

For Luke, the church is inherently a missionary movement. Luke intends to provoke and motivate believers into missional activities and lifestyles by presenting various stimuli for mission. The narrative of Acts functions as rhetorical instruction in this regard, vividly expressing Luke's missional and ideological purposes.

If Christ-followers are to live missional lives, they must employ structures that facilitate this mission and aid in its advance, and Luke aims to help his readers understand what these structures are. Part 2 has identified the church assembly (ἐκκλησία) and the home/household (οἶκος) as the primary missional structures which Luke advocates in Acts, particularly as they combine in the form of the house church. Luke instructs his readers to maximize the strategic opportunities presented by living in an οἶκος society, with its patronage system of benefaction and householders. For Luke, the house church is the ideal missional structure, and he weaves it into his narrative in a comprehensive way that encourages his readers to build and nurture house churches everywhere they go.

Ἐκκλησία is not a new concept in the first-century Greco-Roman world. Yet early Christians take this familiar word and infuse it with new meaning: the called-out ones, the assembly of the gathered Christ-followers. This new eschatological community functions within the structural framework of the ancient οἶκος society, and thus positions itself for sustained long-term missional success as the hands and feet of the mission. In Acts, the house church finds its ultimate efficacy in the Pauline mission. It is also in Luke's description of Paul's ministry in Acts that the missional strategies of the early church come to maturity. This is the subject of part 3 of this work.

PART 3

Missional Strategies in Acts

A strategy at its most basic level is a plan of action designed to achieve a certain goal. The overriding goal of the early Christians in Acts is the success of the mission, manifested in the expansion of the church. This part examines how missionaries achieve this goal in Acts. Although there may be missional strategies in earlier portions of the narrative, they are minimal and mission is mostly incidental rather than plannedin the first twelve chapters of Acts. Throughout Paul's journeys (Acts 13–21) the central missional strategies of Acts develop, for it is from Antioch that genuinely intentional mission emerges. However, can Paul be said to actually have a strategy in Acts?

> Much depends on the definition of strategy. If by strategy is meant a deliberate, well-formulated, duly executed plan of action based on human observation and experience, then Paul had little or no strategy; but if we take it to mean a flexible *modus operandi* developed under the guidance of the Holy Spirit and subject to His direction and control, then Paul did have a strategy.[1]

Luke uses repeated themes and patterns in Paul's journeys to shed light on Paul's *modus operandi* in this broader sense. Schnabel maintains that, "Paul planned his missionary initiatives in the context of a general strategy

---

1. Kane, *Christian Missions*, 73. Others are more skeptical about Paul having a missional strategy, such as Green, *Evangelism*, 174.

that controlled his tactical decisions."[2] The following chapters explore Paul's general strategies as Luke portrays them in Acts 13–21.

If mission in Acts is conceived of as a body, these strategies are the brains of the operation. They determine the tactics to be employed, direct the whole body at crucial points of decision, and keep all the members coordinated and working well together. Luke's stimuli are the beating heart of the mission, his structures are the hands and feet of the outreach, but the strategic brain advances and coordinates all missionary efforts in Acts.

This analysis presupposes that Luke's presentation of Paul's mission is not rhetorically neutral, as if this were even possible. Luke's underlying agenda in these journey sections is to portray his main character Paul as a model to be imitated by his readers in their own missional endeavors. In Acts, Luke is not merely describing "what was" from his perspective, but he is advocating "what should be." The repetitive tactics and approaches in the Pauline journeys reveal the missional strategies which Luke is endorsing in Acts. These stories will be analyzed first in chronological/text order one journey at a time in the next three chapters, and then the findings will be summarized in chapter 11.

---

2. Schnabel, *Mission*, 2:1293; for discussion of strategy and tactics in the ancient world and in the early church's mission, see 1:499–517.

Chapter 8

Paul's First Journey (13:4—14:26)

*While they were worshiping the Lord and fasting, the Holy Spirit
said, "Set apart for me Barnabas and Saul for the work to which
I have called them." Then after fasting and praying they laid their
hands on them and sent them off.*

—ACTS 13:2–3

In Acts, Paul travels extensively before his missionary journeys,[1] and quite
a lot afterwards.[2] This travel establishes Paul as a "professional traveler" *par
excellence*.[3] However, the substance of Paul's missional strategy is found in
his three missionary journeys.[4]

---

1. Luke notes Paul in Jerusalem (8:1; 9:1), Damascus (9:2–3, 8), Tarsus (11:25; his
birthplace, 9:12; 21:39), Syrian Antioch (11:26), Jerusalem again (11:30), and back in
Syrian Antioch (12:25). Between each of these is a lengthy journey by foot.

2. Within the constraints of captivity Paul travels from Jerusalem to Caesarea
(23:33, by horseback), to Sidon (27:3), Myra (27:5), Fair Havens on Crete (27:8), Malta
(28:1), Syracuse (28:12), Rhegium and Puteoli (28:13), all by ship, or shipwreck, then
on foot to the Forum of Appius and the Three Taverns, and to Rome (28:15–16).

3. Rapske, "Acts, Travel and Shipwreck," 3–6.

4. The chapters in part 3 follow the chronological and geographical outline of Acts
in the main section headings (with Acts references) and identify strategic missional
themes in the sub-headings.

Table 8.1 The First Itinerary (13:1—14:26)[5]

13:1	Syrian Antioch	14:6	Lystra, Derbe, and region
13:4	Seleucia	14:8	Lystra
13:5	Salamis, Cyprus (by ship)	14:20	Derbe
13:6	Paphos	14:21	Lystra, Iconium, Pisidian Antioch
13:13	Perga in Pamphylia (by ship)	14:24	Throughout Pisidia to Pamphylia
13:14	Pisidian Antioch	14:25	Perga, Attalia
13:51	Iconium	14:26	Syrian Antioch (by ship)

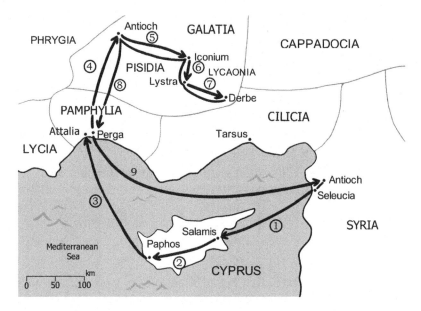

Marshall's assessment of this first journey should be remembered:

> Paul's missionary work [during] this period has the best claim
> to being called a "missionary journey," as is customary on Bible
> maps. The later periods were much more devoted to extended
> activity in significant key cities of the ancient world, and we gain
> a false picture of Paul's strategy if we think of him as rushing
> rapidly on missionary *journeys* from one place to the next, leav-
> ing small groups of half-taught converts behind him; it was his
> general policy to remain in one place until he had established

5. Paul walks on foot unless otherwise specified. These are the locations that Luke
reports in Acts; for other cities and areas that Paul would visit along his journeys, see
Schnabel, *Mission*, 2:1073–292.

the firm foundation of a Christian community, or until he was forced to move by circumstances beyond his control.[6]

CYPRUS (13:4–12)

Led by the Spirit

Barnabas and Paul travel first to Cyprus, which is about sixty miles offshore from Antioch's port city, Seleucia (13:4).[7] Luke emphasizes that they are "sent out by the Holy Spirit" (ἐκπεμφθέντες ὑπὸ τοῦ ἁγίου πνεύματος, 13:4), after saying that the Spirit has set them aside for the mission (13:2).[8] This underscores a frequent theme in Acts: the Spirit does not just initiate the mission for Luke, but directs and empowers it as well (13:9; 15:28; 16:6–7; 20:22–23). "The Spirit is not only intimately connected with their mission but is its author (1:8; 2:17–18) . . . This new mission further exemplifies Luke's emphasis on the Spirit's power for mission."[9]

Urban Centers

The Cypriot account focuses on the two urban centers of the island, Salamis on the east and Paphos on the west.[10] This is a repeated strategic pattern; Paul focuses on the larger cities he encounters, especially the regional capitals and Roman colonies. Salamis is a famous city on the mouth of the river Pedieos, which had been an ancient city-state dating back to at least the eleventh century BCE. It was the capital of Cyprus for many years, but the Romans moved the capital to Paphos in 22 BCE and made it a senatorial province.

---

6. Marshall, *Acts*, 214.

7. Five miles from the mouth of the Orontes River, and with the regional Roman fleet stationed there, it is easy to obtain passage to many destinations from Seleucia; Witherington, *Acts*, 394. That they go to Cyprus first may signify that Barnabas is considered the senior missionary partner at this point.

8. Cf. 20:28, where Paul claims that the Spirit directly appoints leaders in the church.

9. Keener, *Acts*, 2:1994–95. See chapter 2 for more on the Spirit's empowerment for mission in Acts.

10. Schnabel, *Mission* has a brief history of Cyprus, 2:1078, Salamis, 2:1079–80, Paphos, 2:1082; see also Johnson, *Paul*, 57–61.

First to the Synagogues

Acts 13:5 reveals their initial strategy when approaching a new place: "When they reached Salamis, they proclaimed the word of God in the synagogues of the Jews" (κατήγγελλον τὸν λόγον τοῦ θεοῦ ἐν ταῖς συναγωγαῖς τῶν Ἰουδαίων). There is a sizeable and established Jewish population on Cyprus by this time.[11] Barnabas has been a part of this Jewish community (4:36), with multiple contacts in the Cypriot synagogues. This habit of offering the message of salvation to the Jews first is a regular Pauline missional strategy throughout Acts.[12]

Part of Paul's motivation in going to the synagogue first may be theological—scholars often argue that this sequence reflects salvation-history priority, as God always offers salvation first to Israel. However, another reason is Paul's pragmatic missional strategy: "where else would he find those who shared his basic premise about Israel's God and history on which the gospel proclamation built?"[13] Paul finds the largest concentration of both Jews and non-Jewish God-fearers in the synagogue, so this is the obvious starting point, where Paul feels most comfortable because of the shared theological common ground. As Keener asks, "where else might Paul have started to obtain an initial hearing and a base for operations (cf. Luke 10:5–7)?"[14] This repeated pattern does not mean Luke is advocating imitating this exact practice in every missionary venture; the strategic principle is about locating an initial audience with as much common ground, rapport, and receptivity as possible. As a Pharisee and traveling rabbi, the synagogue is Paul's optimal starting point.

"After they had *gone through the whole island*" (διελθόντες δὲ ὅλην τὴν νῆσον, 13:6), they reach Paphos. Διέρχομαι hints that they engage in outreach along the way between the two main cities, as Luke uses the same word to describe missional activity in 8:4.[15] Luke does not report on the outcome of this activity, but the return of Barnabas and John Mark a few years later

---

11. Cf. Philo, *Embassy*, 282: "not only are the continents full of Jewish colonies, but also all the most celebrated islands are so too; such as . . . Cyprus"; Josephus, *Ant.*, 13.284–7.

12. See 13:14; 14:1; 17:1, 10, 17; 18:4, 19; 19:8. Cf. Rom 1:16: "to the Jew first but also to the Greek."

13. Keener, *Acts*, 2:2002.

14. Keener, *Acts*, 2:2002.

15. Barrett, *Acts*, 1:612. "The whole island" is another hint; they probably evangelize in other Cypriot population centers such as Kition, Amathos, Neapolis, and Kourion; Schnabel, *Mission*, 2:1074, 1080–83.

(15:36–39) suggests that there are multiple young Cypriot churches which they intend to support and strengthen.[16]

Miraculous Demonstrations of Power

After arriving in Paphos, Paul and Barnabas rebuke a sorcerer named Elymas who is attempting to prevent the proconsul Sergius Paulus from believing, and he is "immediately" (παραχρῆμα) struck blind (13:6–11).[17] Demonstrations of God's power through signs and wonders such as this are commonplace in Acts, particularly when Christianity is in direct conflict with magic, sorcery, or other religious competitors.[18] Cases of healings and other miracles in the narrative are also relevant examples, for they validate the message being proclaimed. Luke emphasizes that Paul is "filled with the Spirit" (πλησθεὶς πνεύματος ἁγίου, 13:9) in this confrontation with Elymas, further confirming the theme of Spirit-empowerment for mission.

Sergius Paulus's response to this display of God's power is significant: "when the proconsul saw what had happened, he believed, being amazed (ἐκπλησσόμενος) at the teaching about the Lord" (13:12). Ἐκπλήσσω has a connotation of being struck with astonishment, to the point of panic or shock.[19] This shows that the miracle is part of Paul's missional teaching because it is a powerful teaching (διδαχῇ) that comes with spiritual authority.[20] The proconsul's amazement and belief (πιστεύω) are logical responses to signs and wonders for Luke. Practically demonstrating the reality and power of the gospel message is at the heart of Paul's missional strategy in Acts.

Peterson unnecessarily minimizes the prevalence and impact of such miraculous events:

> It was not this display of the supernatural that converted the proconsul . . . even in Acts they [such miracles] are rare and are

16. See their stated intention: "let us visit the brothers in every city (πᾶσαν πόλιν) where we proclaimed the word of the Lord, and see how they are" (15:36). In Acts 21:16 Luke mentions "Mnason of Cyprus, an early disciple," who could be a convert from this missionary trip to Cyprus, or from Barnabas's later trip.

17. Elymas "Bar-Jesus" (Βαριησοῦ, son of Jesus/Joshua) is ironically named, and later called "son of the devil" (υἱὲ διαβόλου, 13:10); Keener, *Acts*, 2.1008–9 notes multiple narrative ironies in this episode, and comments that this scene "fits Luke's polemic against Jewish spirituality without Jesus."

18. Witherington, *Acts*, 397–98.

19. BDAG, 308.

20. Cf. Luke 4:32: "they were amazed (ἐξεπλήσσοντο) at his teaching (διδαχῇ), for his message was with authority (ἐξουσίᾳ)." Note the parallel use of ἐκπλήσσω and διδαχή, implying that Paul, like Jesus, also has ἐξουσία.

usually related to the movement of the gospel into some new area, the overcoming of some form of spiritual opposition, or the winning of some particularly significant figure for Christ ... [Luke] does not even suggest that signs and wonders were a necessary aspect of the progress of the word in every context.[21]

While it is true that miracles are not required for the mission's success, they are so frequently repeated in Acts that it is unhelpful to minimize them in this way.[22] Additionally, the text explicitly links the miracle with Sergius Paulus's belief, which is a direct result of his amazement (13:11–12). Luke is wanting his readers to understand that miracles central to Paul's missional effectiveness, and to encourage them that this kind of power is available through the Spirit for their own ministries.

A Person of Influence

The proconsul Sergius Paulus is a focal character (13:7–12).[23] The title ἀνθύπατος correctly designates the administrator of a Senatorial province, which Cyprus became in 22 CE.[24] Luke stresses that he is a "man of intelligence" (ἀνδρὶ συνετῷ, 13:7). In addition to being a head of household, Sergius Paulus has widespread credibility and influence across the island of Cyprus as an established leader within the local aristocracy.

Sergius Paulus's belief has social significance because it presents Paul as a person accepted in circles of higher society.[25] His life transformation would also make an impact on many others and give social credibility to the new Christian movement in Cyprus. By reaching Sergius Paulus, the gospel indirectly gains access to many others, making him an ideal example of the strategic "person of peace" which Jesus describes in his mission discourse

21. Peterson, *Acts*, 382–83. This might be driven by a desire to reassure missionaries today that they do not need to be reliant on such miraculous confirmations.

22. In addition to this scene, see the following 7 examples in Paul's travels: 14:3, 8–10; 15:12; 16:16–18, 25–26; 19:11–12, 13–16; 20:9–10. There are many other examples in other parts of Acts (2:4–13, 43; 3:6–10; 4:31; 5:3, 9, 12–16; 5:19; 6:8; 8:6–8, 17; 9:34–35, 40–42; 12:7–10; 28:5–6, 9), which indicate that for Luke this is a normative and crucial aspect of Christian witness. See discussion in chapter 4, part of the apostolic ethos.

23. Keener, *Acts*, 2:2014–16 provides background to Sergius Paulus.

24. Johnson, *Acts*, 222. Luke also uses ἀνθύπατος for the administrators in Corinth (18:12) and Ephesus (19:38). By contrast, imperial provinces are administered by military prefects (ἡγεμών) such as Pontius Pilate (Luke 2:2; 3:1), Felix (Acts 23:24, 26), and Festus (24:27).

25. Witherington, *Acts*, 404, 430–38. Paul's missional strategy in Acts includes reaching people of influence.

(Luke 10:6). This proconsul's new faith may be why Paul leaves Cyprus so quickly (Acts 13:12-13). Though he is facing no apparent persecution, and has no observable reason to leave, Paul believes that Sergius Paulus's conversion will ensure the continued growth of the church on the island.[26] Here and elsewhere, Luke emphasizes that missionaries can impact an exponentially larger group of people by reaching a person of influence.

Following Existing Relationships

Cyprus is Barnabas's home (4:36), which means John Mark also has family connections there.[27] They go initially to a location where they have existing relationships, a social network of family and friends who know them, are ready to offer them hospitality, and will be more open to hear and receive their message. It is the logical first choice, for at this point Luke apparently considers Barnabas the leader of the expedition (13:7), and Saul has already spent time in his hometown Tarsus (9:30; 11:25).

Archaeological evidence has revealed a family with the name Lucius Sergius Paullus with connections in Cyprus at this time, which also owns extensive property in the region of Pisidian Antioch.[28] It is possible that Sergius Paulus urges Paul and Barnabas to go next to his family in Pisidian Antioch, though Luke does not mention this.[29] At this point Paul and Barnabas do not appear to have a precise travel plan. They begin where they have relationship in Cyprus, and then follow where those relationships lead. This is a strategic theme in Acts—missionaries go to places where they have a relational connection or invitation, operating along the lines of existing social networks even as they follow the Spirit's leadership.[30]

---

26. Schnabel, *Mission*, 2:1088.

27. Mark, Barnabas's cousin (Col 4:10), is also traveling with them (Acts 13:13; 15:38).

28. Ramsay, *Recent Discovery*, 150–72 has found inscriptions bearing the name L. Sergius Paullus; Hemer, *Acts*, 109. Many conclude that this is the proconsul of Acts and has connections to Pisidian Antioch. See Sergius Paulus's family tree, Schnabel, *Mission*, 2:1084–89.

29. Johnson, *Acts*, 227; Fox, *Pagans and Christians*, 293–94; Keener, *Acts*, 2:2037–38. He may write a letter of recommendation to help them along, cf. Apollos going to Corinth (18:27).

30. The Diaspora synagogue communities would be connected relationally, and there are undoubtedly other social networks linking Paul's destinations of which early readers of Acts would be aware.

PISIDIAN ANTIOCH (13:13–52)

This Antioch is designated "of Pisidia" (Ἀντιόχειαν τὴν Πισιδίαν, 13:14) to distinguish it from the fifteen other cities named Antioch in the Empire at this time.[31] It is an urban center of some significance, and the civil and administrative capital of its immediate area within the larger political province of Galatia, in the ethnic region of Phrygia.[32]

The Synagogue and the God-Fearers

As is their custom, Paul and Barnabas first go into the synagogue in Pisidian Antioch, where they are asked to give a word of exhortation and encouragement (λόγος παρακλήσεως, 13:15; cf. Heb 13:22). The synagogue is a natural first point of contact, for Paul and Barnabas receive instant credibility as itinerant Jewish preachers and are invited by the local Jewish community to teach as guest speakers.[33]

This invitation leads to Paul's first speech in Acts (13:16–47), which is addressed to two groups: "men of Israel" (ἄνδρες Ἰσραηλῖται) and "those who fear God" (οἱ φοβούμενοι τὸν θεόν, 13:16). The first represents ethnic Jews or proselytes to Judaism, and the second refers to God-fearing Gentile sympathizers, who are synagogue adherents on the fringes of the Jewish community, but not full Jewish converts.[34]

God-fearers are a frequent narrative theme in Acts,[35] as is with the Jewish synagogue itself.[36] This episode highlights the Pauline practice of

31. Witherington, *Acts*, 404. Paul likely goes through the seaport of Attalia, and then to Perga, before arriving at Pisidian Antioch (13:13). This is also when John Mark leaves them (15:37–39 shows Paul's dissatisfaction).

32. Luke properly refers to this area as "the Phrygian and Galatic region" (16:6), Witherington, *Acts*, 405. For the history of Pisidian Antioch, see Schnabel, *Mission*, 2:1098–103. Galatians is probably written to churches Paul begins in places like Pisidian Antioch and Iconium on this journey.

33. Meeks, *Urban Christians*, 26–27, 80–81.

34. Scholars debate the historicity of the God-fearers, with some claiming they are a Lukan invention: Hemer, *Acts*, 444–47 discusses the Aphrodisias Inscription, which supports Luke's usage of φοβούμενοι τὸν θεόν; Overman, "God-fearers," 24; Gager, "Jews, Gentiles," 99; Levinskaya, *Diaspora Setting*, 51–126.

35. E.g., the Ethiopian Eunuch (8:27–39); Cornelius (10:2, 28–29, 44–48); the discussion at the Jerusalem council (15:7–11). If σεβόμενοι is an abbreviation of the full formula σεβόμενοι (φοβούμενοι) τὸν θεόν, the phrase is mentioned 8 times in the book of Acts: 13:16, 26, 43, 50; 16:14; 17:4, 17; 18:6–7, covering Pisidian Antioch, Caesarea, Philippi, Thessalonica, Athens, and Corinth. Levinskaya, *Diaspora Setting*, 52–58, 120–26, discusses Luke's change in terminology.

36. Συναγωγή: 6:9; 9:2, 20; 13:5, 14, 42, 43; 14:1; 15:21; 17:1, 10, 17; 18:4, 7, 19, 26;

going to strategic groups of people who are most receptive to his message. Paul can expect a degree of kinship and openness from his Jewish audience in this setting, and thus finds it relatively easy to establish rapport and affinity with strangers. This can be seen in the informal way Paul begins his speech (13:16) and in his use of "brothers" (ἀδελφοί, 13:26); Paul is appealing here to the bond created by their shared ethnic and religious heritage.[37]

The general receptiveness of the God-fearers points to the appeal the Christian message has to Gentiles who are drawn to monotheistic Judaism, but have not embraced all of its cultural requirements, such as circumcision and dietary restrictions.[38] Because Christianity is a monotheistic religion with the same scriptural and theological roots and similar ethical standards, but without the cultural trappings, it is attractive to God-fearers within the Jewish Diaspora, who become the foundation of multiple early non-Jewish Christian communities. They are a bridge from Jew to Gentile, for as Gentiles enjoying close relationship with Jews and frequenting Jewish synagogues, they are the first group of Gentiles to hear and respond to the Christian message. Once again, Luke shows Paul strategically maximizing his missional effectiveness.

A Relevant Message

Paul delivers an exhortational speech in the synagogue at Pisidian Antioch (13:16–41) which is filled with allusions to the Hebrew Scriptures and introduces another strategic theme: as a masterful orator and rhetorician, Paul always preaches in a way that is relevant to his hearers.[39] At least one third of this speech recounts stories from the Hebrew Scriptures, capturing the big picture of Israel's history, which would be familiar to his Jewish hearers (13:16–22). Towards the end, Paul quotes four OT passages (13:33–41): Ps 2:7; Isa 55:3; Ps 16:10; Hab 1:5. He additionally laces his speech with references to Moses (13:39), Abraham (13:26), David (13:22, 34, 36), the prophets (13:26, 37, 40), and Israel (13:27, 23, 24). "Like Stephen, Paul begins with a sweep of biblical history; Luke's Paul wishes it to be clear that his message is grounded not solely in isolated proof texts but in the pattern

---

19:8; 22:19; 24:12; 26:11. Ἀρχισυνάγωγος (synagogue leader): 13:15; 18:8, 17.

37. Witherington, *Acts*, 409.

38. See Juvenal's scorn of Gentiles taking an interest in Judaism, *Satires*, 14:96–103. Most religions have groups with varying levels of commitment and conformity, including fringe adherents like the God-fearers.

39. Witherington, *Acts*, 407–14.

of God's working throughout biblical history."⁴⁰ Paul delivers a thoroughly Jewish speech, building his case for Christ from Scripture that is relevant and authoritative to his synagogue listeners.⁴¹

Many Jews respond favorably, but some incite the crowds to turn against Paul and Barnabas (13:42–45). This causes Paul and Barnabas to turn to the Gentiles, justifying this from Isa 49:6 (13:46–47), and once again "speaking the language" of their synagogue listeners, the Hebrew Scriptures. Luke underscores the significance of Isa 49:6 in his universal inclusion of all peoples at this pivotal turning point. Meek studies this OT quotation in detail, concluding it is in keeping with the text's original contextual meaning (in both the LXX and the Masoretic text), and that it functions as a "proof from prophecy," validating the divine legitimacy and necessity of the Gentile mission.⁴² This also confirms Paul's standard missional strategy: present the message first to the Jews, then to the Gentiles. The results in multiple Gentiles believing in Christ in Pisidian Antioch, and a new church is born (13:48).

Planting Local Churches to Impact Regions

Because of this initial group of believers in Pisidian Antioch, "the word of the Lord *spread* (or was carried, διεφέρετο) *throughout the entire region*" (δι' ὅλης τῆς χώρας, 13:49).⁴³ Διαφέρω in Acts has the connotation of being carried or borne throughout an area, from one locality to another.⁴⁴ This phrase should be understood to mean that the word of the Lord spreads by being carried by specific messengers throughout the entire region; the area that Pisidian Antioch controls is large, including over 50 villages.⁴⁵ Luke implies that the disruption of synagogue life resulting in a new community here presents an opportunity to explain what has happened, which becomes the vector for the word of the Lord to be carried elsewhere.

40. Keener, *Acts*, 2:2050.

41. Cf. the Areopagus speech (17:22–31), where Paul does not mention the Hebrew Scriptures, but references Greek poets and proverbs. Paul does not deliver a "stock message," but preaches in a relevant way that meets his audience where they are.

42. Meek, *Gentile Mission*, 24–55.

43. This is a typical Lukan way of notifying the reader of the mission's success in a region or period, e.g., Acts 2:41, 47; 6:7; 9:31; 11:24; 12:24. Johnson, *Acts*, 242.

44. Cf. the ship being carried or driven about (διαφερομένων) in the Adriatic Sea (27:27); BDAG, 239.

45. Schnabel, *Mission*, 2:1107.

This highlights a geographical strategy in Acts which is repeated throughout this part of Acts. Paul's goal is to establish the initial nucleus of believers in an urban center or regional capital, such as Pisidian Antioch. He stays long enough to establish foundations of faith and mission in this new group, but then leaves them to reach out to their own region. Luke makes no claim that Paul and Barnabas are directly involved in this regional outreach, and reports that they are expelled from the city quickly (13:50–51).[46] Paul plants a "seed" (a new house church, or embryonic community of Christ-followers) in the fertile spiritual soil of an influential urban center, and then leaves it to take root, grow, and spread into the surrounding region, in part propelled by the news of the initial missional encounter.[47]

It can be presumed that un-named messengers not originally sent with Paul and Barnabas carry out this regional mission to Pisidian Antioch's surrounding district, probably drawn from the recently established churches.[48] They have local social networks and credibility that Paul does not have and are therefore better placed for long-term missional effectiveness in their home regions. When local believers are empowered to take responsibility for outreach in their surrounding areas this initiates a reproducing strategy, capable of impacting large areas relatively quickly, as local missionaries are trained and mobilized. This center-oriented regional approach is central to Paul's missional success in Acts and facilitates the noteworthy spread of the Word throughout a whole region (13:49).

The Backlash of Persecution and the Unstoppable Advance of the Church

The success of the Word incites further opposition, which results in a wave of persecution that "threw out" (ἐξέβαλον) Paul and Barnabas from that region (13:50). This is another theme in Acts; opposition often forces missionaries to leave an area. Paul and Barnabas shake the dust from their feet (13:51), expressing in sober action their warnings about rejecting the Word (13:40–41, 46–47) and following Jesus's instructions (Luke 9:5; 10:11). "It is likely that this was a particular warning to their Jewish opponents, who would understand the significance of this prophetic-type action, rather than a wholesale condemnation of the city."[49]

46. In opposition to Schnabel, *Mission*, 2:1107, who seems to think that Paul and Barnabas evangelize the surrounding villages and towns.

47. Cf. 1 Cor 3:6: "I planted, Apollos watered, but God was causing the growth."

48. Barrett, *Acts*, 1:659.

49. Peterson, *Acts*, 400.

Luke immediately follows this by saying that "the disciples were continually filled with joy and with the Holy Spirit" (ἐπληροῦντο χαρᾶς καὶ πνεύματος ἁγίου, 13:52), which is a Lukan indicator that a group's conversion is genuine (e.g., 8:38; 10:44–46).[50] "Luke is concerned to show how the word spread, but also how local communities prospered (see 14:21–23). The code words used here by Luke indicate that this foundation is an authentic realization of the Church."[51] Thus, Paul and Barnabas leave a newly founded Christian community in Pisidian Antioch, undeterred by persecution and missionally expanding into the entire region (ὅλης τῆς χώρας, 13:49).

ICONIUM (14:1–7)

Paul and Barnabas then travel to Iconium, a journey of at least ninety miles,[52] which raises the question of Paul's methods of transport.

Following Established Transport Routes

On Paul's first journey, he sails from Seleucia to Salamis, a common shipping route, and then walks along one of the two main roads from Salamis to Paphos. He then sails from Salamis to Pamphylia, almost certainly disembarking at Attalia, the entry port of Pamphylia.[53] From Attalia, he takes a paved road to Perga, the metropolis of Pamphylia.[54] At Perga, he joins the *Via Sebaste*, a broad and well-paved road connecting the Roman colonies in the region, designed to accommodate wheeled vehicles, which runs all the way from Perga (maybe even Attalia), to Pisidian Antioch, and then on to Iconium, and likely Lystra as well.[55] Paul follows the *Via Sebaste* to Iconium, and then flees from Iconium to Lystra on the same road. He then follows

---

50. "Whereas the opponents of God's servants were 'filled up' (a functional synonym) with jealousy in 13:45, the new believers here are 'filled' with joy . . . outsiders, who receive the message rejected by the insiders, are filled with joy and the Spirit," Keener, *Acts*, 2:2112–13.

51. Johnson, *Acts*, 243. In Acts, the genuine church is filled with joy (13:48) and the Holy Spirit (2:4; 4:31; 8:17; 9:31; 10:44; 13:2).

52. Witherington, *Acts*, 417.

53. French, "Roman Roads," 52. Acts only mentions Attalia in Paul's departure from Pamphylia (14:26).

54. One such road was built under Tiberius, and probably repaired under Claudius; French, "Roman Roads," 52.

55. It was built in 6 BCE by the emperor Augustus; French, "Roman Roads," 52.

another road, perhaps unpaved, to Derbe and the surrounding region.[56] Finally, he follows the same roads back to Attalia, before returning to Syrian Antioch by ship.[57]

"Only the simplest of all possible reconstructions is necessary for an exposition of Paul's first journey into Asia Minor."[58] He travels on paved Roman roads and sails on common shipping routes wherever possible along his route. These established transport and trade routes influence his next destination, particularly when navigating difficult terrain.[59] Paul takes the easiest route into Asia Minor, and then focuses on cities where there are Jewish Diaspora communities who will offer him hospitality.[60] This method of travel minimizes his expense, expedites his progress, reduces exposure to the dangers of overland travel, and naturally brings him to the significant urban centers within his locality.

Local Jewish Communities

The missional progression at Iconium follows that at Pisidian Antioch: "as usual/as is their custom" (κατὰ τὸ αὐτό),[61] Paul and Barnabas begin their outreach by entering the synagogue and speaking in a similar fashion (14:1). This confirms a strategic pattern Luke is endorsing. A "great multitude" (πολὺ πλῆθος) of Jews and Gentiles believe in Iconium in response to their preaching. Persecution again emerges, stirred up by antagonistic Jews, but here Paul and Barnabas stay for a "considerable time" (ἱκανὸν μέν οὖν χρόνον), speaking boldly (παρρησιαζόμενοι) for the Lord and the message of his grace (14:2–3).[62]

---

56. French, "Roman Roads," 53.

57. Keener, *Acts*, 2:2018–19 has a map of these roads, "The Pisidian Taurus." Cf. map at beginning of this chapter.

58. French, "Roman Roads," 52. It is somewhat more difficult to reconstruct the exact routes of the second and third journeys, "Roman Roads," 53–58.

59. Such as the mountainous regions between Perga and Pisidian Antioch, French, "Roman Roads," 50–51.

60. E.g., the synagogues in Pisidian Antioch (13:14), and Iconium (14:1). There is no reason to doubt that Paul continues to follow this same basic travel pattern throughout his journeys.

61. Cf. 17:2; Peterson, *Acts*, 403.

62. This involves teaching and mentoring the new Christians ("the brothers," 14:2).

Signs and Wonders

"The Lord confirmed the message of his grace by enabling them to do (διδόντι, lit. giving) miraculous signs and wonders" (σημεῖα καὶ τέρατα, 14:3). Σημεῖον means a sign or distinguishing mark whereby something is known, or a confirmation.[63] Τέρας is something that astounds because of its transcendent association, such as an omen, portent, or wonder.[64] These concepts summarize the role of the miraculous in the mission: it confirms the message that is being preached, and causes people to wonder in astonishment. "Jesus commanded his agents to heal the sick when they were proclaiming the nearness of the kingdom (Luke 9:2; 10:9). Luke's Paul and Barnabas have been following the model found in those instructions."[65] The strategic importance of signs and wonders is underscored in Barnabas and Paul's summary of this first journey before the Jerusalem Council: the one thing they relate is the "signs and wonders (σημεῖα καὶ τέρατα) God had done among the Gentiles through them" (15:12).

Luke is not interested in miracles for their own sake, but in miracles that confirm the truthfulness of the word being proclaimed and make people wonder what is behind it. "The powerful deeds here as elsewhere serve to certify the message being proclaimed."[66] This theme points to another of the central missional strategies in Acts: signs and wonders authenticate the gospel proclamation.[67]

Bold Regional Outreach, Despite Persecution

Missional success leads to persecution in Iconium (14:5), so Paul and Barnabas flee to the Lycaonian cities of Lystra and Derbe, outside of the Phrygian region (14:6).[68] This continues the pattern of going to the chief cities

63. BDAG, 920.

64. BDAG, 999. All nine occurrences of τέρας in Acts are coupled with σημεῖον: 2:19; 2:22; 2:43; 4:30; 5:12; 6:8; 7:36; 14:3; 15:12. Σημεῖον occurs four additional times: 4:16, 22; 8:6, 13.

65. Keener, *Acts*, 2:2122–23.

66. Johnson, *Acts*, 246. Cf. 2 Cor 12:12. "If such reports in ancient historical documents . . . offend our modern sensibilities, this disconnect reflects our cultural philosophic presuppositions no less than theirs," Keener, *Acts*, 2:2123.

67. E.g., Acts 2:19, 22, 43; 4:16, 22, 30; 5:12; 6:8; 7:36; 8:6, 13; 13:22; 15:8; 20:23. Witherington, *Acts*, 419. Note that in the final three the Lord also "bears witness" (μαρτυρέω) through signs and wonders.

68. Lystra is about a six-hour journey by foot, about eighteen miles. Derbe is at least a further fifty-five miles away. These are two of the principal cities of the region of Lycaonia, along with Laranda and Parlais. Both are beyond the jurisdiction of the Phrygian

of a region, which are connected by well-traveled roads and transport links. Luke adds that they continue to preach the good news (εὐαγγελιζόμενοι) not just in Lystra and Derbe, but also in "the surrounding regions/circumjacent vicinity" (τὴν περίχωρον, 14:6–7), which again hints at the regional strategy Paul intentionally pursues in Acts (cf. 13:49).[69] He focuses on leading population centers, where the majority of the people are concentrated, knowing such urban mission strategies will have an expanding ripple effect on the wider vicinity (περίχωρος) and surrounding populations.

Another of Paul's core strategies is to preach the good news continuously, wherever he happens to be. Even when opposed, he remains undaunted by threats and "continually preaches the good news" (εὐαγγελιζόμενοι, 14:7).[70] He is convinced that the Spirit is leading his journey, and therefore he constantly communicates the gospel message wherever he finds himself. Even while fleeing persecution in Iconium, Paul and Barnabas still boldly evangelize in Lystra, Derbe, and the surrounding regions.

LYSTRA AND DERBE (14:8–21A)

Miracles and Relevant Proclamation

Paul and Barnabas arrive in Lystra, where Luke tells a colorful story about the healing (σωθῆναι) of a man lame from birth (14:8–10).[71] This reemphasizes one of Paul's missional approaches; miracles such as healings confirm the truth of the message he is preaching. However, in this instance, the miracle leads to the unintended result of Lystrans worshipping Paul and Barnabas as Hermes and Zeus (14:11–13).[72]

Paul and Barnabas rush into the crowd to stop this and preach briefly (14:14–18). There is no mention of Jews or a synagogue in Lystra, which helps to explain the dissimilar nature of this speech, which seeks to find common ground with a Gentile audience through natural theology and contains no direct Scripture quotations, in contrast to 13:16–47. They argue

---

officials threatening Paul and Barnabas, and therefore safer. Barrett, *Acts*, 1:672–73; Witherington, *Acts*, 420.

69. Περίχωρος pertains to being around an area, neighboring; BDAG, 808.

70. The present participle emphasizes continual action.

71. This story intentionally parallels Peter's miracle narrative in 3:1–10: both start with an identical description of the lame man, who leaps up and walks once healed, each healer looks intensely at the lame man, each uses ἀτενίσας. Witherington, *Acts*, 422–23. Luke is highlighting the divine plan and Paul's authority as a healer.

72. Cf. the parallels with the myth in Ovid, *Metamorphoses*, 8.626–724, also set in the Phrygian country.

that God is present in creation, which is a silent witness (μάρτυς) of his goodness, and that God seeks to satisfy (ἐμπιπλῶν) the needs of people and give them joy (εὐφροσύνης), because he cares about them (14:15–17).[73] Relevant preaching tailored to his audience is one of Paul's distinctive missionary strategies in Acts; "the ability to adapt one's form to the audience was essential for good rhetoricians."[74]

Persecution and Divine Providence

Jews from Pisidian Antioch and Iconium arrive and convince the crowd to stone (λιθάσαντες) Paul, drag him out of the city, and leave him for dead (νομίσαντες αὐτὸν τεθνηκέναι, 14:19).[75] Luke may be elevating Paul as the "noble sufferer" here, but is primarily highlighting that this is sometimes the result when one takes the mission of God seriously (cf. 14:22; 9:16).[76] Luke's purpose is to reassure his readers when they undergo similar experiences; they should not be surprised when they suffer, and God will care for them, as he cares for Paul.[77]

"The disciples" (μαθητῶν) who surround (κυκλωσάντων) Paul's body to protect him are probably the new Lystran converts (14:20).[78] This and Paul's two follow-up visits show that a new church is established in Lystra (14:21–23; 16:1–3). Paul gets up, rests for a day in Lystra, then departs for Derbe (14:20).[79] Once again, human opposition does not defeat the mission, but divine providence sustains and furthers it.

73. Schnabel, *Mission*, 2:1117–18. This anticipates the famous Areopagus speech (Acts 17:24–31).

74. Keener, *Acts*, 2:2157–58.

75. Luke avoids saying Paul dies, but implies that Paul is unconscious or semi-conscious after a severe beating; Jesus's prophecy concerning how much Paul would have to suffer for the sake of his name is being fulfilled (9:16). Cf. Paul's own words in 2 Cor 11:23–25, also using ἐλιθάσθην. This episode reinforces Luke's theme of persecution and the suffering of the messenger of the word, discussed previously, and the apostolic ethos of the early church as a primary missional stimulus.

76. There is no doubt that the bravery of Christian sufferers is impressive to observers; Galen writes of Christians that "their contempt of death is patent to us every day," Stark, *Rise of Christianity*, 165. See Stark's discussion on suffering and martyrdom as rational choice, *Rise of Christianity*, 163–89: "How much more credible witnesses could be found than those who demonstrate the worth of a faith by embracing torture and death?" (188). On the "righteous sufferer," see Pesch, *Apostelgeschichte*, 1:250.

77. See part 4 for more on this theme.

78. They could be Paul's unnamed traveling companions (13:13), though this is less likely. Johnson, *Acts*, 253.

79. Luke continues to focus on the mission and establishment of churches,

In Derbe, Paul and Barnabas preach the good news (εὐαγγελισάμενοι) and "made many disciples" (μαθητεύσαντες ἱκανούς, 14:21a).[80] These phrases imply that they establish the nucleus of another new church and regional mission with many disciples in Derbe, though Luke provides no additional details.[81] This repeats their established strategic pattern.

RETURN TO SYRIAN ANTIOCH (14:21B-28)

It would probably be easier for Paul and Barnabas to continue southeast in the direction they are going and return to Syrian Antioch overland via Tarsus, the city of Paul's birth.[82] However, their goal is not to return home quickly, but to complete the task they have received, and ensure that their efforts are not in vain.[83] For this reason, Paul and Barnabas return through every city they have visited, even though they have suffered threats in most of them, and actual violence in Lystra. "This return through the cities already evangelized is far from a flight; it is a pastoral visitation . . . the image of the apostles is of truly philosophical courage as they return to the places where they had been so badly treated."[84]

Strengthening the Churches

As they go back through Lystra, Iconium, and Antioch, they strengthen (ἐπιστηρίζοντες—establish, strengthen, render firmer) the disciples by encouraging (παρακαλοῦντες—exhort, admonish, comfort, instruct) them to persevere in the faith (ἐμμένειν τῇ πίστει, 14:21-22). Ἐπιστηρίζω only occurs in the NT in Acts.[85] Luke relates it to the pastoral follow-up and en-

---

Witherington, *Acts*, 428. "Luke draws our attention here not so much to the personality or power of Paul as to the process by which early Christian communities came into being and were nurtured. The value of this text lies . . . in the feel it gives us for the pastoral practices of the early Messianists," Johnson, *Acts*, 256.

80. Derbe is about 60 miles southeast of Lystra, on the road between Iconium and Laranda; Keener, *Acts*, 2:2178; Schnabel, *Mission*, 2:1121. This is the only time when the verb μαθητεύω is uses in Luke-Acts; cf. Matt 13:52; 27:57; 28:19: "make disciples of all the nations." Johnson, *Acts*, 253.

81. Their success in Derbe is underscored by Gaius, a later representative from that church (20:4; cf. 16:1).

82. They take this overland route at the beginning of their second journey.

83. Barrett, *Acts*, 1:685. The time of year and mountainous terrain may also be factors.

84. Johnson, *Acts*, 253.

85. Cf. Jesus's command to Peter after he has been restored (Luke 22:32): "strengthen your brothers" (στήριξον τοὺς ἀδελφούς σου). Στηρίζω is the root of ἐπιστηρίζω, and

couragement of the churches, and it happens in each of Paul's journeys: they strengthen the souls (ψυχάς) of the new disciples here (14:22); Judas and Silas strengthen the brothers at the church at Antioch through prophetic encouragement (15:32); Paul and Silas strengthen the churches throughout Syria and Cilicia (15:41); and Paul strengthens the disciples throughout the Galatian and Phrygian regions (18:23). This four-fold repetition of ἐπιστηρίζω underscores its strategic significance in Luke's mind. Their message to the fledgling communities is sobering: "We must go through many hardships to enter the kingdom of God" (14:22b).[86] This reference to the persecution the new converts are enduring is an attempt to reassure them that this is not abnormal. "The task for Paul and Barnabas is the stabilization of new communities in the face of opposition."[87]

The visiting of already founded churches represents a new stage in Paul's missional strategy. After the founding of the core of a Christian community, Paul tends to leave quickly (though see Acts 14:3), often forced out by threats and persecution. He presumably wants to prevent these new churches from growing overly dependent on him and allow them to learn how to function independently. However, he does not leave them permanently, but returns for pastoral visits to train and strengthen them in their faith and mission.[88]

Paul does not personally lead these infant churches long-term in Acts. However, he is willing to sacrifice, even to the point of personal endangerment, to support and equip them so they can survive and flourish.[89] These initial house gatherings are meant to become bases for regional outreach, so Paul also trains them to impact their surrounding areas and to respond to persecution with resilience. Luke portrays Paul as a leader worth imitating, who does everything within his power to assist these young house churches in becoming influential permanent hubs for regional missional movements.

---

implies permanence, or being established. Paul uses στηρίζω for such pastoral behavior, and the desire to "establish" new churches and believers (Rom 1:11; 16:25; 1 Thess 3:2, 13; 2 Thess 2:17; 3:3). Johnson, *Acts*, 254. Cf. 1 Pet 5:10; 2 Pet 1:12.

86. Cf. 1 Cor 6:9–10; 15:10. Part 4 will examine this theme in more detail.

87. Johnson, *Acts*, 254.

88. Such visits are more useful after a period on their own, in which these new communities can discover questions and challenges with which they need Paul's help.

89. This missional priority can also be seen in Paul's second and third journeys; he returns to each of these cities, "strengthening the churches/disciples" (15:41; 16:1–5; 18:23). He is determined that the newly founded churches will flourish and visits them at least three times to follow-up and strengthen them.

Appointing Local Leadership

It is not enough to strengthen and encourage the new churches; they also require a long-term, local leadership structure, which will help them to develop in a healthy way. To provide this stability, Paul and Barnabas appoint elders for each new congregation (κατ'ἐκκλησίαν πρεσβύτερους, 14:23a).[90] This results in recognized local leadership and direction as the churches grow: "As with the visitation and exhortation, Luke is showing how the early communities were nurtured and stabilized."[91]

Paul and Barnabas solemnly commission the new elders in each church, presenting (παρέθεντο) them to the Lord in whom they had recently put their trust (14:23c). Παρατίθημι has the connotation of presenting to another or "entrusting," usually in deposit or for safekeeping.[92] Luke emphasizes the soberness of this occasion, saying they do this, "having prayed with (multiple) fastings" (προσευξάμενοι μετὰ νηστειῶν, 14:23b), and with the laying on of hands (χειροτονήσαντες, 14:23a).[93] The commissioning of these elders echoes that of Paul and Barnabas as they began this very journey (13:2-3). This episode completes a ministry cycle for Luke; Paul and Barnabas have been appointed and sent out on mission with prayer, fasting and the laying on of hands at Antioch, and now they are doing the same for new leaders appointed to lead the churches their efforts have produced. These leaders will presumably repeat this missional cycle as their churches grow.

The appointing of elders in every church is another aspect of Paul's missional strategy in Acts. Individual congregations require local leadership and pastoral care. In this case Paul waits briefly, perhaps to see who will prove faithful and capable, emerging as natural leaders within the new communities. However, Paul selects local overseers relatively quickly, to help lead the

---

90. Πρεσβύτερος may be borrowed from the Jewish synagogue, and is common in the NT (e.g., Acts 4:5; 11:30; 15:6; 1 Tim 5:17; 1 Pet 5:1-2; 2 John 1; 3 John 1; and esp. Tit 1:5); Witherington, *Acts*, 429.

91. Johnson, *Acts*, 254.

92. Johnson, *Acts*, 255. See Lev 6:4; Ps 30:5; Luke 12:48. Jesus commits (παρατίθεμαι) his spirit into the Father's hands (Luke 23:46); Paul later commends (παρατίθεμαι) the Ephesian elders to God and his grace (Acts 20:32).

93. Κειροτονέω literally means to stretch out the hands, and is used for the raising of hands in an election (Plato, *Laws*, 763E); Josephus uses it of being "appointed" to the chief priesthood (*Ant.*, 13.45). Cf. with the appointment of the Seven (6:5-6), Paul's commission and receiving the Spirit (9:17; 8:17), and the appointment of Paul and Barnabas themselves (13:1-3). This is an important aspect of the leadership development process of the early church. Paul uses κειροτονέω for the "appointment" of Titus as representative of the churches (1 Cor 8:19). Johnson, *Acts*, 254.

church forward; this provides the young communities with much-needed stability, sustainability, and direction for further missional growth.

Speaking the Word Everywhere

Paul and Barnabas make their way down to Perga, where they "were speaking the word" (λαλήσαντες τὸν λόγον, 14:25). This "aside" sheds insight into Paul's missionary strategy in Acts—he speaks the word everywhere he goes. Paul and Barnabas are simply passing through Perga, on their way home to Antioch; this does not seem to be a strategic or intentional stop. Yet even after the lengthy trip and the suffering they have endured, they actively speak the word. Acts also mentions this practice in Salamis (13:5), Paphos (13:12), Pisidian Antioch (13:16–49), Iconium (14:1), Lystra and Derbe (14:6–7), and again in Derbe, after being nearly stoned to death (14:21).[94] This narrative pattern rhetorically reinforces the importance of speaking the gospel to anyone who will listen, no matter where one may be or what obstacles one may encounter. This resolute evangelistic commitment is fundamental for Luke.[95]

Returning to Home Base

Upon leaving Perga, Paul and Barnabas travel to Attalia, and sail back to Antioch, the origin of their journey (14:24–26). This detail reveals another aspect of Paul's comprehensive missional strategy in Acts. For Luke, when a church sends missionaries to accomplish a task, they must return to report on their progress.[96] Luke emphasizes this in the way he describes Antioch, "from which they had been commissioned (παραδεδομένοι—handed over) to the grace of God for the work that they had accomplished/completed" (τὸ ἔργον ὃ ἐπλήρωσαν, 14:26). This accountability aspect is crucial. Paul and Barnabas are responsible to return to their sending congregation to give an account of what has happened since they left. This is underscored by Luke's use of ἀναγγέλλω (to give a report, 14:27). Paul and Barnabas are not traveling haphazardly on their own; they have deep roots, are attached to a local

94. On the first journey, only in Seleucia and Attalia (both port cities) is there no mention of Paul preaching the word (two out of nine destinations). The reader can assume Paul follows this pattern there as well.

95. And for the epistolary Paul, cf. Rom 10:15: "How will they believe in him whom they have not heard? And how will they hear without a preacher?"

96. This practice is repeated at the end of Paul's second journey (18:22), and likely would be at the end of his third, were Paul not taken captive in Jerusalem.

congregation in Syrian Antioch, and must return to that fellowship to give an account. "Throughout this narrative, Paul and Barnabas are portrayed as loyal and active members of the local Antiochean congregation; they had been commissioned by it, and now they report back."[97]

Upon arriving in Antioch, "they gathered the church together and reported all that God had done through them and how he had opened the door of faith (θύραν πίστεως) to the Gentiles" (14:27).[98] This gathering presumably includes quite a lot of dramatic stories and celebration, as Paul and Barnabas share the events that have transpired on their expedition. Here is a church that has participated in Paul and Barnabas's epic journey as their senders and "home base," and that has a personal stake in its outcome. They sacrificially gave them up for the Spirit's assignment, and now they eagerly receive reports about the mission. "The whole church had been involved in sending them out, in response to God's call. Reporting back was a way of encouraging those believers to see how God had been answering their prayers."[99]

Recovery and Relationships

Luke emphasizes that Paul and Barnabas stay in Antioch for "no little time" (χρόνον οὐκ ὀλίγον, 14:28).[100] They doubtless take this time to rest, as well as re-engage with life in Antioch.[101] The travel they have returned from would have been exhausting on its own, not to mention the challenges and persecution which they have endured. To be effective missionaries for the long-term, they must couple the times of intensive work with periods of recuperation. This cycle of exertion and recovery is important—Luke does not portray Paul as "super-human," able to continually live the intensive lifestyle of these journeys. He requires times of rejuvenation to prepare for the next missional excursion.

97. Johnson, *Acts*, 255. There are also theological reasons: "In a work that emphasizes the continuity of ethnically mixed churches with Israel's biblical heritage, Paul's return to Syrian Antioch (14:26) reinforces his connection with a center that, in turn, was birthed by the Jerusalem church (11:19–20)," Keener, *Acts*, 2:2190.

98. The use of "door" (θύρα) is a distinctively Pauline expression (e.g., 1 Cor 16:9; 2 Cor 2:12; Col 4:3), not found elsewhere in the NT; Johnson, *Acts*, 255.

99. Peterson, *Acts*, 416.

100. The duration of this stay is uncertain, Barrett, *Acts*, 1:693. This is a figure of speech called litotes, an affirmative expressed by the negative of the contrary (cf. 12:18), Peterson, *Acts*, 416.

101. This strategic theme is repeated in 18:23, at the end of Paul's second journey. They probably also re-enter the church's leadership.

Luke also clarifies that they stay for this extended time "with the disciples" (σὺν τοῖς μαθηταῖς, 14:28). Paul and Barnabas spent a significant amount of time leading and ministering together in Syrian Antioch prior to embarking on their first journey (at least a "whole year," ἐνιαυτὸν ὅλον, 11:26), and will have formed substantial relationships within that church. Many of these would be refreshing friendships with whom they enjoy shared experience and history, and therefore beneficial to their rest and recovery.[102]

CONCLUSION

Keener comments on the significance of this first journey: "Although the short-range results of Paul's mission seem small compared with his later ministry in more cosmopolitan Ephesus or Corinth, this southern Anatolian mission provided Paul necessary experience and laid the foundation for a growing movement."[103] Multiple repeated themes and patterns emerge in these foundational episodes, revealing the missional strategies which Luke advocates to establish and expand the church. Tannehill highlights some of these:

> Acts 13–14 presents a representative picture of Paul's mission and includes many themes that we will encounter again. He preaches first in the Jewish synagogues but turns to Gentiles when the synagogue preaching is no longer possible. He announces the one God to Gentiles who have no contact with Jewish monotheism. He repeatedly encounters persecution and moves on when necessary, but he does not abandon his mission. He works signs and wonders. He strengthens the new churches.[104]

Luke implies that many of these strategies develop incrementally in Paul's practice as he proceeds. There is a discernible developmental progression in his missionary habits, particularly in the second and third journeys. Nevertheless, even in this first excursion his core missional strategies are already in place. Paul flexibly follows the Spirit, existing relationships, and local transport routes in his travel. He focuses on synagogues where Jews

---

102. Paul likely writes his letter to the Galatians during this time in Antioch, before going up to Jerusalem for the council on the Gentiles (Acts 15); Witherington, *Acts*, 430. His success is one of the primary causes of the Council; the Jerusalem leaders need to reconsider the church's structures and missionary efforts in light of such widespread Gentile involvement (15:1–5).

103. Keener, *Acts*, 2:2184.

104. Tannehill, *Narrative Unity*, 2:182.

and God-fearers are concentrated within larger population centers and seeks out people of influence within strategic social networks. He boldly and continually preaches a contextualized gospel message, relies upon miraculous confirmations of his message, and establishes new churches with a wider vision for regional impact. Finally, he is undeterred by persecution, intentionally strengthens the new churches through pastoral visits and appointing local leadership, and maintains a beneficial connection to his home base in Antioch. Through these carefully crafted stories Luke is urging his readers to note and imitate these strategies in their own missional contexts, and he will further develop them in Paul's subsequent journeys.

Chapter 9

Paul's Second Journey (15:30—18:23a)

Do not be afraid, but speak and do not be silent; for I am with you, and no one will lay a hand on you to harm you, for there are many in this city who are my people.

—ACTS 18:9–10

Table 9.1 The Second Itinerary (15:30—18:23a)[1]

15:30	Syrian Antioch		17:1	Amphipolis, Apollonia, Thessalonica
15:41	Syria and Cilicia			
16:1	Derbe and Lystra		17:10	Berea
16:6	Phrygia and Galatia (but not Asia)		17:15	Athens (by foot or ship)
16:7	Mysia (but not Bithynia)		18:1	Corinth
16:8	Troas		18:18	Cenchrea
16:11	Samothrace and Neapolis (by ship)		18:19	Ephesus (by ship)
16:12	Philippi		18:22	Caesarea (by ship), Jerusalem, Syrian Antioch

---

1. Unless otherwise noted, it can be assumed that Paul walks from place to place.

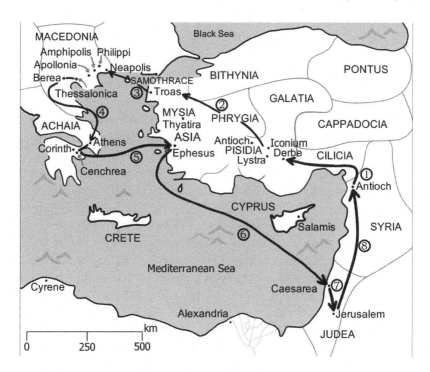

In the first journey Luke emphasizes that the conversion and inclusion of Gentiles in the church is genuine; this is not an idiosyncratic development, but a permanent shift. These new churches are "filled with joy and the Holy Spirit" (13:52), "disciples" (14:20–21), experience "signs and wonders" (14:3), undergo suffering to test their faith and trustworthiness (14:22; cf. Luke 8:13–16), and have "faith to be saved" (14:9). These all point to the genuineness of their faith and identity as the true church of God.[2] Paul and Barnabas's unprecedented success among Gentiles provokes controversy in the Jerusalem church (15:1–5), and this leads to the Jerusalem Council (15:6–35), which brings clarity to many of the questions about Gentile inclusion and the Jewish Law.[3] Plans for Paul's second journey take shape in the context of this affirmation and endorsement of his Gentile mission.

2. Johnson, *Acts*, 257.

3. The issue at hand for the Council is not *if* Gentiles are to be admitted into the new fellowship of God's people, but *on what basis*; do they need to become Jewish proselytes, including circumcision and observance of the law, or has the new reality inaugurated by Jesus the Messiah rendered these proselyte requirements unnecessary?

THROUGH SYRIA, CILICIA, AND GALATIA (15:30—16:5)

The First Priority—Strengthening the Churches

After the resolution of the Jerusalem Council, Paul says to Barnabas, "let us go back and visit (ἐπισκεψώμεθα) our brothers in every city where we preached the word of the Lord and see how they are" (15:36). Ἐπισκέπτομαι means to visit, and carries the connotation of being concerned about, inspecting one's progress, and looking after in order to provide for and help.[4] All of these are motivations for Paul's desire to "visit" the churches, and this suggestion prompts Paul's second journey. These include the places they went in Cyprus, which Barnabas ends up visiting (15:39). This journey is first a pastoral journey, as Paul does not enter new territories until 16:6–12; he seems unclear about continuing his pioneering ministry at this stage, only mentioning plans to visit the churches from his first visit (15:36). This underscores Paul's strategic priority: pastoral care of the new churches and continued relationship with them is his first concern.[5] Barnabas takes John Mark with him to Cyprus after a sharp disagreement (παροξυσμός) with Paul over Mark's suitability for the task,[6] and Paul selects Silas to travel with him (15:37–40).[7]

Paul and Silas's first task is to "go throughout Syria and Cilicia, strengthening the churches" (ἐπιστηρίζων τὰς ἐκκλησίας, 15:41).[8] What ἐπιστηρίζω means in Acts and the NT has been seen in the previous chapter, but in the LXX it also has the connotation of causing to rest on, or supporting.[9]

---

4. BDAG, 378.

5. One can feel Paul's tenderness towards these young churches in the way that he speaks of them as "our brothers," and in his eagerness to check on them and remain close to them. Cf. this theme in Paul's letters, Rom 1:11; Phil 1:3–8; 1 Thess 2:8; 1 Cor 4:15; 2 Cor 11:28–29.

6. Caused by Mark's "desertion" in 13:13. "Luke does not portray his heroes as free from human passions; he uses a strong term to describe this quarrel," Bruce, *Acts*, 249. See also 15:1–2.

7. Silas is an excellent choice; he can represent the Jerusalem church (15:32), interpret the Jerusalem decree (16:4), is a capable co-worker and possible co-author of some of Paul's letters (1 and 2 Thess; 1 Cor 1:19), and is a Roman citizen (16:37–38). Witherington, *Acts*, 473.

8. Ἐπιστηρίζω is used in Acts 4 times in this sense: 14:22; 15:32, 41; 18:23. Luke uses the related word στερεόω, to strengthen, make firm, make solid, in the same sense in 16:5.

9. Liddell and Scott, *Lexicon*, 660. E.g., Ps 31:8: "You have *set* my feet [caused them to stand] in a large place"; Exod 17:12: "Moses' hands were heavy . . . and Aaron and Hur *supported* his hands, one on one side and the other on the other. Thus, his hands were steady until the sun set."

Luke may be drawing on this tradition to create an image of Paul's pastoral effect on the churches: Paul provides support and stability to these young congregations by allowing them to metaphorically lean on the strength and maturity of his life and faith.

This journey parallels the pastoral circuit of 14:22–23, though the cities are in reverse order because they are approaching from the opposite direction, and this one includes Paul's hometown of Tarsus in Cilicia (9:11; 21:39; 22:3).[10] It is notable that just as in the first journey (13:4), they begin with the more hospitable audience of a hometown. After passing through the Cilician gates and some rugged mountainous territory, Paul and Silas reach Derbe and then go to Lystra and the other cities in the area where there are newly founded churches. "As they traveled from city to city, they delivered the decisions reached by the apostles and elders in Jerusalem . . . so the churches were strengthened (ἐκκλησίαι ἐστερεοῦντο) in the faith and grew daily in numbers" (16:4–5). Luke uses στερεόω, related to ἐπιστηρίζω, which has the nuance of causing to become firmer, often in matters of conviction or commitment.[11] Their visit and news of the Jerusalem decree strengthens the churches and reassures them of their legitimacy; Luke is keen to show that they are healthy and strong in faith, conviction, and commitment, resulting in daily growth (an intentional echo of 2:47). "Once again, Luke makes the important point that resolution of doctrinal and practical issues in the churches promoted the work of the gospel and led to rapid growth (cf. 6:7; 9:31)."[12]

Team Ministry

In Lystra, Paul recruits Timothy to join him in his travels (16:1–3).[13] Timothy probably had been converted on one of Paul's two previous visits to Lystra

10. 9:30; 11:25—Did Paul himself help to establish the church in Tarsus, shortly after his conversion? Gal 1:21, 23 indicates that Paul carried out early ministry in the area. They also appear to be following the areas to which the Jerusalem letter is addressed (15:23); Peterson, *Acts*, 449.

11. BDAG, 943. Cf. Acts 3:7, where the lame man's ankles are strengthened (ἐστερεώθησαν); 1 Kgdms 2:1 LXX: "My heart exults (ἐστερεώθη—is strengthened and established) in the LORD"; Xenophon, *Cyropaedia*, 8.8.8: "to *harden* the body by labour and perspiration." Στερεός, the root word, means firm, hard, solid.

12. Peterson, *Acts*, 452.

13. Timothy becomes one of the most important figures in the Pauline mission. He is mentioned in Acts 17:14–15; 18:5; 19:22; 20:4, and is acknowledged as Paul's "fellow worker" (Rom 16:21), special delegate (1 Cor 4:17; 16:10; Phil 2:19; 1 Thess 3:2, 6), and one of the co-sponsors (co-writers?) of several of Paul's letters (2 Cor 1:1; Phil 1:1; Col 1:1; 1 Thess 1:1; 2 Thess 1:1; Phlm). Paul (or a later writer, perhaps Luke) writes 1 and 2 Timothy to him, revealing the fond filial relationship between Paul and his loyal helper.

(14:6–18, 21–23).[14] Luke emphasizes that Timothy comes highly recommended (ἐμαρτυρεῖτο) from the brothers at Lystra and Iconium (16:2).[15] Timothy's addition to Paul's traveling team is a milestone: for the first time, one of Paul's (direct or indirect) converts is joining him full-time in his missionary work. This is a mutually beneficial relationship; Timothy is an excellent Pauline co-worker and a tireless assistant to the ministry, and he undoubtedly receives significant mentoring and training along the way.[16]

Timothy's addition highlights another of Luke's strategic missionary distinctives: team ministry. Paul almost never travels or ministers alone in Acts.[17] Over the course of three journeys, Paul travels with at least thirteen specified co-workers: Barnabas (first journey), John Mark (13:4–13), Silas (second journey), Timothy (16:1; 17:14, 15; 18:5; 19:22; 20:4), the author of Acts (three "we passages"), Aquila and Priscilla (18:1–4, 18–20), Sopater, Aristarchus, Secundus, Gaius, Tychicus, and Trophimus (19:29; 20:4).[18] Paul likely looks to these traveling companions for personal support and encouragement, as well as seizing opportunities to train them for future ministry as his apprentices.

Paul also depends on his companions for protection, as travel in the ancient world poses multiple dangers, such as attacks from bandits and pirates.[19] Much evidence of wide-spread banditry in the Roman Empire exists, largely in the form of tombstone inscriptions,[20] and the great lengths to which the Romans go to provide protection for those using the roads,

---

Johnson, *Acts*, 283.

14. In 1 Cor 4:17 Paul calls Timothy his "beloved and faithful son in the Lord." 2 Tim 1:5 speaks of the conversion of his grandmother and mother.

15. He may have been one of the disciples that stood around Paul's body after his stoning in Lystra (14:20). Luke uses μαρτυρέω in a similar way, to speak well of someone who is highly regarded, in 6:3; 10:22, 43; 22:12.

16. Timothy goes on to lead the Ephesian church, as one of Paul's most trusted associates (2 Tim 4:9–13). Why Luke has Paul circumcise Timothy here is a point of significant debate, Keener, *Acts*, 3:2311–22.

17. Possible exceptions: 17:14–34; 18:21, 23. Paul is uncomfortable when alone, as his "command" (ἐντολήν, 17:15) that they bring Silas and Timothy to him in Athens as soon as possible shows.

18. There are others who travel with Paul unnamed in Acts, e.g., Titus (2 Cor 2:13; 7:6; 2 Cor 8:23; Gal 2:3; Tit 1:4), Demas and Crescens (2 Tim 4:10), Artemas (Tit 3:12), and Erastus (2 Tim 4:20).

19. E.g., the bandits/thieves (λῃσταῖς) in the story of the Good Samaritan (Luke 10:30–37); the soldiers traveling on the ship with Paul to Rome (Acts 27:21, 32, 42), who are not only meant to keep the prisoners in captivity, but also to protect the ship from pirate attacks.

20. Shaw, "Bandits," 10–11.

building guard posts, watchtowers, and advance stations.[21] A traveling group provides security from such hazards, and people rarely travel alone for this reason.[22]

As Paul and his companions travel together, they form bonds of friendship, trust, and brotherly love through the dramatic shared experiences Acts describes; they survive riots, beatings, imprisonment, storms, and sleepless nights together, along with months spent on ships, along roads, and around campfires.[23] Luke presents this as an opportunity for Paul to personally mentor and train these young Christians by instilling his distinctive values and strategies into his companions, as well as discerning their strengths, weaknesses, callings, and potential. Teacher/pupil connections develop, similar to the rabbi/student relationship.[24] "It was common for younger men to be disciples of rabbis or to be apprentices in a chosen field . . . If Timothy had any interest in ministry, this invitation provided an exceptional opportunity . . . For Timothy to travel with him [Paul] was to assume a role similar to the disciple role that Jesus's disciples filled in the Gospel."[25] As Paul's "disciples," Timothy and many of these team members apprentice and then go on to become leaders in the network of churches which Paul and his associates establish and oversee.[26] Luke mentions Paul's multiple co-workers to emphasize the strategic value of team ministry, mentoring, and leadership development; this creates personal bonds and expands the trusted leadership base that Paul can draw upon within the emerging church-planting movement.[27]

21. Though some of these are meant to repel enemy armies, they are also solutions to low-level regional threats to security, such as bandits; Shaw, "Bandits," 12.

22. Jesus rarely travels alone, partially for this reason.

23. This sort of adventurous travel is a shared "team experience," which would be common knowledge to Luke's earliest readers (cf. 2 Cor 11:23–27, with its catalogue of hardships). This parallels Jesus's approach: "He appointed twelve, so that *they would be with him* and that he could send them out to preach" (Mark 3:14).

24. Jesus is often called "Rabbi" (ῥαββί) or "Teacher" (διδάσκαλε) in the Gospels; Neusner, "Rabbi," 1–20.

25. Keener, *Acts*, 3:2320–21. Ancient readers would implicitly understand this, so Luke has no need to explain it.

26. E.g., Tychicus: Acts 20:4; Eph 6:21; Col 4:7; 2 Tim 4:12; Tit 3:12.

27. E.g., Timothy, Titus, Silas/Silvanus, Tychicus, and Trophimus. Luke is also probably a Pauline co-worker (Col 4:14; 2 Tim 4:11; Phlm 24) and arguably has the greatest long-term impact by writing Luke-Acts.

INTO EUROPE—PHILIPPI (16:6-40)

Paul and his companions travel throughout the region of Phrygia and Galatia (16:6). This indicates that they plan to travel directly across Galatia and into the province of Asia, perhaps on to Ephesus, but the Spirit has other things in mind.

Following the Guidance of the Holy Spirit

They are "kept (χωλυθέντες—forbidden) by the Holy Spirit from preaching the word in the province of Asia" (16:6).[28] So they travel north, where this happens a second time: "they tried to enter Bithynia, but the Spirit of Jesus did not permit them" (οὐκ εἴασεν αὐτοὺς τὸ πνεῦμα Ἰησοῦ, 16:7). "What these verses show is that Paul was not clear in advance of the beginning of this journey what direction God had in mind for him to go once he completed the circuit of the already founded churches in Syria, Cilicia, and southern Galatia. Paul would thus try various possibilities until divine guidance opened a door and showed him the way."[29] The Holy Spirit is "squeezing" Paul and his companions down a western path, by preventing them from going south into Asia, or north into Bithynia: "The Spirit blocked every direction sought by human initiative, and left only an opening to Europe."[30] As they go west into Mysia they follow standard protocol and go to the port city of Troas, the nearest urban center to which they are permitted to travel (16:8).[31]

The positive guidance they are seeking materializes in Troas, in the form of a night vision (ὅραμα διὰ [τῆς] νυκτός):[32] "A man from Macedonia" begs Paul, "Come over to Macedonia and help us" (διαβὰς εἰς Μακεδονίαν βοήθησον ἡμῖν, 16:9).[33] Luke emphasizes that this new direction is not based

---

28. This could be a prophetic word or vision, an internal leading from the Spirit, or circumstances such as a "closed door." Perhaps Paul is not ready for ministry in Ephesus but requires more development before his extraordinarily fruitful stay there (19:10, 20); Keener, *Acts*, 3:2331.

29. Witherington, *Acts*, 478–79. See map at beginning of this chapter.

30. Johnson, *Acts*, 286.

31. Troas is a center of commerce and communication; Hemer, "Troas," 79–112. Later there is a Christian church there, possibly founded by Paul (2 Cor 2:12–13; 2 Tim 4:13; Acts 20:7–12); Witherington, *Acts*, 479.

32. This vision could be a dream, as it comes at night; dreams and visions are common in antiquity and in the NT. Visions (ὅραμα) in Acts: 9:10–12; 10:3, 17, 19; 11:5; 12:9; 16:9–10; 18:9; related trances (ἔκστασις): 3:10; 10:10–16; 11:5; 22:17. Paul reports having revelations (often calling them ἀποκάλυψις), e.g., 2 Cor 12:1–7; Gal 1:12; 2:2; Eph 3:3.

33. Scholars have proposed everything from this man being Luke, Ramsay (*Paul the Traveller*, 202), to Alexander the Great (Barclay, *Acts*, 131–32). Luke only reveals that

on human plans, but is a divine commissioning, which parallels their original Spirit-led commission (13:4).[34] An important aspect of Paul's strategy is to follow the Spirit's guidance. The Spirit may lead indirectly through relationships, roads, or shipping routes. However, the direct leadership of the Holy Spirit supersedes all else, and Paul is willing to abandon his travel plans when the Spirit unequivocally intervenes. This is a progressive revelation: The Spirit first tells them two places they are not to go, so they keep moving in the only available direction, following their *modus operandi* of travel and urban centers. The destination does not become apparent until they arrive in Troas, across the Aegean Sea from Macedonia. This underscores Luke's conviction that the Spirit guides and empowers the mission, and for this reason missionaries should always follow the Spirit's leadership, however it comes.[35]

"Once again, the narrator shows keen interest in the dialogue between human purpose and divine purpose, indicating that Jesus's witnesses, too, must patiently endure the frustration of their own plans in order to discover the opportunity that God holds open. This opportunity may not be the next logical step by human calculation."[36] This carefully crafted episode reveals that the Spirit's guidance can take various forms, both leading positively and inhibiting; it can also emerge progressively over time, to be followed step by step. It also emphasizes the importance of timing in following the Spirit's leadership—it is not yet time for Paul's Ephesian ministry. Finally, it directs missionaries to hold their plans loosely while continually being open to the redirection of the Spirit, even when it seems counterintuitive.

An Urban Center

In response to this vision, Paul and his companions sail to Samothrace and then Neapolis,[37] the port of Philippi (16:11–12), and another strategic urban center in which Paul ministers.[38] It is a Roman *colonia* (κολωνία),[39] and its

---

he is Macedonian.

34. Tannehill, *Narrative Unity*, 2:195.

35. Witherington, *Acts*, 480.

36. Tannehill, *Narrative Unity*, 2:195.

37. From Troas to Neapolis is 156 miles, and Philippi is 10 miles further inland, Witherington, *Acts*, 488.

38. Here they enter "Europe," though this might not mean much to them, as Macedonia and Asia are merely two provinces of the Empire, closely related in language and character, Ramsay, *Paul the Traveller*, 199. Luke is interested to show the gospel crossing ethnic and geographical boundaries in Acts.

39. A *colonia* frequently originated as a settlement of Roman citizens in a conquered territory, to help subdue the local population. Then often it became a place

influence is widespread, particularly in travel, communication, population, and cultural trends.[40] Though it is not a capital, Luke calls Philippi "the leading/first city of Macedonia" (πρώτη[ς] μερίδος [τῆς] Μακεδονίας πόλις, 16:12).[41]

Cultural and Religious Points of Contact

On the Sabbath they go to a "place of prayer" (ἐνομίζετο προσευχήν) outside the city gate, find a group of Jewish women assembled there, and speak with them (ἐλαλοῦμεν, 16:13). Once again, Paul goes to spiritually open places, where he has a naturally receptive point of cultural and religious contact. There is probably no synagogue in Philippi, so this Jewish prayer gathering is his natural entry. He continues with his *modus operandi*: to the Jews first.

People of Influence—Householder Mission

Paul meets Lydia, a dealer in purple cloth from the city of Thyatira (16:14).[42] Luke portrays Lydia as a person of ample social status and financial means. The Lord "opens her heart" (διήνοιξεν τὴν καρδίαν) to respond to Paul's evangelistic words, which emphasizes the divine initiative in her conversion. She and her household are then baptized (ἐβαπτίσθη καὶ ὁ οἶκος αὐτῆς, 16:15), including at least any household servants and children. She "urges/exhorts" (παρεκάλεσεν) Paul and his fellow travelers to come and stay in her home, extending a crucial invitation of hospitality which Luke notes is very persuasive (παρεβιάσατο ἡμᾶς). Paul and his companions stay in her home, training the new Philippian believers and assisting in the emerging outreach

---

where discharged soldiers gained land as their pension (true for Philippi). It enjoyed *libertas* (autonomous government), *immunitas* (from tribute and taxation), and *Ius Italicum* (considered to be part of Italian soil, with a Roman administration, law, and judicial procedure). Barrett, *Acts*, 2:780. Philippi is basically a microcosm of Rome itself; Johnson, *Paul*, 74–76.

40. Thessalonica is the capital of Macedonia, and Amphipolis is the capital of the local district.

41. There are multiple textual variants in this verse; Keener, *Acts*, 3:2382–83. Luke is probably referring to Philippi's "honor rating" in that part of Macedonia. Luke may also be from Philippi, as the first "we" section begins here, which might explain a partiality to it. Interestingly, Philippi is famous for its medical school (Col 4:14; Phil 4:3). Philippi lies on the *Via Egnatia*, the main east-west road across Macedonia, connecting Rome with its eastern provinces, Witherington, *Acts*, 488–90. On "we passages" see Keener, *Acts*, 3:2350–74, who concludes they most likely signify the author's presence.

42. Keener, *Acts*, 1:598–605 discusses Luke's interest in balancing male and female characters.

to the city, while continuing to reach out to the same strategic social network by going to the Jewish place of prayer (16:16).[43]

A growing church is born in Lydia's home, emphasized when after being released from prison Paul and Silas meet with "the brothers" (τοὺς ἀδελφούς) in Lydia's house and encourage them (16:40). Paul, an outsider, succeeds in establishing a missional base in Philippi surprisingly quickly, and the Philippian church begins, all through Lydia's faith and involvement. Luke's implicit strategic missional instructions are apparent: search for natural cultural and religious points of contact, where there will be most openness to the message; focus on householders; and look for influential leaders of status and means within larger social networks (such as the place of prayer).[44] Keener comments on this tendency:

> Luke's consistent interest [is] in persons with occupations of relatively high status. Though Luke emphasizes that the rich cannot be saved (Luke 18:24–25; cf. 3:11; 12:33; 14:33) without divine intervention (18:26–27), he frequently reports the conversion of people of means, who sometimes sacrificed or risked much for their conversion (19:8–9; 24:50–52; cf. Acts 8:27–39; 13:12). All four of Luke's accounts of "household" conversions (Acts 10:2, 24, 44–48; 11:14; 16:15, 34; 18:8) probably concern households of ample means (by the standards of most of the population).[45]

This strategy is highly effective, and Lydia's conversion is an example of the results of such an intentional approach to mission in Philippi.

Table 9.2 Lydia—An Ideal Person of Influence (16:13–40)

- A God-fearer (σεβομένη, 16:14b), with substantial cultural and religious common ground with Paul which provides natural rapport and points of connection (16:13, 14c).

- A householder (οἶκος); by reaching Lydia, Paul reaches into the power-center of an entire household network, illustrated by her household's baptism (16:15).

---

43. They must stay for at least a week, possibly much longer, as the next episode is again on their way to the place of prayer.

44. Befriending the head of a social network is the easiest way to enter a new network as an outsider; a householder usually fits this description in the ancient world. See the previous part for households in the mission.

45. Keener, *Acts*, 3:2399.

- A "person of peace" (Luke 10:5–6), highlighted as spiritually interested and responsive to the Lord's initiative of "opening her heart" (16:14c).

- Lydia's friendships, social status, and business contacts provide a social base for Philippian outreach; her reputation and influence in the community provide Paul and his message social credibility (16:13, 16).[46]

- Lydia's house provides hospitality during Paul's stay, a physical base for mission, and a home for the new church in Philippi (16:15b, 40).

- Lydia's relative wealth provides a financial base for outreach into Philippi and the region, and she becomes a patroness and benefactor of the new Philippian house church (16:14a, 40).[47]

Demonstrating God's Power

In Philippi Paul casts a "python spirit" (πνεῦμα πύθωνα) out of a fortune-telling slave girl (16:16–18).[48] This demonstration of God's power appears to backfire, and Paul and Silas are arrested (16:19–21), stripped, flogged with rods (ῥαβδίζω), and locked in the inner cell of the local jail, with stocks around their feet (16:22–24).[49] Their response is inspiring—"about midnight Paul and Silas were praying and singing hymns of worship to God" (16:25). Once again, their willingness to suffer advances the mission, and their spiritual devotion sustains them through danger and pain. They believe God has providentially led them to Philippi (16:9–10), and "it is possible that they worship God not only in but *for* their sufferings, as a faithful expression of confidence in God's love and sovereignty (cf. Eph 5:20) . . . Paul may have connected suffering with proclamation as a necessary corollary (cf. Acts 14:22); certainly, it was to be expected with it (4:25; 5:41)."[50]

"Suddenly a violent earthquake" (ἄφνω δὲ σεισμὸς . . . μέγας) shakes the prison's foundations, causing the prison doors to fly open and the chains

46. Even if being a foreigner (Thyatiran) lowers her perceived status amongst the Philippian elite.

47. Keener, *Acts*, 3:2408–20 discusses patronage and hospitality in the ancient world.

48. For more details on this incident, see Fontenrose, *Delphic Oracle*; Barrett, *Acts*, 2.784–90; Witherington, *Acts*, 493–96. Rom 15:18–19 and 2 Cor 12:12 indicate that Paul performed such miracles.

49. Miracles do not always achieve their desired end, as at Lystra when the crowds worship Paul and Barnabas as gods (14:8–18). Paul's mission often damages the fortunes of pagan worshippers and craftsmen, as in Ephesus (19:23–41). Cf. Paul's references, 1 Thess 2:2; 2 Cor 11:25 (beaten by these Roman rods, ῥαβδίζω, three times).

50. Keener, *Acts*, 3:2488.

to come loose (16:26).[51] This is another example of the miraculous confirmation of Paul's message (cf. 2 Cor 12:12). The jailer certainly interprets the earthquake this way, for after almost killing himself in despair and being reassured that his prisoners have not fled, he rushes in and cries out, "What must I do to be saved?" (τί με δεῖ ποιεῖν ἵνα σωθῶ;, 16:30). The supernatural validation of the message continues to be central to its advancement in Acts.

Household Conversion

Paul and Silas do not escape, but preach to the traumatized jailer, who is a householder: "Believe in the Lord Jesus, and you will be saved—you and your *household*" (ὁ οἶκός σου, 16:31). This is the οἶκος formula, and Luke emphasizes it two further times by saying that they, "spoke the word of the Lord to him together with all who were in his *house*" (τῇ οἰκίᾳ αὐτοῦ, 16:32), and "he and all those with him were baptized" (16:33). This episode echoes the household conversion stories of Lydia (16:15) and Cornelius (11:14).[52] By reaching a householder, Paul again reaches a household network and establishes another base for further expansion in Philippi, emphasizing this normative pattern in Acts.[53] This story also confirms Paul's missional habit—he preaches to everyone, everywhere, even after physical suffering and being dramatically freed by an earthquake.

Strengthening the New Church

When the magistrates realize that Paul and Silas are Roman citizens, they are alarmed and request that they leave Philippi (16:35–39). However, they do not leave immediately, but return to Lydia's house where there is now a young and growing church. "Lydia's significance was not confined to her being a disciple or hostess to traveling disciples. Luke wishes us to understand that what began as a lodging for missionaries, became home of the embryonic church in Philippi."[54] They meet "the brothers/believers" (τοὺς ἀδελφούς), and encourage them (παρεκάλεσαν, 16:40). Παρακαλέω indicates encouragement, exhortation, and comfort, and represents a stock consolation argument involving the expectation of difficulties and loss so as

51. Earthquakes are often interpreted as the visitation of a god to an area. See Ovid, *Metamorphosis*, 9.782–783; 15.669–679; Lucian, *Lover of Lies*, 22. See Keener, *Acts*, 3:2494–97.

52. Johnson, *Acts*, 301.

53. As Lydia is a Thyatiran, the jailer is a significant Philippian convert.

54. Witherington, *Women*, 149.

to not be overwhelmed by grief.[55] Luke reiterates Paul's priority of comforting, strengthening, and encouraging newly formed communities here as he pauses to console and further establish the church he has recently founded before leaving Philippi.

The Philippian episode is a Lukan masterclass in missional strategy. In full rhetorical flourish, Luke shows how Paul effectively plants a church in a city where he has no existing attachments, and where there are very few Jews; his success is astonishing in a situation that one would expect to be immensely difficult. Once again, Paul establishes the first cells of a church in an influential city, trains them for a time, and then leaves quickly.[56]

Table 9.3 Missional Strategies in the Birth of the Philippian Church
(16:12–40)

- *Strategic points of contact*—the place of prayer (16:13–14).

- *Team ministry*—with Silas (and Luke and others?) throughout.

- *Social networks*—the place of prayer, Lydia and the jailer's households (16:13, 15, 31–34).

- *Householder evangelism*—Lydia, the jailer (16:15, 31–34).

- *Responsive people of influence, status, and means*—Lydia, the jailer (16:14, 33–34).

- *Continual preaching*—at the place of prayer, in the jail (16:13, 28–32).

- *Willingness to suffer*—stripped, flogged, locked in the inner jail with stocks (16:22–24).

- *A lifestyle of prayer, worship, and personal devotion*—even in jail (16:25).

- *Miraculous confirmation of the Word*—exorcism, earth-shaking release from jail (16:18, 26–27).

- *Intentional consolation, strengthening, and encouragement*—at Lydia's house, leaving quickly (16:40).

---

55. The young Philippian church must have found Paul's arrest traumatic. Παρακαλέω is regularly related to building up and strengthening churches in Acts: Barnabas at Antioch (11:23), Paul and Barnabas to the churches from the first journey (14:22), Judas and Silas at Antioch (15:32), and Paul throughout Macedonia (20:2).

56. Paul later writes "the letter of joy" to this church (see Phil 1:3–8 for Paul's affection for this community).

THESSALONICA AND BEREA (17:1–14)

Roads and Cities

After leaving Philippi, Paul and his companions travel along the *Via Egnatia* to Thessalonica, a journey of nearly 100 miles (17:1).[57] As is their practice, the traveling missionaries take the main paved Roman roads through this area. Thessalonica is the capital of the Roman province of Macedonia, confirming that Paul continues the pattern of targeting urban centers on primary road networks.[58]

Jews and God–Fearers

Thessalonica has a large Jewish Diaspora population, and Paul, "as was his custom (κατὰ δὲ τὸ εἰωθός, as was normal), went into the synagogue, and on three successive Sabbath days reasoned/discussed (διελέξατο) with them from the Scriptures, explaining (διανοίγων) and demonstrating (παρατιθέμενος) that the Christ had to suffer and rise from the dead" (17:2–3).[59] Paul is again targeting a potentially receptive group, with whom he has common ground, and preaching a message of relevance to his hearers, built upon the authority of the Hebrew Scriptures. "Luke evidently thinks it possible that three Sabbaths might suffice to gather men into the new brotherhood; having been nurtured in the synagogue they would probably need little instruction beyond the simple identification of the Messiah with Jesus."[60] The initial response is positive: some Jews, a "large number of God-fearing Greeks," and "not a few prominent women" join Paul and Silas in Thessalonica (17:4).

Persecution and Households

However, the Jews grow jealous, start a riot (ἐθορύβουν), and go to the house of Jason (οἰκίαι Ἰάσονος, a householder), assuming Paul and Silas are staying with him (17:5).[61] The mob drags Jason and "some other brothers" before the city officials to accuse them (17:6–9). These hint at a small Thessalonian

57. Keener, *Acts*, 3:2534–35.

58. Stark estimates Thessalonica has a population of 35,000 around CE 100, and summarizes its history and character, *Cities of God*, 51–52; also Johnson, *Paul*, 76–80.

59. These three witness words refer to the process of opening the hearer's mind and presenting proofs in rhetorical format.

60. Barrett, *Acts*, 2:814.

61. This may be the Jason of Rom 16:21, a Pauline co-worker; Barrett, *Acts*, 2:813.

house church, already formed around Jason's household: "As in the case of Lydia's, we are to picture a house-church already in existence."[62] Paul and Silas evade capture and are sent to Berea that night under the cover of darkness (17:10).[63]

Table 9.4 Missional Patterns in the Birth of the Thessalonian Church
(17:1-10)

- *Team ministry*—with Silas throughout (17:4-5, 10).

- *Strategic points of contact and social networks*—the Jews and God-fearers (17:1-2).

- *People of prominence*—within those social networks, Jews, God-fearers, prominent women, who give Paul credibility in the community and the material support and resources his mission requires (17:4).

- *Relevant proclamation*—from the Scriptures, focusing on the Messiah (17:2-3).

- *Embryonic house church*—implied at Jason's house, gathered for discipleship and training in faith and mission (17:5-6, 10).

- *Willingness to suffer*—Paul expects persecution and is prepared when it comes (17:5-8).

- *Rapid departure*—Paul leaves the Thessalonian church, trusting that the foundations he has laid will enable them to impact their city and the surrounding regions with the good news (17:10).

The Thessalonica story confirms multiple familiar strategic patterns. That there is already a congregation of believers at Paul's departure is underscored by the two mentions of "the brothers" in Thessalonica, particularly when they send Paul and Silas off to Berea (17:6, 10).[64] The second reference should be understood as the collective newly founded Christian community, acting in defence and protection of the missionaries. This Thessalonian church grows into one of the significant churches in the region; Paul visits

---

62. Johnson, *Acts*, 306. This is only implied, possibly analogous to Acts 18:6-7. See discussion of house churches in chapter 7.

63. Paul has no problem fleeing danger, as he likewise does in Damascus (9:23-25), Jerusalem (9:30), Pisidian Antioch (13:50-51), and Lystra (14:20). It is also interesting to note how much of the action in Acts takes place at night (5:19; 9:25; 12:6; 16:33). Johnson, *Acts*, 307.

64. Οἱ ἀδελφοί (the brothers) is not a gendered term, as it is in English (e.g., 16:40).

again on his third journey (20:4), confirming his pattern of strengthening and following up.[65]

There is much common ground in Paul's strategies in Philippi and in Thessalonica, including the emphasis on team ministry, significant urban centers, strategic points of contact and social networks, householder outreach amongst prominent people, the embryonic house churches, and a willingness to suffer. Paul likely relies on supernatural confirmations of his message in Thessalonica as well, though Luke does not record any miracles there. Such often repeated patterns highlight Luke's rhetorical narrative in these sections of Acts.

Paul's Missional Strategies in Berea

Paul and Silas flee from Thessalonica to Berea, a city not on the *Via Egnatia*, but fifty miles southwest of Thessalonica by a lesser road.[66] Berea is the most significant city in its district of Bottiaea, though smaller than Philippi and Thessalonica.[67] It also has a synagogue, which Paul and Silas visit immediately, as is their custom (17:10). It is doubtful that Paul had planned to visit Berea, but he perseveres despite this setback.[68] Persecution again affects the trajectory of Paul's travel, but Luke presents this as God's providence, and shows Paul continuing undaunted with his missional task.

The Berean Jews are of more noble character (εὐγενέστεροι) than the Thessalonians and receive Paul's preaching with interest (17:10–11). Many (πολλοί) believe, including several prominent women and men (γυναικῶν τῶν εὐσχημόνων καὶ ἀνδρῶν οὐκ ὀλίγοι, 17:12).[69] Again, Paul targets people of prominence within his most accessible social network, the local synagogue. These converts provide stability as well as vital resources for the fledgling Berean church.

---

65. Paul also writes two letters to them, addressing the inevitable problems and conflicts of a new community.

66. Witherington, *Acts*, 509.

67. Barrett, *Acts*, 2:817.

68. Paul may have planned to continue along the *Via Egnatia* all the way to Rome (cf. Rom 1:13; 15:22–24); he is clear that he wants to visit Rome but has been prevented from doing so.

69. Εὐσχημόνων means "decent" or "proper," but Luke uses it here to designate social standing, in contrast to the Thessalonian "rabble"; Johnson, *Acts*, 308. On prominent women converting, see Castelli, "Gender, Theory," 227–57; Osiek and MacDonald, *A Woman's Place*. This can also be seen in Judaism, Josephus, *J.W.*, 2.560; *Ant.*, 18.81–84; 20.35; Ilan, *Jewish Women*, 211–14.

The riotous Thessalonian Jews hear of Paul's activity in Berea and go there to agitate the crowds (17:13). A core of believers is established by the time Paul leaves, because "the brothers" (ἀδελφοί) send Paul on to Athens, and multiple people escort him (οἱ δὲ καθιστάνοντες, 17:14–15).[70] Paul leaves Silas and Timothy behind, presumably to strengthen the young Berean church and help it endure the crisis of persecution.[71] Paul's first thought is for the welfare and strengthening of the new churches in Acts, even when this requires sacrifice on his part.[72]

ATHENS (17:15–34)

After leaving Berea, Paul arrives alone in Athens,[73] where he waits for Silas and Timothy to re-join him. While in Athens, he becomes greatly distressed (παρωξύνετο—a strong anger or irritation) by the many idols he sees (17:16).[74] Paul reasons (διελέγετο) in the synagogue with the Jews and the God-fearing Greeks, as is his clear pattern by this point. However, he also reasons day by day in the marketplace with anyone who happens to be there (17:17). Paul's strategy once again takes him first to the Jews, yet he also proclaims the word to anyone who will listen. A group of Epicurean and Stoic philosophers debate with him, take him to the Areopagus, and ask him to explain his new teaching (17:18–19).[75] Paul then stands up and delivers one of the most famous and studied messages in Scripture.[76]

70. "The brothers" is Luke's stock term for believers in these new congregations (14:2; 15:36, 40; 16:2, 40; 17:10; 18:18, 27). The "sea" (θάλασσαν, 17:14) points to Paul traveling by boat. This takes him into a new political jurisdiction, safe from his violent pursuers.

71. Paul visits Berea two other times on his next journey (20:1–3). The only further mention of Berea is Paul's traveling companion Sopater of Berea (20:4). This may be the same person as Sosipater (Rom 16:21), who is mentioned with Jason, probably the one from nearby Thessalonica (Acts 17:5).

72. This is shown in Paul's "command" for Silas and Timothy to join him (17:15)—he is uncomfortable alone.

73. Another city of significance and history which Paul visits, Athens is a city of great learning, and a showcase for the grandeur of Greek culture. Witherington, *Acts*, 513; Johnson, *Paul*, 85–93.

74. In the LXX παρωξύνετο refers to God's extreme anger at the idolatry of his chosen people, e.g., Deut 9:18; Ps 106:29; Isa 65:3; Hos 8:5. Witherington, *Acts*, 512.

75. Here ἐπιλαμβάνομαι (apprehend) implies formal or informal arrest; Pesch, *Apostelgeschichte*, 2:134–5.

76. This passage has attracted more scholarly attention than any other in Acts; Bruce, *Acts*, 379–80; Witherington, *Acts*, 511; Barrett, *Acts*, 2:823–84; Johnson, *Acts*, 311–21.

A Relevant and Authoritative Message

This educated, philosophical, Gentile audience is quite different than the familiar synagogue setting. But as always, Paul presents his arguments in a way that is uniquely relevant and tailored to his hearers, connecting purposefully with his audience:[77]

> Throughout the speech, Luke or Paul is using various somewhat familiar notions to pass judgment on and attack idols and the idolatry involved in polytheism. In other words, what we see here is not an attempt to meet pagans halfway, but rather a use of points of contact, familiar ideas and terms, in order to make a proclamation of monotheism in its Christian form . . . This subtle but unwavering approach comports with Paul's commitment to the [Jerusalem] decree, the essence of which was to make sure Gentiles are led away from idolatry and immorality.[78]

Paul begins by calling the Athenians "religious" (δεισιδαιμονεστέρους), a phrase which has an ambiguous double meaning, denoting either pious or superstitious (17:22). He hopes to gain a hearing by appearing complimentary, yet probably actually means the negative sense, that they are overly superstitious, as evidenced by the next verse (cf. 25:19). He then refers to an altar "to an unknown god" (ἀγνώστῳ θεῷ) and declares that he intends to tell them who this god is (17:23).[79] He references something familiar to them, using words and images they can grasp. Paul continues by arguing from natural theology that there is a Creator who created all things and all peoples (17:24–26). "God did this so that people would seek him and perhaps reach out for him and find him, though he is not far from each one of us" (17:27). Paul relates this to poetry familiar to the Athenians: a quote from the Cretan poet Epimenides,[80] and from the Cilician poet Aratus (17:28).[81] Paul always

77. Cf. Acts 14:15–17, in a similar setting in Lystra. Tannehill points out that Luke highlights three kinds of Pauline speeches in Acts: "a mission speech to Jews (13:16–41), a mission speech to Gentiles (17:22–33), and a farewell speech to the elders of the Ephesian church (20:18–35)," *Narrative Unity*, 2:210. These should be seen as example speeches, which would be imitated in other similar settings. A fourth kind of speech in Acts is when on trial before a court (Acts 24–26).

78. Witherington, *Acts*, 518–19.

79. Witherington, *Acts*, 520–23 and Keener, *Acts*, 3:26, 30–32 summarize the scholarly debate about this altar.

80. Epimenides (c. 600 BCE), *Cretica*: "In him we live and move and have our being." Tit 1:12 quotes this same poem; the original no longer exists.

81. Aratus (c. 315–240 BCE), *Phaenomena*, 5.1: "From Zeus let us begin; him do we mortals never leave unnamed; full of Zeus are all the streets and all the market-places of men; full is the sea and the heavens thereof; always we all have need of Zeus. *For we*

cites an authority recognized by his audience to support his argument. In the synagogues, Paul quotes the Hebrew Scriptures extensively, but here his audience would not know these scriptures, so Paul never even mentions them. Persuasive arguments only work within the hearers' frame of reference, so Paul builds his argument in a way that is familiar and authoritative to the Athenians.

Paul ends with a declaration of Jesus, and a call to repentance and belief in him (17:29–31). Luke records three different responses: some reject the message and "sneer" (ἐχλεύαζον), some are unsure and say, "we want to hear you again on this subject," and "others join him and believe" (17:32–34). Among those who believe are Dionysius the Areopagite,[82] a member of the council before which Paul has just spoken, and certainly a householder of some social standing in Athens who would act as a person of peace (Luke 10:5–7) and patron for the church in Athens, and a woman named Damaris.[83] The "others with them" (ἕτεροι σὺν αὐτοῖς) who are converted may be their extended family, or other observers, and would be enough to form a small house church in Dionysius's home.[84]

Some believe that no Christian community forms at Athens at this time.[85] However, Luke's language hints at the beginnings of a house church (17:34): "Luke typically notes the success that leads to the foundation of a community. In this case, the success is obviously modest."[86] More positively, Athens is one of the only places on this journey where Paul is not threatened with violence.[87]

---

are also his offspring." Aratus and Paul are both Cilicians.

82. Eusebius, *Hist. Eccl.*, 3.4.11; 4.23.3, claims that Dionysius becomes the first bishop of Athens. Witherington, *Acts*, 532. The designation Ἀρεοπαγίτης suggests that Dionysius is a member of the Athenian council, and therefore of high social rank. Cf. Aristotle, *Politics*, 1273b–1274a. Johnson, *Acts*, 318.

83. Damaris may be a foreign woman, an educated woman who would serve as a companion of an Athenian at a public occasion, or even a God-fearer who had heard Paul at the synagogue (17:17). Hemer, *Acts*, 232.

84. There would be a larger audience at the Areopagus listening to Luke's speech. Ramsay, *Paul the Traveller*, 248.

85. 1 Cor 16:15 refers to the household of Stephanas of Corinth as the first converts in Achaia (Greece). This may mean the first house church in Achaia, or it may not be literal. Witherington, *Acts*, 533.

86. Johnson, *Acts*, 318.

87. Paul may renounce or modify this intellectual approach when he moves on to Corinth (1 Cor 2:1–5). Relying on God's power rather than wise words appears to be Paul's new methodology, after a less fruitful missional effort in Athens than at most other destinations (1 Cor 1:22–25; Acts 18:9–10).

CORINTH (18:1-18)

Cities and Trade Routes

Upon arriving in Corinth (18:1), Paul continues "his [strategic] policy of sharing the gospel in major cities in the Empire, including especially Roman colony cities."[88] Marshall explains that, "Corinth and Ephesus were the two most important cities visited by Paul in the course of his missionary work, and he stayed in each for a considerable period in order to establish churches which would then evangelize the surrounding areas."[89]

When Paul arrives in Corinth in the early fifties, it is the largest, most prosperous city in Greece.[90] Aphrodite is the patron goddess of the city, and while Greek Corinth is known for its high levels of immorality, it provides Paul the ideal base in Greece for making contacts with many kinds of people and founding a new religious group.[91] Paul spends at least eighteen months in Corinth establishing a congregation of Jews and non-Jews (18:11).

Ministry Partnerships, Households, and Social Networks

In Corinth, Paul meets a Christian couple named Priscilla and Aquila who have recently arrived from Rome (18:2).[92] He shares their occupation as tentmakers (σχηνοποιοί, more likely leather workers[93]), living and working with them initially while he reasons (διελέγετο) in the synagogue every

---

88. Witherington, *Acts*, 535.

89. Marshall, *Acts*, 291; note the emphasis on establishing churches which then reach their surrounding areas. Luke probably does not have access to the Corinthian letters when writing Acts, for he fails to mention Stephanas, Fortunatus, Achaicus, or Gaius (1 Cor 1:14-16; 16:17). However, there are still multiple points of convergence, seven of which Witherington itemizes, *Acts*, 537.

90. Corinth has ports on either side of the Isthmus of Corinth, which give it a commercial advantage because shippers can save time by transferring their cargo overland from one port to the other, Stark, *Cities of God*, 50. See Johnson, *Paul*, 94-105, for more on Corinth.

91. Partly because it hosts the Isthmian games every two years, attracting foreign travelers from all over the Empire; Witherington, *Acts*, 538.

92. This couple is always mentioned together in the NT (18:18, 26; Rom 16:3; 2 Tim 4:19). They must be welcome companions for Paul after a lonely period of travel and ministry in Athens. Their home is another example of the strategic value of hospitality as a beachhead for mission (18:3).

93. Keener, *Acts*, 3:2732-36 concludes leather worker is the more probable meaning, though this is debated. Paul is willing to engage in manual labor, looked down upon by the Corinthian elites, to engage the city missionally.

Sabbath (18:3–4).[94] Luke is hinting here at another strategic type of social network in the ancient world, the workplace network: "Associations and guilds formed on the basis of shared crafts were a common feature of the Hellenistic world; the partnership of Aquila, Priscilla, and Paul appears as an informal example."[95] Many of Paul's initial Corinthian contacts may come from Priscilla and Aquila's trade networks.[96]

When Silas and Timothy arrive from Macedonia, Paul devotes himself to full-time proclamation (διαμαρτυρόμενος) in Corinth (18:5). However, the Jews oppose him, so Paul leaves the synagogue and goes next door to Titius Justus's house, a God-fearer (σεβομένου τὸν θεόν) who has recently believed (18:6–7).[97] "As in the case of Lydia (16:15), a center for the new community is found in the household of one who was a God-fearer."[98] Soon Crispus the synagogue ruler (ἀρχισυνάγωγος) converts, along with his entire household (ὅλῳ τῷ οἴκῳ αὐτοῦ, 18:8a).[99] This is another οἶκος formula, and an additional instance of intentional householder mission focusing on Jews and God-fearers in Acts.

The conversion of a synagogue ruler is a notable achievement for Paul and has ramifications in the larger Corinthian community. When "many other Corinthians heard" (πολλοὶ τῶν Κορινθίων ἀκούοντες) about the conversion of Crispus, they "believed and were baptized" (ἐπίστευον καὶ ἐβαπτίζοντο) as well, following his leadership (18:8b).[100] As a householder, his household follows him, and this is explicit in the text, but as a synagogue ruler, he also has influence within a more widespread network of relationships. Because they hear about his experience, Crispus's household *and* wider social network follow his lead in converting, which shows the missional potential of social networks. By reaching Crispus, a person of influence, Paul reaches many others as well.[101]

94. Corinth has a large and long-established Jewish colony which adds to its religious diversity.

95. Johnson, *Acts*, 322.

96. "[The gospel travels] along the natural networks of relationship in each city and between cities. The families and houses of certain individuals seem to have been the starting points, and connections of work and trade seem to have been important," Meeks, *Urban Christians*, 28.

97. Probably also a Roman citizen and prosperous homeowner, likely Gaius (Rom 16:23); Keener, *Acts*, 3:2745.

98. Johnson, *Acts*, 323.

99. 1 Cor 1:14–16 confirms his baptism.

100. Their "hearing" could refer to Paul's preaching, but the text seems to imply hearing about the conversion of Crispus. Regardless, Crispus's conversion has a noticeable impact on the growth of the community.

101. Meeks explains this dynamic of influence within and between household

A Reassuring Vision and the Foundations for Regional Mission

Paul has another vision (ὅραμα) in Corinth, in which Christ inspires him to stay and finish the work there: "Do not be afraid (μὴ φοβοῦ),[102] but speak (λάλει) and do not be silent (μὴ σιωπήσῃς); for I am with you, and no man will attack you in order to harm you, because I have many people in this city" (18:9-10). Jesus wants Paul to stay, where in the past he has fled from impending danger (9:23-25, 30; 13:50-51; 14:20). Christ's declaration that he has "many people" in Corinth highlights another function of social networks: they are also for protection.[103] Jesus offers Paul the reassurance that there are many people in the city who will be available to protect and defend him if needed.[104]

This vision gives Paul reassurance and fortitude, and he stays in Corinth for a total of eighteen months, "teaching (διδάσκων) the word of God among them" (18:11). This is the longest he has stayed in any one place up to this point in his journeys. Διδάσκω implies that during this time Paul lays crucial foundations and develops the Corinthian church into a place of maturity where it is equipped to impact its surrounding area.[105] Paul's strategic goal is always to establish a nucleus of Christ-followers and then train them to impact their surrounding regions, and his extended Corinthian stay allows him to accomplish this.

The predicted persecution materializes, and Paul is brought to court (18:12-13). However, he is released, and the crowd turns on another synagogue ruler, Sosthenes, and beats him (18:14-17).[106] Paul stays in Corinth

---

networks, *Urban Christians*, 30.

102. Cf. 1 Cor 2:3: "I came to you in weakness and fear and much trembling." Paul is clearly afraid in Corinth.

103. E.g., the Derbe disciples surround and protect Paul when he is stoned (14:20); the Thessalonians protect Paul from attacks (17:10); the Bereans escort Paul safely to Athens (17:15).

104. This could be understood as an evangelistic promise: "I have many people who will be saved in this city" (Johnson, *Acts*, 324, most other commentators). However, given that it directly follows the statement about Paul's safety, protection is a better interpretation. Jesus could be saying that many people are yet to believe, and they will be the ones available to protect Paul. Keener, *Acts*, 3:2756-58 concludes it most likely "refers to those who will be supportive though they are not yet believers (Luke 10:6; cf. Matt 10:11)."

105. Paul's Corinthian correspondence reveals much of this content and reminds them of the miracles that confirmed his apostolic ministry there (2 Cor 12:12).

106. Possibly because they perceive Sosthenes to be a Christian sympathizer. Sosthenes may convert to the faith, then leave town with Paul; if so, he is mentioned later helping to write to the Corinthians (1 Cor 1:1). This would mean Paul converts two synagogue rulers in Corinth (18:8, 17), quite a triumph. Keener, *Acts*, 3:2778-79 discusses Sosthenes's identity, which remains uncertain.

for many more days (ἡμέρας ἱκανάς), presumably continuing in mission, teaching Christian foundations, training emerging leaders, and equipping the Corinthian church to impact its city and wider Achaean region (18:18).

RETURN TO ANTIOCH (18:19–23A)

Laying Foundations for Future Ephesian Ministry

While returning to Syria, Paul sails to Ephesus with Priscilla and Aquila (18:19a). Paul lays the groundwork for future outreach by visiting the Ephesian synagogue to "reason/converse with the Jews" (διελέξατο τοῖς Ἰουδαίοις, 18:19b). This underscores Paul's commitment to missional engagement at every opportunity. Luke implies that Paul has a brief window of time while waiting for his ship to leave for the Jerusalem area, and even at the end of a long and exhausting trip, he is quick to pursue receptive synagogue contacts in this new city.

Paul has a positive initial response in the Ephesian synagogue and is asked to return. He declines but promises that he will come back later if God allows (18:20–21). This favorable reaction encourages Paul that the Jews in Ephesus are relatively sympathetic to the gospel, and that he has found another urban center in which to establish a reproducing church, setting the stage for what is to come in his third journey. Paul leaves Priscilla and Aquila in Ephesus to help establish contacts and prepare for future outreach in the city, though they probably carry out business there as well.[107]

Returning Home for Accountability, Rest and Relationships

After landing in Caesarea Paul visits the "mother-church" in Jerusalem. "This visit was not an expression of Paul's subordination to the twelve apostles or to the church in Jerusalem. Rather, it was part of his strategy to maintain good links between the Gentile churches and the centre from which the gospel first came (cf. 11:29; 15:1–4; 19:21; 20:16, 22; Gal 1:18—2:10)."[108] After maintaining good relationships in Jerusalem, Paul returns home to Syrian Antioch (18:22), as he did at the end of his previous journey (14:26–28). Paul takes accountability seriously, and again gives his sending

---

107. Witherington, *Acts*, 558. Priscilla and Aquila also help to train Apollos in Ephesus (18:24–28).

108. Peterson, *Acts*, 522. Though Paul is later accused in Jerusalem of teaching the abandonment of the Jewish "ethos" (ἔθεσιν, 21:20–24), Luke has shown that this charge is false.

church an account of his journeys and all that God has done in the last few years that he has been away. They have played a direct role in all of Paul's exploits, through sending him out and praying for him in his absence (15:40). Luke emphasizes that Paul wants to keep in close contact with the church's old centers, in Jerusalem and Caesarea, but especially in Antioch: "Paul is not a loner, founding a separate, Pauline church, but a major figure in the one mission which began in Jerusalem and was effectively continued from Antioch . . . [While in] Jerusalem he simply greets the church . . . in Antioch he spends some time (18:22–23). The stay in Antioch appropriately rounds off a missionary journey that began there (15:35–41)."[109]

Luke says that Paul spends "some time" at home in Antioch (χρόνον τινά, 18:23a). It is important for Paul to rest and be rejuvenated after a long and exhausting journey, full of danger, opposition, and stress. Though this is not explicit in the text, it is an implied aspect of Paul's missional strategy in Acts. It is also imperative for Paul to re-connect with his home-base, and with core relationships there, for a lot has doubtlessly transpired in his absence. He may have to "straighten out tangled relations with the church" as well.[110] Keener suggests "he probably had timed the arrival so as to be with his friends there and perhaps to meet the church's new adherents."[111] These long-term relationships are essential to Paul's recovery and personal stability.

The Vital Role of the Church at Antioch

Luke emphasizes the strategic importance of the church at Antioch to the Pauline mission multiple times. As Johnson explains, "despite the special side-trip to greet the Jerusalem Church, it is obvious that Antioch, which had sponsored him as an apostle in the first place, remains Paul's 'home community,' and it is there he consistently spends the most time (11:26–30; 13:1–3; 14:26–28; 15:30–35 [18:22–23])."[112] For an itinerant missionary like Paul, having a home base is an emotional and psychological priority, which provides roots to an otherwise transient lifestyle.

Luke implies that the Pauline mission owes much of its success to the Antioch church. Paul trains there with Barnabas, they commission and send him on missional journeys, and they continue to receive him back, help

---

109. Tannehill, *Narrative Unity*, 2.230.

110. Barrett, *Acts*, 2:881; cf. Gal 2:11–14.

111. Keener, *Acts*, 3:2796. Inclement weather not conducive to travel may also contribute to this pause in Antioch.

112. Johnson, *Acts*, 331.

him recuperate, and then send him out again. The Pauline mission emerges directly out of this Antiochene community (13:1–3). Luke portrays the Antioch church as a strongly mission-minded, well-resourced, and expansive congregation (11:20–30), which provides the longevity and stability which Paul requires to negotiate the turbulence of his missionary exploits. This influential church at Antioch may also provide social contacts with people in Paul's destination cities.[113]

In this section of Acts Luke encourages missionaries to emulate Paul and churches to imitate Antioch. His message is unambiguous: "Pauls" do not emerge without "Antiochs." If the next generation of pioneering missionaries is to emerge in Luke's day, the churches of his day must emulate this church at Antioch by becoming communities infused with the power of the Holy Spirit, capable of developing, sending out, and supporting their own international missionaries.[114] Such congregations provide the strength and support necessary to sustain church-planting movements over extensive geographical areas.

CONCLUSION

Luke has carefully crafted these journeys to showcase the missional strategies he is advocating in Acts. Paul's second expedition confirms and develops many of the themes which the first introduced, including: team ministry, following the Spirit's guidance, focusing on strategic cities, social networks and people of influence, continual relevant preaching, confirming miracles, resilience in the face of opposition, establishing church nuclei which impact their surrounding region, strengthening the churches, and maintaining a connection to home base. Luke highlights the Antioch church as an ideal model for churches of his day to imitate, for it directly leads to Paul's effective ministry. Paul's strategies are maturing, and he is now ready for the explosive climax of his mission at Ephesus, which also displays Luke's missional strategies most transparently; this is the focus of Paul's third journey.

---

113. Through links of trade, travel, kinship, political alliances, the Jewish Diaspora, and other church and leadership connections, e.g., with Cyprus, Paul's first destination (4:36; 11:19–20; 13:4). Such relational connections likely help to facilitate Paul's initial approach to a new city or area.

114. According to Paul, there was also conflict at Antioch in the early days, surrounding the issue of Jewish food laws (Gal 2:11–14). Luke does not mention this conflict and is therefore selectively idealizing the church at Antioch. This strengthens the rhetorical argument; in Acts Luke presents Antioch as a model church for later churches to imitate, even if this means overlooking aspects of its early life.

Chapter 10

Paul's Third Journey (18:23b—21:17)

All the residents of Asia, both Jews and Greeks,
heard the word of the Lord.

—ACTS 19:10B

Table 10.1 The Third Itinerary (18:23b—21:17)[1]

18:22	Syrian Antioch	20:5-6	Troas (by ship)
18:23	Galatia and Phrygia (Tarsus, Derbe, Lystra, Iconium, Pisidian Antioch)	20:13	Assos (by foot, others by ship)
		20:14	Mitylene (by ship)
19:1	By "upper parts" to Ephesus (avoiding Colossae)	20:15	Chios, Samos (by ship), Trogyllium and Miletus (by foot)
19:10	2–3 years in Ephesus	21:1	Cos, Rhodes, and Patara (by ship)
20:1	Macedonia (by land, or ship, via Troas?)	21:3	Syria—Tyre (by ship)
		21:7	Ptolemais (by ship)
20:2	Greece (by land?)	21:8	Caesarea (by ship)
20:3	Macedonia (by land?)	21:17	Jerusalem
20:6	Philippi (via Neapolis?)		

1. As before, any mode of travel other than by foot is noted, as well as when it is uncertain.

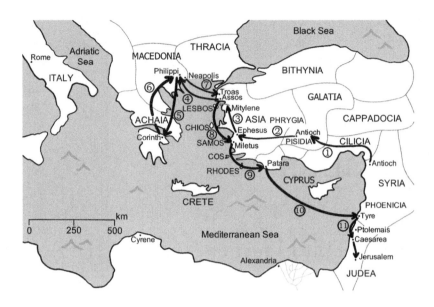

GALATIA AND PHRYGIA (18:23B–28)

Paul begins his third trip by traveling "from place to place in succession (καθεξῆς) throughout the region of Galatia and Phrygia (Γαλατιχὴν χώραν καὶ Φρυγίαν), *strengthening all the disciples*" (ἐπιστηρίζων πάντας τοὺς μαθητάς, 18:23).[2] Paul likely retraces the path he took through these regions on his second missionary journey, stopping at his hometown of Tarsus, passing through the Cilician gates, and then traveling on to Derbe, Lystra, Iconium, and Pisidian Antioch to encourage and strengthen the churches. "The use of 'in succession' (καθεξῆς) here suggests a picture of Paul systematically moving through all the communities that had been established by the earlier mission (14:6), conducting a pastoral visitation similar to those described in 14:21–22 and 15:41."[3]

---

2. "Galatia and Phrygia" has been much debated, though it probably means the same thing as "Phrygian and Galatian region" (16:6). Hemer, *Acts*, 120 makes the point that Phrygia extends into the province of Asia, beyond Galatia, and dismisses the notion of new destinations in "north Galatia," as some have proposed. This also follows Paul's pattern of strengthening churches from previous journeys.

3. Johnson, *Acts*, 331. This is a mountainous journey of some 1,500 miles, probably undertaken completely on foot. It is only possible to pass through the Cilician gates in the spring and summer, so Paul likely embarks in late spring, not arriving at Ephesus until that autumn; Witherington, *Acts*, 560.

Strengthening the Churches

Paul's first priority on this third trip is strengthening the multiple churches that he has helped to establish. As previously seen, ἐπιστηρίζω, "to strengthen" is a word unique to Acts in the NT, and Paul engages in this kind of strengthening on each of his three journeys (14:22; 15:41; 18:23). It is derived from ἐπί (upon, at, by), and στηρίζω (to fix firmly in place, establish, support; to cause to be inwardly firm or committed, confirm, strengthen).[4] When Paul "strengthens" the churches and disciples he is attempting to give them the ability to remain firmly "fixed" to God and his cause, no matter what comes against them.

Paul sees this strengthening of the churches as a core part of his calling. "Once churches have been established in an area, Paul will visit them again to strengthen them. Only then is Paul's work in an area relatively complete."[5] He knows that difficulties will come, and he is determined that the new churches will survive and even prosper, so he visits them surprisingly often.[6] Paul's goal is to establish thriving local congregations, and if they do not prosper and grow then his mission will ultimately fail. As their founder and spiritual "father," Paul does everything he can to ensure that the young churches will remain healthy and strong in his absence.[7]

Leadership Development, Relational Mentoring, and an Expanding Mission

A Jew from Alexandria named Apollos lives in Ephesus, a zealous and eloquent missionary, "boiling over in spirit/enthusiasm" (ζέων τῷ πνεύματι), who receives further instruction from Priscilla and Aquila (18:24–26). It is unknown how Apollos first becomes a Christian, or how Aquila and Priscilla (from Rome) convert, which points to the reality that there are other

---

4. BDAG, 945. Στηρίζω occurs 13 times in the NT, including Luke 9:51; 16:26; 22:32. Paul uses στηρίζω similarly, of strengthening and establishing the church (Rom 1:11; 16:25; 1 Thess 3:2; 3:13; 2 Thess 2:17; 3:3). The NT also uses στηρίζω to refer to an individual strengthening of faith or resolve (Luke 22:32; Jas 5:8; 1 Pet 5:10).

5. Tannehill, *Narrative Unity*, 2:230.

6. Paul visits the churches in Galatia and Phrygia on three later occasions (14:21–23; 16:1–5; 18:23), and those in Macedonia and Achaia two subsequent times (19:21; 20:1–3). Presumably his associates and ministry partners also visit for further training and instruction.

7. Such fatherly affection is implicit in Acts, but explicit throughout his letters (e.g., Phil 1:7–8; 2 Cor 7:3); it is also apparent in the prayers he prays for them (e.g., Eph 1:15–21; 3:14–19), and the exhortations he gives them (e.g., Rom 1:11; Col 1:23; 2:7).

missionaries in early Christianity.[8] Luke chooses to focus on Paul, perhaps the most prominent of them, for narrative reasons, but he is not wholly unique; multiple pioneering leaders and church planters such as Apollos are emerging during this period.[9]

Priscilla and Aquila take Apollos aside (προσελάβοντο αὐτόν), and explain (ἐξέθεντο—expose, expound) to him the way of God (τὴν ὁδὸν τοῦ Θεοῦ) more accurately (ἀκριβέστερον—precisely, exactly, thoroughly, 18:26). These descriptors point to the intentional mentoring found in a teacher/pupil relationship between these three, and ἀκριβῶς echoes Luke's introduction, hinting at Luke's larger rhetorical purposes in writing to train his readers.[10] Here it indicates informal, relational teaching, largely done in the home; such training develops new leaders such as Apollos, and is another strategy for expanding the mission which Luke advocates in Acts.[11]

Apollos desires to go to Achaia, so the disciples in Ephesus write him a letter of commendation to take to Corinth (18:27).[12] Apollos helps the new church in Corinth, publicly debating and refuting the Jews and demonstrating from the Scriptures (ἐπιδεικνὺς διὰ τῶν γραφῶν) that Jesus is the Christ (18:28).[13] This episode shows the broadening of the effort to strengthen the new churches. Apollos's missional visit to Corinth and Achaia is not orchestrated by Paul, but is indirectly influenced by him, in that he helped to train Aquila and Priscilla, who then mentor Apollos. "The effect of [this story] is to make Apollos a helpful but secondary participant in the messianic

---

8. Alexandria is the second largest city in the Empire, and has a large Jewish population, so it is a natural missionary destination. Barnabas and Mark may go there after their time in Cyprus (Acts 15:39) and help to convert Apollos. Additionally, the array of peoples assembled in Jerusalem at Pentecost (including some from Rome, Acts 2:10–11) also contributes to an initial distribution of Christ-followers throughout the Roman and Parthian Empires, as many of them return to their homes (Acts 2:5–12, 41).

9. Other churches and leaders who appear unexplained are evidence of this—there is much more happening missionally in early Christianity than Acts reveals.

10. The word accurate/precise (ἀκριβῶς) refers to the previous verse and description of Apollos, and to Luke's stated intention in his Gospel prologue of providing an "orderly/accurate account in succession" (ἀκριβῶς καθεξῆς, Luke 1:3); Johnson, Acts, 332. Where Priscilla and Aquilla are training informally here, Luke sees his entire narrative as a more formal kind of curriculum for the accurate training of missional leaders.

11. The length of this mentoring relationship is unknown, but Luke mentions it as a model for his readers. Behind the scenes this same pattern is surely repeated across the networks of young house churches, as emerging leaders are trained and mentored by more experienced leaders.

12. Such letters are common in the NT: 2 Cor 3:1; Rom 16:1; Col 4:10; cf. Acts 15:22–29. Barrett, Acts, 2:890.

13. Apollos's use of Scripture is identical to that of Paul in 17:2–3; see also 9:22 of Paul. Johnson, Acts, 333.

movement . . . a teacher instructed by the Pauline school and commissioned by the churches. But Apollos is also, we should note finally, another part of Paul's team—like Priscilla and Aquila themselves."[14] Apollos plays an important role in the growth of the team of Pauline missional partners, as the newly formed network of churches continues to develop in Acts.[15]

EPHESUS (19:1–41)

While Apollos is in Corinth, Paul takes the road "through the interior" (ἀνωτερικὰ μέρη) and arrives back at Ephesus (19:1).[16] Ephesus dominates Luke's account of Paul's third journey, for Paul helps to birth the church and expanding movement there over a period of nearly three years and returns to speak to the new Ephesian elders on his way home. "Ephesus is not just another stop in a series. It is Paul's last major place of new mission work as a free man . . . The fact that Paul's farewell speech will be addressed to the Ephesian elders is a further indication of the special importance of Ephesus."[17]

An Influential Urban Center

Ephesus is a city of great importance in the ancient world, second only to Corinth of the cities which Paul seeks to evangelize.[18] It is the hub of all culture and commerce in western Asia, for from there the Roman roads spread out into the interior.[19] The main road connecting the eastern and western portion of the Empire also originates from Ephesus.[20] It is a major connecting link within the Empire's communication network, because of the land

14. Johnson, *Acts*, 335.

15. Paul's letters show that Apollos's visit to Corinth also creates division within that young church (1 Cor 1–4), prompting Paul to argue that he and Apollos are not in competition but work together (1 Cor 1:12; 3:4). This may explain why Apollos is later reluctant to return to Corinth (1 Cor 16:12). Witherington, *Acts*, 568–69.

16. He probably leaves the main road towards Ephesus at Apamea, and therefore does not go through Colossae. Col 1:7 and 2:1 suggest that Paul's co-worker Epaphras is the founder of the Colossian community, and Col 1:4 and Phlm 1:22 indicate that Paul has never been there. Bruce, *Acts*, 405.

17. Tannehill, *Narrative Unity*, 2:231.

18. For background information on Ephesus and its devotion to Artemis, see Johnson, *Paul*, 113–24.

19. The seven churches of Rev 2–3 are in the order one would reach them following the main road from Ephesus.

20. Witherington, *Acts*, 563.

routes that lead to the interior of Asia, the sea routes from Asia west, and the nearby mouth of the Cayster River. It is the seat of provincial government, which means that the proconsul lives there, along with 200,000 to 250,000 residents, making it the largest city in Asia.[21] The temple of Artemis, one of the great wonders of the ancient world, is in Ephesus, causing it to be a major destination for the religious tourist trade. It is famous as a center for magic arts and the occult, and there is also a large Jewish colony in the city.[22] All of these factors make Ephesus an ideal and strategic base for the Christian mission in Asia and continue Paul's normative pattern of focusing on major urban centers in Acts.

The Legitimizing Power of the Holy Spirit

In Ephesus, Paul meets some "disciples" (μαθητάς) who have received John's baptism but have not heard of the Holy Spirit (19:1–3).[23] Paul explains that John's baptism is a baptism of repentance and that John pointed people towards believing in and following Jesus (19:4). Upon hearing this, they are baptized into the name of the Lord Jesus, receive the Holy Spirit when Paul lays hands on them, and begin to speak in tongues and prophesy (19:5–6).[24]

This is another miraculous demonstration of power validating the message, though this time it comes after the disciples believe, confirming the truth of their choice. Luke emphasizes that the Spirit comes upon them "at the hands of Paul" (τοῦ Παύλου [τὰς] χεῖρας, 19:6). God's power validates the message and messenger, and authenticates these new believers: "The fact that it is the apostle Paul who is the medium for this bestowal has a legitimating function: these erstwhile Johannine disciples are brought within the apostolic community and authority."[25] There are "about twelve men" in this group (ἄνδρες ὡσεὶ δώδεκα, 19:7), which "implies a considerable number of family members with similar beliefs . . . A sizeable group of new Christians is thus

---

21. Witherington, *Acts*, 563.

22. See Josephus, *Ant.*, 14.225–227; 16.162–168, 172–173. Witherington, *Acts*, 564.

23. There is debate about who these "disciples" are. Luke seems to be attempting to clarify John's role as pre-cursor to Jesus, and the relationship between the Johannine sectarian Jewish baptizing movement and Paul's church-planting movement. See also 1:5; 11:16; 13:25; 18:25. Luke is probably claiming that they are not actually Christians yet. Witherington, *Acts*, 570; Marshall, *Acts*, 305; Keener, *Acts*, 3:2815–24; Peterson, *Acts*, 529–33: "their answer showed that they were definitely not Christians" (*Acts*, 530).

24. The Spirit accompanies the laying on of hands rather than baptism, as in the Samaritan mission (8:15–17).

25. Johnson, *Acts*, 338.

indicated."[26] Luke hints that these men and their families become an initial core of the church in Ephesus, and provide the credibility, plus a household and hospitality invitation, which Paul requires to begin his Ephesian outreach.

Establishing the Initial Core Group

Paul returns to the Ephesian synagogue where he was previously well received (18:9), continuing his practice of going to the place where he has the most natural rapport and connection. He begins the task of "discussing and persuading (διαλεγόμενος καὶ πείθων) about the Kingdom of God" and continues to do this for three months (19:8).[27] Some of his listeners refuse to believe and publicly malign the Way, so Paul leaves the synagogue and enters the school of Tyrannus (τῇ σχολῇ Τυράννου), which Paul uses as a lecture hall (19:9).[28]

Paul "took the disciples with him" (ἀφώρισεν τοὺς μαθητάς) to this hall, indicating that there is already a Christian core group at this point, composed of the initial converts from Paul's preaching in the Ephesian synagogue, plus probably the twelve who have received the Spirit and been baptized (19:5–7). Paul has already succeeded in gathering a group of Ephesian believers, made up of receptive Jews and God-fearers. The most crucial part of the mission has now been accomplished: a strategic "beachhead" has been established in Ephesus. This embryonic church functions as the foundation for an emerging city-wide network of house churches, and eventually for a widespread regional outreach to the surrounding areas of Asia.[29]

Developing a City-Wide Church

In the past, Paul would probably have left Ephesus at this point, leaving the church to grow on its own, as he did in most previous locations he visited. However, this time he takes this group into the school/hall of Tyrannus for further teaching and missional proclamation (19:9). Luke implies that Paul's

26. Peterson, *Acts*, 533. Keener claims this is a subtle reference to Jesus's 12 disciples, *Acts*, 3:2824.

27. Three key witness words (19:8): παρρησιάζομαι (speak fearlessly), διαλέγομαι (discuss, argue), and πείθω (persuade).

28. Witherington, *Acts*, 574–75; Luke here portrays Paul as a popular speaker or philosopher seeking to persuade an audience on a subject. Keener, *Acts*, 3:2827–35 discusses this "school" in more detail.

29. Luke does not mention house churches explicitly here, but this is the form of every new Pauline church; see also Paul's later statement about his Ephesian ministry "publicly and from house to house" (20:20).

experience in Corinth has altered his strategy. Jesus instructed him to stay longer in Corinth, and he saw the fruit of perseverance (18:9–11), in the form of a more established congregation, capable of impacting a city and region. This convinces Paul to stay longer in Ephesus and leads to his unprecedented success there.

Paul preaches and teaches "daily" (καθ' ἡμέραν) in the lecture hall for two years (19:9–10a); the change of venue allows a multiplication of gatherings, publicity, and influence within the city, leading to an acceleration of the Ephesian church's growth.[30] Tyrannus's school is an ideal venue, which gives the growing church exposure to the wider public. Paul stays in Ephesus for nearly three years (20:31),[31] implying that he settles there semipermanently, and sees Ephesus as a secondary home base. In these years of intensive teaching and training, the Ephesian church transitions from a small gathering to a city-wide network of house churches.

Starting a Regional Missional Movement

Paul's focused strategy in Ephesus is so successful that after over two years Luke can make the stunning claim that "all those who lived in the province of Asia heard the word of the Lord, both Jews and Greeks" (πάντας τοὺς κατοικοῦντας τὴν Ἀσίαν ἀκοῦσαι τὸν λόγον τοῦ κυρίου, Ἰουδαίους τε καὶ Ἕλληνας, 19:10b). Luke is implying that the word spreads from Ephesus all over the province of Asia, to all the major areas and population centers. "There is no reason to think that anything less than the whole province is intended."[32] Reaching an entire province requires an intentional regional strategy involving the training and sending of multiple missionaries to other key centers throughout the province.[33] In Asia "we begin to see the emergence of Christianity as a separate movement."[34]

---

30. Barrett, *Acts*, 2:905. "Daily preaching" for two years in one location is unheard of for Paul. The longest he ever stayed in any destination before was in Corinth for about 18 months.

31. Adding two years (19:10) to three months in the synagogue (19:8) and "some time longer" (ἐπέσχεν χρόνον) (19:22), arrives at approximately three years (20:31). It is customary to count any part of a year as a full year.

32. Barrett, *Acts*, 2:905. For Paul's hyperbolic way of generalizing the extent of his missionary activity, see Rom 15:19; these are not necessarily meant to be taken literally but neither are they misleading.

33. Epaphras is one example of a Pauline missionary who plants a church in Colossae, and then in neighboring Laodicea and Hierapolis (Col 1:7–8; 4:12–13; Phlm 23). There are likely others like him throughout Asia.

34. Johnson, *Acts*, 339.

Acts implies that Paul uses his prolonged daily teaching in Ephesus to train the believers to reproduce their church into the surrounding areas and give them a vision for outreach into all of Asia (19:10, 20). When he eventually leaves, the Ephesian church continues in this mission of reaching the entire Asian province.[35] The result of Paul's ministry in Ephesus is a large network of relationally connected, rapidly reproducing house churches throughout the province of Asia, covering its significant population centers. Because of this, Luke can claim that all within the province of Asia hear. As Barrett explains, "Luke simply affirms [in 19:10b] widespread evangelistic activity, and the affirmation could be based simply on the fact that Asia as he knew it was one of the most developed Christian mission fields."[36] This implies that once Christianity is established in a few strategic population centers it emanates quickly throughout Roman Asia along trade and communication routes, until even smaller villages are reached.[37]

The church at Ephesus thus becomes another kind of "Antioch church" (13:1–3), a dynamic hub for training and sending missionaries to areas unreached by the gospel. At Ephesus, this model of training and sending comes to full maturity and has the greatest regional impact. In addition, there is no reason to believe that these newly trained missionaries remain only in Asia; they may also go to areas farther afield, even as Paul has done in coming to Ephesus from Antioch.

Miraculous Power

The power of the Spirit fuels this expansion Luke says that God performs "no ordinary powerful deeds" (δυνάμεις οὐ τὰς τυχούσας) by Paul's hands (19:11). He then relates stories of Paul's handkerchiefs (σουδάρια) and aprons (σιμικίνθια) healing the sick and casting evil spirits out of them (19:12).[38] God moves potently through Paul in Ephesus, continuing to confirm Paul's message through signs and wonders. This sort of miraculous ministry undoubtedly attracts large numbers to listen to Paul's daily preaching and

35. The epistle to the Ephesians reflects the vitality of the Ephesian church, which is capable of impacting an entire region. Ephesians is the only NT letter that contains no rebuke or theological correction. Whether Paul wrote it or not, it likely circulates throughout Roman Asia, testifying "to the continuing vibrancy of Pauline Christianity in Asia," Keener, *Acts*, 3:2838.

36. Barrett, *Acts*, 2:906.

37. Keener, *Acts*, 3:2837–38.

38. People come to Paul as he works, and he gives them items of clothing used in his trade (18:3). Witherington, *Acts*, 580.

accelerates the rate of conversions in Ephesus, contributing to the church's rapid expansion locally and regionally.

Luke also tells the memorable story of the seven sons of Sceva, who attempt to imitate Paul and cast out demons in the name of Jesus but are overpowered by evil spirits (19:13–16).[39] The spirit's response about knowing Jesus and being acquainted with Paul emphasizes that Paul's authority is fully attributed to Jesus. Luke underlines this with the reaction of the Ephesians: "Fear (φόβος) fell upon them all, and the name of the Lord Jesus was magnified" (ἐμεγαλύνετο—esteemed, enlarged, honored, 19:17).[40] Luke here reiterates that the power at work is of divine origin, and Jesus deserves the honor for all that is happening in Ephesus.

This incident provokes many who had become Christians to openly confess their evil deeds (19:18) and voluntarily burn valuable scrolls related to magic (βίβλους, 19:19).[41] This scene shows partially socialized Christians who have not given up all their old practices making further commitments to Christianity and abandoning their pagan ways.[42] God is drawing in the fringes of the Ephesian church and expanding the core of highly committed disciples.[43] Some of these newly devoted believers probably train as leaders and missionaries, further accelerating the expansion of the Ephesian movement. The influence of social networks can be seen in this episode, culminating in "many" (πολλοί, 19:18; ἱκανοί, 19:19) coming and confessing their practices. It also demonstrates the triumph of the power of the Christian God over all the "false powers" of magic, witchcraft, and the occult. Ephesus is infamous throughout the Roman world as a center for magic and sorcery; for Christianity to defeat witchcraft on its "home-turf" is a significant victory.[44]

For Luke, these acts of public renunciation are the proper response to pagan religion, particularly in light of the Jerusalem decree (Acts 15:29). They allow the gospel to take deeper root in Ephesus, and to spread more

39. Commentators often refer to this as comic relief in the middle of an otherwise serious narrative.

40. Such φόβος is a sign of church health and flourishing in Acts (2:43; 5:5, 11; 9:31).

41. Bruce, *Acts*, 412 explains that the power of spells lies in their secrecy, so to bring them into the open is to render them powerless. The total value of these scrolls is fifty thousand pieces of silver, a fortune that Luke regards as impressive. Johnson, *Acts*, 342.

42. Witherington, *Acts*, 582. Crossley, *Why Christianity Happened*, 150–72 discusses varying levels of commitment, observance, and conformity in the religious world of antiquity.

43. Many of Paul's letters deal with this issue of how to draw spiritually immature converts into more comprehensive levels of commitment and conformity to the Christian life (e.g., 1 Cor 7).

44. Witherington, *Acts*, 581–83.

rapidly throughout the region. This is underscored by the next verse, which is connected to the previous episode in a causative way: "*therefore* (οὕτως) the word of the Lord continued to spread widely and grew in power" (κατὰ κράτος τοῦ κυρίου ὁ λόγος ηὔξανεν καὶ ἴσχυεν, 19:20). This re-emphasizes the triumph of God's Word over other powers and also refers geographically to the larger regional mission. Because of these dramatic spiritual encounters, which confirm the veracity of the message being preached, the Word triumphantly spreads from city to city.[45] This reminds the reader of the missional advance fueled by God's miraculous power taking place across Asia (19:10). The healings by Paul's handkerchiefs, the increasing fear of God after the sons of Sceva incident, and the burning of the sorcery scrolls all quicken the church's growth in Ephesus and throughout the surrounding areas.[46]

The Ephesus account portrays Paul as a man of mighty deeds and authoritative words, like Jesus and Peter before him. "Paul's ministry has certainly come a long way from the small and resistant beginnings Luke recorded in locations such as Philippi."[47] In many ways this is the narrative climax of Paul's ministry as a free man: "The Ephesian Church, established by an apostle, triumphant over the demonic powers of magic, independent of the synagogue yet drawing into itself both Jews and Gentiles, is the final evidence within Luke's text for the success and integrity of Paul's mission."[48] Luke presents all that happens in Ephesus as a missional movement that invites emulation by his readers.

Table 10.2 The Pauline Mission in Asia: A Reproducing Movement
(19:1–40)[49]

1. Paul proclaims the gospel of the Kingdom of God to receptive people of influence in the Ephesus synagogue and elsewhere (εἰσελθὼν δὲ εἰς τὴν συναγωγὴν ἐπαρρησιάζετο ἐπὶ μῆνας τρεῖς διαλεγόμενος καὶ πείθων περὶ τῆς βασιλείας τοῦ θεοῦ, 19:8; also, the "twelve men" in 19:1–7).

---

45. See chapter 1 and the unstoppable advance of the Word in Acts—the vivid personification of the Word is one of Luke's most potent missional stimuli, and this scene dramatically captures this emphasis.

46. The reader can imagine how word of these things would spread rapidly all over the province of Asia (see 19:17); Luke portrays the Word gaining quite a reputation, of power, authority, and triumph.

47. Keener, *Acts*, 3:2838; not to mention Lystra and Derbe.

48. Johnson, *Acts*, 344.

49. A summary of how "everyone in Asia hears" (19:10) from Paul's Ephesian ministry in Acts.

2. He draws these early believers into an embryonic church—"having withdrawn from them he separated off the disciples" (ἀποστὰς ἀπ' αὐτῶν ἀφώρισεν τοὺς μαθητάς)—and teaches them his values, beginning to equip them for mission and spiritual leadership (19:9).

3. Paul teaches them daily in the school of Tyrannus for two years (καθ' ἡμέραν διαλεγόμενος ἐν τῇ σχολῇ Τυράννου, 19:9–10a).

4. As the community grows the initial church gathering develops into many others, led by the leaders Paul is training (Silas, Priscilla, and Aquila are perhaps primary early leaders).

5. Many are attracted by the "never experienced miracles" (δυνάμεις οὐ τὰς τυχούσας) being done in the name of the Lord, such as healing handkerchiefs and the encounter with the sons of Sceva (19:11–17).

6. The news about these signs and wonders spreads, and the reputation of Jesus and the church becomes "known to all living in Ephesus, both Jews and Greeks" (τοῦτο δὲ ἐγένετο γνωστὸν πᾶσιν Ἰουδαίοις τε καὶ Ἕλλησιν τοῖς κατοικοῦσιν τὴν Ἔφεσον, 19:17a).

7. The fear of God comes over "them all," and the name of the Lord Jesus is praised; wonder turns to worship (καὶ ἐπέπεσεν φόβος ἐπὶ πάντας αὐτοὺς καὶ ἐμεγαλύνετο τὸ ὄνομα τοῦ κυρίου Ἰησοῦ, 19:17b).

8. Multiple converts are drawn closer into the core of the church and increase their commitment by publicly confessing and renouncing their former lifestyles and pagan practices, further strengthening the church (πολλοί τε τῶν πεπιστευκότων ἤρχοντο ἐξομολογούμενοι καὶ ἀναγγέλλοντες τὰς πράξεις αὐτῶν, 19.18–19).

9. With time the congregations in Ephesus gain a city-wide scope and impact, and house churches are established throughout many different areas of the city, as the Word grows in power and prevails (κατὰ κράτος τοῦ κυρίου ὁ λόγος ηὔξανεν καὶ ἴσχυεν, 19:20).

10. High-caliber house church leaders emerge out of this network, some of whom help Paul to oversee the city-wide Ephesian church—Luke specifically mentions Timothy and Erastus (19:22), Gaius and Aristarchus (19:29), and possibly the Asiarchs (19:31).

11. Some of these outstanding emerging leaders are sent to other regional cities in Asia to reproduce this process. These new missionaries establish their own rudimentary churches (implied by 19:10b, 20; Epaphras is a Pauline example in Colossae, Col 1:5–7).

12. These new churches follow the Ephesian pattern by growing to form city-wide house church networks and hubs for regional mission, planting other churches in surrounding towns (repeat above steps; Epaphras plants from Colossae to neighboring Laodicea and Hierapolis, Col 4:12–13).

13. This results in exponential church growth in a relatively short amount of time (19:10, 17, 20; churches of Revelation are examples of the Asian church planting movement, Rev 1:11; 2:1—3:22).

14. In time, every significant population center in Asia has at least one missional house church, so that "all who live in Asia hear the word of the Lord" (πάντας τοὺς κατοικοῦντας τὴν Ἀσίαν ἀκοῦσαι τὸν λόγον τοῦ κυρίου, Acts 19:10b).

Opposition in Ephesus

Although Paul has enjoyed a relatively peaceful existence in Ephesus thus far, a riot develops (19:23–40). The workmen who make idols are angry because demand for their silver shrines of Artemis (ναοὺς ἀργυροῦς Ἀρτέμιδος) has diminished due to Paul's ministry in the city (19:24–27). This re-emphasizes the divine Word's triumph over paganism, particularly vital in view of the Council's prohibition of idolatry (15:20, 29). This is Luke's final persuasive evidence for the gospel's superiority over pagan practice.

In the Ephesian riot scene Luke reveals that Paul has gained friends (φίλοι) among the "Asiarchs" (Ἀσιαρχῶν, 19:31), a prestigious upper-class group in Asia.[50] Some of these may be members of the Ephesian or Asian churches, and as likely patrons they are sources of funding, property, social contacts, and credibility for Paul's public teaching and growing congregations. Their support only strengthens the growing missional movement and indicates how thoroughly Asia's social culture has been affected. Though Paul is detained, he is not harmed and is eventually released peacefully (19:41).

---

50. Though scholars are not sure of their precise function, the "Asiarchs" in Asia are well attested (Strabo, *Geog.*, 14.649–65; *Martyrdom of Polycarp*, 12). Luke again shows a masterful grasp of local political and social arrangements (cf. 16:20; 17:6, 22; 18:12), and demonstrates the mission's further success among the upper classes (cf. 17:4, 12, 34). Johnson, *Acts*, 349. Keener, *Acts*, 3:2908–18 suggests they are Paul's patrons and cover the costs of his public teaching activity. Their request that he not enter the theater to defend himself calls upon Paul's obligation to honor them as his benefactors, and Paul quickly leaves the city, partly as a result of their intervention.

TOWARDS MILETUS (20:1–17)

While in Ephesus, "Paul purposed in the Spirit (ἔθετο ὁ Παῦλος ἐν τῷ πνεύματι) to go to Jerusalem after he had passed through Macedonia and Achaia" (19:21).[51] This is an extremely roundabout way to return to Jerusalem from Ephesus, particularly since Paul has already sailed directly from Ephesus to Jerusalem before (18:21–22).

Caring for the Churches

Paul has a motivation for this long and wearisome itinerary: he longs to see his churches and build them up.[52] Paul's care for the church is re-emphasized as he leaves Ephesus; he does not leave immediately but makes a point of sending for the Ephesian disciples (μαθητάς), encouraging them (παρακαλέσας—comfort, console, exhort) and saying an affectionate goodbye (ἀσπασάμενος—embrace, enfold in one's arms, wish well, 20:1). He has spent a significant amount of time with these believers, sharing many experiences and challenges with them. Though Paul is ambitious, he is not overly quick to progress to the next thing but prioritizes saying goodbye and continuing to train and strengthen them for the Asian missional movement. This will be seen most unmistakably in his later farewell speech to the Ephesian elders (20:17–38).

Paul then embarks on the long journey through Macedonia and Achaia to bless the churches he has recently founded. "It was Paul's practice to reinforce and strengthen churches he had already founded, and this we see him doing in 20:1–5 as he travels back through Macedonia and Achaia."[53] In Acts 20:2, "he went throughout those districts (διελθὼν δὲ τὰ μέρη ἐκεῖνα), speaking many words of encouragement to the people (παρακαλέσας αὐτοὺς λόγῳ πολλῷ), and finally arrived in Greece."[54] This involves retracing his steps through Troas, Neapolis, Philippi, Amphipolis, Apollonia, Thessalonica,

51. This could be Paul's spirit, or the Holy Spirit, or both. See map of this journey at beginning of this chapter.

52. Though Luke does not mention it, Paul's other motivation is to collect the offering for the Jerusalem church; 24:17 shows that Luke is aware of it (cf. Rom 15:23–25). He may know it does not accomplish what Paul hoped for (cf. Rom 15:16, 27, 31); Witherington, *Acts*, 588. Luke's rhetorical priority is Paul's care for the churches.

53. Witherington, *Acts*, 601. "Paul is shown engaging in the same sort of pastoral visitation of churches that he had previously founded, as in 14:21–22; 15:36; 16:4–5; 18:23," Johnson, *Acts*, 354.

54. According to 2 Cor 1–7, this verse covers a prolonged time period, and Luke is telescoping and summarizing; Paul may also go up to Illyricum at this point (Rom 15:19). Bruce, *Acts*, 423.

Berea, and Athens, before arriving in Corinth, where he stays for three months (20:3).[55] Paul's teaching to each of these churches surely focuses on expanding the mission and training the primary leaders in each location. He encourages and consoles them (παρακαλέσας, 20:2), telling them about what God has recently done in Ephesus and Asia, and how they can imitate this regional strategy in their own locales. For Paul (and Luke), such recent and resounding success in Asia needs to be shared as widely as possible.

The Corinthian Jews threaten Paul, so he decides to go back overland through Macedonia, rather than sailing from Corinth back to Syria (20:3).[56] This means that he likely visits the churches in that area once again, checking on their progress and strengthening them. This visit is Paul's third to these churches: once to found them and twice to strengthen them.

Paul's Co-Workers and Missionary Teams

Three episodes around this stage in the narrative shed light on the team of missional co-workers Paul develops. Before he leaves Ephesus, he sends two of his "helpers" (διακονούντων—deacons, ministers), Timothy and Erastus, on ahead of him, presumably to help with the collection he is taking for the Jerusalem church (19:22).[57] There are two others with Paul, "traveling companions" (συνεκδήμους) from Macedonia named Gaius and Aristarchus, who are seized with Paul during the Ephesian riot (19:29).[58] Luke emphasizes that Paul is not traveling alone, but has multiple companions helping him in his mission.

These are probably two different ways of describing similar roles: helpers/co-workers (διακονία) and traveling companions abroad (συνέκδημος). These four fellow travelers are converts from four different Pauline

55. Though the text says Greece ('Ελλάδα, 20:2), most commentators agree that this is not the provincial designation, but the popular term, and that Paul ends up in Corinth. Witherington, *Acts*, 601; Bruce, *Acts*, 423.

56. Keener, *Acts*, 3:2952–53 explains that a lengthy sea voyage would make evading capture and murder much more difficult than remaining on the busy roads of Achaia, surrounded by supporters.

57. This may be the Erastus of Rom 16:23, the treasurer of Ephesus, or of 2 Tim 4:20 in Corinth.

58. Συνέκδημος only occurs here and in 2 Cor 8:19, which speaks of an unnamed Pauline traveling companion who has been appointed by the churches to travel with him, particularly to help administer the offering, and who could be one of these two (Acts 19:29) or one of those in Acts 20:4. Συνέκδημος comes from σύν (with, a marker of accompaniment and association), and ἔκδημος (abroad), meaning those who are with Paul abroad, on a long journey. 'Εκδημέω means to leave on a long journey or be in a strange land (cf. 2 Cor 5:8, 9); BDAG, 300.

churches, and are therefore the direct fruit of his missional labors.[59] They are recruited to travel with Paul and to assist him in his missionary efforts. This shows Paul intentionally mentoring future church leaders and missionaries by allowing them to travel with him, build relationship with him, and learn from him in a rabbi/student relationship, like Silas and Timothy previously (16:1; 18:5). In this way, Paul strategically expands the leadership base of his church networks, even as he goes about the practical responsibilities of the mission. These young leaders are also surely helpful in bearing the demands of Paul's ministry.

Acts 20:4 lists seven Pauline co-workers who accompany him:[60] Sopater from Berea, Aristarchus[61] and Secundus from Thessalonica, Gaius from Derbe,[62] Timothy from Lystra,[63] and Tychicus[64] and Trophimus[65] from the province of Asia. "The most obvious feature of the list is its inclusion of representatives from the diverse geographical areas in which Paul worked. The passage testifies to the complexity of the Pauline mission."[66] As Paul travels, he builds close relationships with many of his converts. Of these, he selects some of the most promising to travel with him and partner with him in his ministry. It seems that most of the churches he establishes are willing

59. Timothy is from Lystra, Gaius is from Derbe (20:4, though Paul seems to say he is from Macedonia here, which could indicate a different Gaius, or only be referring to Aristarchus), Aristarchus is from Macedonia (Thessalonica, 20:4), and Erastus is probably from Corinth (Rom 16:23).

60. On the seven of 20:4 see Pervo, *Acts*, 508–9; Keener, *Acts*, 3:2954–56. Scholars usually view them as delegates of Pauline churches who are bearing the collection for Jerusalem; Haenchen, *Acts*, 581; Witherington, *Acts*, 603.

61. Aristarchus becomes a trusted co-worker, with Paul from Ephesus through Paul's Roman imprisonment. He is mentioned in Acts 19:29 (at the Ephesian riot, and therefore would be known to the Colossians); 27:2 (with Paul when he leaves by sea for Rome); Col 4:10 (a "fellow prisoner" in Rome); Phlm 24 (a "fellow worker").

62. Probably not the Gaius of Rom 16:23 and 1 Cor 1:14, who is from Corinth, and is likely Gaius Titius Justus (Acts 18:7), Paul's host while he stays in Corinth.

63. Timothy may represent multiple churches by this point (1 Cor 16:10–11; Phil 2:19–23). He is one of Paul's most trusted co-workers, and his beloved son in the faith (1 Tim 1:18; 2 Tim 1:2; 2:1).

64. Paul later sends Tychicus to Ephesus (Eph 6:21) and to Colossae (Col 4:7) as his representative (cf. 2 Tim 4:12). Later, Paul may send Tychicus to Crete to relieve Titus, so that Titus can come to Paul (Tit 3:12). Tychicus is in Paul's "inner circle," a trusted representative capable of leading a church.

65. Trophimus is with Paul in Jerusalem (Acts 21:29, which also reveals he is an Ephesian and a Gentile), and later Paul leaves him sick at Miletus (2 Tim 4:20). It is significant that Paul travels with Gentiles in his inner circle.

66. Johnson, *Acts*, 355.

to give him one or a few full-time workers, who represent their church and assist Paul in his work.

These co-workers form a network of apprentices and junior leaders in Paul's ministry and have various responsibilities including assisting Paul, extending the mission, collecting offerings, delivering letters, and helping to care for and instruct the churches. Some are more permanent, such as Timothy and Silas (and Titus), and go on to oversee churches and regional mission bases. Many are more temporary, but still become trusted Pauline co-laborers. As they travel, minister, and endure difficulty together, they become a tight-knit group, with a substantial bond and commitment to one another. These leaders also continue Paul's mission and message once he is imprisoned and no longer able to directly lead the ministry (21:33—28:31).

By traveling and training in this way, Paul empowers the next generations of leaders in the movement, instilling his distinctive values and equipping them to continue in the mission even after he is gone. This deliberate recruitment and development of co-workers is an innovative aspect of the Pauline church-planting movement in Acts which gives it a degree of permanence and sustainability.[67]

Another Urban Congregation and Example of Divine Power

Paul sails from Philippi for Troas, where he stays for seven days (20:6). Troas is another strategic Roman city, which became a Roman colony under Augustus.[68] The church in Troas may be a congregation Paul founded on a previous visit (20:1; 16:8–11; or another visit), though Luke does not mention this and the Pauline evidence is ambiguous.[69] Witherington claims, "here we have another example of the Pauline urban missionary strategy, establishing congregations in major cities in the Empire, particularly in Roman colonies such as Troas, Philippi, or Corinth."[70]

Paul seems to know this church at Troas, for he speaks to them "a long time" (ἐπὶ πλεῖον, 20:7–12). No doubt he tells stories of missionary exploits in various places, including recently in Ephesus and Asia; it is easy to imagine Paul's excitement about this. Around midnight Eutychus falls asleep and

67. In the ancient world it is common for teachers to take companions with them on their travels, Keener, *Acts*, 3:2953. Paul approaches this practice with increasing strategic intentionality throughout his travels. This is all, of course, following Jesus's instructions to travel at least in pairs (Luke 10:1).

68. Witherington, *Acts*, 605. For more on Troas, see Trebilco, "Asia," 357–9; Hemer, "Troas," 79–112.

69. Keener, *Acts*, 3:2958; see 2 Cor 2:12–13; 2 Tim 4:13.

70. Witherington, *Acts*, 606.

drops from a third story window, dying on impact.[71] Paul throws himself on him, puts his arms around him, and he returns to life. This story re-emphasizes the divine power flowing through Paul's life, presenting him as a great leader, equal in authority to Peter, who also raises the dead (9:36–43). This is the last miracle Paul performs as a free man in Acts (cf. 28:5–9), and further evidence Luke uses to rehabilitate Paul's reputation.

MILETUS (20:18–38)

Paul travels on foot to Assos, and then the entire group sails to Mitylene, Chios, Samos, and Miletus (20:13–15).[72] Paul avoids Ephesus because he is in a hurry to get back to Jerusalem by Pentecost (20:16).[73] So he calls the Ephesian elders to join him at Miletus (20:17). This sets the stage for Paul's third major speech in Acts.[74]

The Priority of Empowering Local Church Leadership

Paul's speech in the synagogue at Pisidian Antioch (13:16–41) is a model for his Jewish synagogue-based proclamation throughout his travels, and allows Luke to only make reference to these settings in other places, rather than describing the message in detail.[75] Similarly, Paul's speech at Athens (17:22–31) is an example of how Paul preaches to a Gentile audience, and it should be assumed that he takes a similar approach in other comparable settings.[76] Paul's third major speech in Acts to the Ephesian elders (20:18–35) is also a "model speech" to his third type of audience: established churches and leaders whom he knows personally.[77] This speech shows the sorts of

71. Εὔτυχος ironically means "lucky," or "good fortune," a humorous attempt to lighten up the narrative.

72. Mitylene is the chief city of the island of Lesbos; Chios is where Homer was born; Samos is the birthplace of Pythagoras. A smaller craft would hug the coastline and put into port at night when the winds die down; Luke seems to be giving a daily account of this sea journey, in which he is a participant. Witherington, *Acts*, 609.

73. The depth of his relationships in Ephesus and accepted hospitality requirements would force him to stay there for some time if he visits the city. He may also want to avoid his Ephesian enemies.

74. See Walton, *Leadership*, 17–32, 52–93.

75. E.g., Salamis (13:5), Iconium (14:1), Philippi (16:13, the place of prayer), Thessalonica (17:2), Berea (17:10), Corinth (18:4), Ephesus (19:8).

76. Such as Lystra and Derbe (14:6–21). The shorter speech at Lystra (14:8–18) has thematic parallels to the Athens speech, particularly in natural theology.

77. Paul's relational bond with the other churches and leaders must also run quite

things Paul says when he visits cities where churches have been planted and "strengthens" these believers, filling in details that have been lacking in the narrative up to this point.[78] Paul's priority is to equip and build up the leadership of each church because he knows that if leaders are healthy their churches will flourish and grow.

This speech also confirms the strategic element of Paul's mission Luke mentions in 14:23: a local team of elders is commissioned to lead newly planted Pauline churches. The way it is taken for granted here that the Ephesian church has elders (πρεσβύτεροι, 20:17) indicates that this is Paul's normative practice in Acts, and therefore the reader should assume each Pauline church has a similar presbyterial leadership body.

A Life Worth Imitating

Paul's speech to the Ephesian elders shows the tenderness he feels towards them and the strategic way he seeks to build them up, using his own life and ministry as a primary example for them to follow. As the only extended speech in Acts specifically addressed to Christians, it is no surprise that this speech sounds more like the Paul of his letters than any other part of Acts.[79] "It is unmistakably Paul, and a Paul who presents himself to this community in terms remarkably like the ones we recognize in the letters we know Paul himself wrote to his communities . . . Luke accurately represents not only a number of distinctively Pauline themes, but does so in language which is specifically and verifiably Paul's."[80]

Paul begins by reminding his hearers of his way of life while among them, and the consistent way he proclaimed the gospel to both Jews and Greeks (20:18–21). He speaks of "teaching you publicly and from house to house" (διδάξαι ὑμᾶς δημοσίᾳ καὶ κατ᾽ οἴκους), which points to two

---

deep by this time. E.g., he has been through Iconium and the other Galatian churches at least four times: to establish them (14:1), as immediate follow-up and to appoint elders (14:21–23), at the beginning of his second journey (16:1–5), and at the beginning of his third journey (18:23).

78. Paul incorporates these pastoral visits into his travel itineraries because he is committed to the health and growth of these new churches (14:21–25; 15:41; 16:1–5; 18:23; 19:21–22; 20:1–3).

79. Witherington, *Acts*, 610 discusses the similarities and the differences. The letters of Paul that have been preserved are pastoral and situational in nature because they are addressed to specific believers and churches. But most of Paul's speeches and activity in Acts are evangelistic, addressed to non-believers.

80. Johnson, *Acts*, 367. Walton, *Leadership*, 140–98 discusses the many parallels between this speech and 1 Thessalonians, and the fewer parallels with Ephesians and 2 Timothy.

instructional strategies: one that is public and more evangelistic in nature, and one that is house to house, focused on building up the community of believers (20:20).[81] Paul urges the Ephesian leaders to imitate his way of life in three particular areas: persevering through trial and persecution (20:19), building up the church (20:20), and proclaiming the word continuously (20:21).[82] These three areas reiterate strategic values and priorities Luke advocates in Acts.

Paul then turns to the future, revealing that he is determined to go to Jerusalem, knowing that prison and hardship await him there (20:22–23). Here he articulates his life's mission statement: "I consider my life worth nothing to me, if only I may finish the race/course (δρόμον) and complete the task/ministry (διακονίαν) the Lord Jesus has given me, to testify solemnly of the gospel of the grace of God" (20:24). Paul is displaying a supreme example of what it means to selflessly follow Christ and sacrificially engage in God's mission, and he urges the Ephesian elders to imitate him. He then says he will not see any of them again, and that he is innocent of the blood of all men because he has not hesitated to proclaim to them the full will of God (20:25–27). "In essence, Paul is arguing that he has successfully discharged his duties in Ephesus, and that therefore they are now responsible for heeding his example and teachings on their own."[83] He is imploring his audience to prepare for the future and act in ways that will help them to fulfil their calling and extend the Asian mission even further.

Paul then exhorts the Ephesian elders to discharge the duties of their position of leadership within the church, and particularly to be on alert for attacks (20:28–30). He tells them to guard themselves and then to guard the flock that has been entrusted to their care. This reveals Luke's/Paul's conviction that spiritual leaders must care for themselves so they can remain personally healthy and capable of caring for the churches they lead. Once again, Paul holds himself up as an example worth imitating, particularly in the way that he continually admonished them over a three-year period with tears (20:31). The repeated motif of this speech is the way Paul points to his own exemplary life.

---

81. The school of Tyrannus may be the public venue.

82. Luke is presenting Paul as a great leader, who leads by example and whose life is worth emulating, similar to the ancient *bios* genre. For Paul's theology of imitation, cf. 1 Cor 4:16; 11:1; 1 Thess 1:6; 2:14; 2 Thess 3:7, 9.

83. Witherington, *Acts*, 614.

The Value of the Local Church and Its Leaders

Luke demonstrates his ecclesiastical understanding when Paul speaks of the church of God which he bought with his own blood (20:28). It is not Paul's church, nor does it belong to its leaders; the church is God's, purchased when Christ died on the cross.[84] Paul sees each individual community of Christ-followers as having been personally purchased by Christ on the cross. This shows Paul's great love for the church, and his fervent belief in its worth and potential: it is worth the death of Christ himself. Paul implies that this is the reason he has devoted his life so wholeheartedly to establishing, building, and developing these congregations, for which Christ died; he understands the value and importance of every particular church.

This also appears to be a reference to the cross, which is rare in Acts.[85] Luke includes it here because he wants to underline the significance of this story, not just theologically, but also in terms of practical missional significance. Empowering church leaders to carry the mission forward is the most strategic thing Paul can do at this point, particularly as he moves toward his own captivity, as it has the potential to multiply the growth of the movement. Every church Paul has established has been possible only because of the cross, and that same power will also protect and guide them in the future.

Paul then commits the elders to God and to the word of his grace, which can build them up (οἰκοδομῆσαι) and give them an inheritance among those who are sanctified (20:32). Paul has committed the church to the care of these leaders, and now he commits the leaders to the care of God. The church and its leaders are in the hands of God and Paul trusts that God will care for them and ensure that they flourish. Paul's responsibilities with the Ephesians are complete; they are now God's responsibility.

Paul reminds them how he supplied his own needs while among them and worked hard to help the weak (20:33–34). He finishes his speech with a quotation from the ultimate authority, Jesus: "it is more blessed to give than to receive" (20:35).[86] This serves as a Christological "proof" and summary of all that Paul has said: the Ephesian elders are called not to receive, but to give their lives away for the sake of the churches that have been entrusted to them, imitating Paul's sacrificial model and Christ's ultimate example on the

---

84. This saying must be primarily about the individual church in Ephesus, and not the universal church, because these elders could not shepherd the worldwide church, though Luke may be making a broader theological observation. See discussion in chapter 5.

85. Witherington, *Acts*, 624.

86. Although this saying is not found in the Gospels, it could be a known saying of Jesus, or the earliest Christian community; cf. Luke 6:35–38; Mark 10:45. Witherington, *Acts*, 626.

cross. "This is Paul, not some other speaker; and he is not evangelizing but recalling an already evangelized community to its deepest insights. In other words, the situation, like the theology, is precisely that of a Pauline epistle, not preliminary evangelism."[87] After speaking, Paul kneels with them and prays, committing them to God (20:36).

Deep Relationships—An Emotional (and Strategic) Goodbye

The reaction of the elders is full of pathos, showing how greatly they love Paul: "They all wept aloud (κλαυθμός) as they embraced Paul around the neck (ἐπιπεσόντες ἐπὶ τὸν τράχηλον) and kissed him repeatedly (κατεφίλουν), with a feeling of deep anguish" (ὀδυνώμενοι μάλιστα, 20:37-38).[88] Here is their spiritual father, the one who brought the gospel to them and transformed their lives. He lived among them for three years, personally trained many of them, and they are attempting to model their lives after Paul. By using such emotive words, Luke is highlighting the deep friendship between Paul and the Ephesian leaders.[89] Luke also notes that the most difficult thing for them is when Paul says they will not see him again (20:25, 38).

Luke is claiming that this close relational connection is another reason for the successful advance of the church. This is emphasized in their emotional farewell from which they must "tear/drag themselves away" (ἀποσπασθέντας), so great is their love for one another (21:1). Paul is no distant leader in Acts; he has built heart-felt friendships with many of these younger leaders, and this relational leadership style strengthens the commitment and longevity of the churches which Paul begins. "Paul is sometimes misrepresented by his critics as a hard and austere man, lacking compassion and kindness. However, this passage is one of several challenging that distorted view."[90] Their relational attachment will cause these leaders to be fiercely loyal to Paul and his mission, even after he is gone. It will ensure the long-term viability and sustainability of the Pauline mission in a way that no amount of strategy or inspirational vision could.

It is no accident that this emotional farewell is the last substantial episode of Paul's missionary journeys that Luke records. Luke is highlighting

---

87. Moule, "Christology," 171.

88. Ὀδυνάω means to suffer intense pain, agony, anguish, torment, distress. Cf. Luke 2:48, when Jesus's parents are looking for him in anguish, and Luke 16:24-25, where Lazarus is twice "in agony in the flames." It is unique to Luke-Acts in the NT and emphasizes their depth of emotion at having to say goodbye; BDAG, 692.

89. For such outbursts of emotion, even in weighty historical accounts, see Philo, *Embassy*, 243; Josephus, *J.W.*, 2.402. Johnson, *Acts*, 366.

90. Peterson, *Acts*, 574.

the significance of such an encounter, which is the narrative culmination of Paul's journeys. When Paul first departed in Acts 13:4, there were no Pauline churches, and he was not even sure where he was going or what he would do when he arrived. About twelve years later, there is a significant network of Pauline churches stretching across large areas of the Empire. Luke wants the reader to understand that this has not simply been a "strategic" process. It has been an emotional journey of exhilarating highs and devastating lows. He emphasizes this through Paul mentioning twice that he "served the Lord with tears" in this speech (20:19, 31).[91] Paul has "poured his life out" for these people, and this reality is tangible in Luke's description of their encounter (cf. Phil 2:17; 2 Tim 4:6). His emotional connection with local church leaders is one of the forces driving the momentum of the movement, and readers of Acts can discern this from the emotion-laden words Luke uses.

This group of "Ephesian elders" is sizeable, which is another Lukan indicator of the success of the Ephesian and Asian mission. They likely represent the leadership of the entire province, and many of them are involved in the expansion of the Asian movement and will go on to plant, lead, and oversee fellowships across the province. These are the emerging leaders of a vibrant church-planting movement, and Paul takes the opportunity to impart something strategic to them that will move them forward in the mission: "The church-planting Paul teaches the key themes of Christian leadership to the Ephesian church leaders, who will later pass the torch on to their successors."[92] These exhortations are his parting words, and the importance of the occasion is not lost on them.

The Rhetorical Function of the Farewell Speech

Paul's speech to the Ephesian elders is significant for Luke on multiple levels. It functions as the dramatic climax of his missionary narrative, and much of Acts culminates with this grand scene. It "enables [Luke] to deliver the final 'insider' interpretation of Paul . . . so that the reader is able to grasp 'how Paul was' for his churches—in effect supplying the sort of intimate portrait that the frantic pace of travels and tribulations had not till now allowed."[93] It also summarizes many of the missional strategies which Luke advocates

---

91. This emotional portrait of Paul comports with his letters (e.g., 2 Cor 2:1–4; 1 Cor 2:1–5; 1 Thess 1:7–8).

92. Walton, *Leadership*, 202.

93. Johnson, *Acts*, 366.

in Acts: "His charge to the Ephesian elders effectively summarizes and concludes the whole presentation of his missionary work in Acts 13–20."[94]

This speech is also an example of a well-known genre of speech acts in the Bible and the wider ancient world: the farewell speech.[95] These farewell speeches function as a call to action, but also as consolation literature, preparing people for inevitable loss. The long biblical tradition of such speeches includes the last words of Jacob (Gen 49:1–33), Joseph (Gen 50:24), Moses (Deut 31:1–13; 32:46–47), Joshua (Josh 24:22–28), David (1 Kgs 2:1–12; 1 Chr 29:10–20), and Jesus himself (Matt 28:18–20; Mark 13:1—15:47; John 14–17). Luke draws on this tradition in composing Paul's emotional farewell speech. The goal of such speeches is moral exhortation, often specifically to imitate the exemplary character of the life that has been lived, to call the audience to a renewal of the covenant ideals and of faithfulness to God, to reaffirm certain community values, and to warn about enemies. It is significant that Paul does each of these things in his speech, in addition to consoling and preparing these Ephesian elders for his impending departure and death. His goal is that these leaders would enter "a new level of moral existence that requires a maturity unaided by the guiding presence of the teacher."[96]

Luke reveals his underlying rhetorical purposes in Acts most translucently in this consolatory farewell speech. Luke wants his readers to put themselves in the position of the Ephesian elders—he is attempting to draw his audience in by his farewell speech rhetoric. *When Paul speaks to these leaders in Acts, Luke is speaking to Christian readers in later generations, potential church leaders and missionaries themselves.* "This represents far more than a collection of vague platitudes; it offers a dynamic, sharply focused model of Christian leadership rooted in Luke's understanding of Jesus, in contrast with other approaches to leadership available in the ancient world (Luke 22:25)."[97] The message Paul speaks is the message Luke is conveying to the reader, and can be summarized simply: "imitate Paul."[98] The farewell

94. Peterson, *Acts*, 523.

95. Perdue, "Death of the Sage," 82 claims the approaching death of a sage is, "an important occasion for the moral exhortation of disciples who are left behind." In addition to examples in the NT and Hebrew Bible, Perdue discusses examples from ancient Egypt, Jewish Testament Literature, Rabbinic Literature, and many examples of Greco-Roman Parenesis ("Death of the Sage," 82–109).

96. Perdue, "Death of the Sage," 82. Perdue discusses the Pauline parenesis in 2 Timothy in a footnote ("Death of the Sage," 101), but never mentions this speech in Acts.

97. Walton, *Leadership*, 136. Walton shows that Luke draws deliberate parallels between Paul's leadership and that of Jesus in his Gospel, including a summary of Christian leadership (*Leadership*, 99–136).

98. In a speech totalling 18 verses, only two do not have some explicit reference to

speech is really a Lukan tribute to Paul's Christlike life and ministry, and this is precisely what Luke holds up to his readers to emulate. "Paul is being presented as the ideal church leader who fulfills Jesus' commands and therefore is an example to others."[99]

> The "Farewell Discourse" is in reality a kind of paraenetic discourse, in which the main point is the instruction of the listener in certain moral values. As always in such discourses, there is the presentation of a model that they are to remember and to imitate, with the specific maxims making the example more explicit. In the present case, all of Paul's actions and dispositions are intended to communicate an example that the elders after him (and the readers of Luke-Acts) can imitate (20:31, 35).[100]

Table 10.3 Luke's Message to His Reader in the Miletus Farewell Speech (20:18–35)

- Imitate all that you have observed of Paul's life and ministry throughout Acts (20:18).

- Serve the Lord with humility and tears, enduring trials as the Lord's servant (20:19).

- Teach what is profitable, in public settings and in private from house to house (20:20).

- Solemnly preach the gospel of repentance and faith in Christ to everyone, both Jews and Greeks (20:21).

- Trust God in all things, following and obeying the Spirit, even when the future appears uncertain or ominous; expect that you will suffer for Christ and be prepared to persevere through this (20:22–23).

- Do not attempt to preserve your own life or comfort but focus on fulfilling your calling and completing the evangelistic and pastoral ministry which you have received from Jesus (20:24).

- Live in such a way that nobody can hold anything against you, always giving people the opportunity to receive Christ and to understand his purposes for their life (20:25–27).

Paul's life (20:28, 30), and those are still about things which Paul has modelled for his hearers in his personal life (shepherding and guarding the flock of God).

99. Tannehill, *Narrative Unity*, 2:250.

100. Johnson, *Acts*, 367.

- Guard your personal life and well-being, as this is essential to your leadership and mission; also guard the whole flock which you oversee, understanding that the church is so precious that Christ gave his life for it (20:28).

- Beware of divisive and perverse people who will arise even from within the church and attempt to divide and destroy it (20:29–31).

- Though this will be difficult, you are in God's hands and he is able to build you up, protect you, and give you an inheritance; he is committed to you and to his church (20:32).

- Do not covet others' possessions or depend on others' generosity, but work hard to provide for yourself and even for your co-workers (20:33–34).

- Remember to help the weak and to follow Christ's instructions that it is better to give than to receive; your calling is not to gain from others but to give selflessly to others (20:35).

Luke's ultimate purpose in Acts is to call his readers to action: to inspire and activate a new generation of Christian leaders and missionaries and equip them to carry out this calling effectively. "Luke's work as a whole may be partly an apologetic for Paul but also partly a deliberative exhortation to continue the same Gentile mission to which he devoted himself."[101] These two purposes are not mutually exclusive but complement each other in the overarching goal of commending Paul's life and mission to Luke's readers, and Luke uses this speech to the Ephesian elders to express this most directly. All his main missional themes are present in this climactic episode. Luke is saying that Paul is the ultimate example of what a missionary is and does, so everything he has written about Paul is worth imitating, including his close relationships with the Ephesian leaders. These Pauline strategies and approaches are not just fascinating practices but have been described in Acts so they can be emulated. "In this passage, Paul's life becomes a model for sacrificial ministry."[102]

Paul has a similar emphasis in his letters. He twice instructs the Corinthians to imitate him: "I exhort you, be *imitators* (μιμηταί) of me . . . be *imitators* (μιμηταί) of me, just as I also am of Christ" (1 Cor 4:16; 11:1). Similarly, he tells the Thessalonians that, "You also became *imitators* (μιμηταί) of us" (1 Thess 1:6), and explains, "how you ought to *imitate* (μιμεῖσθαι) us,

101. Keener, *Acts*, 3:2996.

102. Keener, *Acts*, 3:2992. Other scholars, such as Gaventa, "Theology and Ecclesiology," 44–50, overly downplay the extent to which Paul's ministry is presented as a model for others to follow in this speech.

because we did not act in an undisciplined manner among you . . . in order to offer ourselves as a *model* (τύπον—type or pattern for imitation) for you, so that you would *follow/imitate* us" (μιμεῖσθαι ἡμᾶς, 2 Thess 3:7, 9).[103] Luke is using a familiar Pauline motif in his speech to the Ephesian elders, and throughout Acts: "imitate/mimic the pattern of my life, faith, and ministry, as I imitate Christ." This is the ultimate responsibility of a disciple: to imitate and follow his or her leader/rabbi. It also captures the exemplary rhetorical approach Luke has taken throughout Acts—Paul is the definitive example to follow in Acts, particularly in his missional strategies.[104]

TOWARDS JERUSALEM (21:1–17)

After their emotional farewell to the Ephesian elders, Paul and his companions sail to Cos, Rhodes, Patara, and Tyre (21:1–3), and stay with the Tyrian disciples for a week (21:4).[105] They beg Paul not to go to Jerusalem, but he is determined (21:5).[106] There is another moving farewell scene at Tyre, as the men and their wives and children escort Paul and his companions to the beach (αἰγιαλόν), kneel to pray together, and say farewell (21:6). This scene again emphasizes the support and admiration for Paul and his mission work among the churches. "These examples represent what Luke expects us to recognize as a larger pattern of the way Paul must have parted in each place he stopped."[107] Paul and his co-workers then sail to Ptolemais, where they greet "the brothers/believers" and stay for a day (21:7),[108] before traveling to Caesarea and staying in the home of Philip the evangelist and his four unmarried "prophesying" daughters (21:8–9).[109] Here again Paul is warned about impending trouble facing him in Jerusalem by a Judean prophet named Agabus, but he will not be dissuaded (21:10–14). Paul is not

103. Μιμέομαι: Heb 6:12; Eph 5:1; 1 Thess 2:14. Μιμητής: Heb 13:7. Cf. Josephus, *Ant.*, 1.68, 109; 6.347; 8.251; 12.203; *Against Apion*, 2.257; Philo, *On the Virtues*, 66; Xenophon, *Memorabilia*, 1.6.3. BDAG, 651–52.

104. See Keener, *Acts*, 3.2993–97 for more on the rhetoric of this particular speech.

105. The origins of this community are uncertain; 11:19 suggests Christians passed through this region much earlier after being scattered due to persecution, and could have begun this church then.

106. Witherington, *Acts*, 630 discusses the controversy of Tyrian Christians apparently urging Paul and his companions "through the Spirit" not to go to Jerusalem.

107. Keener, *Acts*, 3:3067.

108. This final itinerary hints at a regional mission approach based in Jerusalem or Caesarea, as multiple surrounding towns have churches.

109. Philip was last seen in Caesarea (8:40) and is still there now, likely one of the primary (founding) leaders of the Caesarean church.

hard-hearted throughout this journey—his tenderness to the people shows in 21:13: "why are you weeping and breaking my heart?" (κλαίοντες καὶ συνθρύπτοντές μου τὴν καρδίαν). But he knows his destiny lies in Jerusalem.

Paul finally arrives in Jerusalem (21:15), and his third journey is complete. He stays in the house of Mnason of Cyprus, an "early/original disciple" (ἀρχαίῳ μαθητῇ, 21:16).[110] Mnason brings the journey cycle to a narrative completion, for what began in Cyprus multiple years ago (13:4) now ends in the home of a Cypriot in Jerusalem (21:16), though Paul would likely return to Antioch had he not been captured in Jerusalem.[111]

CONCLUSION

Paul's missional strategies come to maturity in this third journey. At Ephesus a regional movement which impacts all of Asia is born. All the strategies employed on earlier journeys are still in operation, but here Paul realizes his ultimate goal: the mobilization of a reproducing missionary movement with a large geographical scope, capable of reaching its entire surrounding area (19:10, 20). The details of Paul's Ephesian ministry in Acts are Luke's ways of generating such a remarkable missional impact. Luke implies that Paul's prolonged time in Corinth has prepared him for this final missional flourish in Ephesus and Roman Asia. Corinth and Ephesus are "two complementary episodes which illustrate a mature stage of development in Pauline mission practice and theology."[112]

Luke has sought to inspire his readers through various missional stimuli (part 1), and to demonstrate the missional structures they are to employ (part 2). Here he equips them by presenting missional strategies in Paul's missionary journeys, culminating in Ephesus. Luke uses Paul's farewell speech to the Ephesian elders to summarize and recapitulate his call to his readers; Paul's strategic words to these leaders *are* Luke's exhortations to his readers. In this speech Luke shows most transparently his rhetorical purpose in writing Acts: he is calling his generation particularly to imitate Paul and his many missionary exploits, including his close relationships with the leaders of the churches he has planted. Paul's life and example are the crux of Luke's call to action in Acts.

---

110. Perhaps Mnason was converted on Paul's first journey to Cyprus (13:4–12), or earlier by Barnabas (4:36–37). Witherington, *Acts*, 635 discusses Mnason's identity and the expanded information in the Western text.

111. Witherington, *Acts*, 635.

112. Towner, "Mission Practice," 433.

Chapter 11

Summary of Paul's Missional Strategy in Acts

Keep watch over yourselves and over all the flock, of which the Holy Spirit has made you overseers, to shepherd the church of God that he obtained with the blood of his own Son.

—ACTS 20:28

Multiple strategic themes have emerged in Luke's account of Paul's journeys. This chapter summarizes Paul's overall missional strategy and methodology as Luke describes it in Acts 13–21, separating the strategies identified in the previous three chapters into broad categories, while generally following Luke's narrative progression.[1]

---

1. To avoid being overly repetitive, this chapter only references the relevant passages and points of discussion in the previous chapters. Because chapters 8–10 follows Acts 13–21 verse by verse, it is easy to find the detailed discussion of any verse or topic in those sections.

STRATEGIC INITIAL PLANNING

Direction and Travel

Paul must first decide where he will go as a traveling missionary. He has multiple directional indicators. The first is the guidance of the Holy Spirit, which he relies upon whenever possible, and which sometimes changes his plans rather abruptly. Luke emphasizes at least four times that it is not Paul who is leading these expeditions, but the Spirit.[2]

However, when the Spirit's guidance is not evident, Paul also goes to places where he or his traveling companions have pre-existing relational connections,[3] or perhaps for which he can obtain a letter of recommendation from mutual friends.[4] Paul also follows existing transport and trade routes, often simply following the best road and sea routes wherever they happen to lead.[5] In this regard, Paul is surprisingly pragmatic about his travel itinerary, holding his plans loosely while often being redirected by circumstances beyond his control.[6] He is portrayed as an experienced traveler who covers at least 12,000 miles in Acts.[7] "Luke's audience would understand the difficulties of travel in ways that we often do not, and hence would recognize the lengths to which Paul went to reach new areas."[8]

---

2. Acts 13:2–4: the Spirit sends Paul and Barnabas from Antioch; 16:6–10: the Spirit prevents Paul from entering Asia and Bithynia, leading him to Macedonia; 19:21: Paul "purposed in the Spirit" to go to Jerusalem; 20:22, 23: he is "bound by the Spirit"; 21:12–14: "may the Lord's will be done." The many references to God's power and miracles are additional evidence.

3. E.g., Cyprus as the initial destination (13:4–12): Barnabas (and John Mark's) connections by birth and upbringing (4:36–37) and the Antioch church's connection (11:20–22). Cf. Paul going through Tarsus (Cilicia) at the beginning of his second journey (15:41).

4. E.g., Sergius Paulus's possible family connections with Pisidian Antioch (13:7–14; cf. 18:27 for a letter of recommendation). Synagogue social networks are linked across regions, as are early churches such as Jerusalem and Antioch.

5. E.g., the *Via Sebaste*, which runs through Perga, Pisidian Antioch, Iconium, and Lystra (13:13—14:23; 16:1–5; 18:23); the *Via Egnatia*, which runs from Rome through Philippi and beyond (16:12; 20:6). French, "Roman Roads," 52–58; Keener, *Acts*, 1:582–89.

6. E.g., going from Iconium to Lystra and Derbe (14:5–6) and from Thessalonica to Berea (17:10).

7. Finegan, *Archeology*, xix, noting that later travels claimed by Christian tradition would add a further 3,000 miles or more. Such extensive travel (mostly by foot) would consume much of Paul's time in ministry.

8. Keener, *Acts*, 1:596. This is another way Luke holds Paul up as an ideal missionary model.

Expect and Adjust to Persecution

Paul also resigns himself to opposition affecting his travel itinerary and displays remarkable resilience. He frequently alters his plans or flees to another place to avoid personal violence or the harm of the new community which has been established.[9] If persecution drives him out of one city, he entrusts those people to God and moves to the next, continuing to proclaim the word (following Luke 10:10–12). Paul's planning is flexible; when persecution changes the course, he accepts this as the Spirit's leading and adjusts accordingly.

Maximum Impact through Urban Centers

As Paul travels in Acts, he looks for places where he can make a maximum impact and recognizes that this is urban centers, particularly capital cities such as Thessalonica, Ephesus, and Corinth. Many of the urbanites in these cities have already shown an openness and attraction to new religious movements, particularly from the exotic east.[10] Such cities exercise a disproportionate amount of influence on their surrounding regions, and if Paul can establish churches in them, their impact will resonate widely and exponentially multiply his efforts. For this reason, Paul *only* stops for ministry in significant towns and cities in Acts.[11]

Paul's urban focus is not unique among new missionary religions:

> All ambitious missionary movements are, or soon become, urban. If the goal is to "make disciples of all nations," missionaries need to go where there are many potential converts, which is precisely what Paul did. His missionary journeys took him to major

---

9. E.g., Acts 13:50–51; 14:5–6; 14:19–20; 16:40; 17:7–10, 13–14; 20:1. Paul flees when persecution breaks out in every city except Corinth and Ephesus, often going just far enough to cross an administrative border where authorities will no longer search for him. See Keener, *Acts*, 1:461–64 on the conflict reports of Acts more generally.

10. The spread of Christianity is inevitably caught up in the wider fascination and even fanaticism in the cities of the Empire with new eastern religious movements, such as the Isis and Cybele cults. This attraction to cultic expressions from Egypt, Asia, and Judea undoubtedly fuels the growth of Christianity. Stark, *Cities of God*, 116 argues that, "Cybelene worship and Isiacism served as important stepping-stones to Christianity by shaping pagan culture in ways that made the Christ story more familiar and credible."

11. E.g., Syrian Antioch, Tarsus, Pisidian Antioch, Salamis, Paphos, Ephesus, Troas, Philippi, Thessalonica, Athens, and Corinth. Iconium, Lystra, Derbe, and Berea are somewhat smaller but are still regional centers that exercise influence over their surrounding areas, largely through being provincial administrative capitals and hubs for local travel and trade routes.

cities such as Antioch, Corinth, and Athens, with only occasional
visits to smaller communities such as Iconium and Laodicea. No
mention is made of him preaching in the countryside.[12]

If a person wants to reach many people, it is logical to go to the large cities,
for this is where potential converts are most highly concentrated.

Another reason early Christians focus on cities is their attitude toward
rural people.[13] As Stark explains, "It was several centuries before the early
church made serious efforts to convert the rural peasantry—although many
were converted by friends and kinfolk returning from urban sojourns. Fully
sharing the views of their non-Christian neighbors, many early Christians
dismissed rural people as subhuman brutes."[14] There is also evidence that
rural people are content with their lives and despise the cities in similar
fashion.[15] Paul is an urbanite who feels most comfortable in cities, though
he has to travel through rural areas on his way to the cities where he stops.

The Roman Empire is a remarkable epoch, for it comes as close to an
urban culture as any until eighteenth-century Europe, largely because cultural and political influence is so concentrated in the cities. Even though
about 80–90 percent of its population lives on farms or in rural villages,
Rome should still be considered an urban empire: "The cities were where
the power was . . . where changes could occur."[16] There are about a thousand
Greco-Roman towns or cities, and by establishing themselves in these urban
centers, Christians find political influence far greater than their size relative
to the population of the Empire.[17] "Even as late as the fourth century the
overwhelming majority of Christians lived in cities; hence their political
importance probably was far greater that their total number might suggest—
which no doubt played a role in Constantine's seeking the support of the
early church."[18] As Pearson summarizes, "Christianity arose in a time and

12. Stark, *Cities of God*, 25–26.

13. Keener, *Acts*, 1:589–96 discusses rural versus urban life, including urban dis-
dain for rural life.

14. Stark, *Cities of God*, 26. Fletcher, *Barbarian Conversion*, 16: "The peasantry of
the countryside were beyond the pale, a tribe apart, outsiders. Such attitudes under-
pinned the failure of the urban Christian communities to reach out and spread the
gospel in the countryside . . . For them the countryside simply did not exist as a zone
for missionary enterprise. After all, there was nothing in the New Testament about
spreading the Word to the beasts of the field."

15. Keener, *Acts*, 1:595–96.

16. Meeks, *Urban Christians*, 15. The rural "population hovered so barely above
subsistence level that no one dared risk change," MacMullen, *Christianizing*, 27.

17. Keener, *Acts*, 1:590.

18. Stark, *Rise of Christianity*, 10–11. "Because the Christian population was

place in history when cities, great and small, were in their ascendancy."[19] This urban ascendancy gives rise to the urban expression of early Christianity seen in Acts.[20]

Travel and transport trends add to this urban focus. As missionaries travel, they naturally arrive in the larger cities of the Empire, for these cities are the hubs for all transportation networks within the Roman world. The Romans designed roads to connect larger population centers together. However, their ships had the greatest impact:

> It was not primarily roads that made people in this era so mobile. It was boats . . . Rome was mainly a waterfront empire surrounding the Mediterranean Sea. Almost a lake, the Mediterranean has very weak tides, is sheltered from storms, and lacks the offshore distances that make sailing far more dangerous on the great oceans. The sailing ships used in this era were quite reliable, capacious, and much faster than any form of land transportation.[21]

The strategic ports of the Empire quickly become larger cities because of their commercial value and the constant influx of people traveling through them. "Although wandering preachers may have been the first Christians to reach Rome, it seems likely that the primary bearers of the new faith were rank-and-file believers who traveled for commercial or personal reasons."[22] The scope of travel in the Empire is massive: "The people of the Roman Empire traveled more extensively and easily than any . . . would again until the nineteenth century."[23] This unprecedented level of travel and mobility, centered on the cities, contributes to the urban focus of the Christian mission in Acts.

---

concentrated and well organized, it could have had far greater impact on the politics of the empire than the absolute numbers might suggest," Stark, *Cities of God*, 71.

19. Pearson, "Rodney Stark's Foray," 172.

20. There was never a total divide between urban and rural, but a continual overlap between these two populations; Fox, *Pagans and Christians*, 41–46, 132, 139, 287–93. E.g., the elite classes straddled both urban and rural populations through their country villas and town houses.

21. Stark, *Cities of God*, 74. Paul uses ships when possible, as they allow him to reach distant destinations much quicker. Keener, *Acts*, 1:587–88 discusses the speed of ancient travel.

22. Stark, *Cities of God*, 73.

23. Meeks, *Urban Christians*, 17. A grave inscription in Phrygia claims that a merchant made 72 trips to Rome, a one-way journey of more than a thousand miles. Stark, *Cities of God*, 74.

In addition to the various factors related to travel and influence, new religions flock to the cities because they find greater receptivity to their message there. Fischer's Theory of Urban Deviancy explains this trend: "The more urban the place, the higher the rates of unconventionality."[24] This shows that the larger the population, the easier it is to assemble the "critical mass" needed to form a deviant subculture, that is, a group of people who sustain unconventional outlooks and activities. Early Christianity is a "deviant" subculture, largely at odds with the conventional norms governing religious expression in the Greco-Roman world. It follows that Christians are able to assemble the critical mass needed to form a house congregation sooner in larger cities than in smaller ones.[25] Paul assembles this critical mass quickly in nearly every city that he travels to in Acts—the large population sizes expedite this process of finding people open to new ideas and ways of living.

STRATEGIC APPROACHES

Receptive Social Networks

Once Paul has arrived at a place to evangelize, he looks for people matching certain criteria. His goal is to find a way into an existing social network, and this involves forming relational attachments with local people who are welcoming and have multiple other relational attachments.[26] Paul looks for the person or group with whom he can have the most rapport in the least amount of time, and who is most receptive to both his friendship and his message. This is preferably a person with whom he already has some connection.

If he has no existing relational "entry points," Paul goes to the most open and receptive people he can find, who are usually in the synagogue.[27]

24. Fischer, "Subcultural Theory," 1328.

25. Stark, *Cities of God*, 81. The idea of a "critical mass" is a helpful way of thinking about Paul's initial goal when approaching a city to establish a church. This is the necessary "beachhead" for a new religion.

26. This parallels the "person of peace" concept (Luke 10:6).

27. E.g., in Salamis (13:5); Pisidian Antioch (13:14, 43); Iconium (14:1); Thessalonica (17:1); Berea (17:10); Athens (17:17); Corinth (18:4, 7); Ephesus (18:19, 26; 19:8). If there is a synagogue in a city, this is always where Paul begins. If not, he looks for Jews and God-fearers in places such as the place of prayer in Philippi (16:13–15). Acts does not mention the mission starting at the synagogue or Jewish place of prayer in three cities: Paphos (13:6–12), Lystra (14:8–18), and Derbe (14:21). This is because there is not a significant Jewish population there, or Luke's account in the location is extremely brief (Derbe).

The synagogue is a natural starting point for Paul, because he shares significant common ground with it culturally and theologically, and it often welcomes him to teach as a visiting speaker.[28] The synagogue also usually provides a hospitable pre-existing social network.[29] The God-fearers are a particularly successful focal group for Paul, for they are drawn to Jewish monotheism, but are not prepared to embrace all the cultural requirements of becoming full Jewish proselytes, and are therefore on the fringes of the synagogue communities.[30] The God-fearers in the synagogues are one of the chief strategic entry points into many of the cities that Paul visits.

People of Influence

Paul also looks for people of influence within these strategic settings. He practices householder evangelism, and targets leaders or influencers within established social networks.[31] In this way he gains friendship and influence with many by gaining it with a few. The missional breakthrough often comes through a person of influence converting in a certain community, which leads to others following their lead.[32] One of the hallmarks of the Pauline mission in Acts is the number of influential, middle to upper class conversions.[33] These people become the social base for an emerging church community, and their home often becomes the material base for the new congregation. By reaching people of good reputation in an area, Paul can also gain good standing within that area.[34]

28. E.g., Paul's synagogue speech in Pisidian Antioch (13:15–43). Paul selects his destinations partially based on their Jewish Diaspora population.

29. Stark, *Cities of God*, 8–15 discusses the role of social networks in the early Christian mission.

30. God-fearers are mentioned in Pisidian Antioch (13:16, 26, 43, 50); Philippi (16:14); Thessalonica (17:4); Athens (17:17); Corinth (18:7). They are often the first Gentiles to hear the Christian message.

31. E.g., Sergius Paulus in Paphos (13:6–12); Lydia in Philippi (16:15); the Philippian jailer (16:31, 34); Dionysius in Athens (17:34); Titius Justus in Corinth (18:7); Crispus in Corinth (18:8); the Troas homeowner (20:7–8).

32. E.g., at Corinth (18:8): when the synagogue ruler Crispus converts others quickly follow.

33. E.g., Sergius Paulus (13:6–12); Lydia (16:13–15); the leading women (17:4); prominent women and men (17:12); Dionysius the Areopagite (17:34); Crispus the synagogue ruler (18:8); Apollos, "a learned man" (18:24); Manaen, brought up with Herod (13:1); possibly the Asiarchs (19:31). When Luke gives details of converts, they are usually people of influence.

34. E.g., Lydia in Philippi: by gaining her friendship, Paul gains credibility in the community and the friendship of multiple others (16:13–15, 40). This theme contrasts with

Continual and Relevant Proclamation

Paul proclaims the gospel everywhere he goes. Even if he is only in a place for a brief stay or travel stopover, he constantly shares the good news with people he encounters.[35] This practice is reminiscent of the "broad seed sowing" in Jesus's parable of the seed and the sower (Luke 8:4–15).[36] But Paul never preaches a stock message—he preaches with precise relevance, tailoring his message to his hearers.[37] He looks for common ground, natural starting points and affinities, and contextualizes his content to build upon the interests and authorities of his audience, while proclaiming the core Christological message.

Miraculous Confirmations of the Message

Finally, Paul does not simply rely on words and convincing arguments about the gospel, but consistently demonstrates the truth of his message through miracles,[38] spiritual power encounters,[39] and signs and wonders.[40] These confirm the veracity of what Paul is preaching and show the superiority of the Christian God above rival religious systems. This is an effective way of gathering an initial core of followers, who are convinced because they see the love and power of the God Paul is speaking to them about and believe based on that experience rather than because of intellectual persuasion.[41]

Luke's Gospel's emphasis on caring for the poor and the least, though that focus surely continues in the ministries of Paul's churches. Paul's focus on people of influence is one of the most distinctive aspects of his mission in Acts, but this does not mean he and his churches do not care for the impoverished, only that Luke chooses not to focus on this.

35. E.g., 14:25; 17:17; 18:19–20; throughout Paul's journeys.

36. One of the points is that the sower must sow as broadly as possible to find the "good soil" which yields a bountiful harvest. Paul compares himself to a gardener who plants seed (1 Cor 3:5–9).

37. Cf. Paul's speech to the Pisidian Antioch synagogue (13:16–41), to Gentiles at Lystra (14:15–17) and Athens (17:22–31), and to the Ephesian elders (20:18–35).

38. E.g., the healing of the lame man in Lystra (14:8–10); release from prison in Philippi (16:25–26); extraordinary miracles in Ephesus, including his handkerchiefs healing people (19:11–12). Luke's listing of miracles is not comprehensive but meant to be a representative selection.

39. E.g., the confrontation with Elymas the sorcerer in Paphos (13:6–12); with the "pythoness" slave girl in Philippi (16:16–18); with the sons of Sceva in Ephesus (19:13–16).

40. E.g., 14:3; 15:12. For more on miracles in Acts, see Keener, *Acts*, 1:320–82; discussion in chapter 4.

41. The connection between supernatural power and belief leading to conversion is explicit in 13:12; 14:1–4; 16:29; 19:17–20. It is implied elsewhere. Cf. 1 Cor 2:1–5.

God does many powerful miracles through Paul in Acts (19:11), which greatly contribute to the expansion of the church.

Another "confirmation" which contributes to Paul and Christianity's success is their appeal to a *translated* religious text of purported great antiquity, the Septuagint (LXX). This text is accessible in the common language and lends a prophetic legitimation to the events proclaimed in the gospel message. Luke emphasizes that appealing to translated Scripture is the church's customary practice throughout Acts.[42] By contrast, Isis devotion expressly forbids the translation of its obscure and ancient holy texts and prefers to leave them shrouded in mystery.[43] This prevents the emergence of missionaries such as the Apostle Paul, who spreads Christianity confirmed by translated ancient texts *and* powerful miracles throughout Acts.

STRATEGIC FOUNDATIONS

The Cell—Embryonic Church

Once Paul has identified a location and begins to build relationships there, his goal is to plant a small nucleus of a church, sometimes called a "cell."[44] He draws converts into fledgling communities of new Christians, never leaving them alone.[45] He preaches until he has a small group of new converts gathered, and then he takes these aside to train and develop into an embryonic church.[46] This equipping involves vision for further mission, for which they take responsibility, and intentional modelling and training in what the Christian life and community entail.[47] This early cell community happens in the home and is based around an οἶκος household structure.[48]

42. E.g., Acts 1:16; 8:30–35; 13:17–41; 17:2, 11; 18:24, 28; Meek, *Gentile Mission* analyzes Luke's use of OT citations, focusing on 2:17–21 (Joel 3:1–5); 3:25 (Gen 22:18); 13:47 (Isa 49:6); 15:16–18 (Amos 9:11–12).

43. Stark, *Cities of God*, 103–4.

44. Gehring, *House*, 179–80.

45. E.g., in Pisidian Antioch (13:43–48; 14:21–22); Iconium (14:1–4, 21–22); Lystra (14:20–22); Derbe (14:21–22); Philippi (16:40); Thessalonica (17:4, 10); Berea (17:12, 14); Athens (17:34); Corinth (18:8, 18); Ephesus (19:9–10). Luke only mentions Sergius Paulus in Cyprus, but this does not mean communities are not begun there, though it may, as this is the very beginning of Paul's developing missional strategies (13:4–12; 15:39).

46. E.g., in Corinth (18:7–8, 18) and Ephesus (19:8–10).

47. E.g., Priscilla and Aquila (18:26). If converts come from the synagogue setting, Paul has a natural foundation to build from, in both theology and practice.

48. E.g., the home of Titius Justus in Corinth (18:7–8). The only explicit exception to this is the hall of Tyrannus, which provides the ideal setting for training and proclamation in Ephesus, but homes are still part of Paul's missional strategy there (20:20).

City-Wide Church Outreach

Paul's time in a city typically results in one or a few small cells or Christian households, which he visits again later to encourage and strengthen them.[49] These cells become nascent bases of missionary operation in their respective cities. Each one reaches outwards, first impacting its city, and then developing mission into the surrounding regions.[50] Paul generally does not stay long enough for the burgeoning cells to become larger church networks, but only until he feels that they are self-reliant, or until he is forced out by persecution.[51] Paul trains these new churches to be responsible for their own community life and for their outreach in the city and surrounding areas.

Regional Church Networks

This results in a network of young congregations, which each become bases for regional mission (18:27–28). They form their own outreach teams, working to assist Paul in his outreach in their areas, and then continuing with the mission once Paul has left. Each of these is an independent congregation, with an increasingly broad geographical strategy for outreach into their surrounding areas and beyond.[52]

These individual new communities are not isolated from one another but are linked together across multiple networks of travel and communication. Thompson famously compares this early Christian network to the modern internet.[53] He discusses the grid of Roman roads and shipping lanes of the first-century world, which make travel safer, easier, and less expensive for early Christian missionaries, letter carriers, and travelers than ever before. The network "servers" are the churches themselves, and the churches at Jerusalem, Rome, Syrian Antioch, Philippi, Corinth, Athens, and Ephesus are particularly significant hubs. Secondary hubs are many of the smaller cities where Paul establishes churches (such as Iconium, Berea or Lystra),

---

49. See previous section. Rom 15:19b refers to this cell-planting concept in key cities; Paul seems to think he has "fully proclaimed the good news of Christ" in these regions when these cells are established. Meeks, *Urban Christians*, 9–10.

50. E.g., Acts 19:17: "this became known to *all residents of Ephesus.*"

51. See 1 Thess 2:1–2 (Philippi); 1 Thess 1:6; 2:13–20; 3:1–13 (Thessalonica). See previous section for examples of Paul fleeing persecution in Acts.

52. For regional mission strategies, see Acts 13:49: "the word of the Lord spread throughout the entire region (ὅλης τῆς χώρας)"; 14:6–7: "and to the surrounding regions (περίχωρον), where they continued to preach the good news"; 19:10: "all the Jews and Greeks in the province of Asia heard the word of the Lord."

53. Thompson, "Holy Internet," 49–70.

which are centers in their own right because the roads of a local district converge there.[54] Hospitality practices prove essential in this growing matrix, and "ensured social cohesion and solidarity for each smaller network within the larger Christian web."[55] Because the existence of many of these young churches is threatened, they grow to rely on each other in a network of communication, travel, attachment, and support.

STRATEGIC DEVELOPMENT

After Paul has been with the new church for a relatively brief period, he leaves them to continue the mission without him.[56] He is wary of allowing them to become too dependent on his leadership and wants them to be autonomous and self-sufficient.

Strengthening the Churches

Despite leaving relatively quickly, Paul is committed to staying connected with these young churches and supporting them however he can. His priority is to visit the new congregations as frequently as possible, to check on their progress and continue to strengthen, encourage, and train them.[57] Paul's goal of establishing reproducing churches requires follow-up and training, as each community learns what it means to be the body of Christ in its locale.[58]

Local Leadership

Paul also establishes a local structure of leadership and oversight for the new churches by appointing elders in the churches he establishes.[59] He often

---

54. Thompson, "Holy Internet," 53–54.

55. Thompson, "Holy Internet," 56.

56. Paul's stays vary from a few days in the earlier cities (e.g., 14:20–21) to nearly three years in Ephesus (19:8–10, 22; 20:31), but he always leaves the young churches to take responsibility for their survival and growth. Paul learns through his experiences at Corinth and Ephesus (and Jesus's intervention, 18:9–11) that staying longer can lead to a more substantial missional impact.

57. E.g., 14:21–22; 15:41; 16:1–5; 18:23; 19:21; 20:1–3.

58. Luke never mentions Paul's letters, another strategic way he strengthens the churches. See Keener, *Acts*, 1:233–37—most scholars doubt that Luke has access to Paul's letters, though this is debated.

59. Though Luke does not explicitly state this in every city, it can be assumed based on 14:23 ("Paul and Barnabas appointed elders for them *from church to church*"), and

does this after a short period of testing to see who remains faithful and is capable of such a role (14:21–23). These new elders are generally leaders within the community, such as householders and business leaders.[60] After being commissioned through prayer and fasting (14:23; cf. 13:2–3), the elders work to guide the local congregation's vision, direction, and strategy for community life, as well as their citywide and regional outreach. They also take responsibility for pastoral care, teaching and preaching, and other leadership duties.

Equipping these elders is an unmistakable priority for Paul.[61] His focus on empowering local leadership in Acts shows how vital healthy leaders are to the development of a healthy church. These elders are pivotal to the emergence of church-planting movements in an area because they are embedded within local social networks and are often people of influence and means. "Paul and Barnabas appointed leaders . . . so that the churches could continue to function and grow in the apostles' absence. Organizing converts would consolidate the mission's results into self-propagating bodies capable of sustained growth."[62]

Co-Workers and Ministry Partners

Paul cannot accomplish such a massive missionary enterprise on his own, so he develops a team of ministry partners who assist him.[63] These co-workers are another innovative element of Paul's missional strategy in Acts.

20:17–38, Paul's farewell to the Ephesian elders. Luke "brackets" his narrative account of Paul's journeys with these two references to church elders, implying that this is Paul's standard practice.

60. On appointing local leaders and elders in the ancient world, see Keener, *Acts*, 2:2182–89.

61. The narrative climax of Paul's journeys is his instruction to the Ephesian elders (20:17–38). The reader can assume this is a practice repeated elsewhere, as Luke often picks one example of a commonly repeated practice to describe in detail (such as the speeches). The other references to "strengthening" and "encouraging" the churches likely follow similar lines (14:21–22; 15:41; 16:1–5; 18:23; 19:21; 20:1–3).

62. Keener, *Acts*, 2:2182, who cites several examples where similar leadership structures have facilitated rapid church growth and multiplication.

63. Gehring, *House*, 180.

Timothy,[64] Silas/Silvanus,[65] and Priscilla and Aquila[66] are examples of this primary team, along with Tychicus[67] and Luke.[68] They are given responsibility for looking after churches, helping with teaching and outreach, and other duties such as organizing collections and delivering personal correspondence.[69] Paul also travels significantly with Barnabas, from whom he may first learn this strategy.[70]

A secondary group of co-workers assists Paul on a more temporary basis, drawn from congregations he has established, particularly to assist in local and regional mission.[71] Among these are Sopater, Aristarchus, Secundus, Gaius (Acts 20:4), and Erastus (19:22).[72] These leaders are released from their local responsibilities within individual congregations to help with Paul's regional outreach for a time, either to travel with Paul or to serve in a Pauline church.[73]

These tiers of co-workers greatly expand the leadership base of the emerging movement of churches. They are a source of support, encouragement, and protection to Paul, and he strategically equips them to further the mission after he departs. Luke also emphasizes the depth of emotional

64. Timothy likely comes to faith on Paul's first journey through Lystra (Acts 14:6–20; cf. 1 Tim 1:2) and joins Paul on his second journey through Lystra (Acts 16:1–5). He helps Paul evangelize Macedonia and Achaia (17:14–15; 18:5), is with him throughout his ministry at Ephesus (19:22), travels with him to Macedonia, Corinth, back to Macedonia, and to Asia Minor (20:1–6), and may accompany Paul all the way back to Jerusalem (21:16–20).

65. Silas is a leader in the Jerusalem church (15:22), a prophet (15:32), and a Roman citizen (16:37–38), who is appointed along with Judas to carry the apostolic decree (15:22, 27), and encourages and strengthens the brothers (15:32). Paul chooses Silas to travel with him on his second journey (15:40), and he travels with Paul through that journey (17:4) to Berea (17:10, 14), before joining him again in Corinth (18:5).

66. They meet Paul in Corinth and accompany him to Ephesus (18:2, 18–20, 26).

67. See Acts 20:4; cf. Eph 6:21; Col 4:7; 2 Tim 4:12; Tit 3:12.

68. Luke probably travels with Paul during the three "we passages" (16:10–17; 20:5—21:18; 27:1—28:16).

69. These details are present in Acts, but more prominent in Paul's letters.

70. First missionary journey and trip to Jerusalem Council (13:2—15:36); earlier trip from Tarsus to Antioch, Jerusalem, and back to Antioch (11:25–30).

71. Gehring, House, 180. Cf. 1 Cor 16:15–18; Phil 2:25–30; 2 Cor 8:18–19.

72. Paul mentions many other partners in his letters, such as Titus, about whom Acts is strangely silent (2 Cor 2:13; 7:6, 13, 14; 8:6, 16, 23; 12:18; Gal 2:1, 3; 2 Tim 4:10; Tit 1:4); Stephanas, Fortunatus, Achaicus (1 Cor 16:17), Chloe (1 Cor 1:11); Epaphroditus (Phil 2:25; 4:18), Phoebe, Priscilla, Mary, Junia, Tryphena, Tryphosa (Rom 16:1–12); Nympha (Col 4:15); Euodia, Syntyche (Phil 4:1–3).

73. They likely also have a vital role to play in the collection for the Jerusalem church (20:1–15; cf. 24:17).

attachment which Paul has to these leaders and to the churches he has found-ed.[74] Paul's missional enterprise would not reach such widespread influence without these networks of ministry partners, which Paul intentionally de-velops during his various journeys.

Regional Movements

Paul continues to practice partner mission and is nearly always part of a larger team. The mission bases emulate him, assembling small teams to send into un-evangelized areas to proclaim the word, start cells, and reproduce the process again.[75] Individual house churches within these cities are the starting point for the entire local and regional missionary enterprise, the seeds of the future movement.[76] This is what makes householders such a priority for Paul. "In the Pauline mission, houses served not only as meet-ing places for the worship services but also as mission support bases that provided the manpower for mission outreach to the city and beyond."[77]

It does not end with these house churches; the goal is a city-wide net-work of congregations, which are able to send mission teams into surround-ing areas. The best example of this in Acts is the church at Antioch. Acts 13:1–3 is a paradigmatic episode on many levels, such as the role prayer, fasting, and prophecy play in the advancement of the mission.[78] But its depiction of the church sending Barnabas and Paul on their mission jour-ney is perhaps most significant. After hearing the Holy Spirit's instruction (13:2), they place their hands on them and send them off (13:3). This formal commissioning emerges directly out of the vibrancy and strength of this local church at Antioch. This relationship is underscored by the way this mission team returns to the Antioch church, "from which they had been commissioned" and "reports" back to them (14:26–27). Paul and Silas leave on the second journey, "commended by the brothers to the grace of the Lord" (15:40), and Paul returns only to be sent out again after staying there for "some time" (18:22–23). Luke is painting a picture of a thriving local community, which sends out teams to start other churches, and there is no

74. E.g., 20:36–38; 21:5–6, 12–14.

75. Paul begins reproducible churches that are easily multiplied into surrounding areas, and this is crucial to his missional success. Epaphras in Ephesus is an example (Col 1:5–7; 4:12–13).

76. Cf. 1 Cor 3:6—the seed is the initial house church gathering, and once that is planted, Paul is often on his way elsewhere, content to let others nurture and water the developing plant.

77. Gehring, *House*, 182. They provide financial resources as well.

78. For more analysis of the pivotal Antioch church, see chapters 7–9.

reason to believe this is not at least partially duplicated in the other churches Paul begins.[79]

As established city-wide house church networks begin sending out mission teams, this grows into regional movements, each reproducing these same basic elements into new areas. There are indications of this at Pisidian Antioch ("the word was carried throughout that entire region," 13:49), as well as at other stages of the Pauline mission such as the "surrounding areas" of Lystra and Derbe (14:6). However, this comes to full development in the way that the Ephesian church has such a significant regional impact that "all who lived in the province of Asia heard" (19:10), and "the word spread widely [geographically] and grew in power" (19:20).[80] *These passages highlight a regional strategy, involving the sending of church-planting teams into surrounding areas from a missional hub.* As further hubs for outreach are established, this process replicates, until an entire area has heard the word and there are missional churches in many of its population centers.

PERSONAL STRATEGIES

Team

Paul also develops personal strategies which enable him to persevere in his ministry and avoid burnout; these strategies are missional in that they sustain the missionary for the long term. A primary personal strategy is the concept of team. Paul almost never travels alone but is always building teams of workers and companions around him, in an intentional practice of partner mission.[81] These individuals help to prevent the loneliness and discouragement that can set in on long and challenging trips. They also provide physical protection and security from bandits, pirates, and other dangers, and help Paul to persevere through many difficulties.[82] These companions are also intentionally developed into vital leaders for the emerging churches. Throughout Acts, Luke emphasizes the importance of team ministry and partner mission to the long-term success of the Pauline movement.

79. Apollos's journey to Achaia hints at this sort of strategy (18:27–28). See Epaphras (Col 1:5–7; 4:12–13; Phlm 1:23) and the seven churches of Revelation in Asia (Rev 2–3), NT examples of a mission strategy towards which Acts points.

80. Cf. 12:24: "the word of God *grew* and was multiplied," also about the church's regional growth.

81. There are only two or three times when Paul may be alone: 17:14–34; 18:21, 23.

82. Paul's letters show how greatly he relies upon this ministry team, and how devastated he is if they abandon him: Rom 16:21; 1 Cor 4:17; 2 Cor 1:9; 1 Thess 3:2; 1 Tim 1:2; 2 Tim 1:2; 4:10, 16.

Connection to "Home Base"

Paul also stays connected to his home-base in Syrian Antioch and returns to report to them on his progress whenever possible.[83] This likely involves times of celebrating together what God has done and re-connecting with deep friendships. This sort of long-term relational history is a stabilizing anchor for Paul, particularly when he is continually forming new relationships on his journeys.

Periods of Rest

At the end of his first two journeys, Paul takes a period to rest and become reenergized for the next step in his mission.[84] He pursues a balanced cycle of exertion and restoration, which enables him to persevere in his mission for the long haul without growing overly fatigued by the intensive work and travel.[85]

Table 11.1 Summary of Lukan/Pauline Missionary Strategies (Acts 13–21)[86]

1. Strategic Initial Planning

    a. *Direction*

        i. Follow the Spirit's guidance (13:4; 16:6–10; 19:21; 20:22–23; 21:12–14)

        ii. Follow pre-existing relational connections (13:4–12)

        iii. Expect persecution and persevere through it, adjusting itinerary accordingly (13:50–51; 14:5–6, 19–20; 16:40; 17:7–10, 13–14; 20:1)

    b. *Travel*

---

83. Acts 14:26–27: "They sailed back to Antioch, where they had been committed to the grace of God for the work they had now completed [note Luke's emphasis on closure]. On arriving there, they gathered the church together and reported. . ." See also 18:22–23.

84. 14:28: "stayed not a short time"; 18:23: "spending some time in Antioch."

85. Paul surely also rests during his journeys, such as while waiting for ships, e.g., 16:12; 18:11; 19:8, 10, 22; 20:31.

86. This should be understood as Luke's teaching to a potential missionary or church leader through his recounting of Paul's missionary journeys, as well as Paul's strategic *modus operandi* in Acts.

    i. Follow the best transport and trade routes (13:13—14:23; 16:1–12; 18:23; 20:6)

    ii. Seek maximum impact by targeting influential urban centers and capital cities (13:5, 6, 14, 51; 14:1, 6; 16:8, 12; 17:1, 10, 15; 18:1, 19; 19:1)

2. Strategic Approaches—Beginning to Impact a City

    a. *Target receptive social networks, where there is natural rapport and connection*

        i. Local synagogues (13:5, 14, 15, 42, 45; 14:1; 17:1, 10, 17; 18:4, 7, 8, 17, 19, 26; 19:8)

        ii. God-fearers (13:16, 26, 43, 50; 16:14; 17:4, 17;18:7)

        iii. Jewish places of prayer (16:13–15)

        iv. Workplace networks (18:1–3)

        v. Spiritually/philosophically "receptive" people (17:17–21; 19.9)

    b. *Focus on people of influence and prominence, who can provide credibility, material support, and other relational connections*

        i. Householders (13:6–12; 16:15, 31–34, 40; 17:34; 18:7, 8; 20:7–8)

        ii. Synagogue Leaders (18:8, 17)

        iii. People of social status and wealth (13:6–12; 16:13–15, 40; 17:4, 12, 34; 18:8, 24; 19:31)

    c. *Proclaim the Gospel*

        i. Continually (14:25; 17:17; 18:19–20; nearly everywhere Paul goes)

        ii. Relevantly (13:16–41; 14:15–17; 17:22–31; 20:18–35)

    d. *Rely on miraculous confirmations of the message*

        i. Miracles (14:8–10; 16:25–26; 19:11–12)

        ii. Spiritual power encounters (13:6–12; 16:16–18; 19:13–16)

        iii. Signs and wonders (14:3; 15:12)

        iv. Translated and accessible ancient Scripture (13:17–41; 17:2, 11; 18:24, 28)

3. Strategic Foundations—Establishing Healthy Churches

    a. *The cell—an embryonic church*

      i. Gather initial believers into a house church, never leave individual converts isolated (13:43–48; 14:1–4, 21–22; 16:40; 17:4, 10, 12, 14; 18:8, 18; 19:9–10)

     ii. Train and equip this group for community and mission, focusing on empowering ordinary members (above, 18:7–8, 26; 19:9)

  b. *City-wide church networks*

      i. Multiply the house churches as they grow (19:9–10)

     ii. Allow the house churches to spread across a city (19:10–20)

  c. *Regional church networks*

      i. Relationally link the new churches with others (18:27–28)

     ii. Encourage churches to develop regional missional strategies (13:49; 14:6–7; 19:10)

4. Strategic Development—Establishing Sustainable Reproducing Movements

  a. *Empower the new church to take ownership for its mission*

      i. Leave relatively quickly (13:13, 51; 14:6, 20, 21; 16:40; 17:10, 14; 18:1)

     ii. Stay longer if the Spirit leads to do so (18:9–11, 18; 19:10)

  b. *Strengthen and support the new churches*

      i. Visit as often as possible for further training and encouragement (14:21–22; 15:41; 16:1–5; 18:23; 19:21; 20:1–3)

     ii. Send or leave ministry partners to support churches (17:14; 18:27–28; 19:22; 20:4–5)

    iii. Forge close relational attachments (20:36–38; 21:5–6, 12–14)

  c. *Appoint local church leadership*

      i. Wait to see who is faithful and capable (14:21–23)

     ii. Commission local elders in each church, with prayer, fasting, and the laying on of hands (14:23; 20:17)

    iii. Focus on empowering and equipping these local elders (20:17–38; the strengthening visits)

  d. *Develop a network of co-workers and ministry partners to help with the mission*

      i. A primary, more permanent team (13:3; 15:36–40; 16:1, 19, 25, 29; 17:4, 10, 14, 15; 18:5; 19:22)

     ii. A secondary, more temporary team (18:1–4; 19:29; 20:4)

e. *Cultivate a movement mentality*

 i. Create vision for regional mission (13:49; 14:6)

 ii. Challenge churches to send missionaries into other areas (13:1–3; 19:10, 20)

 iii. Commission new church planters (implied in 19:10, 20; Col 1:5–7; 4:12–13)

 iv. Repeat all the above steps in new locations to reproduce the entire process

5. Personal Strategies

a. *Minister in teams—recruit traveling companions, never travel alone*

 i. Personal encouragement, companionship, protection (Paul is only alone in 17:14–34; 18:21, 23)

 ii. Intensive training and mentoring (18:1–4; 19:29; 20:4)

b. *Maintain beneficial connection to "home base"*

 i. Accountability and reporting back (14:26–27; 18:22)

 ii. Supportive long-term relationships (14:28; 18:23)

 iii. Emotional/psychological stability (14:28; 18:23)

c. *Set aside periods of rest and rejuvenation*

 i. Briefly during journeys (hints—16:12; 18:11; 19:8, 10, 22; 20:31)

 ii. For extended periods after journeys (14:28; 18:23)

PART 3

Conclusion

The Pauline Mission as A Missionary
Training Narrative

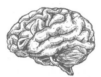

Paul's journeys contain patterns and themes which point to intentional missional strategies Paul employs in his ministry, as Luke reports it. These strategies undergird the rapid expansion of the early church throughout the Roman Empire. Luke weaves these strategies into his account of the Pauline mission to motivate and equip his readers to do these very things, that they might be successful in their own missional efforts.

The Pauline mission in Acts functions as a training narrative for a new generation of missionaries. Nearly every step which Paul takes is strategic and is meant to be a roadmap for Luke's readers, as they seek to emulate their role-model. Many of these strategies exist in seed-form in Paul's first journey, and are developed in his second journey, particularly at Corinth, before coming to full maturity at Ephesus on his third journey. Luke's rhetorical purposes are most explicit during Paul's farewell address to the Ephesian elders, during which he articulates most of these missional approaches (20:17–38). Luke is urging his readers to imitate Paul, and calling his church to action, by provoking them to join the advancing mission in their day.

Acts is not a "how-to-guide" for successful Christian mission and growth, and it does not claim to have all the "answers" about being church and doing mission. It is not a technical manual, but a witness and a narrative.[1] Yet its story contains much practical missional instruction. Luke paints a vivid picture of Paul's mission, using detailed and poignant narrative strokes. Perhaps Luke believes this will be more effective in achieving his overarching goals and mobilizing his church for mission, for the narrative picture he develops is memorable, inspiring, and more easily contextualized to the various contexts of its readers than a didactic training manual might be.

If Luke's missional instruction in Acts is a body, the strategies found in Paul's journeys are the brain. They guide, direct, and provide a roadmap for how to go about the mission, including what practices to implement and models to emulate at key points of decision. Some of Luke's strategic themes relate to persecution, and the final chapters of Acts focus primarily on this motif. Any rigorous endeavor such as Luke is advocating requires an extraordinarily strong backbone, and Luke's instruction about suffering provides this very need. Part 4 of this work turns to this missional spine.

---

1. Robinson and Wall, *Called to Be Church*, 13.

PART 4

Missional Suffering in Acts

Luke goes to great lengths in Acts to inspire and equip his readers for mission. He provides the motivation for it (part 1), the structures they should employ (part 2), and suggests strategic instruction for effective missional engagement (part 3). He also addresses the highly relevant theme of suffering and persecution. While this is part of Luke's strategies, the narrative time he devotes to suffering justifies examining it as a separate part of this work. Luke recognizes that if Christians of his generation follow the missional examples he provides in Acts, they will invariably experience opposition of various kinds.

When thinking of Luke's missional instruction in Acts as a body, his teaching on suffering and opposition represents the backbone, the fundamental support structure of the body. It gives strength and rigidity to the entire system, and provides the toughness and resilience required for long-term missional success, particularly under the pressure of suffering and persecution. The spine also houses the spinal cord and works together with the brain to form the central nervous system, which controls and coordinates the strategic elements of the whole body. Luke establishes this theme in his Gospel, and uses important episodes scattered throughout Acts to develop it. However, his depictions of Paul the prisoner in Acts 22–28 supply the clearest rhetorical training. Throughout Luke-Acts, Luke provides practical teaching about how to deal with various kinds of opposition when they arise, particularly how to view opposition, imprisonment, and trials as invaluable evangelistic opportunities, and how to make the most of such occasions. For Luke, suffering for the gospel is a central aspect of the church's missional vocation.

Chapter 12

Mission and Suffering Prior to Acts 21

They will arrest you and persecute you; they will hand you over to synagogues and prisons, and you will be brought before kings and governors because of my name. This will give you an opportunity to testify.

—LUKE 21:12–13

Luke devotes significant space to Paul the prisoner; nearly 25 percent of Acts concerns Paul's final arrest and imprisonment.[1] Maddox claims that the last section about Paul's arrest and incarceration "is slightly longer than that describing his mission,"[2] and concludes that "when we read Acts as a whole, rather than selectively, it is Paul the prisoner even more than Paul the missionary who we are meant to remember."[3] This calls into question the overall thesis of this work, for as Maddox explains, "if in Luke's eyes the main thing about Paul was his mission, then the final section of Acts is

---

1. This is 11 percent of Luke-Acts, when calculated by verse numbers. When Paul's earlier Philippian imprisonment is included (16:16–40), this is close to 30 percent of Acts, and more than 12 percent of Luke-Acts. Rapske, *Roman Custody*, 2; Maddox, *Purpose*, 66.

2. Maddox, *Purpose*, 66.

3. Maddox, *Purpose*, 67.

disappointing, for in the last nine chapters no one is converted."[4] Similarly, Krodel claims that, "for Luke, Paul the imprisoned, suffering witness and defender of the faith is even more important than Paul the missionary."[5]

These claims can be disputed in at least two ways. First, the numbers Maddox refers to are questionable. The total number of verses devoted to recounting Paul's missionary journeys is 279,[6] while Luke uses 240 verses to describe Paul's imprisonment.[7] If such numbers matter, the balance is slightly in favor of Paul's mission travels.

However, this entire argument is missing the point; as Rapske explains, scholars making this kind of argument, "clearly miss the Lukan emphasis, for the dichotomy, 'either missionary, or prisoner' is a patently false one."[8] Witherington also articulates this fallacy: "Prior to Acts 20 we have chronicles about evangelism and missionary work . . . by contrast, from Acts 20 on we have not missionary chronicles but apologetics in various forms."[9] By imposing this false dichotomy on the text of Acts, scholars fail to comprehend what Luke has already made plain: *a vital part of Paul's mission is his imprisonment and suffering*.

> While Maddox contends for a sharp distinction between Paul's work as a "missionary" during the first half of his career in Acts and his situation as a prisoner or defendant during the second half, it may be the case, instead, that what changes is not Paul's activity but the settings in which he finds himself and the audiences they permit . . . Luke presents Paul's custody as a redirection of the apostle's witnessing mission.[10]

Rather than being distinct aspects of Paul's life and calling (*either* missionary *or* prisoner), the two are inseparable (*both* missionary *and* prisoner). Paul's incarceration, trials, and sufferings should be regarded as another important dimension of the missional agenda which Luke pursues throughout Acts; his fundamental paradigm is that witness and prisoner are complementary, rather than antithetical.

---

4. Maddox, *Purpose*, 76. This is incorrect (Acts 28:23–24), but also misses the point.

5. Krodel, *Acts*, 397.

6. Only verses explicitly recounting the Pauline journeys: 13:4–14:28; 15:36—21:16.

7. Acts 21:27—28:31. Luke presents Paul's Philippian imprisonment (16:16–40) as part of his mission. However, even these 25 verses only bring the total to 265 verses, still less than the 279 total of Paul's missionary journeys.

8. Rapske, *Roman Custody*, 435–36. See also Skinner, *Locating Paul*, 186–89.

9. Witherington, *Acts*, 661.

10. Skinner, *Locating Paul*, 3, 5.

SUFFERING AS MISSION IN LUKE'S GOSPEL

Luke establishes this paradigm in Jesus's prophetic predictions (Luke 21:12–19):

> But before all this occurs, they will arrest you and persecute you; they will hand you over to synagogues and prisons (συναγωγὰς καὶ φυλακάς), and you will be brought before kings and governors (βασιλεῖς καὶ ἡγεμόνας) because of my name. *This will give you an opportunity to testify* (ἀποβήσεται ὑμῖν εἰς μαρτύριον). So make up your minds not to prepare your defense in advance; for I will give you words and a wisdom that none of your opponents will be able to withstand or contradict. You will be betrayed even by parents and brothers, by relatives and friends; and they will put some of you to death (θανατώσουσιν ἐξ ὑμῶν). You will be hated by all because of my name. But not a hair of your head will perish. By your endurance (ὑπομονῇ) you will gain your souls/ lives (τὰς ψυχὰς ὑμῶν).[11]

This passage is Luke's attempt to prepare his readers for the suffering and imprisonment still to come in Acts, and for their own persecution. It is significant that the words "and prisons" (καὶ φυλακάς, 21:12) are not found in the corresponding sayings in Mark 13:9 or Matt 10:17.[12] It is also crucial that Jesus summarizes this sort of suffering as "an opportunity to testify/witness" (literally, "it will result for you in witness," ἀποβήσεται ὑμῖν εἰς μαρτύριον, 21:13). This clearly articulates Luke's fundamental paradigm: *Christ's followers should see persecution such as this as a unique and strategic opportunity for missional witness.* These verses predict the coming persecution (21:12), the trials that will follow (21:12, 14), the unique empowerment for testimony that will accompany those trials (21.15), the betrayals and martyrdom that will befall some (21:16, 17), and God's ultimate protection (21:18, 19).[13] Later in Acts, Luke depicts Paul as the preeminent fulfillment of Christ's prophetic words.

This explicit link between persecution and bold missional testimony is echoed in an earlier passage in Luke's Gospel (12:8–9, 11–12):

---

11. Rapske, *Roman Custody*, 398–401 discusses each of these phrases.

12. Rapske, *Roman Custody*, 399. These words particularly point to Paul's frequent imprisonment in Acts.

13. In light of the martyrdom predicted for some (21:16), "not a hair on your head will perish" (21:18) must be referencing God's ultimate spiritual/eternal protection (ψυχὰς ὑμῶν, 21:19), cf. Luke 9:23–27.

> And I tell you, everyone who acknowledges me before others, the Son of Man also will acknowledge before the angels of God; but whoever denies me before others will be denied before the angels of God . . . When they bring you before the synagogues, the rulers, and the authorities (τὰς συναγωγὰς καὶ τὰς ἀρχὰς καὶ τὰς ἐξουσίας), do not worry about how you are to defend yourselves or what you are to say; for the Holy Spirit will teach you at that very hour what you ought to say.

This saying also anticipates the coming persecution, including being brought before rulers and authorities. And it reiterates a similar reassurance: The Holy Spirit (rather than Jesus, 21:15) will teach Jesus's followers what to say "at the very hour" when they are in front of these threatening authorities. This implies that inspiring and empowering speech should be interpreted as the Spirit's activity in Paul's defense speeches (Acts 22–26), and in defense speeches throughout Acts.[14] Both passages emphasize that it is unnecessary to prepare a defense beforehand, or indeed to worry about what to say, for divine guidance will be given when it is needed. This helps to explain the extemporaneous nature of most speeches in Acts.

Luke 12:8-12 is not as explicit about the various kinds of suffering Jesus's followers will undergo as Luke 21:12–19, but it does emphasize the importance of acknowledging Christ before others, and the corresponding danger of denying him. Jesus's specific promise to testify on behalf of his witnesses before the angels of God links to the scene where Jesus stands at God's right hand to honor Stephen's death (Acts 7:56).[15] Once again, imprisonment and trials are strategic opportunities for testimony about Jesus to people of significant authority and status. This repeated theme in Luke establishes the following principle: imprisonment and persecution are essential aspects of Christ's missional calling to his people (cf. Luke 6:22–23). This prepares readers to reject the suffering *or* mission false dichotomy and to embrace the suffering *as* mission paradigm.

The most immediate embodiment of this paradigm is Christ's death on the cross, undoubtedly the most missionally significant act of suffering in history for Luke (Luke 22:47—23:49). This is not what Jesus is referring to in the above two passages, which explicitly refer to his followers, but his trial and death remain an important model.[16] Luke depicts a relevant epi-

---

14. Keener, *Acts*, 1:525; Rapske, *Roman Custody*, 398–401; also true of the apostles before the Sanhedrin (Acts 4–5), and Stephen before the Synagogue of the Freedmen (6:9–10) and the Sanhedrin (7:1–53).

15. Keener, *Acts*, 2:1442.

16. There are also differences, e.g., in his trial Jesus is noticeably quiet before Pilate and Herod, only making minimal responses (Luke 22:67—23:4), while Luke 12:8–12

sode just before Jesus's arrest, on the Mount of Olives, when Jesus grapples with his impending suffering and pleads, "Father, if you are willing, remove this cup from me" (22:42a). This human picture of Jesus struggling would resonate with any Christian facing persecution or suffering, and Luke constructs this scene in a relatable and reassuring way.[17] Jesus's resolution is also instructive: "yet not my will but yours be done" (πλὴν μὴ τὸ θέλημα μου ἀλλὰ τὸ σὸν γινέσθω, 22:42b; cf. 12:47). Luke depicts Jesus demonstrating emotional honesty about his desire to avoid looming pain and suffering, and yet embracing God's will with strength to endure the way of the cross nonetheless.[18] Each of these passages in Luke's Gospel prepare the reader for the development of this theme, which is to come in Acts.

RHETORICAL PERSECUTION THEMES IN ACTS 1–12

Although Paul's imprisonment and trials are the most prominent examples of missional suffering in Acts, they are by no means the only such examples. Luke establishes that persecution is a normal part of following Christ in earlier parts of his Gospel and Acts, in an attempt to reassure his readers when they undergo violent opposition.[19] He describes specific scenarios that his readers will face in their mission, using demonstrative rhetoric to supply instructive examples of how to respond to them.[20]

The two Sanhedrin trial episodes (4:5–22; 5:27–42) are the first instances of persecution in Acts, and function as equipping narratives in *how to respond when on trial*. Luke's message is straightforward in both, and there

---

and 21:12–19 both emphasize verbal proclamation.

17. Later scribes understand the significance of this moment and add the following to emphasize Jesus's psychological agony and God's reassurance: "Then an angel from heaven appeared to him and gave him strength. In his anguish he prayed more earnestly, and his sweat became like great drops of blood falling down on the ground" (Luke 22:43–44).

18. The narrative parallels with scenes of suffering in Acts are obvious—missionaries follow the example of Christ in submitting to evil treatment, embracing the way of the cross, and trusting God for vindication.

19. E.g., Luke 6:22–23; 12:8–12; 21:12–29; 22:47–23:46; Acts 4:1–22; 5:17–40; 7:54–60; 8:1–4; 9:23–25; 11:19; 12:1–5; 13:50–51; 14:5–6, 19–20; 16:40; 17:7–10, 13–14; 20:1; 21:27–36. This is one of the major themes of Luke-Acts; House, "Suffering," 317–30; Rapske, "Opposition," 235–56; Cunningham, *"Many Tribulations."* Luke is of course drawing on multiple OT traditions here, including the suffering servant passages in Isaiah, certain psalms of lament, and various portions of Hebrew wisdom literature.

20. Cf. Paul's own persecution reports, e.g., Rom 8:35; 1 Cor 15:9; 2 Cor 12:10; Gal 1:13, 23; Phil 3:6; 1 Thess 1:6; 2:14–16; 3:3–7; 2 Thess 1:4; cf. Heb 10:33; Rev 1:9; 2 Tim 3:12.

are multiple parallels between the two.[21] Each passage shows the apostles boldly proclaiming the message about Jesus to their captors, teaching readers to never compromise in their courageous preaching, and to view public trials as unique opportunities for missional proclamation (4:8–13; 5:30–32). Both also use nearly identical language to emphasize that followers of Jesus must always obey God rather than people (4:19–20; 5:29), following Jesus's example, who accepts human authority, but always in subordination to God's rule (Luke 20:25).

The first time Peter and John are before the Sanhedrin, they respond to the warning to stop speaking and teaching in the name of Jesus by saying, "it is impossible for us not to speak about what we have seen and heard" (οὐ δυνάμεθα γὰρ ἡμεῖς ἃ εἴδαμεν καὶ ἠκούσαμεν μὴ λαλεῖν, 4:20). "Peter is here confronting religious as well as civil authority, preferring truth to authority."[22] The second Sanhedrin episode inverts honor and shame expectations by claiming that anyone being persecuted should rejoice because they have been found worthy of suffering disgrace on behalf of Christ's name (5:40–41).[23] Finally, even when they suffer cruelly, they should "never stop teaching and proclaiming the good news that Jesus is the Christ" (οὐκ ἐπαύοντο διδάσκοντες καὶ εὐαγγελιζόμενοι τὸν Χριστὸν Ἰησοῦν, 5:42).[24] Luke here explicitly links trials before authorities with opportunities for proclamation, and provides practical instruction about how to respond to persecution. Using these twin stories, and particularly their repeated concepts and language, Luke drives home his rhetorical points that suffering for the name of Christ is an honor and a central part of the missionary calling, trials are opportunities for bold witness, and opposition will not hinder the providential spread of the gospel.

Luke similarly presents Stephen as the *ideal Christian martyr* to be imitated in comparable situations (6:8—7:60). "The challenge for readers of

---

21. Keener, *Acts*, 2:1126 discusses the literary parallels and argues that the second is a reduplication of the first, in a deliberate "echo effect" that advances the plot further towards crisis and requires Gamaliel's intervention to save the lives of the apostles, 2:1039–40.

22. Keener, *Acts*, 2:1162: This passage endorses Spirit empowered boldness for Christians beyond the apostles (4:29–31) and has often been used as a model for Christians when the state (or even the established church) seeks to suppress the message.

23. Jesus has already established this theme in Luke's Gospel (Luke 6:22–23); this suffering makes the apostles successors of the biblical prophets, something worth celebrating.

24. "An interesting innovation at this point is the introduction of the word 'evangelising' . . . This verb becomes a key term in subsequent chapters (8:4, 12, 25, 35, 40; 10:36; 11:20; 13:32; 14:7, 15, 21; 15:35; 16:10; 17:18), where it is sometimes combined with the notion of proclaiming the kingdom of God, as in the ministry of Jesus himself (cf. Luke 4:43; 8:1; 16:16)"; Peterson, *Acts*, 228.

Acts is to mirror the authentic witness of those early Christians in whatever context they find themselves, knowing that the outcome for some could even be martyrdom (cf. Luke 9:23–26)."[25] Stephen is wise and filled with the Spirit in his evangelistic arguments (6:5, 8–10), eloquent and uncompromising in his spoken convictions (7:2–50), scathing in his judgment of the religious authorities who killed the prophets and Jesus himself (7:51–53), serene and full of the Spirit ("with a face like the face of an angel," τὸ πρόσωπον αὐτοῦ ὡσεὶ πρόσωπον ἀγγέλου, 6:15), offering nonviolent resistance in the face of violent and corrupt opposition (7:54–56), and even forgiving of the very ones who stone him to death (7:59–60; cf. Jesus's similar response, Luke 23:34, 46).[26] Most significantly, he sees Jesus standing at the right hand of God, ready to receive his faithful witness; this is a promise of Christ's reassuring presence to any Christian threatened by martyrdom (7:55–56).[27] In all these ways, Stephen is the exemplary Christian martyr, "a rare example of a man dying in a godly and holy way,"[28] and worthy to be emulated by later followers of Christ facing similar persecution.[29] It is easy to imagine later Christians threatened with martyrdom finding consolation, help, and inspiration in Luke's story of the original martyr-witness (μάρτυς—the extreme fulfilment of 1:8).[30]

When many of the Jerusalem believers are scattered abroad (διεσπάρησαν, "diaspora-ed," 8:1, 4) by persecution after Stephen's death, they go "from place to place, proclaiming the word" (εὐαγγελιζόμενοι τὸν λόγον), even when fleeing death themselves (8:4).[31] Luke's language here is inclusive, implying that many unnamed missionaries are evangelizing; the text specifically excludes the apostles (8:1). "In a book that concentrates on the evangelistic efforts of apostles and prophetic figures such as Stephen, Philip, and Paul, this is a significant point. Here and in 11:19–21 Luke implicitly challenges his

25. Peterson, *Acts*, 270.

26. Neudorfer, "Speech of Stephen," 275–94 is a literary and theological analysis of the main themes of this speech, which comprises about 5 percent of Acts.

27. This may be a reference to Jesus standing ready to acknowledge Stephen's witness before the angels of God (Luke 12:8); Witherington, *Acts*, 275.

28. Calvin, *Acts*, 1:221. The contrast in detail with the death of James the brother of John is extreme—Luke only casually mentions it in passing (12:1–2).

29. Scholars note the parallels with Christ's death, e.g., Witherington, *Acts*, 253; Keener, *Acts*, 2:1294–95, 1430. This is not to say Christians should seek out martyrdom, Keener, *Acts*, 2:1421–22.

30. Keener, *Acts*, 2:1296 discusses the thousands of modern martyrs each year: "To readers in many places, Luke's account of a single martyr is far more restrained than their normal experience."

31. Most scholars conclude that the Hellenists are primarily those scattered here, Keener, *Acts*, 2:1467–69.

readers about their own involvement in this great work of God."[32] This story narratively leads directly into Philip's ministry throughout Samaria, which is characterized by bold proclamation, dramatic miracles, and divine appointments (8:4–13, 26–40). Luke presents Philip and the unnamed missionaries as ideal examples of *how to respond to persecution induced scattering*, for they carry the gospel with them as they flee from threats, crossing new ethnic and geographical boundaries with the missional power of God (8:40; 21:8–16).

This persecution ironically brings about the expansion of the Word and the activity of Hellenist missionaries throughout Samaria, Damascus, Phoenicia, and Cyprus, eventually resulting in the establishment of the strategic church at Syrian Antioch, from which Barnabas and Paul's wider journeys are launched. Luke links the scattering of 8:1–4 with the founding of the Antioch church in 11:19–21, referring again to the same scattered people (διασπαρέντες). These developments herald the beginnings of reaching Samaria through Philip (8:4–40), and then the ends of the earth through Paul and Barnabas, both direct realizations of Acts 1:8. "The scattering of the Christians led to the most significant step forward in the mission of the church. One might say that it required persecution to make them fulfil the implicit command in 1:8."[33]

There is one final relevant scene: after James is executed by King Herod, Peter is arrested and imprisoned (12:1–4). Luke's focus here is on the church community, who are "earnestly/fervently/continually in prayer (προσευχὴ ἐκτενῶς) to God for him" (12:5). Peter's subsequent release at the hands of the angel of the Lord is an amusing and memorable story, typical of divine rescue narratives in Acts (12:6–19).[34] When Peter arrives at Mary's house, "many" are gathered "continually praying" (προσευχόμενοι—present participle, 12:12). Peter is a largely passive participant in this story, who does nothing other than depart immediately after being freed. Luke here twice encourages believers to continually pray for loved ones in prison and awaiting trials, and to believe that because of such fervent prayer, God can provide a miraculous rescue, even through dramatic angelic intervention.

Luke's primary message through this sequence of episodes is that Christians must continue to evangelize unapologetically, even when they are fiercely opposed and forced to flee. In fact, geographical scattering often leads to new opportunities in places which were not previously accessible if the scattered can perceive these openings for the gospel. Once again, suffering in

---

32. Peterson, *Acts*, 279.

33. Marshall, *Acts*, 152.

34. Witherington, *Acts*, 381; e.g., 5:18–20; 16:23–29; 27:13–44.

Acts is not antithetical to the mission but directly facilitates it, and Christians are called to pray fervently to this end. God guarantees the advancement of the Word, despite the suffering its messengers must endure, and his larger purposes will be fulfilled even in painful situations. This is certain to provide consolation to Luke's audience when they experience similar circumstances.

PAUL'S MISSIONAL SUFFERING BEFORE HIS JERUSALEM IMPRISONMENT (ACTS 13–20)

Paul's experiences are Luke's chief evidence about these suffering themes, for he suffers and proclaims the gospel more than anyone else in Acts. Even before his final imprisonment and trial narratives in Acts 22–28, this is a prominent theme in his life.

Just after Paul's conversion, Christ reassures Ananias about Paul's calling: "he is an instrument/vessel (σκεῦος)[35] whom I have chosen to bring my name (βαστάσαι τὸ ὄνομα μου) before Gentiles and kings and before the people of Israel; *I myself will show him how much he must suffer for the sake of my name*" (ἐγὼ γὰρ ὑποδείξω αὐτῷ ὅσα δεῖ αὐτὸν ὑπὲρ τοῦ ὀνόματος μου παθεῖν, Acts 9:15–16). Paul is a divinely chosen witness in various sufferings, and "the reader is assured that the apostle's sufferings are within the divine spotlight's beam; these *are* his mission."[36] Even at Paul's conversion, his calling to suffering is predicted, and Christ underscores the inevitability of it by emphasizing that "it is necessary (δεῖ) for him to suffer" as his missional vessel. Such distress is an unavoidable aspect of Paul's divine vocation as he testifies of Jesus's name before both Jews and Gentiles. This passage deliberately echoes Christ's prediction in Luke 21:17, who uses identical language to claim this is "for my name's sake" (ὑπὲρ τοῦ ὀνόματος μου). It is ironic that the one who inflicted suffering on those who bear Christ's name will now suffer for that name: "The great antagonist of the gospel will become its outstanding protagonist. The persecutor will become the persecuted and suffer like Jesus himself."[37]

Thereafter, Paul's mission unfolds in Acts with an array of divinely ordained suffering, including six cities from which he is violently expelled: Pisidian Antioch (13:50–51), Iconium (14:5–6), Lystra (14:19–20), Thessalonica (17:7–10), Berea (17:13–14), and Ephesus (20:1). There are at least

---

35. "A vessel does not belong to itself but is an instrument of another, employed wholly for another's purposes," Keener, *Acts*, 2:1656. Peterson translates σκεῦος ἐκλογῆς μοι, "a vessel of choice for me," *Acts*, 309.

36. Rapske, *Roman Custody*, 399. It is better to say that Paul's sufferings are a vital *aspect* of his mission.

37. Peterson, *Acts*, 309.

four additional destinations where Paul experiences some opposition, even if his ministry there ends more peacefully: Cyprus (13:13, Elymas the sorcerer opposes him), Philippi (16:40, he is imprisoned), Athens (18:1, the philosophers dispute him), Corinth (18:18, he is brought to court). It is only in Derbe (14:21), an extremely brief account, that Luke mentions no opposition of any kind.

Paul attracts riots like a magnet in Acts; he suffers the threat of or actual mob violence in each of the six cities from which he is expelled, as well as in Jerusalem (21:27–35). Paul varies his response to the situation. In Pisidian Antioch, he shakes the dust from his feet in protest against them, following Jesus's instructions (13:51; Luke 9:5). Paul usually escapes when he is able, realizing that once unrest in a city has grown to the point where a mob has formed his presence is no longer helpful to the local believers. Only in Jerusalem does Paul finally make a public defense of himself before the crowd, probably partly because there is no new Pauline church to endanger (22:1–21).

Luke is sending a message to his readers through these repeated narrative themes: they must be prepared for violent opposition, even at the hands of mobs. If the apostle Paul suffers this level of opposition in most places he visits, they should expect the same sort of treatment. Most often, the opposition takes the form of threats, and Paul is able to flee and avoid suffering actual violence. This gives implicit permission to Luke's readers to follow suit and flee when tensions boil over, though his caveat is that following Christ's direct leadership to remain must take precedent over escape. In such cases, Luke indicates that staying longer despite opposition can lead to greater missional effectiveness, as is the case at Corinth and at Ephesus (18:9–11; 19:8–10).

Of Paul's frequent threats, one is particularly vicious and descends into severe bodily harm: Jews from Pisidian Antioch and Iconium come to Lystra and incite mob violence (14:19–20). They stone (λιθάσαντες) Paul and drag him outside the city, thinking he is dead (νομίζοντες αὐτὸν τεθνηκέναι).[38] The Lystran disciples gather around (κυκλωσάντων) Paul in defense and prayer, and he is revived (ἀναστάς—raised up) and leaves the next day for Derbe. The next verse describes Paul preaching the good news (εὐαγγελισάμενοι) in Derbe and winning a large number of disciples (μαθητεύσαντες ἱκανοὺς), before courageously returning through Lystra, Iconium and Antioch, the very places from which this malicious threat had emerged (14:21). Here Luke is showing that even when someone has suffered a life-threatening

---

38. Keener, *Acts*, 2:1453–55 discusses stoning as mob violence in the ancient world: "stoning was simply the most ready-to-hand form of public violence available."

attack, while of course recovering physically, they should remain unde-terred in their determination to continue the mission, even willing to return to the very places where they have suffered. In this scene, Paul is the model suffering-missionary, a heroic example for Luke's readers to imitate in com-parable situations. "Recounting triumphs over sufferings might constitute an adolescent luxury [Pervo's claim for scenes such as this, which Keener calls 'pure prejudice'] for culturally dominant groups that face little oppres-sion, but oppressed groups in much of the world generally find them more meaningful."[39]

The imprisonment of Paul and Silas in Philippi is another instance of missional suffering in Acts (16:22–39). They are stripped of their clothes, severely flogged ("they laid many stipes on them," πολλάς τε ἐπιθέντες αὐτοῖς πληγάς) and beaten with rods (ραβδίζειν), and then placed in the inner cell with stocks on their feet (τοὺς πόδας ἠσφαλίσατο αὐτῶν εἰς τὸ ξύλον, 16:22–24). Witherington claims this is a public beating, "meant to humiliate those involved and perhaps also to discourage their followers."[40] Although this is certainly painful, the narrative directs the reader's focus to their response, which is not dictated by their circumstances: they pray and sing hymns of worship to God throughout the night (κατὰ δὲ τὸ μεσονύκτιον Παῦλος καὶ Σιλᾶς προσευχόμενοι ὕμνουν τὸν Θεόν, 16:25). Paul and Silas are ideal prison-ers, who respond to pain and opposition with prayer and worship, and their subsequent earth-shaking rescue and the salvation of their jail keeper and his household are evidence of God's approval of their actions (16:26–34). The jailer's household is a significant missional breakthrough and follows directly from their model conduct while in prison. The other prisoners hear the good news as well, through Paul and Silas's enthusiastic night prayers and proclamation to the jailer.

In this scene Luke is reassuring his readers of God's presence and protec-tion in times of imprisonment and encouraging them to respond to suffering with prayer and praise and to make the most of any missional opportunity presented by persecution. "These events vividly illustrate Paul's own claim in his Philippian letter that imprisonment, far from being an obstacle to his mission, poses a unique opportunity to spread the gospel boldly to Roman guards and others who come his way (Phil. 1:12–14)."[41]

As Paul is making his final journey to Jerusalem, Luke focuses on his impending suffering in Paul's farewell speech to the Ephesian elders: "And

39. Keener, Acts, 2:2174, referencing Pervo, Profit, 27.

40. Witherington, Acts, 496–97.

41. Spencer, Acts, 168. Paul sees imprisonment as a fortuitous missional window of opportunity; his words in Philippians are probably about his later Roman house arrest (Acts 28:14–31).

now, bound by the Spirit (δεδεμένος . . . τῷ πνεύματι), I am on my way to Jerusalem, not knowing what will happen to me there, except that the Holy Spirit solemnly testifies to me in every city, saying that bonds and afflictions await me" (δεσμὰ καὶ θλίψεις με μένουσιν, 20:22–23).[42] Paul's response to these warnings confirms his willingness to reject self-preservation as his highest priority, and to embrace this divine calling as a prisoner-witness: "But I do not consider my life of any account as dear to myself, so that I may finish my course and the ministry/mission which I received from the Lord Jesus (ὡς τελειῶσαι τὸν δρόμον μου καὶ τὴν διακονίαν ἣν ἔλαβον παρὰ τοῦ Κυρίου Ἰησοῦ), to testify solemnly of the gospel (διαμαρτύρασθαι τὸ εὐαγγέλιον) of the grace of God" (20:24).[43] Note that for Paul to value his life by avoiding incarceration and affliction would be to refuse the ministry of solemn witness which he has received directly from the Lord Jesus himself (cf. 9:15–16).

Shortly after this, the Tyrian disciples keep telling Paul through the Spirit not to set foot (μὴ ἐπιβαίνειν) in Jerusalem (21:4), which heightens the sense of impending suffering. This is confirmed when the prophet Agabus comes from Jerusalem to Caesarea, takes Paul's belt, binds his feet and hands with it, and says, "This is what the Holy Spirit says: 'In this way the Jews at Jerusalem will bind (δήσουσιν) the man who owns this belt and deliver (παραδώσουσιν) him into the hands of the Gentiles'" (21:11). This prophetic declaration causes the observers to beg (παρεκαλοῦμεν) Paul not to go to Jerusalem with weeping (21:12), and this deeply affects Paul, who asks why they are causing him such great sorrow. But Paul once again emphasizes his willingness to submit to his divine calling: "I am ready not only to be bound (δεθῆναι), but even to die (ἀποθανεῖν) at Jerusalem for the name of the Lord Jesus" (21:13).[44] This episode is partly about the suffering caused when well-meaning friends attempt to persuade a person to avoid God's will because it is painful, a situation many of Luke's readers could surely relate to.

Paul's unshakeable resolve to fulfill the mandate leaves his observers finally to say, "The Lord's will be done" (τοῦ Κυρίου τὸ θέλημα γινέσθω, 21:14).

---

42. Skinner, *Locating Paul*, 100, claims that this use of θλῖψις refers to physical suffering, in light of its uses in Acts 7:10, 11; 11:9.

43. There are multiple parallels in this passage with Jesus's willingness to suffer (e.g., Luke 9:24; 14:26–27; 17:33); Peterson, *Acts*, 566. "His sufferings extend over a long period of imprisonment and stretch from the Jewish to the Gentile capital. Paul follows his master in suffering, but there is a new twist that corresponds to the new dimensions of Paul's universal mission," Tannehill, *Narrative Unity*, 2:259.

44. Paul's suffering is "on behalf of the name of the Lord Jesus" (ὑπὲρ τοῦ ὀνόματος τοῦ κυρίου Ἰησοῦ, cf. 5:41; 9:16; 15:26; Luke 21:12, 17). Throughout Acts "the name (ὄνομα) of the Lord" has power and spiritual authority (19:17), for salvation (2:21; 3:16; 4:12; 10:43; 22:16), for baptism (2:38; 8:12, 16; 10:48; 19:5), for healing (3:6; 4:10, 30; 16:18), for preaching (4:18; 5:28, 40; 8:12; 9:27, 28), and is even worthy of suffering and death.

These words recall Jesus's prayer in his time of personal agony and wrestling with God's will (Luke 22:42), and are "not an expression of resignation, but a positive affirmation of the will of God."[45] As Rapske explains, "No other expression could fix more firmly in the readers' minds the assurance that . . . Paul . . . will be a prisoner witness in accordance with the divine will. In this, the Lord leads Paul and Paul unswervingly obeys . . . Paul is not simply a witness who has been imprisoned but one who fulfills the divine will as prisoner witness."[46]

CONCLUSION—PAUL, THE IDEAL SUFFERING MISSIONARY

These episodes establish the framework for understanding Paul's prison and trial narratives that follow in Acts 22–28. Paul's incarceration does not end Paul's missionary work; instead, it furthers it, as a divinely ordained and unavoidable extension of it. Paul is *both* a missionary witness *and* a suffering prisoner at the end of Acts—Rapske's designations of the "suffering witness" and the "missionary-prisoner" are helpful ways of understanding what Luke is meaning to convey throughout Acts, and particularly in Acts 22–28. As Rapske concludes:

> Paul is declared at the outset to be destined to prosecute his missionary labour throughout Acts as *suffering witness*. We have a vigorously asserted synthesis. The spotlight of God's choice of Paul to be his witness and to be involved in a ministry of suffering as he is involved in missionary labour is focused upon Paul at the very outset of his ministry. And if there is any change whatsoever, it is not in the move from missionary to suffering witness, but in the focus and intensity of the divine spotlight of God's choice upon his life which demonstrates, to any who might doubt, that *as prisoner-witness Paul fulfils his missionary vocation*. Paul is indeed the *missionary-prisoner* for Luke; effective, appreciated and divinely approved in his free doings with all the struggles that attended in the earlier phase of his ministry as described in Acts and effective, appreciated and divinely approved in the tribulations of his bonds in the later phase of Acts.[47]

45. Conzelmann, *Acts*, 178; also Marshall, *Acts*, 341. Paul's impending suffering in Jerusalem and beyond *is* God's will.

46. Rapske, *Roman Custody*, 411.

47. Rapske, *Roman Custody*, 436; emphasis added.

All these experiences of suffering and opposition illustrate Paul's teaching to the churches in Galatia, and presumably other churches he visits as well: "It is through many afflictions/tribulations/persecutions/pressures that we must enter the kingdom of God" (διὰ πολλῶν θλίψεων δεῖ ἡμᾶς εἰσελθεῖν εἰς τὴν βασιλείαν τοῦ θεοῦ, 14:22).[48] Luke views these hardships as divinely ordained aspects of Paul's mission, and as opportunities to extend it ever further. By depicting Paul teaching this to the churches in 14:22 and elsewhere, he extends this concept to other Christians as well. Persecution is an unavoidable part of God's missional calling, just as Jesus had predicted (Luke 12:11–12; 21:12–19): "Tribulation is the normal lot for Christians."[49]

In light of this inevitability, Luke goes to great lengths to equip his readers in how to respond to these difficult situations. He gives examples of being on trial, facing martyrdom, being scattered by persecution, and praying for imprisoned witnesses in Acts 1–12. Then in the stories of Paul's journeys in Acts 13–21, he describes how to respond to mob violence, being expelled from a city, being stoned, being arrested and imprisoned, and companions attempting to dissuade a person from God's will. All nine of these are discrete experiences of suffering and persecution which Christians have faced throughout history, and Luke includes narrative episodes that focus on each of them. In every story, his goal is to strengthen and inspire his readers by providing an example which they can learn from and follow. This reassurance extends beyond overt physical suffering to other hindrances and obstacles as well: nothing can obstruct the expansion of the gospel, which is God's sovereign plan. Such opposition is an inevitable feature of the divine mission, and if a missionary responds rightly to it, can even lead to further opportunity.

While each of these stories is important to Luke's rhetorical purpose in Acts, they also effectively pave the way for the climax of these missional suffering themes, which comes in Luke's stories of Paul the missionary-prisoner (Acts 21–28). The following chapter deals with this final section of Acts in detail, highlighting the frequent continuities with the persecutions stories that have come in earlier parts of Luke-Acts.

---

48. Θλῖψις literally means pressing together or pressure, metaphorically the "trouble that inflicts distress, oppression, affliction, tribulation," BDAG, 457.

49. Bruce, *Acts*, 296.

Chapter 13

Paul The Missionary-Prisoner in Acts 21–28

I pray to God that not only you but also all who are listening to me today might become such as I am—except for these chains.

—ACTS 26:29

Why does Luke devote so much time to Paul's multiple trials and end a book which is intended to inspire and equip his readers for mission in such a disconcerting way?[1] As has been the case throughout his work, Luke has a definite rhetorical purpose in composing this concluding section of Acts, including its enigmatic ending. He is aware that the church of his day is undergoing a degree of persecution and that if Christians increasingly engage in mission this persecution will only intensify, resulting in imprisonment and legal proceedings.

In light of this, Luke is teaching his readers how to respond when they are incarcerated and brought to trial by their persecutors in the final episodes of Acts.[2] This is a common type of consolation argument in the

1. Acts 21–28 can be understood as a parallel to Luke's Gospel's passion narrative, Dunn, *Acts*, 277–78.

2. Luke's rhetorical purposes in Acts 21–28 are complex and multi-faceted. He is also interested in the early church's relationship with Judaism in this trial section: "the overwhelming impression left by the speech material in the last quarter of Acts is that

ancient world, aimed at preparing people for future calamity and suffering.[3] "Luke makes clear that Paul was not the first of God's servants to face a miscarriage of justice. The implications would likely encourage and warn his audience: God's servants would probably face further miscarriages of justice, but (like Jesus) they ultimately would experience divine vindication one way or another."[4] Because imprisonment, trial, and sometimes martyrdom are probable results for missionaries who heed Luke's instruction, following in Jesus, Peter, and Paul's footsteps, it is logical for Luke to end Acts this way.

Luke's missional paradigm does not merely have space for persecution, it expects it as part of the divine plan. This is why the end of Acts should be regarded as thoroughly missional—*Paul's tribulations are his mission in this section, for they provide the context for new and pioneering missional opportunities.*

> Within places of custody Paul's missionary activity continues, albeit with such distinct characteristics as a limited or elite audience and predominantly indifferent responses to Paul's evangelistic efforts. These places thus emerge not as obstacles to be conquered but as settings that create new vistas, new cultures of contact for the gospel that Paul preaches . . . Paul's custody settings thus function to make the case that the divinely commissioned mission of witness in Acts can and will operate in any place, wielding more power (or wielded by a God more powerful) than any human effort to constrain it via force or relegation to exile . . . They present avenues for proclamation to pursue in different directions, now toward a limited and eminently powerful audience.[5]

'the Way's' relationship to non-Christian Judaism is still very much a live issue for the author, requiring repeated instruction to his audience on this subject . . . who is the Messiah, what is God's plan for his people, who are included in that people, by what means are they included?," Witherington, *Acts*, 659–60. However, such purposes are included within Luke's overarching missional interests, which continue unabated until the end of his narrative.

3. "To avoid being caught off guard, the Cyrenaics advocated meditating on possible future calamities, the so-called *praemeditatio futuri mali*. For individuals already afflicted with grief, they claimed that comfort could be found in the thought that misfortunes are a normal part of human existence and so 'nothing unexpected has happened' (*Tusc.* 3.23.55), supported by the observations that others have suffered similar things." Holloway, *Philippians*, 5–6. A similar consolatory approach underlies Luke's choice to include so much material on Paul's imprisonment and suffering in Acts.

4. Keener, *Acts*, 3:3159.

5. Skinner, *Locating Paul*, 186–87.

Paul's trial and prison narratives in the last eight chapters of Acts reveal a prisoner who continues to actively evangelize. This is the best way to understand Paul as a missionary-prisoner and as a suffering witness—both facets of his calling are not mutually exclusive but complement each other and continue simultaneously from his conversion to the end of Acts. The paradigm that mission involves suffering is not new to the final section of Acts, but is presented first by Jesus (Luke 21:12–19; 12:8–12) and then found throughout all of Acts , as the previous chapter has shown. However, in Acts 21–28 Luke turns to more specific equipping about what to do when his readers are brought to trial because of the name of Jesus. In this process, he revisits and develops many of the missional themes he has already initiated in previous parts of Acts. He does this once again through characterization and epideictic rhetoric, presenting Paul as the ideal missionary-prisoner, worthy to be emulated by later readers.

PREACHING IN JERUSALEM (21:17—22:21)

After arriving in Jerusalem, Paul greets James and the Jerusalem elders and reports to them "in detail (καθ' ἓν ἕκαστον, one by one) what God had done among the Gentiles through his ministry" (21:17–19). At their urging, Paul undergoes a purification ritual at the Jerusalem temple (21:20–26). During this time, Jews from the province of Asia see Paul and his companions in the temple and stir up a riot, which seizes Paul and drags him outside the temple confines, attempting to kill him (21:27–31). In another example of narrative irony, Paul's ritual cleansing has the opposite than intended effect: "Rather than clearing Paul of a charge before Jewish Christians, it leads to a lengthy imprisonment with repeated accusations and trials."[6] Luke emphasizes the extreme level of violence the crowd resorts to—they are trying to kill Paul (ἀποκτεῖναι, 21:31), beating him (21:32), even pressing so violently that Paul has to be carried by the soldiers (21:35), and screaming "Away with him!" (21:36). Αἶρε αὐτόν literally means "do away with him!," and intentionally echoes the cry against Jesus: αἶρε τοῦτον ("do away with this man!" Luke 23:18). Paul's detention is "a parallel to Christ's passion, a sharing of his sufferings."[7]

In this volatile environment Paul reveals his Jewish identity and Tarsian citizenship to the Roman commander and receives permission to speak

---

6. Tannehill, *Narrative Unity*, 2:271. Nevertheless, Acts implies that this is part of God's plan.

7. Keener, *Acts*, 3:3167.

to the crowd (21:37–40).[8] Luke depicts Paul as a man of heroic missional courage and eloquence here, who does not back down from his violent persecutors but wants to preach to them.[9] Paul stands on the steps of the Jerusalem barracks and motions boldly (κατέσεισεν τῇ χειρί) to the crowd. What follows is a classic example of proclamation in Acts (22:1–21), which once again shows opposition leading directly to a missional opportunity which could not have happened otherwise.

As has been seen throughout Luke's recounting of Paul's mission, Luke portrays Paul expertly crafting a message of precise relevance to his hearers. In a deft example of *prosopopoeia*, Paul begins by attempting to establish rapport with his audience through speaking in Aramaic (Ἑβραΐδι διαλέκτῳ), which gets their attention and causes them to "become very quiet" (21:40; 22:2, emphasized twice).[10] He then addresses them as "brothers and fathers" (Ἄνδρες ἀδελφοὶ καὶ πατέρες, 22:1), establishing himself as an insider. Further, Paul emphasizes his strong Jewish credentials: a Jew, born in Tarsus of Cilicia, brought up in Jerusalem, and trained in the law of the Jewish fathers under Gamaliel. He accents this with the audacious claim that he is "just as zealous for God (ζηλωτὴς ὑπάρχων τοῦ Θεοῦ) as any of you are today" (22:3). Paul has now succeeded in getting their attention, establishing significant commonality with his audience, and convincing them of his authority to speak to them. He articulates his pedigree to a Jewish audience zealous for the Law by boldly using every possible personal qualification to his missional advantage.

Paul then begins to tell his personal story, continuing to accentuate his thorough Jewishness. He explains how he used to persecute "the followers of this Way," arresting and beating many of them (22:4–5, 19). He even emphasizes his role in the death of Stephen, a local event some of his hearers would remember, in an attempt to identify with his audience by showing that he is one of them (22:20). He then speaks in detail of his dramatic experience on

---

8. Rapske, *Roman Custody*, esp. 9–112 is a summary of the many legal debates and implications in this section of Acts. On Paul's claim of Tarsian citizenship, see Keener, *Acts*, 3:3185–87.

9. "Paul knew he had a mission. Unless deterred by allies (9:29–30/19:30–31), Paul was normally ready to keep speaking even in the face of danger (20:34)," Keener, *Acts*, 3:3187.

10. *Prosopopoeia* is an ancient rhetorical exercise which involves recomposing a story from one character's point of view and adapting it to a particular audience or setting. There is some debate about whether Hebrew or Aramaic is implied here, but most conclude it is Aramaic: "Except in Rev 9:11; 16:16, where 'Hebrew' is meant, such expressions in the NT refer to Aramaic, which was the Palestinian vernacular and 'the *lingua franca* of non-Greek speakers in the eastern Roman world and in the Parthian Empire,'" Peterson, *Acts*, 593, quoting Bruce, *Acts*, 453; also Keener, *Acts*, 3:3190–95.

the road to Damascus, of encountering Jesus of Nazareth, and of Ananias's early influence on him (22:6–16). When he mentions the Lord sending him "far away to the Gentiles" the crowd grows violent again (22:17–22).

Most commentators consider this speech unsuccessful: "as a defense speech it is a failure, for the verdict from the crowd, which is the judge here, is very negative."[11] Why does Luke deliberately portray Paul making a speech that makes a credible connection with his audience but is finally a failure? One reason may be Luke's continuing explanation for the failure of the Jewish people to embrace Jesus and the mission to the Gentiles which his followers are pursuing. Luke here portrays Paul as a kinder, gentler version of Stephen (7:51–54), still holding out Christ's offer of salvation to the resistant Jerusalem Jews.

While this speech may be a failure from an apologetic perspective, in terms of the response Paul receives, it is more successful when viewed from a missional perspective. Paul relishes the opportunity to speak so boldly of "Jesus of Nazareth" (22:8), telling how his personal life has been transformed by Christ's intervention to a massive crowd of Jews in the spiritual and geographical heart of the Jewish faith. Luke makes a point of saying "the whole city was aroused, and the people came rushing together" (21:30), emphasizing that this is a vast crowd, easily numbering into the thousands.[12] Luke means for readers to see this speech as missional and deliberative, for his readers' sake as well as for the presumed audience. Against all expectation, it is not defensive or forensic—Paul hardly pursues any organized legal defense. Instead, he takes the unique opportunity to proclaim Jesus as the Messiah to the Jewish multitudes gathered for worship in the temple, using the story of his transformed life as the primary evidence. Though Luke does not report any immediate success, many will have clearly heard the good news of Jesus, and this episode should be seen as Paul taking advantage of a significant and unusual circumstance. In this regard, Paul achieves a strategic missional victory, in keeping with his continual desire to proclaim the gospel message to as many people in as many places as possible.

In addition to the singular significance of such a missional opportunity, this speech functions as an equipping speech for Luke's audience when attacked in similar ways. "While Paul's intention in the narrative world is partly evangelistic (24:25; 26:27–19), part of Luke's purpose in including the speeches for a probably Christian audience (cf. Luke 1:4) seems to

11. Witherington, *Acts*, 675.

12. This is not necessarily exaggerated, as such a mob is not an unprecedented phenomenon when a slight against Jewish customs and the Temple is perceived: Josephus, *J.W.*, 1.88–89; 2.8–13, 42–48, 169–74, 223–27, 229–31, 315–20, 406–7, 449–56. Johnson, *Acts*, 381.

be to offer them tools for defending themselves against widely circulated slanders."[13] Luke crafts Paul's speech in a way that challenges his readers to follow Paul's example and defend their own missional purpose robustly, using every potential advantage and prioritizing telling their story above personal safety and national or cultural identity.

BEFORE THE SANHEDRIN AND DIVINE REASSURANCE (22:22—23:35)

When the crowd revolts again at mention of the Gentiles, the Roman commander takes Paul into the barracks, presumably for his own protection, and then brings him before the Sanhedrin and the Jewish chief priests the next day. Paul is not afraid to stand up for himself and boldly proclaim what he believes to be true, as shown by his aggressive and argumentative interchange with the high priest Ananias (23:2–3) and with the Sanhedrin as a whole (23:1, 6–9). After realizing that he will not get a fair trial, Paul shrewdly uses his belief in the resurrection of the dead to divide the Pharisees and the Sadducees in the assembly, provoking another intense dissension (στάσις) in the assembly (23:7). The assessment of the Pharisees about Paul is pivotal: "We find nothing wrong with this man; suppose a spirit or an angel has spoken to him?" (23:9). This statement reveals that there is still hope that these Jewish leaders will be receptive to the claims about the resurrection which Paul is making. That the Pharisees think it possible that Paul has some special revelation from God or a spiritual being shows a promising degree of openness to the gospel, and that Luke has not written off the Jews or their leaders. It also shows Luke's apologetic on Paul's behalf, as a key part of his ongoing rehabilitation of Paul. The verdict of Paul's innocence will be a recurring theme throughout the remainder of Acts, from the lips of both Jews and Gentiles (e.g., 23:29; 25:18–20, 25; 26:31, 32).[14] Paul is taken back into the barracks because the commander fears he will be torn in two by the violent dispute (23:10).

After the intensity of Paul's appearance before the Sanhedrin, Paul is in need of reassurance, which comes when the Lord stands near (ἐπιστὰς αὐτῷ)[15] to Paul and says, "Take courage (θάρσει); as you have testified

---

13. Keener, *Acts*, 3:3197. See 3:3197–240 for Paul's rhetorical strategies in this speech.

14. Soards, *Speeches*, 116.

15. This may be a technical phrase for a dream experience, Aune, *Prophecy*, 267 (cf. Acts 12:7); or it may indicate a wakeful revelatory experience (cf. Luke 2:9; 24:4). "Whether the Lord comes to Paul in a vision as he sleeps, or appears to him as he is praying at Acts 23:11 cannot be determined," Rapske, *Roman Custody*, 419.

(διεμαρτύρω) about me in Jerusalem,[16] so you must also testify (μαρτυρῆσαι) in Rome" (23:11). This is a theme of Paul's story in Acts—such dramatic visions or reassurances consistently come at times of crisis or turning points.[17] However, the reader also realizes that there are no more miraculous escapes for Paul; this imprisonment is God's will, and Paul will have to see it to its end, whatever it may be. "The Lord's reassurance must take the place of miraculously opening doors. The divine power that rescues from prison has become a powerful presence that enables the witness to endure an imprisonment that lasts for years."[18]

This verse is an important clue to interpreting the trial and captivity sequences in Acts 21-28—Luke emphasizes through Christ's words that Paul's appearances in court are to be understood as explicitly missional testimony, as shown by the witness verbs μαρτυρέω and διαμαρτύρομαι. Luke also clarifies that just as this witness has happened in Jerusalem (21:37—23:10), the center of Judaism, so it must also happen in Rome, the heart of the Empire,[19] and that the completion of this mission in the Roman courts will require Paul to possess divinely given courage. Luke means for the reader to understand this trial sequence as a central part of Paul's missionary calling, and this comes from the authoritative mouth of Christ himself. "As Paul has been a prisoner-witness before groups and authorities in Jerusalem, so in the same way he will be a prisoner-witness in Rome."[20]

This divine message must strengthen and encourage Paul. He needs this courage, for the Jews quickly form a conspiracy to kill Paul (23:12–15), which is thwarted when Paul's nephew overhears word of their violent plot (23:16-22). After hearing of their plans, the commander Lysias transfers Paul to a more secure location in Caesarea that very night, under the protection of a large armed guard (23:23–35).[21]

What is Luke's rhetorical purpose in this portion of Paul's trial narrative? Luke is presenting Paul as a model prisoner-witness, worthy of

16. This almost certainly refers to Paul's experiences and activities in Jerusalem just a few days before, rather than his much earlier preaching in Jerusalem at Acts 9:28–30, Rapske, *Roman Custody*, 420. Marshall, *Acts*, 367, and Krodel, *Acts*, 429 both note that the emphasis here is not on self-defense, but on evangelistic witness.

17. E.g., 9:4; 16:9; 18:9; 22:17; 27:23–24. Bruce, *Acts*, 467.

18. Tannehill, *Narrative Unity*, 2:292.

19. This saying is set in parallel terms and framed by the expression "as . . . so" (ὡς . . . οὕτω), highlighting a direct comparison between Paul's past missional activity in Jerusalem and his future evangelism in Rome.

20. Rapske, *Roman Custody*, 421.

21. Lysias opts for a change of venue, but not a change of jurisdiction, which is beyond his authority.

emulation when his readers find themselves in similar circumstances. They also ought to be bold in their proclamation, particularly when they are facing violent persecution. They should preach in a way that is relevant to their hearers, adapting it to fit their circumstances, and looking for ways to establish rapport, commonality, and credibility with their audience. In this sort of combative setting, they should emphasize their own personal story and testimony as a missional priority, which is more difficult to dispute or debate than contentious theological concepts. They should never be afraid to stand up for themselves, and even to defend themselves legally where required, using every possible advantage at their disposal. They should be confident that Christ is with them and will give them the strength and courage they need. Above all, Luke urges his readers to view their suffering and imprisonment as an essential part of their mission, opening new opportunities to proclaim Christ as they follow in the footsteps of Paul, the archetypical prisoner-witness.

Throughout these trial sequences Luke also portrays Paul as a deft political operator. In earlier parts of Acts Paul has undergone localized suffering in brushes with the law, but here it crystallizes into a long-term relationship with the authorities. Luke shows Paul using various identities in his speech to reconfigure the situation he finds himself in, always with the goal of negotiating a favorable outcome in the service of the mission. Paul's announcement of his belief in the resurrection before the Sanhedrin is a way to self-identify as a Pharisee, though the reader knows this is not the case, and this astute move prevents the assembly from making a determination. His speech serves to reorient his audience by upending stable cognitive frames and showing that a situation may be creatively reappropriated to bring a dynamic new state of affairs. Such fraught political situations are an acute form of missional suffering, but also an important form of consolation, for they provide witnesses with the example of Paul, a person who has given everything for the mission of the kingdom of God and is able to challenge the current reality to introduce a new state of affairs. The way the missional imperative creatively reconfigures these situations and reorients Paul's audience sheds light on the political/missional strategy which Luke is commending to his readers.

BEFORE FELIX (24:1–27)

Acts 24 contains the account of Paul's first Roman trial before Felix, the governor (ἡγεμών) of Judea.[22] Paul's accusers present their arguments (24:1–9),

22. Felix is a freedman, and Tacitus, *Annals*, 12.54 says that he "practiced every kind

some of which have a ring of truth to them, at least in that Paul has stirred up riots (στάσεις—dissensions, insurrections) among the Jews all over the world, and that he is a ring-leader of the Nazarene sect (πρωτοστάτην τε τῆς τῶν Ναζωραίων αἱρέσεως).[23] However, what is patently false from Luke's perspective is that Paul is a troublemaker (λοιμόν—pest, plague) and that he has tried to desecrate the temple (τὸ ἱερὸν ἐπείρασεν βεβηλῶσαι, 24:5–6).[24]

Paul defends himself vehemently from these unjust accusations, directly responding to the claims about the temple and saying, "they cannot prove to you the charges they are now making against me" (24:10–13). However, he admits that he worships God as a follower of "the Way, which they call a sect" (τὴν ὁδὸν ἣν λέγουσιν αἵρεσιν, 24:14). He emphasizes that this Way is a part of Judaism, and that he has the same basic hopes in God as his accusers (24:14–16). Then he recounts his personal story again, explains why he is in Jerusalem, and stresses that he was ceremonially clean when they found him in the temple, and was not involved in any disturbances (24:17–21). Paul is responding directly to the accusations made against him point by point here, emphasizing his personal journey, and expertly defending himself. "The author of Acts intended his readers to see Paul handling his defence with great dexterity, and refuting these charges. He had done this by prescribing the limits of the evidence based on Roman law proscribing the charges of absent accusers, using forensic terminology, and not least of all, presenting a well-argued defence, even if preserved in summary form."[25]

Felix adjourns the proceedings and "after some days" he and his wife Drusilla return to listen to Paul speak about faith in Jesus Christ (περὶ τῆς εἰς Χριστὸν Ἰησοῦν πίστεως, 24:22–24), a clear indication of missional speech. Luke further emphasizes this by adding that Paul discourses on righteousness, self-control, and the coming judgment (δικαιοσύνης καὶ ἐγκρατείας καὶ τοῦ κρίματος τοῦ μέλλοντος), to the point where Felix becomes terrified (ἔμφοβος—an intensified form of fear) and dismisses Paul (24:25).

This exchange between Paul and Felix and Drusilla can only be understood as an evangelistic conversation in which Paul expounds on faith in Jesus Christ, God's requirements of righteousness and self-control, and

---

of cruelty and lust, wielding the power of a king with all the instincts of a slave." Like many Romans, he is anti-Semitic, and deals with the Jewish zealots brutally and cruelly, alienating most Jews. Witherington, *Acts*, 699.

23. Keener, "Paul and Sedition," 201–24 analyzes this charge of sedition (στάσις), and what it reveals about Luke's apologetic purposes in defending Paul's reputation.

24. Λοιμόν implies that Paul is like a contagious disease or plague, spreading disruption and even revolution everywhere he goes throughout the Roman world. Cassidy, *Society and Politics*, 104.

25. Winter, "Official Proceedings," 327.

his impending judgment of all people. It is not a formal legal setting, but an informal verbal exchange. Even in custody, before possibly the most powerful person in Judea, who holds Paul's fate in his hands, Paul boldly proclaims the gospel. Once again, Paul is the ideal prisoner-witness, actively furthering the mission even when he is in prison and awaiting trial. "Although the narrative is brief, it contains significant terms which indicate how Paul presented the gospel to this couple in a way that was relevant to their background and situation."[26]

This scene before Felix emphasizes to Luke's readers that they should actively defend themselves when accused unjustly in court. It recalls Christ's promise in Luke 21:15 that when his followers come to trial, he will give utterance and wisdom which none of their opponents will be able to resist or refute. Luke stresses again that the Christian defendant should recount their story, in their own words. Moreover, Luke sees the chance to speak about Jesus with a person of such clout as an opportunity full of missional potential and urges his readers to take maximum advantage of any similar opportunities they may encounter. This episode further illustrates how Paul's incarceration "operates as the continuance of his missionary work, not the end or suspension of it. The places in which he must remain in custody display themselves as suitable arenas for proclamation and avenues for God to guide the gospel into the heart of the Roman world."[27]

Felix leaves Paul in prison for more than two years as a favor to the Jews, until Festus comes into office (24:26–27).[28] This highlights another facet of Paul's missional suffering in Acts—except for the timely warning from Paul's nephew in Jerusalem (23:16–22), Luke records no visits from friends or supporters during this lonely period of incarceration in Jerusalem and Caesarea (though cf. 24:23; 27:3).[29] This is surprising, particularly given the way that Luke highlights Paul's multiple co-workers and companions throughout his previous journeys. Have they all deserted him in his time of greatest need? During this lengthy period of Paul's life, the only supportive visits Luke highlights are those of Christ himself in Jerusalem (23:11; cf. 18:9–10), and an angel of the Lord just before the shipwreck (27:23–24). No associates take the initiative to aid Paul until the Roman "brothers" travel to the Forum of Appius to meet Paul and accompany him to Rome, and Luke makes a point of noting here how thankful and encouraged Paul is by their

26. Peterson, *Acts*, 639.

27. Skinner, *Locating Paul*, 138.

28. The length of this delay, and the reasons for it, are unclear.

29. Keener, *Acts*, 4:3427–29 speculates that multiple associates visit Paul in Caesarea, including Luke and Aristarchus (27:2); if this is the case, Luke fails to mention it. As ever, he has rhetorical reasons for constructing this aspect of his narrative as he does.

support (28:15). Luke is offering consolation to his readers through these stories, particularly when they find themselves similarly imprisoned, abandoned, and isolated. His rhetorical reassurance is that divine support will be available in such situations, even when human aid is lacking.[30] Friends may be capricious and even betray one another, but God is faithful to supply what is needed.[31]

BEFORE FESTUS AND AGRIPPA (25:1—26:32)

When Festus succeeds Felix another trial scene transpires in Caesarea.[32] After the Jews from Jerusalem have made their accusations against Paul (25:1–6), Luke describes an adversarial scene: Paul is surrounded by his accusers, who make many serious charges (πολλὰ καὶ βαρέα αἰτιώματα) against him (25:7). Paul once again strongly and comprehensively defends himself (ἀπολογουμένου—to exculpate oneself legally): "I have done nothing wrong against the law of the Jews or against the temple or against Caesar" (οὔτε εἰς τὸν νόμον τῶν Ἰουδαίων οὔτε εἰς τὸ ἱερὸν οὔτε εἰς Καίσαρά τι ἥμαρτον, 25:8). When Festus brings up the idea of returning to Jerusalem for trial, Paul again forcefully insists that he has done nothing wrong, as Festus himself knows (25:9–10). To avoid the dangerous trip back to Jerusalem, Paul successfully appeals as a Roman citizen to Caesar himself (25:11–12).[33] Though he does not do this flippantly, Paul is again not afraid to make the most of his legal rights, particularly when his life is unjustly at stake (25:12).[34]

30. This may also be a subtle way for Luke to acknowledge that relationships between Paul and the Jerusalem Christians, led by James and the elders, have not been as substantially reconciled as his readers might hope (cf. 21:17–26; 15:1–2, 13–21).

31. Friendship and conflict are significant themes throughout Acts, from the Jerusalem summaries which present friends navigating multiple conflicts (2:42–47; 4:32—5:11; 6:1–7), to Paul and Barnabas (11:25–26; 13:2—14:28; 15:36–40), to the inter-Christian tensions surrounding non-Jewish inclusion (11:1–24; 15:1–11, 24–32; 21:19–26).

32. Little is known about Porcius Festus; sources are limited to Acts 25–26 and Josephus, *Ant.*, 20.182–197; *J.W.*, 2.271. He appears to be more honest and honorable than his predecessor Felix.

33. The governor may not be able to refuse this appeal under the *Lex Iulia de Vi Publica*, passed in the time of Augustus; for more discussion of Paul's appeal see Witherington, *Acts*, 722–26; Keener, *Acts*, 4:3462–68.

34. "Paul does not lightly or cavalierly exercise his right of appealing to Caesar. Similar to the earlier two instances in which he claimed his rights of citizenship, Luke again depicts Paul asserting his right to appeal before a small, predominantly Roman, group and only at the point in the proceedings when he could no longer tolerate a course of action being proposed by a Roman official . . . Paul exercised his right of appeal only under considerable pressure." Cassidy, *Society and Politics*, 109. Cf. Acts 16:37–39; 22:25–29; 23:27.

When King Agrippa and Bernice arrive in Caesarea, they request to hear Paul themselves (25:13–22). This sets the stage for the great trial message in Acts, which Festus dramatically introduces (25:23–27). This episode brings about a further fulfillment of what Jesus promised long ago—that his witnesses (Luke 21:12–13), and specifically Paul (Acts 9:15), would testify before kings and governors.[35] The following scene is not technically a trial, for Paul's appeal to Caesar has already been granted, but judicial inquiry (ἀνακρίσεως—preliminary investigation, 25:26). Paul's speech is in certain ways the climax of all his speeches in Acts, and a succinct summary of the Christological gospel message that Luke is conveying in Acts.[36]

When Paul receives permission to speak, he immediately turns to recounting his own personal story in detail, beginning with his childhood and his training as a Pharisee (26:1–5). He then focuses on the contentious theological issue at hand—the resurrection of the dead (26:6–8). Paul resumes his individual story by speaking of his zeal "to oppose the name of Jesus of Nazareth" (26:9), and his widespread early persecution of Christians (26:10–11). This leads to the second re-telling of his Damascus Road conversion experience (26:12–18), where Christ himself comes to Paul and calls him to be a witness: "I have appeared to you to appoint you as *a servant and a witness* (ὑπηρέτην καὶ μάρτυρα) of what you have seen of me and what I will show you . . . I am sending you to them (τῶν ἐθνῶν—the Gentiles or nations) to open their eyes and turn them from darkness to light, and from the power of Satan to God" (26:16–18). In this summary of his missionary call, Paul articulates his dual vocation, as a servant and a witness of Christ. Luke also implies that Paul's appearance before Festus and Agrippa is a partial but significant fulfillment of this calling.[37]

Paul then continues to tell his story, and to summarize his postconversion mission to both Jews and Gentiles (26:19–21). Significantly, Paul has declared (ἀπήγγελλον) to those at Damascus, and "at Jerusalem, throughout all the districts of Judea, and to the nations/Gentiles" (τοῖς ἔθνεσιν, 26:20). It is not coincidental that Paul's mission after Damascus follows the programmatic course that Jesus prescribed for his witnesses in Acts 1:8: "It begins in Jerusalem, spreads to the surrounding region, and then moves out to encompass the world (a gigantic development that both

---

35. "The tradition of Paul's testimony before rulers was not soon forgotten (1 *Clem.* 5.7)," Keener, *Acts*, 4:3484.

36. Tannehill, *Narrative Unity*, 2:315–29; Witherington, *Acts*, 735–53.

37. Paul seems to feel that his calling applies as much to his current audience as to any other he has had. This reassures the reader that God's hand continues to be on Paul and that God's will will be done (21:14). Paul's identity as a "witness" is a further fulfillment of Christ's promise in Acts 1:8.

statements summarize in a brief phrase). Thus, it is probably that Paul is be-ing presented as sharing the mission given to Jesus's first witnesses in 1:8."[38] This description underscores the ethnic and geographical inclusiveness of Paul's mission.

This mission has caused the Jews to seize him, but Paul has had God's help throughout, "and so I stand here and testify to small and great alike (μαρτυρόμενος μικρῷ τε καὶ μεγάλῳ) . . . that the Christ would suffer and, as the first to rise from the dead, would proclaim light to his own people and to the Gentiles" (τοῖς ἔθνεσιν, 26:22–23).[39] This statement reminds the reader that Paul is on trial chiefly to testify (μαρτυρέω) about the gospel of Christ, and that he sees this as a unique missional opportunity before rulers, kings, and other people of influence (μεγάλῳ), and before people of less significance as well (μικρῷ).[40] Once again, Paul the model prisoner-witness employs a missional strategy of gaining maximum impact by reaching out to influential people, while offering the gospel to everyone.

Festus and Agrippa's dramatic reaction to this statement clarifies that this is Paul's intending meaning, for they are immediately defensive, and Festus accuses Paul of going insane. Paul responds that he is not a "maniac" (οὐ μαίνομαι) but is speaking words of sober and rational truth (ἀληθείας καὶ σωφροσύνης ῥήματα), and boldly asks whether Agrippa believes the prophets (26:24–27). King Agrippa then asks Paul an astounding question: "Do you think that in such a short time you can persuade me to become a Christian?" (ἐν ὀλίγῳ με πείθεις Χριστιανὸν ποιῆσαι, 26:28).[41] Agrippa real-izes that this is exactly Paul's hope, and Paul's uncompromising response confirms his true purposes: "Short time or long—I pray God that *not only you but all who are listening to me* today may become what I am (οὐ μόνον σὲ ἀλλὰ καὶ πάντας τοὺς ἀκούοντάς μου σήμερον γενέσθαι τοιούτους ὁποῖος καὶ ἐγώ εἰμι), except for these chains" (26:29).

38. Tannehill, *Narrative Unity*, 2:326. There are also parallels with Jesus's commission to his first witnesses in Luke 24:44–48.

39. "Here we have one of the more compact and helpful summaries of the essential apostolic kerygma, proclaimed by Peter, Paul, Philip, and others, as the first fourteen chapters of Acts have revealed," Witherington, *Acts*, 747. There are also multiple deliberate parallels with Jesus's last speech, in Luke 24:44–48.

40. Luke again accentuates the inclusiveness of the mission, which is for all social classes.

41. 26:28 is a complex verse to interpret, Witherington, *Acts*, 750–51. Agrippa may be saying "with so few arguments, do you hope to convince me to be a Christian?" The tone does not seem to be bitter or sarcastic, but incredulous. Some interpret Agrippa's tone to be ironic or joking, but whatever his intentions Paul embraces his question positively, Keener, *Acts*, 4:3544–48.

Paul's statement is a hermeneutical key to interpreting these trial sequences. Paul acknowledges that there are many people listening to his testimony and affirms that his ultimate desire is that whether it takes a short or long time (or little or much argument), every one of them would become a follower of Christ, including King Agrippa.[42] "Paul's interest in them is less judicial than evangelistic."[43] Paul views his trials as opportunities for missional proclamation, to an audience that would have little or no other chance to hear the message about Jesus Christ. He turns the tables on his accusers and judges, and challenges them to consider the truth claims he is making: "In the end, Festus gets frustrated, and it is Agrippa who is backpedaling and on the defensive!"[44] Witnessing to kings and rulers is the culmination of Paul's (and Luke's) distinctive missional strategy of sharing with people of influence in Acts, and he realizes that if people such as Festus and Agrippa believe, this will have a dramatic effect on the spread of the Christian mission throughout Judea and the larger Roman world. "In a world where social status proved highly influential both in courts and in public opinion, Paul's exalted audience here is significant . . . he now had the rare opportunity to expose his message to prominent people who would have a bearing on the tolerance accorded the movement."[45]

Haenchen argues that "Luke no longer hoped for the conversion of the Jews . . . though Paul speaks in Chapter 22 to the Jewish people, in 23 to the Sanhedrin and in 26 to King Agrippa. Luke with all this is not canvassing for a last-minute conversion."[46] This is inaccurate, for Luke goes to great lengths in this episode to present Paul as the model evangelist, including to Jews. Tannehill's missional interpretation of this exchange is more accurate:

> The vivid portrait of Paul seeking to convert a high-ranking Jew is more than a memorial to a lost past. Heroic figures (like Paul in Acts) inevitably become models of behavior, and Paul's farewell to the Ephesian elders (20:18–35) indicates awareness that Paul could be an effective model for the later church. Paul's exemplary behavior includes his dedicated witness to both Jews and Gentiles (cf. 20:21). The portrait of Paul before Agrippa

42. "On Luke's presupposition that the Christians proclaim only the same message as Moses and the prophets, namely the Messiah and his resurrection, such a conversion is by no means inconceivable," Haenchen, *Acts*, 692.

43. Keener, *Acts*, 4:3549.

44. Witherington, *Acts*, 736.

45. Keener, *Acts*, 4:3484–85.

46. Haenchen, *Acts*, 693. However, his following suggestion that "Luke wanted to help the Christians of his own age with their defence," has more merit, as a part of Luke's rhetorical motivation in this scene.

has, in part, the same exemplary function. The previous defense scenes lay the foundation for this portrait of Paul as model evangelist . . . Paul is being presented as a dedicated and resourceful evangelist who is able to keep the mission to Jews alive in difficult times.[47]

Paul's speech is not a technical defense speech, but a testimonial witness speech. "The whole speech leads forward toward . . . an appeal to Agrippa and others to become as Paul is, except for the chains. Paul is bearing witness to a Jewish king by means of a rehearsal of his own life, in the context of a judicial hearing."[48] Luke is advocating trials such as this as ideal and rare opportunities for proclamation. "Paul, the captive, momentarily has a captive audience."[49] Rather than focusing on personal survival, Luke challenges his readers to grasp the potential of such circumstances, which provide their own "captive audiences." Even though there is no recognizable conversion response in the narrative, the strategic value of Paul's interaction with this Roman court is apparent. Luke continues to instruct his readers that when they are on trial for their faith and mission they are prisoner-witnesses with a divine mandate to boldly proclaim the gospel in that uniquely strategic environment, and the promise of divine assistance in such an arduous task (Luke 12:8–12; 21:12–19).

Luke has gone to great lengths throughout Acts to show that the gospel is for everyone, everywhere, and this must include the upper-class elite and the politically mighty.[50] He concludes this argument by showing the gospel reaching the powerful Jewish and Greco-Roman nobility through Paul's bold witness. For Luke, Paul's ability to testify freely before the high priest and the Sanhedrin, and before elite rulers such as Felix, Festus, and Agrippa, is the ultimate "proof" of the Christian movement's access to the highest classes. Luke repeatedly emphasizes the significance of such opportunities. Though Felix, Festus, and Agrippa do not immediately accept the gospel, Sergius Paulus in Paphos did accept it (13:12), providing a degree of hope for such elites.

Paul's journey to Rome underscores this point—Paul's ultimate strategic and influential audience is Caesar himself. When Festus exclaims, "You have appealed to Caesar. To Caesar you will go!" (25:12), he is granting Paul

---

47. Tannehill, *Narrative Unity*, 2:328–29.

48. Witherington, *Acts*, 736.

49. Skinner, *Locating Paul*, 137.

50. See chapter 3 for Luke's universalized theology, and examples of the "upper" classes in Acts; and part 3 for multiple examples of the strategy of targeting people of influence.

the right to bring his gospel message before the ruler of the entire Roman Empire, arguably the most powerful person on earth (cf. 23:11; 27:24). This helps to explain why Paul does not accept the offer of his own personal freedom—Paul could travel to Rome on his own, even risking the dangers of violence at the hands of the Jews, but he will only be granted an audience with Caesar through the Roman legal system (26:31–32). Testifying before Caesar represents the ultimate fulfillment of the missional strategy of focusing on people of influence which Luke advocates throughout Acts. Luke implies that Paul recognizes this once-in-a-lifetime opportunity, and is therefore content to wait on the sluggish Roman judicial system.

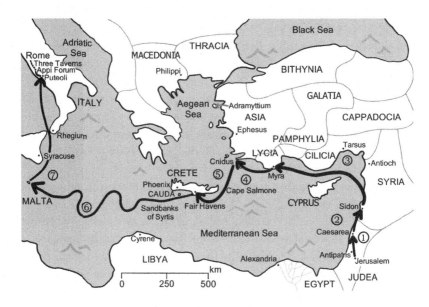

Paul's Journey from Jerusalem to Rome

STORMS AND SHIPWRECK (27:1–44)

After a private positive verdict from Agrippa and Festus which vindicates Paul again (26:31–32), he finally sails for Rome along with multiple other prisoners, under the centurion Julius (27:1–12). A fierce "northeaster" (εὐρακύλων) overtakes their ship off the shore of Crete and drives them across the storm-tossed Adriatic Sea for two weeks (27:13–26). Finally, the ship runs aground on a sandbar near Malta, and all its occupants swim or float safely to the island on planks and pieces of the ship (27:27–44). Luke vividly describes this adventurous journey in one of the most famous and dramatic passages in Acts.

During the storm, an angel appears to Paul and confirms how crucial it is for Paul to testify to Caesar: "Do not be afraid Paul. You must stand before Caesar" (μὴ φοβοῦ Παῦλε· Καίσαρί σε δεῖ παραστῆναι, 27:23–24a).[51] Luke affirms Paul's divine mandate to appear before the center of Roman power and government; the δεῖ confirms that this is necessary. The implication is that God is sovereignly orchestrating circumstances to bring this missional encounter to pass. Paul has apparently been praying for the preservation of his shipmates, and the angel also reassures him that the lives of all who sail with him are given to him as a gracious "gift" (χαρίζομαι, 27:24b). "The divine assurance given specifically to Paul at Acts 27:23f. is to be the hermeneutical tool with which Luke's readers interpret the remaining threats of storm, summary execution, shipwreck and snakebite which Paul experiences."[52]

Just before the shipwreck, Paul publicly breaks bread: "he took some bread and gave thanks to God in the presence of them all (λαβὼν ἄρτον εὐχαρίστησεν τῷ Θεῷ ἐνώπιον πάντων). Then he broke it (κλάσας) and began to eat. They were all encouraged and ate some food themselves" (27:35–36).[53] Paul has not withheld his Christian identity throughout this journey (27:3, 10, 21–26, 34), but Luke emphasizes the public nature of this act of thanksgiving, and implies that all 276 of the ship's occupants witness Paul breaking the bread (ἅπας or πᾶς, "all" is repeated four times, 27:33, 35, 36, 37). Some argue that this is intended to evoke the Eucharist,[54] while others understand it to be a typical Jewish introduction to a meal.[55]

Whether it is eucharistic in the formal sense or not, this is a sacramental act of hope and gratitude (εὐχαρίστησεν) which certainly recalls other "breaking of bread" allusions in Luke and Acts, and it takes on a subtle but

51. The parallels with Paul's earlier divine reassurances are unmistakable (23:11; 18:9–10); Aune, *Prophecy*, 268.

52. Rapske, *Roman Custody*, 421.

53. Scholars debate whether this is the Christian Eucharist, partly because there is no mention of wine; Witherington, *Acts*, 772–73. Gaventa, *Acts*, 355: "Paul's insistence on taking food at this stage, when the very people charged with sailing the vessel have just demonstrated their own hopelessness [27:30], constitutes a sign of hope and confidence in God . . . If it is not the bread of the Eucharist, it is the bread of hope."

54. "Had the narrator not wished to evoke the sacrament, he could simply have said 'Paul ate.' The meal is not itself a Eucharist, since those present are not believers, but it evokes the Eucharist . . . The action symbolizes the life brought by God through Jesus. The means for bringing people to faith is mission. Acts 27:33–38 . . . has a universal, missionary thrust," Pervo, *Acts*, 664; also, Tannehill, *Narrative Unity*, 2:335.

55. Peterson, *Acts*, 693–94; Keener, *Acts*, 4:3645–46; Witherington, *Acts*, 772–73; Barrett, *Acts*, 2:1208–10.

important missional dimension.[56] The symbolic action of publicly breaking bread is Paul's way of "preaching" hope to his fellow travelers appropriately in this traumatic situation.[57] His message is confirmed when Paul's prophetic prediction that the ship will run aground and be destroyed but none of them will die comes to pass, affirming its divine origins (27:22, 26, 34, 41–44). "It will be clear that Paul's God, whom he thanks, is the one to whom he has already attributed their coming deliverance."[58] Even in such dire circumstances, Paul continues to be the suffering prisoner-witness.

MALTA (28:1–10)

After surviving shipwreck and reaching land safely, a surprising miraculous missional episode occurs. Paul is bit by a poisonous viper (ἔχιδνα) on Malta while gathering brushwood for a fire, and miraculously suffers no harm (ἔπαθεν οὐδὲν κακόν, 28:1–5). The people assume this is Justice (ἡ δίκη) catching up to Paul (28:4) but change their minds and decide he is a god after seeing Paul survive the deadly snake bite (28:6). Luke portrays Paul's survival as a naturally unexplainable miracle, in direct fulfillment of Luke 10:19, which has quite an effect on the Maltese. "In Luke's Gospel, Jesus delegates to the disciples the authority to 'tread on' snakes and serpents, creatures associated with Satan, without themselves being harmed . . . Paul is not healed from the viper's attack so much as he is simply immune to it, and his immunity comes not from his own resources, but from the God who called him and delivered him safely from shipwreck."[59]

This miracle causes Publius, the chief official of the island (τῷ πρώτῳ τῆς νήσου), to welcome them into his wealthy estate for three days (28:7).[60] Paul prays for Publius's father, who has fever and dysentery, and after placing his hands on him, he is healed (προσευξάμενος ἐπιθεὶς τὰς χεῖρας αὐτῷ ἰάσατο αὐτόν, 28:8). This miracle only adds to Paul's burgeoning reputation on the

---

56. Luke says Paul εὐχαρίστησεν (gave thanks). This is particularly true in light of Luke 22:19, and the four breaking bread references in Acts, all using the identical words (κλάω or κλάσις, and ἄρτος): 2:42, 46; 20:7, 11.

57. Luke highlights the public nature of this meal and follows it by saying that there are 276 people onboard.

58. Keener, Acts, 4:3646.

59. Gaventa, Acts, 358–59.

60. Publius is probably the governor/magistrate of Malta, though he could also be the wealthiest citizen of the island, and thus the patron/benefactor of the region. Johnson, Acts, 462. Luke typically associates Paul with the leading figures of a location (e.g., 13:7; 16:22; 17:19; 18:12; 19:31).

island, and the rest of the sick on the island come to him and are cured (οἱ λοιποὶ οἱ ἐν τῇ νήσῳ ἔχοντες ἀσθενείας προσήρχοντο καὶ ἐθεραπεύοντο, 28:9).

This explosion of miracles on Malta is an unexpected missional encounter. Although Luke does not specifically say that Paul evangelizes in Malta, Luke has established this pattern many times in Acts, and it is inconceivable to think of Paul failing to explain the gospel to people as he prays for and ministers to them. In Acts, signs and wonders are the confirmation of the gospel, and the validation of Paul's message. Luke implies that Paul enjoys missional success on Malta through the miraculous validations of his ministry in the form of surviving a venomous snakebite and the healing of many across the island. This is also another example of the unfolding of God's sovereign will; even in the apparent disaster of the storm and shipwreck, "God's plan leads Paul to such open people."[61]

Luke underscores this by emphasizing that the locals "honored us with many honors (πολλαῖς τιμαῖς) and when we were ready to sail, they furnished us with the supplies we needed" (28:10).[62] This is the material benefit offered to someone from whom one has benefitted spiritually and implies that the islanders regard Paul and his traveling companions as "holy men." It is uncertain whether a church community begins in Malta, but because the sharing of possessions is a sign in Luke-Acts of sharing in the good news, Luke almost certainly means for the reader to understand that Paul does share the gospel in Malta.[63] "It is hard to imagine Paul failing to preach in this place."[64]

The Malta episode reiterates many of the missional strategies seen throughout Paul's journeys in Acts. Publius is an ideal person of influence/peace, as a wealthy householder and the head of the elite ruling class. By inviting Paul and his companions into his οἶκος, he extends the hospitality invitation and explicitly endorses Paul and his message. Publius's influence and reputation open the way for Paul to minister in a widespread way across the island. Paul relies on miraculous signs and wonders to assist in the spread of the message and to validate his ministry. He quickly gains a

---

61. Keener, *Acts*, 4:3681.

62. Πολλαῖς τιμαῖς can mean many honors or gifts/payments (Acts 4:43; 5:2–3; 7:16; 19:19); the next phrase spells out the gift of possessions from the islanders.

63. Johnson, *Acts*, 463. E.g., Luke 6:32–36; 8:3; 12:32–34; 14:13–14; 18:22; 21:1–4; Acts 2:42–47; 4:32–37. "Since Paul has elsewhere preached, [many interpreters] assume that he preaches here also. Given the character of these chapters as a reprise of earlier elements of Acts, and given the clear declaration at the end of chapter 28 that Paul continues to preach and teach, the traditional view has some force," Gaventa, *Acts*, 362. It is easy to imagine Paul establishing a Maltese house church in Publius's home.

64. Peterson, *Acts*, 698.

regional influence across the island, underscored by the way "the rest of the sick on the island" come to him for healing.[65] Luke claims that Paul's missional presence impacts the entire population of Malta over three months, whatever the result (28:11).[66] However, Luke is eager to move his story on to its true culmination.

ROME (28:11–31)

Paul and the traveling group depart by ship after three exciting months in Malta, and following multiple brief stops, finally arrive in Rome, the Imperial capital (28:11–15). Paul is allowed to live by himself under house arrest in Rome, with a soldier to guard him (28:16). After nearly three years of captivity, trials, and travel, Paul the missionary-prisoner has at last arrived in the power center of the Empire.

After three days Paul calls together the leaders of the Jews in Rome and begins to defend himself (28:17–20). He emphasizes his own personal story (28:17) and his innocence (28:18), and concludes by declaring, "It is because of the hope of Israel that I am bound with this chain" (28:20).[67] While they might understand this ambiguous reference to be to Yahweh, Paul is referring to Jesus the Christ/Messiah, and to the resurrection of the dead (26:6–8, 22–23). Paul also reassures them that he has no charge to bring against the Jews (28:19), and the overall effect of this speech is "to indicate the true Jewishness of Paul (vv. 17, 20), make clear his innocence, and place the ultimate blame for his predicament on the Jewish authorities in Jerusalem, not on the Roman Jewish leaders, against whom Paul had nothing."[68] The Jews reply that they have not heard anything about Paul, and would like to hear more about what his views are, for "people everywhere are talking against this sect" (αἱρέσεως, 28:21–22; cf. 17:6).[69] So a larger number of Jews

65. Luke may be implying that a local house church begins in Publius's home, and that this influential οἶκος provides the social networks and relational connections which catalyze a regional church-planting movement, carried forward by miraculous healings (part 3), though the actual results on Malta are unknown. Tannehill, *Narrative Unity*, 2:340 claims that Luke's focus here is on "images of cooperative relationships between Christians and non-Christians, to the benefit of all."

66. "Luke is showing how the giving and receiving of acts of kindness built bridges for the gospel with good-living pagans," Peterson, *Acts*, 702.

67. This interaction between Paul and the Roman Jews is Luke's way of clarifying Paul's relationship with Judaism and insisting that Paul's missionary work (and those following him in subsequent generations) is not anti-Jewish in any way. Witherington, *Acts*, 793.

68. Witherington, *Acts*, 799.

69. Luke is still locating Christianity within Judaism, as a "sect," an insider word (cf. 24:5, 14; 26:5).

meet with Paul at a later time. This is in keeping with Paul's missionary strategy in a new location, to go to the Jews first, and then to the Gentiles (13:42–48; 18:5–7; 19:8–10). Paul senses an opportunity within the Roman Jewish Diaspora.

This leads to the most explicit missional activity in the final section of Acts. Luke reports that, "from morning till evening he explained (ἐξετίθετο) and declared (διαμαρτυρόμενος) to them the kingdom of God and tried to convince (πείθων) them about Jesus from the Law of Moses and from the Prophets" (28:23). It is significant that Paul is able to preach to these Roman Jews about the kingdom of God for an entire day. Their response is predictably varied: "Some were convinced (ἐπείθοντο) by what he said, but others would not believe" (28:24). This partially positive response importantly highlights the only unambiguously successful missionary activity in the final nine chapters of Acts.[70] Πείθω is used elsewhere in Acts to indicate heartfelt conviction and conversion.[71] The contrast between those who are persuaded and the "unbelieving" (ἠπίστουν) also points towards faith on the part of some of these Roman Jews. Here in Rome, Paul is still actively engaged in his mission, proclaiming the gospel in a way that requires a response from his hearers.

When Paul quotes Isa 6:9–10 and speaks about God's salvation being sent to the Gentiles, many of them begin to leave (28:25–27). As has happened in multiple other locations, Paul has given the Jews an opportunity to hear and respond to the gospel, but after many have rejected the message, he turns to the Gentiles, for he knows from experience that, "they will listen!" (ἀκούσονται, 28:28). Luke sums up Paul's calling at the end of Acts by saying, "God's salvation has been sent to the Gentiles" (28:27), and reminds the reader that even though Paul is not a free man, and is awaiting trial in Rome, he is still carrying out a divinely ordained mission. Luke presents Paul as the primary instigator of this Gentile outreach, and the archetypal missionary to emulate, but he is also seeking to involve his readers in the ongoing mission to the Gentiles in his day. By emphatically adding "and they will listen," he is encouraging readers that they will find a receptive and responsive audience among the Gentiles, even as Paul does.

---

70. Missional success is relative. Although there are no conversions mentioned in Jerusalem or the trial scenes, Luke implies that the proclamation of the gospel to these high (and huge) audiences is a success in its own right. The goal is to declare the good news; the response of the hearer is a separate issue. Understood this way, the final eight chapters of Acts are full of missional success.

71. E.g., 13:43; 14:1–2; 17:4; 19:8–9; Polhill, *Acts*, 542. The parallels between this scene and 13:44–47 also point towards genuine conversion on the part of certain Roman Jews; Witherington, *Acts*, 800–802.

This saying need not be understood as a categorical rejection of mission to the Jews,[72] particularly given that multiple Jews have just responded positively to the gospel (28:24), but should be interpreted as the continuation of the paradigm which Paul has always possessed: to the Jew first, and then to the Gentile. It is likely that as Luke is writing Acts the issue of Jewish inclusion has not been fully resolved. Luke is calling his church back to the practice of the Pauline mission as he presents it in Acts and advocating that Christ-followers reach out to both Jews and non-Jews everywhere they go.

Luke summarizes that "for two whole years Paul stayed there in his own rented house (ἐν ἰδίῳ μισθώματι) and welcomed all who came to see him" (28:30). Here is Paul, under house arrest, bound with a chain and guarded continually by a soldier (28:16, 20), making even this house a base for ministry. As there is already a church in Rome (28:14–15), these visits may partly be for the building up of this community. Paul is no longer mobile, yet he makes his private οἶκος into a hub for mission and edification. He remains the ideal missionary-prisoner in Rome, faithfully ministering to all who come his way.

This is underscored by the final verse in Acts, which ends the narrative on a triumphant note by depicting Paul, "preaching the kingdom of God (κηρύσσων τὴν βασιλείαν τοῦ Θεοῦ) and teaching concerning the Lord Jesus Christ (διδάσκων τὰ περὶ τοῦ Κυρίου Ἰησοῦ Χριστοῦ) with all boldness, unhindered" (μετὰ πάσης παρρησίας ἀκωλύτως, 28:31). Each of these words is pregnant with meaning for Luke. Paul has a two-fold ministry in Rome: evangelistically preaching (κηρύσσω) the Kingdom of God, and teaching (διδάσκω) about the Lord Jesus, presumably to new Christians and the existing Roman church. Significantly, Paul is doing these things boldly (μετὰ πάσης παρρησίας, with all freedom and boldness of speech) and freely (ἀκωλύτως, unhindered). "The final words 'with all boldness and without hindrance', further typify the appropriate character of Christian witnessing. Throughout Acts, the witnesses to Jesus' resurrection have spoken 'boldly' (4:13, 29–31). 'Without hindrance' intensifies the description."[73] There is a confidence and freedom in Paul's Roman ministry; no person or persecution will hinder him. Ironically, although Paul is in captivity and awaiting trial, he is still free and unfettered in his outreach, as Jesus's missionary-prisoner.

This final verse functions as a paradigmatic statement, which summarizes what Luke is rhetorically advocating throughout Acts, somewhat like 1:8. It epitomizes Luke's ideal wish for his readers, namely that they would

---

72. Jervell, *Apostelgeschichte*, 631 sees this passage marking the separation of the church from "the unbelieving component of Judaism."

73. Gaventa, *Acts*, 369.

also preach the kingdom of God and teach about Jesus Christ with freedom and bold confidence, just as Paul does. As Marguerat explains:

> This portrayal of the ideal pastor [28:30–31] points to the men and women, with Luke or close to him, who through their missionary engagement, perpetuate the memory of the apostle to the Gentiles. In this way, they were associated with the witness of the Risen One "to the ends of the earth" (1:8)—a programme which remains open. *The summary offers an anticipation of it, as it waits to be reconstituted in the life of the reader the moment when he or she finishes the reading of the book.*[74]

It is significant that Acts 28:31 comes in the context of Paul's Roman house arrest; Luke is claiming that effective mission can happen even when persecution is severely limiting mobility and freedom. In fact, Luke is advocating that this kind of "unhindered" outreach and building up of the church should happen particularly in times of imprisonment, trial, and other forms of persecution. This verse summarizes the final part of Acts: persecution is an unavoidable part of the mission, and regardless of the difficulty a person may encounter, they can be an effective and unhindered messenger of the gospel in every circumstance. Paul is the ultimate example of such a missionary-prisoner paradigm, and Luke hopes that his audience will be inspired by his example and emulate him in their own practice.

THE ENDING OF ACTS

The Apostle Paul embodies the apostolic ethos which carries the message and movement forward in Acts. Even when imprisoned, on trial, and severely limited, he continues to exemplify the ideal prisoner-witness. The narrative appears to be moving towards some grand climax in which the gospel takes on the Empire, and wins. However, the enigmatic conclusion of Acts disappoints such expectations. Luke has hinted four times that Paul would appear before Caesar (25:11–12, 21; 26:32; 27:24), so the reader looks forward to this confrontation, and towards learning how Paul's life and mission resolve. Yet none of this materializes in Acts. Luke does not even describe the outcome of Paul's impending trial in Rome, much less the grand finale of his vast mission, if there is one. Instead, Paul is preaching and teaching with all boldness, unhindered (28:31). Thus, this epic missionary narrative ends.

---

74. Marguerat, *Historian*, 230. Emphasis added.

In fact, it does not really end, it simply quits. On reading these last words, one wishes to turn the page and discover what becomes of Paul, or at least what happens next. "Perhaps, instead of a final period, the book should end with ellipsis points . . ."[75] Scholars have repeatedly discussed why the book of Acts does not actually end.[76] Perhaps Luke is planning a third volume? Perhaps he writes as Paul is on trial, and does not know the outcome?

From a rhetorical perspective, the explanation for the ending of Acts is simple: the narrative does not end because the mission does not end. If the "Acts of the Apostles" was really about the apostles, Luke would reveal what becomes of them, particularly Peter and Paul. However, Acts is about mission, and Luke is employing an intentional literary strategy by not properly ending Acts: he is implying that the story continues to his present day and beyond. He avoids putting a fixed ending point on his narrative because his conviction is that it is still ongoing. The overarching promise of Acts 1:8 (and 13:47) that the gospel will reach the ends of the earth remains unfulfilled.[77] The "ending" of Acts is a rhetorical device designed to "hand the baton" on to the readers of Acts, that they might take their turn in God's unfolding mission.

Luke attempts to draw his readers into participating in the missional story of Acts by leaving multiple narrative details unresolved and many questions unanswered, and by departing abruptly from the on-going story-line. Early commentators recognized this:

> Chrysostom was one of the first interpreters to recognize the literary implications of the ending of Acts: "The author [Luke] conducts his narrative up to this point, and leaves the hearer thirsty so that he fills up the lack by himself through reflection" (*Hom. Act.* 15). How would the audience be expected to "fill up the lack"? By completing the story in accord with what has preceded (cf. Aristotle, *Poet,* 7.21).[78]

Many since Chrysostom have understood the final verses of Acts similarly:

75. González, *Acts,* 280.

76. E.g., Hemer, *Acts,* 383–87; Marguerat, *Historian,* 205–30; Pervo, *Acts,* 668–70.

77. Some see Rome as Luke's implied "ends of the earth" because the Acts narrative "ends" there, Stevens, *Acts,* 581. However, if Luke intentionally leaves his narrative incomplete, it makes more sense to see the Christological promise of Acts 1:8 as unfulfilled and requiring further missional action on the part of future Christ followers. Peterson, *Acts,* 722; Keener, *Acts,* 4:3775: "Luke also provides indication that the gospel will reach the ends of the earth (1:8); if it has reached the heart of the Roman Empire, it will prevail despite the obstacles."

78. Parsons, *Acts,* 366.

What response might his [Luke's] original readers well have had when they reached the end of his second volume? . . . They must have been encouraged to continue in faithful witness to their risen Lord by all that Luke related in his second volume concerning the apostles and Paul . . . Whatever their time and place, whatever their particular circumstances, how could they not have been inspired to manifest within their own lives the same faithfulness and the same resoluteness which Paul himself had manifested in his own surpassing witness to the risen Jesus, the Lord who had called them all?[79]

The important unfinished business in this situation is for the witness of the new community to press forward. Still to be accomplished in the contemporary life of the church is the divine intention revealed to Paul and Barnabas at Pisidian Antioch midway through the narrative of Acts (13:47): "I have set you to be a light for the Gentiles, that you may bring salvation, to the uttermost parts of the earth."[80]

Through a variety of rhetorical strategies, Luke-Acts manoeuvres its readers into alignment with the "witnesses" (*autoptai* or *martyres*) who constitute the insiders in the story. That is, the Lukan text is designed to persuade the readers to become believing witnesses.[81]

Rosner substantiates this claim by examining the ending of Acts in terms of ancient rhetoric and modern literary theory.[82] He also helpfully cites N. T. Wright's analogy of how biblical narrative carries authority for Christians: if the fifth act of a play of Shakespeare has been lost, "highly trained, sensitive and experienced Shakespearian actors, who would immerse themselves in the first four acts," would be well qualified to re-compose it.[83] As Rosner concludes, "Acts, to adopt the model, is about the spread of the gospel and it challenges its readers to press ahead with the unfinished task."[84] It could be said that Luke understands his readers to be living in "Acts 29," the subsequent episodes of his narrative, and the open-ended conclusion of Acts deliberately includes them in the task of continuing the

79. Cassidy, *Society and Politics*, 170.

80. Kee, *Good News*, 107.

81. Darr, *Character Building*, 53, also 147.

82. Rosner, "Progress," 230–32.

83. Wright, *New Testament*, 1:140.

84. Rosner, "Progress," 233.

spread of the word.[85] The many missional methods and strategies Luke has depicted throughout Acts are his suggested way to go about this in the following generations. Peterson summarizes this idea:

> In the narrative of Acts, Peter, Paul, Stephen, and Philip have their own unique function in salvation history, but in certain ways they also function as models of faithful discipleship for others. Many others are involved in the growth of the word as divine agents. Some, such as Barnabas, Silas, and Mark, are named; others are not (e.g., 8:4; 11:19–21). By implication, the conclusion of Acts challenges readers to consider how they themselves will continue the story of the gospel's progress. Acts 27–28 . . . highlight again the importance of persisting in ministry to Gentiles and Jews—whatever the indifference or hostility—using the variety of approaches that Luke has illustrated. They suggest that the ascended Lord is still working through his Spirit to empower his gospel agents to proclaim and teach *with all boldness* and—as the situation permits—*without hindrance*.[86]

CONCLUSION

One of the fundamental tenets of Christianity is the suffering of Christ. Similarly, one of the chief characteristics of the early church is its own suffering, as Christians follow in the footsteps of their Lord. This suffering in Luke's Gospel and in Acts provides an important and "profound link" between Luke's two-volume work.[87] As Peterson explains, "Readers are encouraged to follow the example of the earliest believers, and Paul in particular, by holding fast to the same gospel and continuing to be active in its dissemination, even in the face of persecution from without and conflict from within the churches."[88]

It would be difficult enough for Luke to inspire his readers to mission in pleasant circumstances, but Luke has the arduous task of motivating them in challenging times. He knows that what he is advocating in Acts will unfold in a climate of frightening and sometimes violent hostility.[89] For this reason, he devotes the final portion of his missional narrative to equipping his audience in how to respond when they face persecution, particularly

85. Though of course Luke would be unaware of later chapter divisions in his work.
86. Peterson, *Acts*, 724.
87. Peterson, "Theological Enterprise," 544.
88. Peterson, "Theological Enterprise," 544.
89. Rapske, "Opposition," 254.

in the form of imprisonment and trial. Christian readers are inspired and equipped by Paul's example in the final eight chapters of Acts, as he demonstrates what it means to remain faithful to Christ and boldly committed to the cause, as the ideal prisoner-witness. "Custody hardly truncates Paul's life as a missionary; instead, it offers new locations and new audiences for his proclamation to continue."[90] By presenting Paul's imprisonment and trials in this way, Luke integrates suffering and persecution into an overarching matrix of outreach and shows his readers that they are not merely compatible, but inseparable. The abrupt "ending" of Acts shows that the mission is not complete, and compellingly invites readers to join the unfolding story in their time, even when it involves pain and sacrifice.

90. Skinner, *Locating Paul*, 109.

PART 4

Conclusion

Equipping Missionaries to Respond
to Suffering and Persecution

If readers of Acts take Luke's missional exhortations seriously, many will face suffering, whether that is opposition, violence, imprisonment, trial, or martyrdom. Luke realizes that if his goal is to motivate and equip his readers to engage in Christian mission, they will require practical instruction about how to respond to persecution when it comes their way. Luke presents the various persecution accounts in his narrative with this purpose in mind.

Table 13.1 Situations of Suffering and Persecution Acts Addresses[1]

1. When on trial before Jewish authorities—before the Sanhedrin (4:5–22; 5:27–42; 22:22—23:35)

2. When threatened with immediate death—the martyrdom of Stephen (6:8—7:60)

3. When scattered by threats—the persecution of Jerusalem believers (8:4–40; 11:19–21)

4. When a loved one is threatened or imprisoned—praying for Peter's release (12:1–19)

1. More detail about each of these scenarios can be found in the relevant sections of the previous two chapters, which follow the chronological timeline of Acts.

5. When suffering the threat of mob violence and being expelled from a place of mission—Paul in Pisidian Antioch (13:50–51), Iconium (14:5–6), Thessalonica (17:7–10), Berea (17:13–14), Ephesus (20:1), Jerusalem (21:27–35)

6. When stoned—Paul and his Christian defenders in Lystra (14:19–20)

7. When imprisoned for local witness—Paul and Silas in Philippi (16:22–39)

8. When urged to stop taking risks by friends—Paul with the Tyrian disciples (21:4–14)

9. When speaking before a violent crowd—Paul in Jerusalem (21:27–35)

10. When on trial before non-Jewish rulers—before Felix (24:1–26), Festus (25:1–12), Agrippa (26:1–32)[2]

11. When in long-term captivity (and alone or abandoned)—Paul in Jerusalem, Caesarea, and *en route* to Rome (21:33—28:14)

12. When threatened by a natural disaster—the storm and shipwreck (27:13–44)

13. When under house arrest—Paul in Rome (28:14–31)

The theme of missional suffering is interwoven throughout Luke-Acts, from Jesus's predictions and promises about it through the early Sanhedrin trial narratives, Stephen's martyrdom, the Jerusalem scattering, Peter's imprisonment, and Paul's Philippian incarceration. However, it is most apparent in Paul's trial narratives (Acts 21–28). Luke advocates that trials and imprisonment are ideal platforms for missional proclamation, and that Christian sufferers should preach the gospel boldly in such situations. Additionally, they should defend themselves vigorously in court, using every possible advantage at their disposal, and emphasize their personal testimony, trusting that God will give them the right words for the moment. "The narratives of Paul's experiences before officials would provide useful models for Christian audiences, who might need to frame their own defenses or public arguments wisely with appropriate precedents."[3]

Above all, missionaries should recognize God's presence in their suffering, and trust that he will intervene on behalf of the gospel message and its messengers. Christ is reassuringly near them, just as he draws near to

---

2. Note that Luke provides three episodes before Jewish authorities (the Sanhedrin) and three corresponding episodes before non-Jewish authorities (Felix, Festus, Agrippa).

3. Keener, "Paul and Sedition," 203.

Paul at key junctures throughout his ministry. God's vindication will ultimately materialize, even if this means dying well for the sake of Christ. Luke knows faithful martyrdom is perhaps the most powerful missional action of them all, and church history bears this out. All of this provides the robust backbone to the missional practice Luke is advocating throughout Acts, and the vital strength to endure victoriously and proclaim the gospel boldly and unhindered, even when under painful pressure and opposition.

Conclusions and Reflection

I have set you to be a light for the Gentiles,
so that you may bring salvation to the ends of the earth.
—ACTS 13:47 [ISA 49:6]

Acts is the most explicitly missional book in the Bible. Readers do not so much analyze as encounter its content: "It tells of the beginnings of Christianity with a vigour and vividness which often leaves the new reader breathless."[4] Filled with stories of dramatic missionary adventures, breathtaking examples of the power of the Spirit, and death-defying risks on behalf of the gospel, Acts presents the reader with a vibrant missional theology in action. Luke is not concerned with precise presentations of doctrine or systematic theology but tells a vivid story about Jews who encounter the living Christ, are filled with the power of the Spirit, and sent on extraordinary journeys of witness to Jewish and non-Jewish peoples. This study has proposed that mission is the basic framework through which Acts should be interpreted and has identified many missional themes and narrative details which Luke emphasizes. These have been organized into an overarching body metaphor, which provides a coherent framework for understanding Luke's missional teaching. The amount of the Acts narrative extolling the missionaries and their churches clearly demonstrates Luke's unequivocal advocacy of the Christian mission.

Readers of the book of Acts still look to this ancient narrative for guidance, and its inclusion in the canon of Scripture means that for many Acts is not simply a story about the first churches, but a divinely inspired text with genuine relevance for their own lives and mission today. However, it is

---

4. Dunn, *Acts*, ix.

not necessarily straightforward to translate the meanings of Acts across two thousand years of history. It establishes a trajectory of meaning, and though modern readers cannot hope to relive its stories verbatim, they can live their own stories following the missional course which Acts suggests. It is a book without a proper ending, and its abrupt departure invites readers to involve themselves in the ongoing epic of the church's mission, empowered by the Spirit to join Paul in proclaiming, "the kingdom of God and the teaching about the Lord Jesus with all boldness, unhindered" (28:31). This compelling invitation still beckons readers today, just as it did in Luke's day.

This study has focused on Luke's meaning and intentions within his ancient context. However, as readers examine the biblical text, they inevitably begin to look through it as through a lens, and see themselves and their own world.[5] As Thiselton explains, "understanding takes place when two sets of horizons are brought into relation to each other, namely those of the text and those of the interpreter."[6] Acts does not present a single pattern for what it means to be church or to engage in mission, and readers must be careful to avoid reading their particular brand of Christianity into Luke's writing. What Acts offers is a compelling set of stories which accentuate the many missional themes discussed in this study, all emphasizing following the guidance of the Spirit, as God's people discover what he is doing in their communities and the wider world and learn to cooperate with this in their particular situation. These stories critique, provoke, and encourage readers and communities today, just as they have throughout church history.

There are no denominations or bible colleges or church buildings in Acts. Readers cannot expect to find the same forms of Christian expression in the book of Acts that they practice today, nor should they attempt to justify their common practices from the example of the early church. Instead, Acts tells the stories of a band of people wholly convinced that Christ is alive, and totally committed to proclaiming this reality. God's Messiah has come, the Scriptures are fulfilled, and everyone is invited to participate in this expanding kingdom experience through the power of the Spirit. The story of Acts is fast-paced and breathtaking, and readers should see it as a Lukan "highlight reel" of the first thirty years of the church, rather than a description of the daily life of the Christian community, lest they become discouraged that their own experience does not constantly mirror these exceptional stories. Yet Acts does challenge its readers to consider the full potential of the missional church, and to compare their own lived experiences with that which it so compellingly describes.

5. Smart, *Interpretation of Scripture*, 34–35.
6. Thiselton, *Two Horizons*, 103.

Luke unveils both the thesis and the geographical outline of all of Acts in 1:8, clarifying that his overarching purpose is to articulate and hasten the spread of the gospel throughout the earth, initiated and spurred on by the Holy Spirit. In doing this, Luke designs a narrative world which functions as a persuasive equipping narrative for mission. Within this overarching ambition are multiple missional sub-purposes, such as healing and maintaining the unity of the Christian movement within increasing diversity, rehabilitating the controversial figure of Paul, and responding to and overcoming opposition and setbacks. But *Luke's primary purpose remains to unleash the missional potential of the united church*, and this gives readers focus as they encounter and interpret this dramatic story. The book of Acts is Luke's attempt to inspire the church to continue the vision and mission of Jesus, Peter, and Paul to the *true* ends of the earth, and to recover the missional vibrancy of the earliest churches and Christian leaders. In today's postmodern and post-Christendom era, this missional provocation is surely as relevant now as it has ever been.[7]

PART 1—MISSIONAL STIMULI

There are four primary missional stimuli in Acts, each of which is a theological and ethical catalyst for advancement and an example to be emulated by Luke's readers. Instead of the Greek or Roman ethics of his contemporaries, Luke's historical narrative proclaims a missional ethic rooted in the teachings of Christ based on a modified Jewish theological outlook. The stimuli he extols can be thought of as the four chambers of the heart of the missional teaching of Acts, for they work together to keep the life-giving blood "oxygenated" with zealous motivation, which flows throughout and supports the rest of the body. These are primary for Luke, for they inspire readers to engage missionally, shaking them out of apathy, and set the stage for the more practical equipping that follows.

Luke presents the *Word* (λόγος) as the first source of missional advancement. The λόγος in Acts combines Luke's Christological, ecclesiological, and missional convictions, and as a narrative character leads the unfolding progression of the early Christian mission, which Luke is implicitly inviting his readers to join. Luke's conception of the λόγος emphasizes that *the leadership of the mission rests in Christ's hands, and is ultimately God's responsibility*. Followers of Christ join with him in the mission, but the divine λόγος is already

7. Robinson and Wall, *Called to Be Church*, 9–13.

accomplishing it, and will carry it to completion. The unstoppable nature of the Word's advance inspires the church with confidence: though there may be setbacks and suffering along the way, Christ's ultimate victory is assured. God's sovereign leadership is foundational to Luke's missional theology.

In Acts, the *Spirit* (πνεῦμα) carries this movement forward, as the central power-source for the mission. Lukan outreach is initiated, sustained, and directed by the Spirit, who as a character in the Acts narrative is also the ultimate prophetic mouthpiece. The πνεῦμα builds and fortifies the church, protecting its unity and transforming the personal character of its members. Luke is not asking his readers to do something for which they have no empowerment. Instead, his narrative beckons believers to live in and draw from the power of the Spirit in their personal lives, and to join with the missional journey of the πνεῦμα throughout the earth.

The church of Acts has a *universally inclusive theological outlook*, in which the Father's offer of salvation is for everyone regardless of location, ethnicity, or social class, and holistically addresses every part of a person's life. This becomes a source of missional urgency in itself—if the message is for all of everyone, everywhere, it must be carried and proclaimed to them, that they might have the opportunity to respond. According to Acts, Christian witness requires a radically inclusive theology: everyone is welcome without exception. When the gospel loses its universal claims to truth and relevance, the mission's efficacy becomes limited. This outreach is orchestrated by the Father, who welcomes all people into his loving family.

Acts invites its reader to be led by the Word, empowered by the Spirit, and caught up in the Father's universally relevant and inclusive offer of salvation. Luke also challenges his readers to develop a missional way of life. The *radical lifestyles* of the earliest Christians, characterized by rigorous discipleship, the apostolic ethos, and enthusiastically disciplined devotion to Christ, are central to their missional success. In Acts, Christians believe so deeply in the importance of the mission that pain, suffering, and even martyrdom on behalf of its advancement are reasonable sacrifices. The early missionaries Luke celebrates are characterized by a pioneering spirit, determined to go to places where the gospel has not yet been proclaimed, continually engage in evangelistic activities, and consistently rely on miracles to confirm and validate their message. Luke invites the church to cultivate all these characteristics, along with a high standard of obedience and a consistent practice of the personal disciplines of prayer, fasting, and worship. In the book of Acts, effective mission flows directly from and is sustained by this personal devotion, nurtured by a close relationship with the Father such as Jesus models throughout Luke's Gospel. Acts portrays a church which lives in spiritual power and grows largely because people experience this reality in their personal lives and are infused with faith and boldness as a result.

Luke depicts many of the characters in Acts as role-models who embody these missional characteristics, and from which Christians can find inspiration and motivation. He also presents the primary churches in his narrative, such as Jerusalem, Syrian Antioch, and Ephesus, as models for local churches to emulate in terms of their missional activity. Luke is convinced that a vision and theology based on the irresistible advance of the λόγος, the unending empowerment of the πνεῦμα, and the universal relevance and inclusion of the Father's salvation must be at the heart of Christian witness. *This Trinitarian mission team is the driving force behind all mission in Acts.*[8] Additionally, a high standard of Christian discipleship, a willingness to suffer for the cause, a pioneering spirit, and an enthusiastic devotion to God are essential ingredients for missionaries in Acts. Luke presents all of this in a rhetorical call to his readers to take action and join the advancing Jesus movement.

A pivotal message for the church today is the *missio Dei,* the idea that Christian mission is grounded in and flows from God's mission as an inherent attribute of his being: God is a missionary God.[9] One way to summarize Acts is to say it depicts Christ-followers attempting to track and keep pace with the Trinity's ever-expanding mission, and this paradigm is crucial to contemporary missiology. God initiates as the missional architect, and his followers do just that, attempting to follow as best they can. With the relatively recent advent of *missio Dei* theology and the Trinitarian renaissance of the last century, these emphases of Acts take on extremely poignant theological resonance today.

The importance of these priorities cannot be overstated. As Bosch says, "mission is not primarily an activity of the church, but an attribute of God."[10] Similarly, Moltmann claims, "It is not the church that has a mission of salvation to fulfill in the world; it is the mission of the Son and the Spirit through the Father that includes the church."[11] Understood this way, mission is not primarily ecclesiological, or even soteriological, but fundamentally

---

8. This is not to say that Luke has a fully developed doctrine of the Trinity, as reflected in the later creeds, but that his conception of Father, Son, and Spirit reflect an embryonic understanding of how these three persons work together within the divine identity and mission.

9. Wright, *Mission of God,* 62–65. Wright's treatment of mission in Acts emphasizes its OT roots and prophetic fulfillment but is unfortunately brief (*Mission of God,* 514–21).

10. Bosch, *Transforming Mission,* 389–90.

11. Moltmann, *Church in the Power of the Spirit,* 64.

Trinitarian, derived from the very nature of God. All true missionary initiative originates from God and has no life on its own apart from the sending hand of God. "Mission is thereby seen as a movement from God to the world; the church is viewed as an instrument for that mission. There is church because there is mission, not vice versa. To participate in mission is to participate in the movement of God's love toward people, since God is a fountain of sending love."[12] Acts calls the church to take up its modest but important part in the Trinity's loving mission today, always following God's initiative and asking first what he is already doing.

Luke intends to draw every follower of Christ into God's mission. They are part of the church, and therefore personally sent by Jesus himself, as the continuation of his own ministry: "The church is sent into the world to continue that which he came to do, in the power of the same Spirit, reconciling people to God."[13] There are "professional missionaries" who provide leadership and inspiration in Acts, but everyone is called to discover a missional way of life: "No one can say: 'Since I'm not called to be a missionary, I do not have to evangelize my friends and neighbors.' There is no difference, in spiritual terms, between a missionary witnessing in his home town and a missionary witnessing in Kathmandu, Nepal. We are all called to go—even if it is only to the next room, or the next block."[14] Whether this is through preaching and teaching, relational evangelism, lifestyle mission, or a combination, Acts offers every Christian the opportunity to ascertain what mission means in their life.

The book of Acts also presents a missional gospel that is radically inclusive and transforming. The church is an instrument of this mission, called and sent as a witness by God's initiative, and rooted in his purposes to restore and heal all of creation. Luke goes out of his way to emphasize that everyone is invited to join in, with no barriers to entry. This extreme inclusivity is an important challenge to today's church, which so often says more about who is excluded than who is invited. The book of Acts challenges Christians to think seriously about how to be and do church in a way that welcomes everyone, and particularly those who are different or other. Who is the Ethiopian eunuch today? Who are the pagan Gentiles? Who is the outsider, the foreigner, the excluded? The invitation to belong, to be welcomed home into the Father's relational family, is one of the primary missional offers the church can make.

---

12. Bosch, *Transforming Mission*, 389–90.

13. Newbigin, *Gospel*, 230.

14. Hale, *On Being a Missionary*, 6. While this is not expressly referring to Acts, it is a fitting reflection.

The story of the book of Acts is an invitation to unity in diversity, and a roadmap to overcoming prejudice and ethnocentrism. Today's Christian church and wider culture are profoundly fractured and polarized, and desperately need the vision of unity which Acts provides. The progression of Gentile inclusion is Luke's story of the church overcoming division; episodes such as the Ethiopian eunuch, Cornelius's household, the church at Antioch, the Jerusalem Council, and Paul's Roman ministry continue to function as important provocations to the contemporary church. As people are welcomed into this unified community of loving acceptance, their lives are transformed and healed by God's love, and they in turn are empowered to become witnesses within their own social networks.

This radical and welcoming inclusivity accelerates the momentum of the mission and generates the kind of apostolic ethos which Acts so compellingly describes. Relational unity undergirds the health of this missional movement. And classic spiritual disciplines such as prayer, worship, fasting, serving, solitude, and silence continue to nourish and feed this movement today. Finally, Acts calls the church to continue to boldly proclaim this good news of healing and reconciliation to everyone. It is increasingly difficult in the western world to speak openly about faith and spirituality. Perhaps today's church needs to discover different platforms and new language; most Christians do not belong to synagogues with audiences waiting to listen as Paul does in Acts. But they belong to many social networks where the Word would be welcome if offered sensitively and relevantly. Luke's narrative is a rebuke of missional apathy and indifference in the church, and calls every Christ follower to unapologetic proclamation, in lovingly relevant word and deed, as they follow their missional God.

PART 2—MISSIONAL STRUCTURES

Christians hold the *church* (ἐκκλησία) as the highest priority in Acts, in terms of the way that they structure and organize themselves. Mission emerges out of the church and results in the establishment and growth of new churches.

Luke uses the ἐκκλησία concept to establish a distinctively Christian identity, and to paint a picture of what the missional church should look like for his readers. In the body analogy, the churches of Acts are the hands and feet, for they are the material and social structures which reach out in mission, welcome others into the church community, and carry the mission forward, in the power of the Spirit.

In a household (οἶκος) society, these gathered groups of believers develop most naturally within the established physical and social structures of the οἶκος, and so the church in Acts takes shape largely within the houses and households of the ancient world, alongside a few public meeting places. The οἶκος is the consistent target for initial house-based outreach in a particular location, and the launching point for further city-wide and regional evangelism in an area. This creates a cycle of outreach, establishing, consolidation, and further outreach in Acts, all based around the οἶκος structure.

The ἐκκλησία and the οἶκος combine to form the house church. Jesus introduces the house church model in embryonic form in his village and regional ministry, the earliest Jerusalem church develops it in its city-wide outreach, those scattered from Jerusalem by persecution adapt it in their urban and regional outreach, culminating at Antioch, and Paul employs it in his center-oriented mission throughout the Empire. Luke stresses in Acts that the spread of the church as a relational network of house church communities is God's desire, and one of the primary reasons for the success of the mission.

> The consistent witness of Scripture . . . is that God's intention is to form a people, a community, a visible body . . . the nature and life of the community of faith is the focus . . . the concern of Scripture is not the spiritual state of individuals, their holiness, or even their salvation. The focus is God's *ekklesia,* God's community taking form in the world.[15]

This focus on "we" rather than "me" is a central theme of the book of Acts, for it pictures the Christian faith as life-lived-in-community, a community out of which mission naturally flows. This also forcefully confronts the Western tendencies towards individualism and isolation, and the prevalent aversion to the communal life of deeply committed relationship. Acts depicts a network of house churches, sharing their possessions and goods, devoted to the apostles' teaching, prayer, and breaking bread, and living in κοινωνία fellowship together in ways that are formative and transformative to those around them. These churches reproduce themselves to plant other

---

15. Robinson and Wall, *Called to Be Church,* 3.

churches, which develop wherever the mission spreads. For Luke, Christ-followers must be gathered into communities of faith and mission. Acts compellingly beckons its readers, both ancient and modern, to discover the transforming power and priority of authentic church community.

> The greatest need in our time is not simply for *kerygma*, the preaching of the gospel; nor for *diakonia*, service on behalf of justice; nor for *charisma*, the experience of the spirit's gifts; nor even for *propheteia*, the challenging of the King. The greatest need of our time is for *koinonia*, the call simply to be the church, to love one another, and to offer our lives for the sake of the world. The creation of living, breathing, loving communities of faith at the local church level is the foundation of all other answers.[16]

Much of today's church does not resemble the church in Acts, at least in terms of its outward structure. Nevertheless, the picture Luke paints can strengthen and critique the modern church. Ecclesial trappings such as advertising campaigns, billboards, even church buildings themselves, can easily become unhelpful distractions from the church's primary missional calling. The book of Acts is not interested in the inward workings or organization of the church, but in its central theological calling into the mission of the Trinity. Throughout Acts it is always the Spirit who sets the stage and provides the leadership; this invites every church and church leader today to prayerfully realign themselves with God's missional initiative.

The modern house-church movement is a relatively recent attempt to return to the structure of the earliest church.[17] There is much to be commended in this approach: it is more financially affordable, it focuses on authentic community and personal relationships, and in certain parts of the world it is the only viable option as public Christian meetings are banned.[18] Some believe smaller house-based fellowships are a deliberate apostolic pattern, advocated by Christ himself. While Acts can be used to support this line of thinking, it must be emphasized that what the church looks like in Acts will always be altogether distinct from anything Christianity experiences today, for the cultural contexts are so fundamentally different. There is a danger of anachronistically assuming that a modern "house church" is the same as the ancient house communities which Acts describes:

16. Wallis, *Call to Conversion*, 109.

17. Gehring, *House*, 302–11 evaluates the strengths, weaknesses, and questions posed by the modern house church model.

18. House-church movements in nations such as China and Iran have experienced recent periods of growth.

> The term "house church/churches" is deeply associated with the modern house church movement, and in applying it to early churches, it is difficult to avoid thereby implying that they are homologous with house churches of modern times. I would go as far as to suggest that the category "house church/churches" should be dropped altogether from New Testament and Early Christian studies.[19]

Acts advocates the vital importance of a deeply relational pattern of community, gathered around God's mission as the guiding principle; small groups meeting locally are its fundamental missional structure. In Mediterranean cultures hospitality is a primary value, and so these groups usually meet in homes. But such small-scale spiritual communities can also meet in public places like restaurants or outdoors, particularly if house-based hospitality is a less prominent cultural value. How this looks today will vary enormously depending on context. The contemporary western church's buildings, megachurch campuses, and extravagantly staged worship performances would be unrecognizable expressions of church in Luke's eyes, but this should not be a surprise; this is a vastly different time and place. Whether these expressions of church should be advocated is another question—Luke would want to ask how focused on relationship they are, and how effectively their social and material structures facilitate local, community-based mission.

The same is true of church leadership in Acts; Luke writes long before the institutionalization of Christian leadership. "For Luke the church as an institution is remarkably free and spontaneous in the impulses of its communal life . . . The church is led not by institutional authorities but by the Holy Spirit. By the Spirit the church is consolidated, but also disciplined and purified, and at the same time kept open to the mysterious and always new demands of God's will."[20] This is a provocative warning to the church—in Acts leaders never exercise authoritarian or institutionalized direction. The Spirit leads and guides the church first and foremost. Church leaders in Acts are relationally and organically trained, emerging from the local communities themselves, and their character and trustworthiness are of paramount importance in their selection. Their vocation is to follow God's Spirit. Leadership teams such as those at Jerusalem, Antioch, and on Paul's journeys

---

19. Adams, *Meeting Places*, 202. While his point is poignant, most scholars are not convinced by his attempt to eradicate this vocabulary from the study of early Christianity.

20. Maddox, *Purpose*, 185.

model vital group leadership structures, always operating in community and accompaniment.

Contemporary Western culture has largely spurned the church. It is common to hear declarations such as, "I am spiritual, but not religious," or "I love Jesus, but cannot bear the church." Spiritual interest is on the increase, but interest in the church as an organized religious community is in multiple places waning dramatically, with privatized spirituality becoming the norm. Acts is a crucial voice in this regard, for nowhere is there any room for individualized or private faith. Instead, Acts continually displays a community of people fully engaged in corporate spirituality and at the same time in justice-focused social-cultural witness. In this regard, Acts is a gift and a challenge to today's church, and to the wider culture that is so often walking away from it. If the church were to take seriously the missional priorities of Acts, this could shift the negative discourse within wider culture, and prompt people to prioritize community and relationship in their spiritual exploration.

Christ's "I am Jesus whom you are persecuting" (9:5) on the road to Damascus intricately links Jesus and his followers together; in Acts, Christ and the church are one. No one can love Jesus without loving the church, for as Paul would say, the church is the body of Christ and they are therefore inseparable. Whatever else the story of Paul's encounter with Christ communicates, Luke intends for readers to understand that Jesus takes personally how people treat his church; to love and serve the church is to love and serve Christ himself, and the same is true of those who mistreat it. Acts is a provocative call for followers of Christ to embrace his church as a mysterious and indivisible extension of himself, and to recover a vision of missional church that gains the trust of people through love and relationship. Church community is undeniably broken and messy, but it is also profoundly and beautifully part of Jesus, and Acts beckons Christ's people to cherish the church as they cherish Christ.

While it does not provide all the answers, Acts speaks with surprising relevance to many of the contemporary questions the church faces today, such as: the role of women; the place of possessions, materialism, and consumerism in the lives of faith communities; decision-making and navigating conflict in the church; responding to loneliness and suffering; mission and contextualization in a pluralistic era; and leadership more broadly in the church. However, its most cherished ecclesiological theme is also perhaps its most relevant, and this is the way Acts shows the church becoming increasingly multicultural. In today's profoundly multicultural world, these narratives of unified multiracial faith and community, and of the contextualization of the gospel as it crosses racial, cultural, and class boundaries, are deeply relevant. A community displaying this kind of unity is a prophetic and coun-tercultural witness. In a world where the church is increasingly marginalized and dismissed, Acts has much to say about today's pressing issues.[21]

Finally, it must be reemphasized that in Acts the church's main calling and organizing principle is God's mission. As Wright claims, "The church exists . . . for what we sometimes call 'mission': to announce to the world that Jesus is its Lord. This is the 'good news' and when it's announced it trans-forms people and societies."[22] The very nature and purpose of the church is missional, and all the above themes are important aspects of this calling.

> A working definition of missional church is a community of God's people that defines itself, and organizes its life around, its real purpose of being an agent of God's mission to the world. In other words, the church's true and authentic organizing principle is mission. When the church is in mission, it is the true church. The church itself is not only a product of that mission but is obli-gated and destined to extend it by whatever means possible. The mission of God flows directly through every believer and every community of faith that adheres to Jesus. To obstruct this is to block God's purposes in and through God's people.[23]

This fundamental paradigm shift involves thinking of the church not as attractional in nature, an institution to which outsiders must come to receive the gospel, drawn by various programs on offer, but as missional in nature, "sent ones" who actively incarnate the gospel outside of the walls of the church within a particular cultural context. "Mission is not just a pro-gram of the church. It defines the church as God's sent people. Either we are defined by mission, or we reduce the scope of the gospel and the mandate of the church. Thus our challenge today is to move from church with mission to missional church."[24] Acts provides a compelling picture of the missional church in action which readers today can creatively impersonate.

21. Gallagher and Hertig, *Mission in Acts*, is a helpful set of essays about how the text of Acts relates to contemporary mission practice and highlights many of these themes in more detail.

22. Wright, *Simply Christian*, 204.

23. Hirsch, *Forgotten Ways*, 82.

24. Guder, *Missional Church*, 6.

PART 3—MISSIONAL STRATEGY

Throughout the Acts narrative, and particularly in the Pauline journeys, Luke is instructing his readers to go about mission in a strategic and effective manner. This comprehensive teaching includes instruction about initial planning and direction, how to approach a new city or area, how to build strategic foundations for the emerging mission, how to develop early cells into reproducing city-wide and regional movements, and even hints at personal strategies for sustainable long-term missional success.[25] These missional strategies culminate in rapidly reproducing regional church-planting movements, as epitomized by the way that Paul's ministry at Ephesus has a direct impact on the entire province of Asia. In the body analogy, the missional strategies of Acts are the brain, for they determine the tactics and approach to be employed, direct the whole body at crucial points of decision, and keep all the members coordinated synergistically with one another.

The details of mission in Acts are not rhetorically innocent but are meant to be understood and interpreted as the very things which undergird the rapid expansion of the church throughout the Empire, and which are to be emulated by its readers in later generations. This is not to say that Acts is a straightforward "how-to-guide," with easy answers for church growth and mission. It is a complex narrative, which must be carefully interpreted. However, its story contains much accessible instruction, presented in vivid stories of normal people taking risks on behalf of Christ and his unfolding mission.

Much has been written in recent times about church growth and decline, including an explosion of interest in how to grow and develop Christian communities effectively. The emphases of Acts, and particularly of Paul's journeys, are vital in this regard. The Paul of Acts does not have a predetermined strategy or approach to his mission but learns and develops as he goes. Paul's strategic approach is not formulaic or predictable but led by a set of guiding principles which result in his surprising and unprecedented success. This kind of experimental and incremental learning approach, sensitive to local contextual and cultural dynamics, is highly relevant and beneficial to any contemporary missional endeavor.

In terms of the particulars of how Paul approaches his mission, Acts urges Christians to prioritize following the Spirit's guidance above all else. It also encourages missionaries to consider existing travel and trade routes

25. Table 11.1 is a comprehensive summary of these missional strategies and where they are found in Acts.

and urban centers where they can make the maximum impact. Similarly, they should think carefully about receptive social networks and who the people of influence within those networks are. Though social networks have changed substantially since the first century, this is still a highly pertinent and strategic missional approach, which recognizes pre-existing relational connections. Luke's narrative invites the church to minister not just to the poor and the least, but to the influential "gatekeepers" within all parts of society. This emphasis might be controversial and unconventional today, but for those called to this kind of ministry, learning how to impact society's influencers is a vital strategy for cultural transformation and widespread impact. The many miraculous stories in Acts also commend a reliance on miracles to confirm the truth of the message, for personal encounters with God's love and grace have the potential to effectively cut through the rational and often confusing cloud of apologetics and rival truth claims. This theme in Acts challenges the church to continue to pray for and expect God to perform miracles today.

Once Paul has selected a city and a network, he establishes strategic foundations through developing a small embryonic church and multiplying this to become a city-wide and then regional church network. This practice continues to have resonance today, particularly in pioneering settings where established churches are rare. Additionally, his various methods of supporting and undergirding this process, including appointing and empowering local leadership, strengthening and visiting the new churches, and developing a network of co-workers and ministry partners are still applicable. One of Paul's more provocative practices is the way he never remains for very long in one location—it is vital that new missional initiatives do not grow overly dependent on outside influences but are able to gain autonomy and self-sufficiency as soon as possible. Paul's emphasis on team ministry is another relevant strategy, and Acts presents crucial leadership teams throughout its narrative, from Peter and John, the seven appointed later in Jerusalem, the Antioch leadership team, and Paul's various co-workers, including Barnabas, Silas, Priscilla, and Aquila. Finally, Paul's emphasis on maintaining his connection with home base and developing a rhythm of missional exertion and rest are also vital personal strategies today.

Acts couches all these missional strategies in vivid and memorable narrative. It reads not as a textbook or how-to guide, but as an exciting and empowering set of stories, easier to recontextualize in various places and times. Just as Paul takes a strikingly different approach to proclaiming Christ to different audiences, such as the Pisidian Antioch synagogue and the Athenian Areopagus, so Acts invites its readers to do the same in their own context. The memorable stories allow readers to glean from Paul's

strategic missionary insights, and then apply them imaginatively and re-
sourcefully to their situation.

One final crucial theme emerges from this examination of missional
strategies in Acts—the significance of church planting. In the last century
there has been an explosion of interest in various church planting models
and methodologies, most of which look to Acts for inspiration and guidance.
Wagner memorably describes church planting as "the single most effective
evangelistic methodology under heaven."[26] When Christian communities
begin to grow, reproduce, and multiply rapidly, led by local and indigenous
leadership, this is often known as a church planting movement.[27] This is
happening in many places and forms today, though it is also controversial
in places.[28] Church planting is growing in influence throughout the world,
largely generated by the strategic missional model which Acts presents.

PART 4—MISSIONAL SUFFERING

Part 4 traced the missional themes previously identified through the end
of the narrative, and concluded that through the final verse, Paul is Luke's
archetypal missionary-prisoner, particularly when he is persecuted and on
trial. Luke constructs the final scenes of Acts rhetorically with the purpose
of equipping his readers for how to respond when they find themselves in
similarly difficult circumstances. Every body needs a backbone, and the instruction from Acts about suffering as mission, and for the cause of mission,
gives instruction on how to respond when this happens. As a spine for the
entire system, it provides bravery, strength, longevity, and resilience to the
mission, and keeps it upright and correctly aligned when confronted with
opposition.

Luke's rhetorical purposes are perhaps most visible in the abrupt ending of Acts. He is attempting to motivate and equip his readers for mission
through the book, and he leaves the early missional calling to the ends of

26. Wagner, *Church Planting*, 5.

27. Garrison, "Church Planting Movements vs Insider Movements," 3. An example
of this is the Training for Trainers (T4T) method in China, Smith and Kai, *T4T: A
Discipleship ReRevolution*, 36.

28. Church planting can be problematic for certain established churches, largely
because of the territorial nature of dioceses. The Anglican church has launched its Fresh
Expressions initiative and has also recently appointed the Bishop of Islington to be the
first bishop for church plants, linked closely to London church planting church Holy
Trinity Brompton; Davies, "HTB planters."

the earth unfulfilled in the hopes that they will pick up the baton and carry on with God's missional task. As this happens, throughout church history and today, missionaries inevitably face trials and suffering of various kinds. It is therefore extremely strategic that Luke includes such extensive training for how to respond to a whole variety of painful situations, including being scattered, attacked by mobs, stoned, imprisoned, brought to trial, and even martyred. Perhaps most significantly, Luke advocates throughout Acts that such experiences of opposition are not just a painful consequence of mission, but an inherent part of the mission, as opportunities to carry it further by continuing to proclaim Christ to all who will hear. Additionally, he underscores the importance of defending oneself when on trial using every legal option available and communicating one's personal story as a means of missional proclamation.

For many contemporary readers, this theme will appear to be the most foreign and irrelevant. Most Christians in the west will never face the overt suffering and persecution which Luke describes. However, all who take God's mission seriously will face rejection, relational breakdown, discouragement, and significant emotional opposition; Luke's instruction is inspiring, relevant, and consoling in these times. Additionally, in many parts of the world the threats of torture and martyrdom are very real, and often even more traumatic than the scenes which Acts describes.[29] While much of the western church shies away from this theme, in the interest of comfort and self-preservation, Acts places a theology of suffering and persecution at the very heart of God's mission and his people's calling. Throughout most of church history, and much of the world today, this is perhaps the most relatable and relevant topic of all. It is so prevalent in Acts that if a Christian never experiences any opposition for their witness, reading Acts might lead them to ask how faithful their witness actually is.

Parts three and four of this study have focused on the presentation of Paul in Acts, and in retrospect this may be one of Luke's greatest successes. He has provided a vivid and memorable portrait of the Apostle Paul's life and ministry which is distinctively his own, and yet sufficiently compatible with Paul's own writings to be credible. In doing so, he has rehabilitated Paul so effectively that Christians throughout history consult the bibliographical details of Paul's life in Acts when they think of Paul. By minimizing Paul's controversies and emphasizing his missional strengths, Luke has given the church an archetypal and exemplary missionary to imitate today.

---

29. Keener helpfully mentions some such examples, including from his own personal experience, *Acts*, 2:1296; 2:2173–74; "Mayhem," 61–64.

FINAL THOUGHTS

The church's mission to carry the gospel to all the world is fraught with overwhelming obstacles; danger, disease, terrorism, loneliness, human stubbornness and greed, church strife and corruption, and persecution can be devastating. What can simple missionaries hope to accomplish in the face of such opposition and contention? Yet the book of Acts depicts a small band of Christ followers who overcome such odds and spark a radical missional movement that is still expanding today. It gives the church hope that the mission is initiated and sustained by God, and thus will prevail; this enables those who partner in the mission to proceed in love, gratitude, confidence, and the Spirit's power, while entrusting the big challenges and obstacles to God.

This work has argued that the mission inaugurated by Jesus and shaped by the early church is the primary theme of the book of Acts and therefore the principal frame of reference for any interpretation of it. Such a missional hermeneutic illuminates many aspects of the story of Acts and helps readers comprehend Luke's intentions in writing this narrative work of art. Understood in this light, Acts is more than a story, and more than history—it is an ancient rhetorical guide to Christian mission which remains surprisingly relevant today.

The narrative of Acts invites followers of Christ to discover (or rediscover) the missional stimuli, structures, strategies, and even the missional suffering of the earliest church, and to apply them to their own situations in relevant and innovative ways. It beckons the church to revisit the transforming experience of the primitive Christian community. Above all, it urges its readers to participate in that mission, and to share in the fulfillment of the programmatic Christological promise which overshadows its entire narrative. Answering the call to action which Acts declares leads readers to receive the Spirit's empowerment to be Christ's witnesses where they are, in their surrounding regions, and even to the ends of the earth. In doing so, they continue the mission of Jesus, Peter, and Paul, and compose the next chapters of this grand story of God's redemptive love for the whole world.

Bibliography

Adams, Edward. *The Earliest Christian Meeting Places: Almost Exclusively Houses?* Revised ed. London: Bloomsbury T. & T. Clark, 2016.

Aland, Barbara et al., eds. *Novum Testamentum Graece.* 27th rev. ed. NA27. Stuttgart: Deutsche Bibelgesellschaft, 1993.

Alexander, Patrick H. et al., eds. *The SBL Handbook of Style: For Ancient Near Eastern, Biblical, and Early Christian Studies.* 2nd ed. Atlanta: SBL, 2014.

Anonymous. *Rhetorica ad Herennium.* Translated by Harry Caplan. LCL 403. Cambridge, MA: Harvard University Press, 1954.

Aratus. *Phaenomena.* Translated by A. W. Mair and G. R. Mair. LCL 129. Cambridge, MA: Harvard University Press, 1921.

Aristotle. *Ars Rhetorica.* Translated by W. Rhys Roberts. Oxford: Clarendon, 1924.

———. *Nicomachean Ethics.* Translated by Harris Rackham. LCL 73. Cambridge, MA: Harvard University Press, 1926.

———. *Politics.* Translated by Harris Rackham. LCL 264. Cambridge, MA: Harvard University Press, 1932.

Artemidorus. *The Interpretation of Dreams: Oneirocritica.* Translated by R. J. White. Park Ridge: Noyes, 1975.

Aune, David E. *Prophecy in Early Christianity and the Ancient Mediterranean World.* Grand Rapids: Eerdmans, 1983.

Baker, Coleman. *Identity, Memory, and Narrative in Early Christianity: Peter, Paul, and Recategorization in the Book of Acts.* Eugene, OR: Pickwick, 2011.

Balch, David L. "Acts as Epideictic History: A Recommendation of and Response to Todd Penner." In *In Praise of Christian Origins: Stephen and the Hellenists in Lukan Apologetic Historiography*, edited by Todd Penner, xi–xxi. New York: T. & T. Clark International, 2004.

———. "Founders of Rome, of Athens, and of the Church: Romulus, Theseus and Jesus. Theseus and Ariadne with Athena Visually Represented in Rome, Pompeii and Herculaneum." In *Seeing the God: Image, Space, Performance, and Vision in the Religion of the Roman Empire*, edited by Marlis Arnhold et al., 177–205.Tübingen: Mohr Siebeck, 2018.

———. "Luke-Acts: Political Biography/History under Rome. On Gender and Ethnicity." *Zeitschrift fur die Neutestamentliche Wissenschaft* 111 (2020) 65–99.

Barclay, William. *The Acts of the Apostles.* Philadelphia: Westminster, 1955.

Barrett, C. K. *A Critical and Exegetical Commentary on the Acts of the Apostles.* 2 vols. International Critical Commentary. Edinburgh: T. & T. Clark, 1994–1998.

Bauer, Walter, et al., eds. *Greek-English Lexicon of the New Testament and Other Early Christian Literature* (BDAG). 3rd ed. Chicago: University of Chicago Press, 2000.

Best, Ernest. "Acts 13:1–3." *JTS* 11 (1960) 344–48.

Blue, Bradley B. "Acts and the House Church." In *Acts in Its Graeco-Roman Setting*, edited by David W. Gill and Conrad H. Gempf, 119–222. AIIFCS 2. Grand Rapids: Eerdmans, 1994.

Bosch, David J. *Transforming Mission: Paradigm Shifts in Theology of Mission*. 6th ed. Maryknoll, NY: Orbis, 1993.

Bovon, Francois. *Luke the Theologian: Fifty-five Years of Research (1950–2005)*. 2nd rev. ed. Waco, TX: Baylor University Press, 2006.

Brown, Peter. *The Body and Society: Men, Women and Sexual Renunciation in Early Christianity*. New York: Columbia University Press, 1988.

Bruce, F. F. *The Acts of the Apostles: The Greek text with Introduction and Commentary*. 3rd ed. Leicester: Apollos, 1990.

———. *Men and Movements in the Primitive Church*. Exeter: Paternoster, 1979.

Calvin, Jean. *The Acts of the Apostles*. Translated by J. N. Fraser and W. J. G. McDonald. Edinburgh: St Andrew, 1965.

Campbell, R. Alastair. *The Elders: Seniority within Earliest Christianity*. Studies of the New Testament and Its World. Edinburgh: T. & T. Clark, 1994.

Capper, Brian J. "The Community of Goods of the Early Jerusalem Church." *Aufstieg und Niedergang der römischen Welt* 26 (1979) 1730–34.

Cassidy, Richard J. *Society and Politics in the Acts of the Apostles*. Maryknoll, NY: Orbis, 1987.

Castelli, Elizabeth A. "Gender, Theory and the Rise of Christianity: A Response to Rodney Stark." *Journal of Early Christian Studies* 6 (1998) 227–57.

Chadwick, Henry. *The Early Church*. London: Penguin, 1967.

Charlesworth, James H., ed. *Old Testament Pseudepigrapha*. Vol. 1: *Apocalyptic Literature and Testaments*. London: Darton, Longman & Todd, 1985.

———. *Old Testament Pseudepigrapha*. Vol. 2: *Expansions of the "Old Testament" and Legends, Wisdom and Philosophical Literature, Prayers, Psalms and Odes, Fragments of Lost Judeo-Hellenistic Works*. London: Darton, Longman & Todd, 1985.

Chen, Diane G. *God as Father in Luke-Acts*. Studies in Biblical Literature 92. New York: Peter Lang, 2006.

Chow, John K. *Patronage and Power: A Study of Social Networks in Corinth*. LNTS. Sheffield: Sheffield Academic, 1992.

Chrysostom, John. *Homilies on the Acts of the Apostles*. Translated by J. B. Morris. Edited by W. H. Simcox et al. Grand Rapids: Eerdmans, 1975.

Cicero. *In Pisonem, The Speeches*. Translated by N. H. Watts. LCL 252. Cambridge, MA: Harvard University Press, 1931.

Conzelmann, Hans. *A Commentary on The Acts of the Apostles*. Translated by James Limburg et al. Edited by Eldon Jay Epp et al. Philadelphia: Fortress, 1987.

———. *The Theology of St. Luke*. Translated by Geoffrey Buswell. New York: Harper & Brothers, 1961.

Crossley, James. *Why Christianity Happened: A Sociohistorical Account of Christian Origins, 26–50 CE*. Louisville: Westminster John Knox, 2006.

Cunningham, Scott. *"Through Many Tribulations": The Theology of Persecution in Luke-Acts*. LNTS. Sheffield: Sheffield Academic, 1997.

Darr, John A. *On Character Building: The Reader and the Rhetoric of Characterization in Luke-Acts*. Louisville: Westminster John Knox, 1992.

Davies, Madeleine. "HTB Planters Seek to Bless the West." https://www.churchtimes. co.uk/articles/2018/10-august/news/uk/htb-planters-seek-to-bless-the-west.

Dio Chrysostom. *Discourses*. 5 vols. Translated by J. W. Cohoon and H. Lamar Crosby. Cambridge, MA: Harvard University Press, 1932–1951.

Diodorus Siculus. *Library of History*. 12 vols. Translated by C. H. Oldfather et al. Cambridge, MA: Harvard University Press, 1933–1967.

Diogenes Laërtius. *Lives of Eminent Philosophers*. Translated by R. D. Hicks. LCL 184 and 185. Cambridge: Harvard University Press, 1925.

Dix, Gregory. *The Shape of the Liturgy*. London: Dacre, 1978.

Drews, Robert. "Ephorus' *kata genos* History Revisited." *Hermes* 104 (1976) 497–8.

Driver, Samuel Rolles. *Notes on the Hebrew Text and Topography of the Books of Samuel*. 2nd ed. Oxford: Clarendon, 1913.

Dunn, James D. G. *The Acts of the Apostles*. Valley Forge: Trinity, 1996.

———. *Baptism in the Holy Spirit*. London: SCM, 1970.

———. *Jesus and the Spirit: A Study of the Religious and Charismatic Experience of Jesus and the First Christians as Reflected in the New Testament*. London: SCM, 1975.

Epictetus. *The Discourses, Books 1–2*. Translated by W. A. Oldfather. LCL 131. Cambridge, MA: Harvard University Press, 1925.

Epimenides. *Cretica*. Translated by J. Rendel Harris. *The Expositor, Seventh series* 2 (1906) 305–17.

Estrada, Nelson P. *From Followers to Leaders: The Apostles in the Ritual of Status Transformation in Acts 1–2*. LNTS. London: T. & T. Clark, 2004.

Eusebius. *Ecclesiastical History*. Translated by Kirsopp Lake and J. E. L. Oulton. LCL 153 and 265. Cambridge, MA: Harvard University Press, 1926–32.

Fletcher, Richard. *The Barbarian Conversion: From Paganism to Christianity*. New York: Holt, 1998.

Filson, F. V. "The Significance of the Early House Churches." *JBL* 58 (1939) 105–12.

Finegan, Jack. *The Archeology of the New Testament: The Mediterranean World of the Early Christian Apostles*. Boulder, CO: Croom Helm, 1981.

Fiorenza, Elizabeth Schüssler. *In Memory of Her*. New York: Crossroad, 1983.

Fischer, Claude S. "Toward a Subcultural Theory of Urbanism." *American Journal of Sociology* 80 (1975) 1319–41.

Fitzmyer, Joseph A. *The Acts of the Apostles*. Anchor Bible 31. New York: Doubleday, 1998.

———. *The Gospel According to Luke I–IX*. Garden City, NY: Doubleday, 1981.

Foerster, W. and G. Fohrer. "σῴζω/σωτηρία." In *Theological Dictionary of the New Testament* 7, edited by Gerhard Kittel and Gerhard Friedrich, translated by Geoffrey W. Bromiley, 965–1024. Grand Rapids: Eerdmans, 1971.

Fontenrose, J., *The Delphic Oracle*. Berkeley: University Press of California, 1978.

Fox, Robin Lane. *Pagans and Christians: Religion and the Religious Life from the Second to the Fourth Century A.D., When the Gods of Olympus Lost Their Dominion and Christianity, With the Conversion of Constantine, Triumphed in the Mediterranean World*. New York: Knopf, 1987.

French, David H. "Acts and the Roman Roads of Asia Minor." In *Acts in Its Graeco-Roman Setting*, edited by David W. Gill and Conrad H. Gempf, 49–58. AIIFCS 2. Grand Rapids: Eerdmans, 1994.

Friesen, Steve. "Poverty in Pauline Studies: Beyond the So-called New Consensus." *JSNT* 26 (2004) 323–61.

Gager, John G. "Jews, Gentiles and Synagogues in the Book of Acts." *HTR* 79 (1986) 91–99.

Gallagher, Robert L., and Paul Hertig, eds. *Mission in Acts: Ancient Narratives in Contemporary Context.* Maryknoll, NY: Orbis, 2004.

Garrison, David. "Church Planting Movements vs. Insider Movements: Missiological Realities vs. Mythiological Speculations." *International Journal of Frontier Missions* 21 (2004) 151–54.

Gaventa, Beverly Roberts. *The Acts of the Apostles.* Abingdon New Testament Commentaries. Nashville: Abingdon, 2003.

———. "Theology and Ecclesiology in the Miletus Speech: Reflections on Content and Context." *NTS* 50 (2004) 36–52.

———. "Towards a Theology of Acts: Reading and Rereading." *Interpretation* 42 (1988) 146–57.

Gehring, Roger W. *House Church and Mission: The Importance of Household Structures in Early Christianity.* Peabody, MA: Hendrickson, 2004.

Giles, Kevin N. "House Churches." *Priscilla Papers* 24 (2010) 6–8.

———. "Luke's Use of the term ΕΚΚΛΗΣΙΑ with Special Reference to Acts 20:28 and 9:31." *NTS* 31 (1985) 135–42.

Gill, David W. J. "Behind the Classical Façade: Local Religions of the Roman Empire." In *One God, One Lord: Christianity in a World of Religious Pluralism,* 2nd ed., edited by Andrew David Clarke and Bruce W. Winter, 72–87. Carlisle: Paternoster, 1992.

González, Justo L. *Acts: The Gospel of the Spirit.* Maryknoll, NY: Orbis, 2001.

Goppelt, Leonhard. *Apostolic and Post-Apostolic Times.* Translated by Robert A. Guelich. Grand Rapids: Baker, 1980.

Green, Michael. *Evangelism in the Early Church.* London: Hodder & Stoughton, 1970.

Guder, Darrell L., ed. *Missional Church: A Vision for the Sending of the Church in North America.* Grand Rapids: Eerdmans, 1998.

Haenchen, Ernst. *The Acts of the Apostles: A Commentary.* Translated by Bernard Noble and Gerald Shinn, revised by R. McL. Wilson. Oxford: Basil Blackwell, 1971.

Hale, Thomas. *On Being a Missionary.* Pasadena: William Carey Library, 1995.

Harland, Philip A. *Associations, Synagogues, and Congregations: Claiming a Place in Ancient Mediterranean Society.* Minneapolis: Augsburg Fortress, 2003.

Harvey, A. E. "Elders." *JTS* 25 (1974) 318–32.

Hatch, Edwin. *The Organization of the Early Churches.* Bampton Lectures for 1880. 6th ed. London: Longmans, 1901.

Hays, Richard B. *The Moral Vision of the New Testament.* London: T. & T. Clark, 1997.

Heath, Malcolm. "The Substructure of Stasis-theory from Hermagoras to Hermogenes." *Classical Quarterly* 44 (1994) 114–29.

Hemer, C. J. "Alexandria Troas." *TynB* 26 (1975) 79–112.

———. *The Book of Acts in the Setting of Hellenistic History.* Edited by Conrad H. Gempf. WUNT 49. Tübingen: J. C. B. Mohr, 1989.

Herodotus. *History of the Persian Wars.* 4 vols. Translated by A. D. Godley. Cambridge, MA: Harvard University Press, 1920–1925.

Hicks, Edward Lee et al., eds. *Ancient Greek Inscriptions in the British Museum (IBM).* 4 vols. Oxford: Clardendon,1874–1916.

Himerius. *Orationes*. Translated by F. Dubner. 2nd ed. Paris: Didot, 1878.

Hirsch, Alan. *Forgotten Ways: Reactivating Apostolic Movements*. 2nd ed. Ada, MI: Brazos, 2016.

Holloway, Paul A. *Philippians*. Minneapolis: Fortress, 2017.

Holmberg, Bengt. *Paul and Power: The Structure of Authority in the Primitive Church as Reflected in the Pauline Epistles*. Coniectanea Biblica, New Testament Series 11. Lund, Sweden: LiberLäromedel/Gleerup, 1978.

The Holy Bible: New Revised Standard Version (NRSV), Containing the Old Testament and the New Testament with Apocrypha. Nashville: Thomas Nelson, 1993.

Homer. *Iliad*. Translated by A. T. Murray. LCL 170–71. Cambridge, MA: Harvard University Press, 1924–25.

———. *Odyssey*. Translated by A. T. Murray. LCL 104–5. Cambridge. MA: Harvard University Press, 1919.

House, Paul R. "Suffering and the Purpose of Acts." *JETS* 33 (1990) 317–30.

Hull, John H. E. *The Holy Spirit in the Acts of the Apostles*. London: Lutterworth, 1967.

Ilan, Tal. *Jewish Women in Greco-Roman Palestine: An Inquiry into Image and Status*. Tübingen: Mohr Siebeck, 1995.

Jervell, Jacob. "The Daughters of Abraham: Women in Acts." Translated by Roy A. Harrisville. In *The Unknown Paul: Essays on Luke-Acts and Early Christian History*, 146–57. Minneapolis: Augsburg Fortress, 1984.

———. *Die Apostelgeschichte*. Kritisch-exegetische Kommentar über das Neue Testament 17. Göttingen: Vandenhoeck & Ruprecht, 1998.

Johnson, Luke Timothy. *The Acts of the Apostles*. Collegeville, MN: Liturgical, 1992.

———. *The Gospel of Luke*. Collegeville, MN: Liturgical, 1991.

Johnson, Sherman Elbridge. *Paul the Apostle and His Cities*. Good News Studies 21. Wilmington: Glazier, 1987.

Josephus. *Jewish Antiquities*. 9 vols. Translated by Ralph Marcus et al. Cambridge, MA: Harvard University Press, 1933–1963.

———. *The Jewish War*. 3 vols. Translated by H. St. J. Thackeray. Cambridge, MA: Harvard University Press, 1927–28.

———. *The Life, Against Apion*. Translated by H. St. J. Thackeray. LCL 186. Cambridge, MA: Harvard University Press, 1926.

Judge, Edwin A. "The Early Christians as Scholastic Community." *Journal of Religious History* 1 (1960–61) 4–15, 125–37.

———. *The Social Pattern of the Christian Groups in the First Century: Some Prolegomena to the Study of New Testament Ideas of Social Obligation*. London: Tyndale, 1960.

Juvenal. *Satires*. Translated by Susanna Morton Braund. LCL 91. Cambridge, MA: Harvard University Press, 2004.

Kane, J. Herbert. *Christian Missions in Biblical Perspective*. Grand Rapids: Baker, 1976.

Käsemann, Ernst. *Der Ruf der Freiheit*. 5th ed. Tübingen: Mohr, 1972.

Kee, Howard Clark. *Good News to the Ends of the Earth: The Theology of Acts*. London: SCM, 1990.

Keener, Craig. *Acts: An Exegetical Commentary*. 4 vols. Grand Rapids: Baker Academic, 2012–15.

———. *Bible Background Commentary*. Downers Grove, IL: InterVarsity, 1993.

———. "Mutual Mayhem: A Plea for Peace and Truth in the Madness of Nigeria." *Christianity Today* (November 2004) 60–64.

———. "Paul and Sedition: Pauline Apologetic in Acts." *Bulletin for Biblical Research* 22 (2012) 201–24.

———. *Paul, Women, and Wives: Marriage and Women's Ministry in the Letters of Paul.* Grand Rapids: Baker Academic, 1992.

Kennedy, George A. *New Testament Interpretation Through Rhetorical Criticism.* Chapel Hill, NC: University of North Carolina Press, 1984.

Kodell, Jerome. "'The Word of God Grew': The Ecclesial Tendency of ΛΟΓΟΣ in Acts 1:7; 12:24; 19:20." *Biblica* 55 (1974) 505–19.

Kraeling, Carl H. "The Jewish Community at Antioch." *JBL* 51 (1932) 130–60.

Kreider, Alan. *Patient Ferment of the Early Church: The Improbable Rise of Christianity in the Roman Empire.* Grand Rapids: Baker Academic, 2016.

Krodel, Gerhard A. *Acts.* Augsburg Commentary on the New Testament. Minneapolis: Augsburg, 1986.

Lampe, G. W. H. "Miracles in the Acts of the Apostles." In *Miracles: Cambridge Studies in their Philosophy and History,* edited by C. F. D. Moule, 165–78. London: Mowbray, 1965.

———. *A Patristic Greek Lexicon.* Oxford: Oxford University Press, 1961.

Levine, Amy-Jill, ed. *A Feminist Companion to Luke.* London: Sheffield Academic, 2002.

Levine, Lee I. *Ancient Synagogues Revealed.* Jerusalem: Israel Exploration Society, 1981.

———. "The Second Temple Synagogue: The Formative Years." In *The Synagogue in Late Antiquity,* edited by Lee I. Levine, 7–31. Philadelphia: The American Schools of Oriental Research, 1987).

Levinskaya, Irina. *The Book of Acts in its Diaspora Setting.* AIIFCS 5. Grand Rapids: Eerdmans, 1996.

Liddell, H. G., and Robert Scott. *A Greek-English Lexicon.* 9th ed. Oxford: Oxford University Press, 1996.

Lohfink, Gerhard. *Jesus and Community: The Social Dimension of Christian Faith.* Translated by John P. Galvin. Philadelphia: Fortress, 1984.

Longenecker, Bruce W. "Exposing the Economic Middle: A Revised Economy Scale for the Study of Early Urban Christianity." *JSNT* 31 (2009) 243–78.

Lucian. *Lover of Lies.* Translated by A. M. Harmon. LCL 130. Cambridge, MA: Harvard University Press, 1921.

———. *The Parliament of the Gods.* Translated by A. M. Harmon. LCL 302. Cambridge, MA: Harvard University Press, 1936.

Lührmann, Dieter. "Neutestamentliche Haustafeln und antike Ökonomie." *NTS* 27 (1981) 83–97.

MacMullen, Ramsay. *Christianizing the Roman Empire, A.D. 100–400.* New Haven, CT: Yale University Press, 1984.

———. *Paganism in the Roman Empire.* New Haven, CT: Yale University Press, 1981.

———. "Women in Public in the Roman Empire." *Historia* 29 (1980) 208–18.

Maddox, Robert. *The Purpose of Luke-Acts.* Edinburgh: T. & T. Clark, 1982.

Marguerat, Daniel. *The First Christian Historian: Writing the Acts of the Apostles.* Cambridge: Cambridge University Press, 2002.

Marshall, A. J. "Roman Women in the Provinces." *Ancient Society* 6 (1975) 108–27.

Marshall, I. Howard. *The Acts of the Apostles.* Tyndale New Testament Commentaries. Leicester: InterVarsity, 1980.

———. *The Gospel of Luke: A Commentary on the Greek Text.* NIGTC. Grand Rapids: Eerdmans, 1978.

———. *Last Supper and Lord's Supper*. Didsbury Lectures. Exeter: Paternoster, 1980.

Marshall, I. Howard, and David Peterson, eds. *Witness to the Gospel: The Theology of Acts*. Grand Rapids: Eerdmans, 1998.

Matson, David L. *Household Conversion Narratives in Acts: Pattern and Interpretation*. LNTS. Sheffield: Sheffield Academic, 1996.

Mattingly, Harold B. "The Origin of the Name Christiani." *JTS* 9 (1958) 26–37.

Mealand, David L. "Community of Goods and Utopian Allusions in Acts II–IV." *JTS* 28 (1977) 96–99.

Meek, James A. *The Gentile Mission in Old Testament Citations in Acts: Text, Hermeneutic, and Purpose*. London: T. & T. Clark, 2008.

Meeks, Wayne A. *The First Urban Christians: The Social World of the Apostle Paul*. New Haven, CT: Yale University Press, 1983.

———. *The Moral World of the First Christians*. London: SPCK, 1987.

Meeks, Wayne A., and Robert L. Wilken. *Jews and Christians in Antioch in the First Four Centuries of the Common Era*. Missoula: Scholars, 1978.

Menzies, Robert P. *Empowered for Witness: The Spirit in Luke-Acts*. Rev. ed. Journal of Pentecostal Theology SS 6. Sheffield: Sheffield Academic, 1994.

Metzger, Bruce M. *A Textual Commentary on the Greek New Testament (UBS4)*. 2nd ed. New York: United Bible Society, 1994.

Moltmann, Jürgen. *The Church in the Power of the Spirit: A Contribution to Messianic Ecclesiology*. Minneapolis: Augsburg Fortress, 1993.

Moore, Thomas S. "'To the End of the Earth': The Geographical and Ethnic Universalism of Acts 1:8 in Light of Isaianic Influence on Luke." *Journal of the Evangelical Theological Society* 40 (1997) 389–99.

Moule, C. F. D. "The Christology of Acts." In *Studies in Luke-Acts*, edited by Leander E. Keck and J. Louis Martyn, 159–85. London: SPCK, 1968.

Murphy-O'Connor, Jerome. "House-Churches and the Eucharist." In *Christianity at Corinth: The Quest for the Pauline Church*, edited by Edward Adams and David G. Horrell, 129–38. Louisville: Westminster John Knox, 2004.

———. "Prisca and Aquila." *Bible Review* 8 (1992) 40–51.

———. "The Cenacle—Topographical Setting for Acts 2:44–45." In *Acts in Its Palestinian Setting*, edited by Richard Bauckham, 303–21. AIIFCS 4. Grand Rapids: Eerdmans, 1995.

Neudorfer, Heinz-Werner. "The Speech of Stephen." In *Witness to the Gospel: The Theology of Acts*, edited by I. Howard Marshall and David G. Peterson, 275–94. Grand Rapids: Eerdmans, 1998.

Neusner, Jacob. *Formative Judaism: Religious, Historical and Literary Studies*. Chico, CA: Scholars, 1982.

———. "The Phenomenon of the Rabbi in Late Antiquity." *Numen* 16 (1969) 1–20.

Newbigin, Lesslie. *The Gospel in a Pluralist Society*. Grand Rapids: Eerdmans, 1989.

Neyrey, Jerome H. "'Teaching You in Public and from House to House' (Acts 20.20): Unpacking a Cultural Stereotype." *JSNT* 26 (2003) 69–102.

Nolland, John. *Luke 1–9:20*. Word Biblical Commentary 35A. Dallas: Word, 1989.

Origen. *Contra Celsum*. Translated by Henry Chadwick. Cambridge: Cambridge University Press, 1953.

Osiek, Carolyn. Review of *The Earliest Christian Meeting Places: Almost Exclusively Houses?*, Biblical Theology Bulletin 45 (2015) 185–6.

Osiek, Carolyn, and Margaret Y. MacDonald. *A Woman's Place: House Churches in Earliest Christianity*. Minneapolis: Fortress, 2006.

Overman, J. Andrew. "The God-fearers: Some Neglected Features." *JSNT* 32 (1988) 17–26.

Ovid. *Metamorphoses*. Translated by Frank Justus Miller. LCL 42–43. Cambridge, MA: Harvard University Press, 1916.

Pao, David W. *Acts and the Isaianic New Exodus*. Grand Rapids: Baker Academic, 2002.

Parsons, Mikael C. *Acts*. Paideia. Grand Rapids: Baker Academic, 2008.

———. "Hearing Acts as a Sequel to a Multiform Gospel: Historical and Hermeneutical Reflections on Acts, Luke and the ΠΟΛΛΟΙ." In *Rethinking the Unity and Reception of Luke and Acts*, edited by Andrew F. Gregory and C. Kavin Rowe, 128–52. Columbia, SC: University of South Carolina Press, 2010.

Parsons, Mikael C., and Richard I. Pervo. *Rethinking the Unity of Luke and Acts*. Minneapolis: Augsburg Fortress, 1993.

Pearson, Birger A. "On Rodney Stark's Foray into Early Christian History." *Religion* 29 (1999) 171–6.

Penner, Todd. *In Praise of Christian Origins: Stephen and the Hellenists in Lukan Apologetic Historiography*. New York: T. & T. Clark International, 2004.

Peppiatt, Lucy. *Unveiling Paul's Women: Making Sense of 1 Corinthians 11:12–16*. Eugene, OR: Cascade, 2018.

Perdue, Leo. "The Death of the Sage and Moral Exhortation: From Ancient Near Eastern Instructions to Greco-Roman Parenesis." In *Parenesis: Act and Form*, edited by Leo Perdue and John G. Gammie, 82–109. Semeia 50. Atlanta: Society of Biblical Literature, 1990.

Pervo, Richard I. *Acts*. Hermeneia. Minneapolis: Fortress, 2009.

———. *Dating Acts: Between the Evangelists and the Apologists*. Santa Rosa: Polebridge, 2006.

———. *Profit with Delight: The Literary Genre of the Acts of the Apostles*. Minneapolis: Augsburg Fortress, 1987.

Pesch, Rudolph. *Die Apostelgeschichte*. 2 vols. Evangelisch-Katholischer Kommentar zum Neuen Testament 1 & 2. Zurich: Neikurchen-Vluyn, 1986.

Peterson, David G. *The Acts of the Apostles*. The Pillar New Testament Commentary. Grand Rapids: Eerdmans, 2009.

———. "Luke's Theological Enterprise: Integration and Intent." In *Witness to the Gospel: The Theology of Acts*, edited by I. Howard Marshall and David G. Peterson, 521–44. Grand Rapids: Eerdmans, 1998.

Philo. *Embassy to Gaius*. Translated by F. H. Colson. LCL 379. Cambridge, MA: Harvard University Press, 1962.

Plato. *Gorgias*. Translated by W. R. M. Lamb. LCL 166. Cambridge, MA: Harvard University Press, 1925.

———. *Laws*. Translated by R. G. Bury. LCL 192. Cambridge, MA: Harvard University Press, 1926.

———. *Phaedrus*. Translated by Christopher Emlyn-Jones, William Preddy. LCL 36. Cambridge, MA: Harvard University Press, 2017.

Pliny the Younger. *Letters and Panegyricus*. 2 vols. Translated by Betty Radice. Cambridge, MA: Harvard University Press, 1969.

Plutarch. *Moralia* [including *De Defectu Oraculorum, Table Talk*]. 16 vols. Translated by Frank Cole Babbitt et al. Cambridge, MA: Harvard University Press, 1927–2004.

Polhill, John B. *Acts*. New American Commentary 26. Nashville: Broadman, 1992.

Polycarp. *Martyrdom of Polycarp*. Translated by Bart D. Ehrman. In *The Apostolic Fathers, Vol. 1: 1 Clement, 2 Clement, Ignatius, Polycarp, Didache*. LCL 24. Cambridge, MA: Harvard University Press, 2003.

Ramsay, William Mitchell. *Bearing of Recent Discovery on the Trustworthiness of the New Testament*. London: Hodder, 1920.

—————. *St. Paul the Traveller and the Roman Citizen*. London: Hodder & Stoughton, 1895.

Rapske, Brian M. "Acts, Travel and Shipwreck." In *Acts in Its Graeco-Roman Setting*, edited by David W. Gill and Conrad H. Gempf, 1–48. AIIFCS 2. Grand Rapids: Eerdmans, 1994.

—————. *Paul in Roman Custody*. AIIFCS 3. Grand Rapids: Eerdmans, 1994.

————— "Opposition to the Plan of God and Persecution." In *Witness to the Gospel: The Theology of Acts*, edited by I. Howard Marshall and David G. Peterson, 235–56. Grand Rapids: Eerdmans, 1998.

Reimer, Ivoni Richter. *Women in the Acts of the Apostles: A Feminist Liberation Perspective*. Minneapolis: Fortress, 1995.

Richards, Earl. "Pentecost as a Recurrent Theme in Luke-Acts." In *New Views on Luke and Acts*, edited by Earl Richards, 133–49. Collegeville, MN: Liturgical, 1990.

Riesner, Rainer. "Synagogues in Jerusalem." In *Acts in its Palestinian Setting*, edited by Richard Bauckham, 179–211. AIIFCS 4. Grand Rapids: Eerdmans, 1995.

Robinson, Anthony B., and Robert W. Wall. *Called to Be Church: The Book of Acts for A New Day*. Grand Rapids: Eerdmans, 2006.

Roller, Matthew B. "Exemplarity in Roman Culture: The Cases of Horatius Cocles and Cloelia." *Classical Philology* 99 (2004) 1–56.

Rosner, Brian S. "The Progress of the Word." In *Witness to the Gospel: The Theology of Acts*, edited by I. Howard Marshall and David G. Peterson, 215–33. Grand Rapids: Eerdmans, 1998.

Rowland, Christopher C. *Radical Christianity*. Eugene, OR: Wipf & Stock, 2004.

Sampley, J. Paul. *Pauline Partnership in Christ: Christian Community in the Light of Roman Law*. Philadelphia: Fortress, 1980.

Schaps, David M. "The Women Least Mentioned: Etiquette and Women's Names." *Classical Quarterly* 27 (1977) 323–30.

Schmidt, Karl Ludwig. "ἐκκλησία." In *Theological Dictionary of the New Testament* 3, edited by Gerhard Kittel and Gerhard Friedrich, 501–36. Grand Rapids: Eerdmans, 1965.

Schnabel, Eckhard J. *Early Christian Mission*, vol. 2: *Paul and the Early Church*. Downers Grove, IL: InterVarsity, 2004.

—————. *Paul the Missionary: Realities, Strategies, and Methods*. Downers Grove, IL: InterVarsity, 2008.

Schneckenburger, Matthias. *Über den Zweck der Apostelgeschichte: Zugleich eine Ergänzungder neueren Commentare*. Bern: Chr. Fischer, 1841.

Schweizer, Eduard. "πνεῦμα." In *Theological Dictionary of the New Testament* 6, edited by Gerhard Kittel and Gerhard Friedrich, translated by Geoffrey W. Bromiley, 404–15. Grand Rapids: Eerdmans, 1968.

Scott, James M. "Acts 2:9–11 as an Anticipation of the Mission to the Nations." In *The Mission of the Early Church to Jews and Gentiles*, edited by Jostein Ådna and Hans Kvalbein, 87–123. WUNT 127. Tübingen: Mohr Siebeck, 2000.

Seim, Turid Karlsen. *The Double Message: Patterns of Gender in Luke and Acts*. Nashville: Abingdon, 1994.

Shaw, Brent D. "Bandits in the Roman Empire." *Past and Present* 105 (1984) 3–52.

Shelton, James B. *Mighty in Word and Deed: The Role of the Holy Spirit in Luke-Acts*. Peabody, MA: Hendrickson, 1991.

Shepherd, William Henry. *The Narrative Function of the Holy Spirit as a Character in Luke-Acts*. Atlanta: Scholars, 1994.

Skinner, Matthew L. *Locating Paul: Places of Custody as Narrative Settings in Acts 21–28*. Atlanta: Society of Biblical Literature, 2003.

Slee, Michelle. *The Church in Antioch in the First Century CE: Communion and Conflict*. LNTS. Sheffield: Sheffield Academic, 2003.

Smart, James D. *The Interpretation of Scripture*. Norwich: Hymns Ancient and Modern Ltd, 2012.

Smith, Steve, and Ying Kai. *T4T: A Discipleship Re-Revolution*. Monument, CO: Wigtake Resources, 2011.

Snowden, Frank M. *Blacks in Antiquity: Ethiopians in the Greco-Roman Experience*. Cambridge, MA: Harvard University Press, 1970.

Soards, Marion L. *The Speeches in Acts: Their Content, Context, and Concerns*. Louisville: Westminster, 1994.

Spencer, F. Scott. *Acts*. Readings: A New Biblical Commentary. Sheffield: Sheffield Academic, 1999.

Squires, John T. *The Plan of God in Luke-Acts*. SNTSMS 76. Cambridge: Cambridge University Press, 1993.

Stark, Rodney. *Cities of God: The Real Story of how Christianity Became an Urban Movement and Conquered Rome*. New York: Harper Collins, 2006.

———. *The Rise of Christianity: How the Obscure, Marginal Jesus Movement Became the Dominant Religious Force in the Western World in a Few Centuries*. New York: Harper Collins, 1997.

Stevens, Gerald L. *Acts: A New Vision of the People of God*. 2nd ed. Eugene, OR: Pickwick, 2019.

Strabo, *Geography*. 8 vols. Translated by Horace Leonard Jones. Cambridge, MA: Harvard University Press, 1917–1932.

Strelan, Richard E. *Strange Acts: Studies in the Cultural World of the Acts of the Apostles*. Berlin: Walter de Gruyter, 2004.

Tacitus. *Annals*. Translated by John Jackson. LCL 312, 322. Cambridge, MA: Harvard University Press, 1937.

Talbert, Charles H. "Martyrdom and the Lukan Social Ethic." In *Political Issues in Luke-Acts*, edited by Richard J. Cassidy and Philip J. Scharper, 99–110. Maryknoll, NY: Orbis, 1983.

Tannehill, Robert C. *The Narrative Unity of Luke-Acts: A Literary Interpretation*, vol. 2: *The Acts of the Apostles*. Minneapolis: Fortress, 1990.

Taylor, Nicholas H. "The Social Nature of Conversion in the Early Christian World." In *Modeling Early Christianity: Social-Scientific Studies of the New Testament*, edited by Philip F. Esler, 128–36. London: Routledge, 1995.

Testament of Joseph. In *Old Testament Pseudepigrapha*, vol. 1, *Apocalyptic Literature and Testaments*, edited by James H. Charlesworth, 819–25. London: Darton, Longman & Todd, 1985.

Thiselton, Anthony C. *The Two Horizons: The New Testament and Philosophical Description*. Grand Rapids: Eerdmans, 1996.

Thompson, J. W. "The Gentile Mission as an Eschatological Necessity." *Restoration Quarterly* 14 (1971) 18–27.

Thompson, Michael B. "The Holy Internet: Communication Between Churches in the First Christian Generation." In *The Gospels for All Christians: Rethinking the Gospel Audiences*, edited by Richard Bauckham, 49–70. Grand Rapids: Eerdmans, 1998.

Thornton, Timothy C. G. "To the End of the Earth: Acts 1:8." *ET* 89 (1977–1978) 374–5.

Thucydides. *History of the Peloponnesian War*. 4 vols. Translated by C. F. Smith. Cambridge, MA: Harvard University Press, 1919–23.

Towner, Philip H. "Mission Practice and Theology under Construction (Acts 18–20)." In *Witness to the Gospel: The Theology of Acts*, edited by I. Howard Marshall and David Peterson, 417–36. Grand Rapids: Eerdmans, 1998.

Trebilco, Paul. "Asia." In *Acts in its Graeco-Roman Setting*, edited by David W. Gill and Conrad H. Gempf, 291–362. AIIFCS 2. Grand Rapids: Eerdmans, 1994.

Turner, Max B. "Jesus and the Spirit in Lucan Perspective." *TynB* 32 (1981) 3–42.

———. *Power from on High: The Spirit in Israel's Restoration and Witness in Luke-Acts*. Sheffield: Sheffield Academic, 1996.

——— "The Spirit of Prophecy and the Power of Authoritative Preaching in Luke-Acts: A Question of Origins." *NTS* 38 (1992) 66–88.

Verner, David C. *The Household of God: The Social World of the Pastoral Epistles*. Society of Biblical Literature Dissertation Series 71. Chico, CA: Scholars, 1983.

Vogler, Werner. "Die Bedeutung der urchristlichen Hausgemeinden für die Ausbreitung des Evangeliums." *Theologische Literaturzeitung* 11 (1982) 785–94.

Wagner, C. Peter. *Church Planting for a Greater Harvest: A Comprehensive Guide*. Eugene, OR: Wipf & Stock, 2010.

Wallis, Jim. *The Call to Conversion: Why Faith is Always Personal but Never Private*. Revised edition. Oxford: Monarch, 2006.

Walton, Steve. *Leadership and Lifestyle: The Portrait of Paul in the Miletus Speech and 1 Thessalonians*. SNTSMS 108. Cambridge: Cambridge University Press, 2000.

Westermann, Claus. *Isaiah, 40–66*. Translated by David M. G. Stalker. London: SCM, 1969.

Westfall, Cynthia Long. *Paul and Gender: Reclaiming the Apostle's Vision for Men and Women in Christ*. Grand Rapids: Baker Academic, 2016.

White, L. Michael. *Building God's House in the Roman World: Architectural Adaptation among Pagans, Jews, and Christians*. Baltimore: Johns Hopkins University Press, 1990.

Winter, Bruce W., ed. *The Book of Acts in Its Ancient Literary Setting*. Grand Rapids: Eerdmans, 1993.

———. *The Book of Acts in Its Graeco-Roman Setting*. Grand Rapids: Eerdmans, 1994.

———. *Paul in Roman Custody*. Grand Rapids: Eerdmans, 1995.

———. *The Book of Acts in Its Palestinian Setting*. Grand Rapids: Eerdmans, 1996.

———. *The Book of Acts in Its Diaspora Setting*. Grand Rapids: Eerdmans, 1996.

———. "Official Proceedings and the Forensic Speeches in Acts 24–26." In *The Book of Acts in its Ancient Literary Setting*, edited by Bruce W. Winter and Andrew D. Clarke, 305–35. AIIFCS 1. Grand Rapids: Eerdmans, 1993.

———. *Philo and Paul Among the Sophists: Alexandrian and Corinthian Responses to a Julio-Claudian Movement*, 2nd ed. Grand Rapids: Eerdmans, 2001.

Witherington, Ben, III. *The Acts of the Apostles: A Socio-Rhetorical Commentary.* Grand Rapids: Eerdmans, 1998.

―――. "The Anti-Feminist Tendencies of the Western Text in Acts." *JBL* 103 (1984) 82–84.

―――. *Women in the Earliest Churches.* Cambridge: Cambridge University Press, 1988.

Wright, Christopher J. H. *The Mission of God: Unlocking the Bible's Grand Narrative.* Downers Grove, IL: InterVarsity, 2006.

Wright, N. T. *The New Testament and the People of God.* 2 vols. London: SPCK, 1992.

―――. *Simply Christian: Why Christianity Makes Sense.* London: SPCK, 2006.

Xenophon. *Cyropaedia.* Translated by Walter Miller. LCL 51, 52. Cambridge, MA: Harvard University Press, 1914.

―――. *Memorabilia, Oeconomicus, Symposium, Apology.* Translated by E. C. Marchant, and O. J. Todd. LCL 168. Cambridge, MA: Harvard University Press, 1923.

Author Index

Adams, Edward, 103, 112, 113, 115, 116, 117, 118, 119, 120, 133, 139, 140, 141, 143, 144, 304
Alexander, Patrick, 1
Aratus, 189, 190
Aristotle, 10, 123, 190, 286
Artemidorus, 108
Aune, David, 268, 279

Baker, Coleman, 7, 9
Balch, David, 8, 10, 48, 49, 64, 127
Barclay, William, 178
Barrett, C. K., 1, 39, 45, 55, 57, 59, 96, 98, 100, 118, 120, 121, 123, 140, 152, 159, 163, 165, 169, 180, 182, 185, 187, 188, 195, 200, 204, 205, 279
Bauer, Walter (BDAG), 15, 13, 20, 77, 92, 93, 153, 158, 162, 163, 174, 175, 199, 211, 218, 223, 262
Best, Ernest, 137
Blue, Bradley, 117, 118, 140, 141
Bosch, David, 299, 300
Bovon, Francois, 24, 28, 32, 33
Brown, Peter, 61
Bruce, F. F., 1, 6, 28, 56, 59, 66, 80, 83, 84, 118, 131, 135, 174, 188, 201, 206, 210, 211, 262, 266, 269

Calvin, Jean, 121, 255
Campbell, Alastair, 129, 130
Capper, Brian, 126
Cassidy, Richard, 7, 271, 273, 287

Castelli, Elizabeth, 187
Chadwick, Henry, 61
Chen, Diane, 45
Chow, John, 105
Chrysostom, 28, 48, 63, 286
Cicero, 10, 11, 123
Conzelmann, Hans, 1, 21, 261
Crossley, James, 106, 206
Cunningham, Scott, 21, 77, 253

Darr, John, 11, 287
Davies, Madeleine, 309
Dio Chrysostom, 48
Diodorus Siculus, 106
Diogenes Laërtius, 92
Dix, Gregory, 122
Drews, Robert, 45
Driver, Samuel, 66
Dunn, James, 1, 29, 34, 43, 263, 295

Epictetus, 84
Epimenides, 189
Estrada, Nelson, 128
Eusebius, 190

Fletcher, Richard, 228
Filson, F. V., 104, 120
Finegan, Jack, 226
Fiorenza, Elizabeth Schüssler, 64
Fischer, Claude, 230
Fitzmyer, Joseph, 1, 6, 68
Foerster, W., and G. Fohrer, 65, 66, 67
Fontenrose, J., 57, 186
Fox, Robin Lane, 155, 229

Subject Index

Scripture Index

Acts (*continued*)

Made in the USA
Monee, IL
01 July 2022